Strathmore

Manuscript

101
R269r

Copyright, 1900
BY
G. P. PUTNAM'S SONS

Copyright, 1909
BY
G. P. PUTNAM'S SONS

The Author.

The Knickerbocker Press, New York

PREFACE

THIS volume, an analysis of the thought in which will be found clearly indicated in the headings of the chapters in the Table of Contents, completes a series of essays begun several years ago on the subject of Comparative Æsthetics. But while the last to be published, the volume is the second in the order in which the members of the series are to be arranged, and was the first to be planned, as also, with exception mainly of Chapters V. to VII. and IX. to XI., the first to be written. The manuscript has been left lying in my desk for so many years for two reasons. In the first place, I was not certain that the general conception of art — indirectly underlying if not directly expressed in the volume — could be applied to all the details of each of the arts; and the only course that could make me certain was to think the subject out to the end of all its possible ramifications. While pursuing this course, I produced the other volumes. In the second place, the particular theory of the relations between the mind's conscious and subconscious actions, which appealed to me at that time as a vague suggestion, I had not verified; and my conceptions of the importance and reach of the subject, as well as of the responsibilities of authorship, were such that I did not feel justified in publishing opinions that were not grounded upon thorough investigation. Such investigation is attended with difficulties; and if pursued with an application of every test which one's mind is capable of devising, is a work of years.

This book contains no records of preparatory processes; but the conclusions reached in it, and the views implied in them would have little value, were they not conformable to results obtained by the broadest feasible outlook over the whole field of phenomena with which they are connected.

There are very evident reasons for the importance of the subject thus studied as applied to art. The transcendentalists of New England who, fifty years ago, were exercising the most pronounced of any effect upon the art and literature of our country were constantly confounding artistic inspiration with religious inspiration. The tendency of this mistake was not only to minimize in religion the importance of the spiritual, because this was conceived to be the same in kind as the distinctively human in art; but to minimize in art also the importance of the material,—*i. e.*, of the material product as given form through skill in technique,—because the whole desired effect was conceived to be attained, as in religion, by merely giving adequate and accurate expression to the results of inspiration. Emerson himself, not only in his practice but in his theory, almost always goes astray when he approaches this subject of art-form. On the other hand, the followers of the French, who, during the last twenty-five years, have occupied in our country the position formerly occupied by the transcendentalists, are constantly confounding artistic observation with scientific observation; and the tendency of their influence is not only to minimize in science the importance of imaginative hypothesis as a prerequisite for the discovery of great underlying principles, because they conceive that science has the same interest in the mere appearances of nature that art has; but to minimize in art also the importance of imaginative construction embodying the great truths of analogy; because they suppose the end to be attained in art, as in science, by an accurate study of the facts of nature as they are, poems or paintings being ranked according to the literal fidelity with which they recall or imitate the details of that which has been observed.

The two tendencies of art thus exemplified, and the constant inclination of the mind, when perceiving the deficiency in the one, to turn altogether away from it to that which, when regarded in itself alone, causes equal deficiency in the other, make one feel, at times, as if it were wellnigh hopeless to try, as has been attempted in these volumes, to introduce into the conceptions of American artists and critics even a beginning of that balance between the two which always characterizes the highest art,—that of ancient Hellenism, for instance, which was equally careful to reproduce only the ideal in thought and only the beautiful in form. I have concluded that nothing could more certainly accomplish the desired end than a practical recognition of the relationship of art both to religion on the one hand and to science on the other, together with a recognition of the natural limitations to art which such a double relationship necessarily involves.

The facts with reference to this relationship could not well be brought out without the thorough discussion in Chapters V. to XII. inclusive. I am free to admit, however, that aside from its bearings upon art, I became interested, as I was writing, in the discussion for its own sake. Many of the conclusions reached are unusual, and may prove satisfactory to few. The materialist may not like them because they concede too much to the spiritualist, and the spiritualist because they concede too little; while the conventional Christian may demur because they seem to let down certain bars which it pleases him to think that the Almighty has put up to separate him from the world to-day, as similar bars separated the Jew from the Gentile of old. However, it is the duty of an author claiming to be a seeker of truth to publish the truth which he thinks that he has found; and if he do so without reserve, he may be confident that the result will be a help to some of his readers whose minds work as his mind does. Besides this, in view of the acknowledged skeptical tendencies of the scientific and historic criticism of the present age, it is not a valueless contribution to general thought to show that all that is needed for the highest spiritual stimulus, all that is vital to practical religion, even to the vaguely guided life of faith which characterizes the Christian religion, can command acknowledgment and acceptance upon its own merits—even with such an one as delegates many of its mysteries to the realm of mystery where, though suggestive and possible, he cannot recognize them to be provable. There are always some who, like a boy whistling through the dark to keep up his courage, imagine that the need of the world in a period of doubt is a strong, emphatic, and even extravagant expression in an opposite direction. Yet if it be never right or wise, or even, in the long run, expedient, to pretend to be certain about that which is merely probable, any method of regarding the subject in question that renders such forms of expression not only unnecessary, but unphilosophical, ought to be welcomed. Besides this—to say nothing of religion—what a revival of art there might be, in an age which many deem too materialistic to be at all poetic, if only what is unfolded in these pages with reference to the subconscious and the spiritual could be widely recognized to be true!

It is hoped that the last half of this volume will prove

especially satisfactory owing to the endeavor, through the thorough analysis of the whole subject, to make the definitions and characteristics of epic, realistic, and dramatic art, together with their various subdivisions in the different arts, appear inevitable. The same may be said of what is unfolded with reference to the particular phases of significance which each art is fitted to express, as, in accordance with the analogies of form in nature, the art-form is presented in space alone, or in time alone, or in both combined. The fundamental thought of this part of the discussion was suggested, of course, by Lessing in " The Laocoön." But the subject has been developed much further than by him; and some of the conclusions are based upon conceptions entirely different from his.

PRINCETON, N. J., January, 1900.

CONTENTS.

I.

PAGE

SIGNIFICANCE ATTRIBUTABLE TO THE ELEMENTS OF NATURAL FORM IN SPACE AND TIME TRACED AS FAR AS TO ORGANISM, LIFE, AND IMPORT . 1–11

Art-Form as Appealing to the Senses and Sense-Influenced Imagination—Significance Includes an Appeal to both Thought and Emotion—Object of the Present Volume—Thoughts and Emotions Derived from Experience—Those of Art Derived from Experience of Nature—Certain Fundamental and General Suggestions of Nature to the Mind—Space, Time, Existence, Matter, Movement, Force, Arrangement, Operation—Method of Operation—Every Object Bears Relations to Space and Time—A Rock—A Musical Tone—Every Object in Bearing Relations to both Space and Time Suggests Methods of Operation—Suggestions of Organism—Of Life—Of Import.

II.

HIGHER SIGNIFICANCE AS ATTRIBUTABLE TO THE ELEMENTS OF NATURAL FORM IN SPACE AND TIME: THE INFINITE, THE ETERNAL, AND THE ABSOLUTE 12–25

An Appearance or Form may be Connected with all Space or all Time—The Apprehension of a Method of Operation in a Small Form may Involve some Apprehension of that in the Whole Universe—Do Forms in Nature Reveal Anything of the Infinite, the Eternal, and the Absolute?—Testimony of Art and Philosophy—Of Religion—These Inferences Drawn from the Forms of Nature, yet not as they Appear in Space alone—Nor in Time alone—But in both—How they Suggest the Infinite—The Eternal —The Absolute—Suggestions of the Absolute not Inconsistent with those of the Infinite and the Eternal—Unity in Mode and Diversity in Operation—Illustrated by a Spiral—Appearances of Nature as Suggesting a Divine Living Intelligence—Men and Animals Express Intelligent Life through Material Appearances in Space and in Time Combined, or by Methods of Operation—Arguing from Analogy to Modes of Expression of Divine Intelligence—Human Expressions of Feeling—Divine Expressions of the Same—Human Expressions of Character—Divine—Application of the Subject to Art.

III.

THE HIGHEST SIGNIFICANCE: THE NATURE OF TRUTH AS INDICATED BY THE SOURCES TO WHICH MEN ATTRIBUTE IT, AND THE TERMS BY WHICH THEY CHARACTERIZE IT 26–38

The Value of Significance Determined by the Truth in it—Scientists and Philosophers Search for Truth behind Appearances in Space—And in Time—Therefore Conceive it to be not alone in the Appearances themselves—But in these as Related to Certain Methods of Operation—Same Facts Shown by the Treatment Given to Formal Statements—The Truth in them Discovered by Regarding Relations to Surrounding Circumstances—Therefore to Methods of Operation—Absolute Truth as Existing without Reference to Relations—Necessity of Considering Methods of Operation Shown by Men's Ways of Characterizing Truth: Meanings of the Adjective *True*—Further Meanings—The Meanings when Material or Bodily Conditions are Compared with Mental or Spiritual—Its Meanings when Applied to Language—The False in Language is a Want of Conformity to a Method of Operation in a Mental Process—Summary of the Meanings of the Word *True*—Of the Word *Truth:* Its Special and General Applications.

IV.

THE HIGHEST SIGNIFICANCE: THE NATURE OF TRUTH AS INDICATED BY THE METHODS IN LANGUAGE AND LIFE, THROUGH WHICH MEN EXPRESS IT 39–60

Objections to the View Presented in the Third Chapter—Truth as Expressed in Language should not be Confounded with the

Formula : Illustrated from Interpretations of the Bible—Its History
Noteworthy for the Methods and Results of Life, etc., which the
Events Exemplify—Its Prophecies Valuable for their Fulfilment
not only, but Applicability to Laws Operating everywhere—Confirmation of this Principle of Interpretation of the Bible in its Explanations—Its Arguments—Its Injunctions—Real Meaning Lost
when Truth is Supposed to be Conformed to Formulæ alone, and
not also to Methods of Operation—Importance of Observing this
Distinction—The Use of the Word *Truth* in the Bible — Illustrations—Truth as Expressed in Life—Truth to the Divine Spirit
is Action in Conformity with the Divine Method—Truth is Perceived in the Process of Searching for it—Dangers of Supposing
Progress or Change Inconsistent with Absoluteness in Truth : The
Source both of Infidelity and Bigotry—Right Views of Truth as
a Corrective of these — The Truth in Revealed and Natural Religion Lies in its Method—He who Recognizes this a Friend to
both Progress and Permanence—Inferences from the View here
Presented — A Few Forms in Space may Reveal Universal
Methods—One Mind may Represent God—And One Life, if Full
of Love—The Mission of the Friend—Comfort in this Suggestion
—The Changes of a Few Moments in Time may Reveal Universal
Methods—Child or Man, with Short or Long Life, may both have
Experience of them.

V.

SIGNIFICANCE, RELIGIOUS, SCIENTIFIC, AND ARTISTIC,
   AS RESPECTIVELY ATTRIBUTABLE TO MENTAL
   ACTION, PREDOMINANTLY SUBCONSCIOUS, CON-
   SCIOUS, AND BLENDED 61–85

Results Reached in the Foregoing Chapters—Mental and Material
Conditions Preceding the Recognition of Truth — Religious,
Scientific, and Artistic Conceptions—How they Differ—Religious
or Spiritual Meaning—The Occult Side of the Mind—Proof of
Subconscious Intellection in Memory, Fright, Fever—Hypnotism
—Its Effects Allied to those of Art—Germs of Hypnotic Sugges-
tion—Subconscious Philosophical and Mathematical Intellection—
Resulting from Previous Conscious Action as in Skill—Not Result-
ing from Previous Conscious Action : Coburn, Mozart, Blind Tom
—Subconscious Diagnosis of Disease at a Distance—Subconscious
Apprehension of Distant Occurrences — Both in Space and in

Time—Mind-Reading and Mediumship — Automatic Writing — The Truth and the Limitations of Spiritualism—Hudson's Theory —The Investigation of the Subject Justifiable.

VI.

SIGNIFICANCE AS ATTRIBUTABLE TO MENTAL ACTION: RELIGIOUS CONCEPTIONS HAVING THEIR SOURCE IN INSPIRATION 86–111

Subconscious and Conscious Influences Found in all Intellection, but the Main Source of it Different in Religion, Science, and Art —Making it in Each Different in Kind—Origin of Religious Conceptions Concerning a Future State of Rewards and Punishments —Often Attributed to Material Causes—Should be Attributed to Influences from Nature's Occult Side—Shown in Susceptibility of the Primitive, Uneducated Man to Such Influences—Instinct and Reason—Instinctive and Reflective as Correlated to Subconscious and Conscious Intellection—Result of Subconscious Intellection Allied to the Teachings of Nature and Religion—To the Mental Action of Animals—Of Negroes, Indians, and those Subject to Hallucinations, with Inferences therefrom—Like Inferences with Reference to the Origin of Religion Drawn from Primitive Religious Customs—With the Growth of Intelligence Physical Occult Manifestations are Considered Less Important than Verbal—But the Verbal Continue to be Associated with Subconscious Intellection—Truth Obtainable from this Depends on Suggestion Developed in it—Truth of the Suggestion Depends on Conscious as well as Subconscious Intellection Exercised by Some One—The Conscious Mind Modifies Everything Received from the Subconscious, Making it not Less Inspired, but More Intelligent— This the Condition in Inspired Writings—Intellectual Progress Resulting from this Form of Inspired Influence.

VII.

SIGNIFICANCE AS ATTRIBUTABLE TO MENTAL ACTION: RELIGIOUS CONCEPTIONS HAVING THEIR SOURCE IN INSPIRATION; ARTISTIC IN IMAGINATION 112–136

Form of Inspiration partly Dependent on the Human Mind as Developed by Environments of Place and Time—This Theory

PAGE

Explains the Gradual Development of Truth in the Revealed Scriptures—Also the Necessity for Spiritual Discernment: no Form is an Adequate and Complete Expression of the Spiritual—Tracing all Inspired Writing to or through the Same Subconscious Mental Processes Need not Impair Authority or Authenticity of the Scriptures—Nor Need the Attributing of Signs and Wonders to Sources not Divine—Conformity of this View to the Theories of Modern Biblical Criticism—The Three Tests of the Truth in the Scriptures: Conformity to Previous Information—To Results of Intuitive Judgment—To Results of Rational Inference—Different Views of Scriptural Inspiration Conformable to the Theory here Presented—Bearings of this Subject upon Artistic Sympathy, the Zeit-Geist, Imagination—Differences between Inspiration and Imagination—Failure to Recognize the Differences Detrimental to Both Religion and Art—Influence of Recognizing it upon Opinions Concerning Religion—Concerning Art—Nevertheless Art Lessens Materialism and Traditionalism, and Aids Religion, but is not a Substitute for it—Religion an Aid to Art.

VIII.

SIGNIFICANCE AS ATTRIBUTABLE TO MENTAL ACTION: SCIENTIFIC CONCEPTIONS HAVING THEIR SOURCE IN INVESTIGATION; ARTISTIC IN IMAGINATION 137-154

Results of Scientific Investigation to be Contrasted with those of Artistic Imagination—Quotation from Huxley Showing Scientific as Contrasted with Religious View-Point—Is equally far from View-Point of Art—The Difference in View-Point is Owing to a Difference between a Desire to Investigate and to Imagine—Scientific Interest is in Preceding Conditions, Artistic in Conditioned Effects—The Detailing of Results of Investigations is Inartistic in Literature—Quotations from Gay—From Scott—Expression of Results of Imagination from Tennyson—Of Investigation from West—Of Imagination from Homer—Criticism upon an Explanation of a Quotation from Shakespeare—This Distinction of Universal Applicability—Thought in Modern Art Different in Range from Ancient—Justification for Introduction of Philosophy and Science in Art—Scientific Investigation Overlooks Nothing: Artistic Imagination Regards only the Prominent and Emphatic—

By its Results: Science Presents Thought Logically; Art, Analogically—This Latter Fact Renders Form Essential in Art—Also Significance, which is the Basis of the Analogy Expressed through the Forms—Difference between that which Looks like and which also Operates like—To Bring out the Latter Involves a Higher Effort of Imagination—Because Making Art in the Highest Sense Natural: Illustrated in the Novel, Drama, Ballad, Descriptive Poetry—In these such Comparisons as are not Based on Analogies Taken from Nature are not Indicative of High Imaginative Gifts—The Same Principles Apply to Conceptions of Poems as Wholes—To the Use of Separate Words—Same Principle Illustrated in Music—When both Artistic and Natural—Illustrated in Painting and Sculpture—Further Explanations—In Architecture—That Art should Represent Analogies through Forms not Inconsistent with its Representing Beauty—Relative Use in Art of Natural Beauty and of Ugliness—Representative Expression a Limitation to Art; yet the Reason why its Products Have such Enduring and Universal Influence.

XIII.

Artistic Significance as Attributable to Bodily Action, and Having its Source Subjectively in Temperament, Objectively in Training 208–232

Connection between the Thought in this and in Preceding Chapters—Subjective and Objective Relationships of Expression—Instinctive, Reflective and Emotive Sources of Mental Effects—Conscious Reflective and Investigative Mental Action Slow—Subconscious Intuitive and Imaginative Action Rapid—The Two Actions do not Differ as Thought and Feeling, but as Unexcited and Voluntary from Excited and Involuntary Thought—The Artistic Involves Much Emotion—The Exciting Cause, being Permanent in Some, is Due to Temperament—Difference between Scientific and Artistic Temperament largely one of Degree—Some necessarily Excluded from the Sphere of Art, Some Included in it—Effects of Education and Practice—They Develop Mental through Physical Nature—Even Develop Possibilities of Genius—Illustrations—Connection between Results of Artistic Inspiration and of Skill—Inspiration, or Unhindered Expression of Subconscious Intellection, Helped by

PAGE

Cultivation of Expression and Memory—Even by Scientific Study—Broad Culture not Injurious to the Æsthetic Possibilities—Here as elsewhere Labor the Measure of Worth—Nothing Necessary in Religion or Science Fails to be an Aid to Art.

XIV.

ARTISTIC SIGNIFICANCE AS ATTRIBUTABLE TO BODILY ACTION, AND CHARACTERIZED SUBJECTIVELY BY A PERSONAL EFFECT, OBJECTIVELY BY A SYMPATHETIC 233–250

Connection between the Thought in this and the Preceding Chapter—The Surmisals of Art those of One Individual, the Artist—Should Have a Personal Effect—A Prose Description that Lacks this: Scott—A Poetic: Crabbe—A Poetic that Exhibits it: Byron—A Prose: Dickens—The Latter Descriptions Show the Effects of an Intervening Human Mind—As Personality is most Apparent in Unconscious Action, to Represent these Effects does not Interfere with consciously Representing Nature — The Personality of Artistic Effects is Recognized in the Universal Proneness to Attribute to Artistic Genius Originality and Eccentricity—Personality of Effect always Appeals to Others through Awakening Sympathy for or against—So the Arts are the Humanities—Illustrations of Artistic Appeal to the Sympathies—Explanation of the Passages—The Principle Involved—Why Artists Seem often Interested in Technique rather than in Significance—Individuality of Effect not Inconsistent with an Appeal to Universal Interest—Yet the Artist must Have a Peculiar Temperament to Fulfil both Requirements—Genius Has a Temperament Congenial to Nature and Man — German Words Corresponding to Genius, Genial, and Geniality—Brilliancy—Art Humanizes Nature according to the Sentiments of One, yet Accords with the Sentiments of All.

XV.

ARTISTIC SIGNIFICANCE AS ATTRIBUTABLE TO BODILY ACTION, AND TENDING SUBJECTIVELY TO THE POSSESSION OF CULTURE, OBJECTIVELY TO THE EXPRESSION OF SENTIMENT 251–269

Connection between Thought in this and in the Preceding Chapter—Culture: its Relation to Training—Its Development through

Poems—Non-Poetic Description of Cathedral—Of Natural Scenery—Even when Imaginative—Passages Illustrating Poetic Conceptions—Another, Illustrating a Painter's Conception—Contrasted with a Poetic One—Different Classes of Poetry Represent Different Degrees of Movement.

XXVI.

SIGNIFICANCE MAINLY ATTRIBUTABLE TO THE ELEMENTS OF ART-FORM IN TIME ALONE AS DIFFERENTLY REPRESENTED IN POETRY, MUSIC, AND ORATORY 454–473

Definite Thought as Expressed in Poetic Words, and Indefinite Emotion in Musical Tones—Words Cause Imagination to See as well as to Hear what is Referred to—Poetry of the Highest Order Presents a Vision of an Ideal Realm—Even when Describing Objects Vague in Themselves—Lack of these Effects in that Poetry which Subordinates the Verbal to the Musical—Such Poetry Common in our Own Day—And does not Exert the Legitimate Influence of Poetry—Contrast between Tennyson and Byron—Reasons why Foreigners Prefer the Latter—Comment on Byron's Methods—Explanations — Expression Appropriate for Musical Tones—Printed Explanations of Scenery Accompanying Musical Compositions no Proof that Limitations of this Form of Expression should not be Recognized—Pleasure from Musical Effects is Independent of these Explanations—And of the Words and Acting in Ballads and Operas—As Shown by Various Facts with Reference to Lovers of Music—Expression in Oratory as Limited on its Poetic or Musical Side—And on its Picturesque Side.

XXVII.

SIGNIFICANCE MAINLY ATTRIBUTABLE TO THE ELEMENTS OF ART-FORM IN SPACE ALONE AS DIFFERENTLY REPRESENTED IN LANDSCAPE-GARDENING, PAINTING, SCULPTURE, AND ARCHITECTURE 474–492

Landscape-Gardening : Difference between the Conceptions Appropriate for it and for other Arts of Sight—Painting Attempting to

Express what can be Represented in Poetry only—Illustrations—
Even in Legitimate Allegoric Paintings the Interest is Greatest in
Single Figures—Some Subjects Appropriate for both Painting and
Poetry, but must be Differently Treated—The Shield of Achilles
as Painted and as Described in the "Iliad"—That which can be
Represented in Painting Distinguished from that in Landscape-
Gardening—In Sculpture—In Architecture—Difference between
that which can be Represented in Sculpture and in Poetry—And in
Landscape-Gardening and Painting: The Material and Lack of
Color in a Statue Emphasizes Individual rather than Associative
Interest—The Large and Grand rather than the Small and Trivial
—The Dignified, Regular, Parallel, etc., rather than the Oppo-
site—The Conception of Architecture should be Peculiar to Itself
—Injurious Influence of its Imitating Methods of Representation
in Painting or Sculpture—Buildings Conceived as Pictures Tending
toward Inartistic Styles—Conclusion—Explanations.

INDEX 493–514

parts of which appeal to the imagination—*i.e.*, the imaging power of the mind—in a clearly articulated, distinctly outlined, or graphic, way, so that one may liken the conception to a thing that the senses can perceive. This is the use of the word that justifies one in speaking of the *form* of an oration or a drama, or of a storm-scene or a battle-scene, which latter he may have only in mind without any intention of ever putting it into the form of a picture. Not all the effects of art, however, are limited to such as can be thus perceived or conceived. There is a clear distinction, the recognition of which is philosophically essential, between the effects of a form physically fitted to produce a certain physiological result in the ear or the eye, as do some of the phenomena of tone or of color, or else artistically fitted to produce a certain psychological result or image in imagination,—there is a clear distinction between these effects and the implicit or suggestive, rather than explicit or arbitrary, effects upon thought or emotion, which, invariably, when the mind perceives art's real or imagined outlines, seem to surround these outlines as by a halo. This halo of thoughts and emotions surrounding the natural form as represented in the art-product, or surrounding the image of this product as represented in imagination, constitutes what, in this volume, will be termed the *representative significance*. As distinguished from the *significant* effects, the *form*-effects might be termed the *sensuous*. But the word *sensuous*, meaning that which is perceived by the senses, is, in the first place, subtly suggestive to some of the word *sensual*, meaning that which is dominated by the senses; and, in the second place, the word *sensuous*, though it is sometimes figuratively attributed, as when speaking of a visually representative style of poetry, to an appeal to the imagination, is not, in other regards, broad enough in meaning for all the uses to which art finds it necessary to put the word *form*. This word, therefore, seems the one best fitted for the conception that has just been indicated.

In ordinary language, when, by using one thing which, owing to its nature, we can see, we indicate another thing which, owing to its nature, we cannot see, nor even imagine as having any particular outlines that could be seen, as when, by hanging out a flag, we indicate our patriotism, we are accustomed to say that the former is the *signal* of the latter, which is the *thing signified*. It is in accordance with this use of language that, in the present volume, the substance of the thought or emotion represented or suggested by any given form of art will be termed its *significance*. In this last sentence, the words *thought* and *emotion* were both introduced intentionally. By significance in art is meant its mental as distinguished from its material effects, whether these material effects be produced by the external form itself, or by the image of this form which reflectively appears in imagination; and thought and emotion are effects as inseparable in mental experience as perception and feeling are in the experience of the senses. Indeed, in the term *humanities*, so often applied to the arts, we may recognize a conception equally suggestive of the sources of understanding and of sympathy. These arts address not only the senses and the sense-influenced imagination, but, through them, the whole range of the mind's activities.

The general fact that all the higher arts are audible or visible forms representing the phenomena—or, as they are technically termed, whether appealing to ear or eye, the *appearances*—of material nature for the purpose, through them, of representing human thoughts and emotions, was brought out and illustrated in the introductory volume of this series, entitled "Art in Theory." The object of that book was to examine the forms of art, as we find them developed in the world about us, in order to detect, inductively, the sources to which their effects are attributable. The present book has for its object to begin the work of tracing, deductively, these effects outward from their sources, and, in doing so, to direct attention to the principal artistic possibilities toward which, when rightly developed, the effects tend. In endeavoring to attain this end, it is evidently logical to start, not as in "Art in Theory," with the art-forms; but to start at the point reached in that book, *i. e.*, with the intellectual or emotional significance which was found to be, as it were, behind the art-forms. But besides being logical, as related to the general course of thought in these volumes, this method is psychological. It conforms to that necessarily pursued by the artist himself the moment that he turns from considerations of art in theory to those of art in practice. In his practical work, he begins with effects of which he is conscious in his own mind, and only later considers the ways in which, through his products, he may make others conscious of the same effects. The present volume is designed to trace the steps of only the earlier parts of this general mode of procedure; in other words, it is designed to show from what the artist derives his thoughts or emotions, what is their character, under what heads they can be classified, and what general methods of expression can represent them. The further applications of the subject to the particular methods peculiar to each of the arts will be left to subsequent volumes.

When we speak of the thoughts or emotions that art is to embody in form, we are reminded, at once, that these themselves, sometimes in whole but always in part, are derived from a man's experience; and that a large proportion of his experience is derived from the appearances of external nature. Moreover, the first condition of art is an audible or visible form; and, as shown in Chapter I. of "Art in Theory," this form is always a reproduction, at least partially, of something perceived in nature, which term is to be understood as including not only non-human but human nature, as manifested in a man's actions and utterances. It follows, therefore, that, in some way, one must always associate with nature whatever thoughts and emotions he puts into artistic form. Otherwise, he could not attribute to nature any possibility of representing these; he could not suppose that, by using natural forms as he does, he could suggest his thoughts and emotions to others.

Accordingly there is a sense in which, without being sensationalists or materialists, we may say that an artist is indebted to nature not only for the forms that he uses, but also for thoughts and emotions. For, even though thousands of these latter may be traceable mainly to his own mind, his mental processes in themselves are inaudible and invisible; and, when he comes to let another know of them, he must convert them into a form which another can hear or see. Especially must he do so when expressing them in art which necessitates form. But notice that this is the same as to say that he can express them at all only so far as somewhere in external nature he has recognized a form that seems fitted to express them, because it has already represented them to himself.

This statement evidently brings us to the question, What are the methods through which the audible or visible forms of nature represent or suggest thoughts or emotions? Evidently, too, this question must be answered before we can be prepared to show the methods through which the forms of art can suggest the same. Evidently, again, it will be logical to determine the answer to the question as applied first to such suggestions as are more fundamental and general, and advance from these to those that are more inferential and particular. In pursuance of this course, the reader will recognize the substantial accuracy of the following:

Space	Matter	Arrangement	Organism
Time	Movement	Operation	Life
Existence	Force	Method of Operation	Import

These four columns are intended to indicate the order of the development of the elementary suggestions of nature, all the later ones in the list being dependent on all that precede them. As will be noticed, the most fundamental of these suggestions are those of *space* and *time*, which, together, are conditions enabling us to form a general conception of *existence*. *Existence*, as conditioned mainly in *space*, *i. e.*, by the effect of one thing standing side by side with another, gives us our impression of *matter*. *Existence*, as conditioned mainly in *time*, *i.e.*, by the effect of one thing following another, gives us our impression of *movement;* and, as conditioned by combined effects in both *space* and *time*, *i. e.*, by combined effects both of *matter* and of *movement*, *existence* gives us our impression of *force*, *i. e.*, of one thing working upon another, as the *movement* of the wind in *matter* affects our cheeks which resist it, or the clouds which are carried along by it. *Force*,—which itself, as must be borne in mind, is a manifestation of *existence* conditioned upon both *matter* and *movement* and in both *space* and *time*,—*force*, when it is manifested mainly in *matter*, gives us our impression of *arrangement*, like that of the clouds which the winds blow together or separate; and, when it is manifested mainly in *movement*, it gives us our impression of *operation*, like that of the wind when fanning our cheeks or when blowing us down. Once more, when conditioned both in *space* by *matter* and *arrangement* and also in *time* by *movement* and *operation*, *force* gives us our impression of the *method of operation*.

This latter impression is very important, for it has to do with suggesting not only the method of operation, but, as will be shown presently, with suggesting almost every other advanced phase of significance. But before the importance of this impression can be recognized, its derivation needs to be clearly perceived. Of course, all that we can learn about *methods of operation* we must derive from appearances; and these can be observed only in *space* or in *time* or in *both together*. Can we gain a knowledge of a *method of operation* by observing an object as manifested in *space* alone or in *time* alone? It is not necessary, except for its bearings upon what is to follow, to argue that we cannot. If we could, the rocks could teach any one who merely looked at them the principles of geology; and moon and stars while standing still, "like Joshua's moon at Ajalon," could manifest the laws of astronomy. But such is not the case. To the study of rocks and stars, as they appear in *space*, must be joined the conception of the influence of *time* upon them. This conception alone can cause the scientist to break apart the rocks in order to detect their evidences of development, or to adjust his telescope to the stars in order to make out their variations of movement. Or again, take an object that assumes different appearances in successive intervals of *time*—could this fact even as a fact be recognized unless at more than one *time* men had observed the material *arrangements* of the parts of the object as it appeared in *space*? And how is it about recognizing the *method* of the change, the connection between one phase of appearance and another? Take, for instance, two trees, the one an "inside-grower" and the other an "outside-grower." How do men detect the different *methods of operation* distinguishing these? Simply through a superficial look at the trees, and noticing the mere fact that changes occur in different years and seasons? Or how do they become acquainted with the *methods of operation* among the fluids? Simply through noticing superficially that different phases—snow, rain, ice, vapor—appear at different intervals of *time?* Evidently not. To learn that for which they are in search, men cut into the trunks of the trees and analyze the fluids. In other words, they examine both as they appear in *space*.

If this be true, *i.e.*, that *methods of operation* can be understood in natural objects so far only as one regards them as affected in both *space* and *time*, it must be true, in addition,—a fact which, as we shall find by-and-by, has an important bearing upon art-methods,—that every object can be thus regarded. Otherwise there might be forms in nature through which it would be impossible for operations to be manifested. In order to show that all things can be thus regarded, two examples only need be instanced.

A rock is recognized in *space*. We never see it move itself, nor any movements in it. And yet the *method of the operation* of life upon it can be ascertained alone when one has recognized the fact that it has reached its present state while passing through successive changes.

From *time*, one needs to instance no example more extreme than that of a musical tone. What *space* can it be said to occupy? And yet, as long ago as when Pythagoras lived, men knew that no one can begin to comprehend the operations of a tone until, in connection with it, certain effects in *space* have been considered; that not until the relative contractions of the spaces through which different quantities of wind must pass, not until the relative proportions of different cords made to vibrate together, have been investigated, can there be any trustworthy theories concerning melody and harmony.

Accordingly, all forms in nature may be said to sustain relations both to *space* and to *time*, the medium through which they appear to us depending not upon their nature, but upon our point of view. If we regard a plant without any consideration of influences exerted upon it before the *time* when we notice it, it appears related only to *space*. But in the degree in which we conceive of it as a product of growth, it appears related to *time*. When, therefore, *methods of operation* are declared to be discoverable so far alone as one regards effects as they appear in *space* and in *time* conjointly, no criterion is given not susceptible of being applied to all appearances of nature whatsoever.

We pass on now to the remaining suggestions indicated on page 6. The first of these is the suggestion of *organism*. An *organism* is an *arrangement* of *matter* resulting in a body, the parts of which form organs, *i. e.*, are mutually operative upon one another. An *organism* therefore involves an *operation* according to a particular *method*, therefore a *method of operation*, in which the suggestive element appears mainly in *space*. It is because there is nothing in the *arrangement* or body of the rock suggesting interaction between one part of it and another that we say that it is inorganic, and it is because of the slight evidences of such an *arrangement* in the plants and lower animals, as contrasted with the higher animals, that we term the latter highly organic.

Again, as indicated on page 6, the *method of operation*, as affected mainly in *time*, gives us the suggestion of *life*. This is a particular *method of movement* or *operation* which takes place in connection with *organism* or a body. But *life* is mainly suggested by an appearance in *time*. If we see something strike the ground and stay where it falls, we are likely to consider it lifeless,—a feather, chip, or stone, as the case may be. But if shortly it begin to *move*, we usually change our opinion, because few things *move* in this way that fail to manifest the *method of operation* characterizing *life*. Moreover, our impression of this latter is frequently increased in the exact degree of the shortness of the time in which different *movements* are manifested. We are more apt to infer the presence of *life* from the rapid changes taking place among the leaves of a tree in springtime, than from noticing the slow development of its trunk; and from the movements of the animal which are physically perceptible, than from those of vegetable growth which are not so. And among the animals, too, other things being equal, we generally attribute the greatest degree of *life* to those whose *movements* are the most rapid,—to the bird or hound, for instance, rather than to the snail or sponge.

In Chapters XXII. to XXIV. will be found indicated the bearings of these natural methods of suggesting effects of *organism* and *life* upon the methods of producing effects of *organic form* and *animation* in art. At present we pass on to the last suggestion indicated on page 6. It is that of *import*. This term has been chosen because it seems to include, equally well with *significance*, both the apprehension of a general emotive tendency and a comprehension of a particular intellectual tendency. At the same time, it is a term indicating greater definiteness of meaning and

—as the word itself indicates—greater importance of meaning than *significance;* and it cannot be applied quite as appropriately as the latter to the elementary suggestions such as we have in the more abstract ideas of *space, time, matter,* or *movement.* Now it is the *method of operation,* as affected both by *organism* and *life,*—both in *space* through *matter* and *arrangement,* and in *time* through *movement* and *operation,*—that mainly furnishes the conditions causing appearances in the world to be suggestive of depth and breadth of *import.* Without *life, organism* alone, as in the dead or petrified animal or plant, has slight significance. The same is true of *life* alone, connected with little or no *organism,* as in the sponge, jelly-fish, or fungus. Only in the degree in which *organism* reveals *life,* or *life* is revealed through *organism,* do the forms of nature appeal in the most rational and profound way possible to intellect and sympathy, to mind and soul. This fact, with its bearings, will be brought out in the chapters following.

CHAPTER II.

HIGHER SIGNIFICANCE AS ATTRIBUTABLE TO THE ELEMENTS OF NATURAL FORM IN SPACE AND TIME: THE INFINITE, THE ETERNAL, AND THE ABSOLUTE.

An Appearance or Form may be Connected with all Space or all Time—The Apprehension of a Method of Operation in a Small Form may Involve some Apprehension of that in the Whole Universe—Do Forms in Nature Reveal Anything of the Infinite, the Eternal, and the Absolute?—Testimony of Art and Philosophy—Of Religion—These Inferences Drawn from the Forms of Nature, yet not as they Appear in Space alone—Nor in Time alone—But in both—How they Suggest the Infinite—The Eternal—The Absolute—Suggestions of the Absolute not Inconsistent with those of the Infinite and the Eternal—Unity in Mode and Diversity in Operation—Illustrated by a Spiral—Appearances of Nature as Suggesting a Divine Living Intelligence—Men and Animals Express Intelligent Life through Material Appearances in Space and in Time Combined, or by Methods of Operation—Arguing from Analogy to Modes of Expression of Divine Intelligence—Human Expressions of Feeling—Divine Expressions of the Same—Human Expressions of Character—Divine—Application of the Subject to Art.

WHEN we speak of the *forms* or *appearances* of nature, as in the preceding chapter, we are using terms that are necessarily indefinite in meaning. Nothing except our own choice or ability need limit the extent in time or in space of that which we designate by them. A man may look at a drop of dew. It alone is an appearance. But while he looks at it, he may look also at the rose on which it rests, or enlarge his field of vision till it embrace the bush, the ground, the ledge beneath it, and, possibly, the whole scope of the horizon. But all this, in spite of many appearances, may still, in a sense, be considered an appearance; and if one could stretch his comprehension far enough, he might extend the outlines to embrace the world, its planetary system, and the universe; and these as developed, too, not only in one moment of time, but through all time. In fact, though our own choice, or the limitations of our physical or mental powers, in view of certain arrangements of outline, color, or tone, may cause an object to seem separate from others, there is a sense in which it may be said that no actual separation, isolation, self-sufficiency, exists in nature. Every smallest object is a partner of all space and a product of all time. What is the little rosebud, which one plucks upon the meadow, but the blossoming of material forces which have been at work on every side of it since the first day of creation?

But if this be so, if every appearance in nature, however small or large our choice or circumstance may make it, be a portion of all the universe, it follows that the apprehension of the *method of operation* in this single portion must involve some apprehension of the *method of operation* in the whole. Each thing is an effect, and when thought searches for the cause of this effect, it journeys sideward toward infinity in space and backward toward eternity in time.

This fact suggests the inquiry, how much nature, fully interrogated, has the power to teach us. Must we stop at limits of the finite, the transient, the concrete, or can our investigation pass beyond these to that which is not finite, but infinite; not transient, but eternal; not concrete, but absolute? This is asked, of course, because of the necessary correspondence that must exist between conceptions like these, as represented through the forms of nature and as represented through the forms of art.

It is a simple fact of history that men of every age have drawn from nature inferences that warrant an affirmative reply to our inquiry. There is no need here of recalling the myths, theories, and various imaginings that prove this to be true of the poet and the artist. But it is equally true of the philosopher and the scientist. Notice a confirmation of this from a source which, on first consideration, might be thought to controvert it, viz., the writings of Mr. Herbert Spencer, the representative of the philosophy of the Unknowable, the philosophy which, as some think, accepts the revelations of the supernatural at their minimum. While he argues, on the one hand, that a natural theology can give man no authority either to affirm or to deny the attributes of the Creator, not even such as intelligence and will, on the ground that ("First Principles," p. 109) "the ultimate cause cannot, in any respect, be conceived by us, because it is in every respect greater than can be conceived," he nevertheless admits, on the other hand (p. 397), that "community of result implies community of cause. It may be that of such cause no account can be given further than that the Unknowable is manifested to us after this mode"; and again, on page 122, that "we must recognize . . . elements in that great evolution of which the beginning and end are beyond our knowledge or conception, as modes of manifestation of the Unknowable."

Thus, both the artist and the philosopher bear testimony to the essential rationality of the claim, universal among religionists, that the outward appearances of nature are, in some sense, symbols suggestive of that behind them, which is greater and grander than they. Religionists, of course, carry their conceptions farther than the others, but only develop the same principle. When they say that nature gives expression to the attributes of a Divine Life, creating and controlling it, they do not claim that these attributes can be perceived in themselves, but merely that they can be inferred from what is perceived. In fact, the spirit or character of the Divine Life, as a whole, is supposed to be recognized, like the spirit or character of the human life about us, not in its essence, but in its effects, "the invisible things . . . being understood by the things that are made" (Rom. i., 20).

It is from the appearances of nature, therefore, that art, philosophy, and natural theology equally derive their conceptions of that which transcends the finite by being infinite, the transient by being eternal, and the concrete by being absolute. Now from what in these natural appearances are these conceptions derived? The appearances themselves, as we have found, must be perceived in space, or in time, or in both. Are the conceptions derived from that which is perceived in space, and in this alone? How could they be? Objects that appear in space are rendered distinct to consciousness by means of outlines that limit their extent. How then could they, of themselves, convey an impression of the infinite, *i. e.*, of space without limits?—or of the eternal, *i. e.*, of time without limits?—or of the absolute, *i. e.*, of totality without limits except so far as they circumscribe all things?

It is evident that if we were confined to appearances in space merely, little could be suggested save the finite, the transient, and the concrete. Of course, it may be answered superficially that the grander notions are suggested by way of contrast. Yes, but what suggests the possibility of contrast? That is the question here. If the inferior conceptions be suggested positively, we should strive, at least, to find a positive suggestion of the greater.

The same is true with reference to appearances in *time*. These are rendered distinct to consciousness through their different changes or phases as assumed in successive minutes, hours, or days. But can appearances in their very nature temporal, constantly changing, convey in themselves alone any impression of the eternal, *i. e.*, of the immutable, of time without intervals or change?—or of the infinite, *i.e.*, of form without limits?—or can the various phases thus assumed in any sense represent the absolute, *i.e.*, totality as distinguished from the partial or the concrete? Manifestly not.

As the conceptions of which we are speaking cannot be derived from effects in *space* alone nor in *time* alone, we are forced by the conditions mentioned on page 7 to try to derive them from effects in both *space* and *time* combined. These effects, as shown on page 7, manifest the *method of operation*. Does the method of operation, then, suggest the infinite, the eternal, and the absolute?

First, does it suggest the infinite? This means the limitless, and, as such, it is apparent that it must be suggested in connection of some kind with effects in *space;* and yet it cannot be suggested by the limits that surround forms as they appear in space alone, for such forms are necessarily limited. Is it not when, in connection with effects in *space*, one thinks of those in *time*,—how during every day and month and year each stream and leaf and rock is changing, and that, therefore, at no separate time or place can one affirm of anything in nature, this or that is really the limit of its size or its influence,—is it not then that the suggestion of the infinite emerges? To the eye regarding an object as it appears in space alone it is finite; but ideally, to the mind, recalling methods of operation, how each object changes constantly in time, and how all objects interact, the impression of infinity, *i. e.*, of a negation of all finiteness, or definiteness in form, is as derivable from a rock matured through ages as from a cloud that is being rent by a hurricane. Suppose that our perceptions of the universe compel us to conceive of it as having limits, our impressions, nevertheless, of changes wrought in time suggest to us how matter, now condensed in order to form worlds and systems of worlds, may be dispersed through space with shapes and sizes infinite; and thus, although the infinite be utterly beyond our comprehension, we are forced to an apprehension of it, since it is as equally beyond our comprehension to conceive of a universe that is finite.

Let us find now, if we can, the source of our conception of the eternal. This must evidently be suggested in connection of some kind with effects in *time*. But notice that, in connection with these effects, the conception inevitably necessitates regard for those in *space* also. Here is a tree. As it appears in time there may be nothing to hint of immutability or eternity; but when we add considerations of effects in space, when we notice how each change is wrought upon the selfsame object, and, with this in view, regard the progress of the tree, what follows? Starting from the seed, we see it pass through sprout, limb, leaf, flower, and fruit, until a new seed is developed looking precisely like the first one. Together with this seed are many others just like it. There has been, therefore, an increase in the number of products. But there has been no change in the character of each product. The tree's development, despite the different phases that it may assume, is discovered in the end to be, so far as concerns the character of results, merely a return to a preceding starting-point. And thus, although the actual appearance of a tree is always changing, the tree conceived of by the mind does not change. It is simply the completed cycle of these different appearances that present themselves in the same order wherever the same kind of tree is found. A like impression is conveyed by everything in nature. Rain may be traced through springs, streams, oceans, vapors, clouds, back to rain again. And thus, though constant changes in the appearances in space indicate the mutable alone, there is something in the conception, whether of a tree, vapor, animal, man, nation, world, or universe, which is suggestive of immutability. At different recurring intervals of time all these objects repeat, each in its own sphere, the selfsame operations. These operations, therefore, seem eternal. And it is because they seem so that so many philosophers have agreed in the distinction made between phenomena and substance. In other words, they have come to consider all things in nature, even when their phases change too slowly to be apprehensible, as the manifestations of a substance underlying them, which substance abides the same through all successive intervals of time, and hence, so far as man can comprehend the term, is unchangeable and thus eternal. Whether philosophers are warranted in this conclusion with reference to substance is a question for them to decide. For the purposes of æsthetics it is enough to know that the conclusion would not be drawn at all unless it were suggested by what is known of *methods of operation*.

Now let us consider the source of the suggestions of the absolute. It has been shown that every object in the universe bears some relation to the whole universe, and, by consequence, that the operation in each object is connected with the operation in the whole. There is no doubt that it is in this fact that we must find that which suggests the conception for which we are now in search.

Portions of the *space*, for example, which a plant occupies develop under the effects of *time*, in a process which we term *growth*. Certain characteristics of the mode of growth in a plant are these: The germ begins by being small, weak, and simple in its structure. It develops to be large, strong, and complex. Now if we notice the phenomena of growth in any relation, even in the results of a man's intellectual or spiritual life, we find a similar order of development. The same is true with reference to the unfoldings of the life in masses of men, *i. e.*, in nations and races. In other words, the methods according to which inanimate things, brutes, men, and families of men develop, all correspond. Thus their many different forms and phases suggest the idea of unity in spite of multiplicity; of something which is absolute in method, in spite of limitless differences in concrete appearance.

The student of philosophy is sometimes reminded of the futility of all attempts to reconcile the conception of the absolute, *i. e.*, of a totality with limits, with a conception of the infinite and the eternal, *i. e.*, of space and time without limits. But the principle here adopted, of referring all suggestions of such conceptions to the *method of operation*, will enable us to perceive a sense in which it is inevitable that both conceptions should coexist. On the one hand, looking mainly at the method according to which operations take place, our minds are carried to the absolute. And this is so, no matter how minute or how extensive may be the effects through which we note the method's influence. The life of an insect, lasting but a day, or that of a bird or a man, the unfolding of a tree's bud or of a world, all equally evince a unity of method which we attribute to the absolute. But when, on the other hand, we notice mainly the operations as they influence the forms, it is next to impossible for us to conceive of any limits to the intervals or to the shapes, to the times or to the places in which these forms may be developed.

All methods of operation in the universe may be resolved into one, but the evolution of new forms according to this method is unceasing. The absolute is a method with limits; but it is a method of operation, not of any force that ends in time or in space; and, by consequence, the operation has no limits. The motive power of the universe may thus be conceived to be an absolute unity, so far as concerns itself alone; but this conception may coexist with the idea that it is possessed of eternal possibilities of operation, unfolding into forms of infinite variety.

To use an old illustration, were we to take a point and represent a method of operation by a spiral line described about this,—a spiral because in nature, although the method remains the same, the extent of its applicability to the number of specimens,—trees, men, whatever they may be,—is increasing with every generation,—were we to represent a method of operation by a spiral line, it is evident that this might extend indefinitely, yet at the remotest distance the law according to which it could be described would remain the same. This is to say that the method of operation indicated in the line would be absolute, although the line itself might be so far extended that the computation of its distance from the point of departure would necessitate considerations of infinity and eternity. Accordingly when we refer suggestions of the infinite, the eternal, and the absolute, to the methods of operation evinced in nature, we notice that the three, so far as apprehensible at all, are apprehensible as co-existing.

Let us turn now to the claims of natural theology. In addition to the infinite, the eternal, and the absolute, as mere abstract conceptions, the advocates of this consider these as attributes of a Divine Life, independent and intelligent, which is everywhere manifested and represented through the appearances of nature. These advocates may not be right in their conclusions; nevertheless the conclusions are made and believed to be warranted; and our present search constrains us to discover what there is in nature which suggests them. Why is it that from the days of fetishism to the present, certain men have drawn from nature the inferences thus indicated? What is there in the appearances of nature to suggest a connection between them and the expressions of intelligent life?

To find this, we must consider, in the first place, how it is that men discover anything about the expressions of intelligent life. Evidently they discover this from expressions that are made by the only being of intelligence with whom they are acquainted. This is the human being. But in what can his expressions suggest the appearances of nature? Of course, in the figures always used in language, and always referring to these appearances. The suggestion, however, is seldom in the appearances—say of trees or clouds—as these are perceived in *space* or in

CHAPTER III.

THE HIGHEST SIGNIFICANCE: THE NATURE OF TRUTH AS INDICATED BY THE SOURCES TO WHICH MEN ATTRIBUTE IT, AND THE TERMS BY WHICH THEY CHARACTERIZE IT.

The Value of Significance Determined by the Truth in it—Scientists and Philosophers Search for Truth behind Appearances in Space—And in Time—Therefore Conceive it to be not alone in the Appearances themselves—But in these as Related to Certain Methods of Operation—Same Facts Shown by the Treatment Given to Formal Statements—The Truth in them Discovered by Regarding Relations to Surrounding Circumstances—Therefore to Methods of Operation—Absolute Truth as Existing without Reference to Relations—Necessity of Considering Methods of Operation Shown by Men's Ways of Characterizing Truth: Meanings of the Adjective *True*—Further Meanings—The Meanings when Material or Bodily Conditions are Compared with Mental or Spiritual—Its Meanings when Applied to Language—The False in Language is a Want of Conformity to a Method of Operation in a Mental Process—Summary of the Meanings of the Word *True*—Of the Word *Truth*—Its Special and General Applications.

THE value of significance of any kind is measured by the degree of its truthfulness. Few can have read the preceding chapter attentively without finding themselves asking how far the conceptions suggested by appearances in space and in time combined, and, therefore, by *methods of operation*, may be supposed to conform to what we term *the truth*. They ask this because they recognize that a vague, general conception of the possibility of there being something infinite, eternal, and absolute is very different from definite, specific indications of the significance of this, such as are needed for practical guidance. They cannot be satisfied, therefore, with what has been said thus far. They desire to know, in addition, whether the same principle that conditions the ascertaining of truth of the more generic character conditions, as well, the ascertaining of truth of the more specific character. In this and the following chapter, an attempt will be made to show that the same principle does apply in all cases,—in other words, that what men mean by *the truth*, whenever they use the term, is a conception or a statement of that which is *true to* something; and that this something, while often a condition which appears upon the surface, is often too, and, in the last analysis, can be proved to be always, itself conditioned upon some method of operation to which it is materially or mentally related.

In order to attain our object, *i. e.*, to determine exactly what it is to which men refer when they use the word *truth*,—what it is that they conceive it to be,—it seems well to start by learning what we can from the sources to which, when searching for truth, men are accustomed to attribute it. Through observing what they seek in such cases, we certainly ought to gather some suggestions with reference to what they think it to be when obtained. Scientists and philosophers investigate, as we say, the appearances surrounding them. But what in these do they investigate? Merely the appearances as appearances? Do they believe that they can obtain the truth thus—even a part of it, to say nothing of the whole of it? Not at all. They often tear each superficial appearance into shreds. To detect its subtle elements, they hunt for them as for hidden treasure. Then, looking, if possible, through the elements, they strain their vision onward and inward, as if, beyond the whole material fabric, were something still for which they are in search. Their efforts often are of no avail. They prove, at least, that each who undertakes them has a firm conviction that the truth can be discovered through the outward forms of nature, else why should he examine them? And they prove, as well, his firm conviction that the truth cannot be attributed to that which is wholly in the outward forms, else why should he, in his examination, try to probe beneath them?

Appearances are not confined to stationary forms alone. Another element is potent in the universe. The folds upon earth's mighty vestment rise and fall. The fickle shadows come and go. The brilliant colors separate and blend. One listens and he hears the bustle of perpetual movement. He infers that somewhere underneath the movement there must throb a heart of life; that there must be a cause, and that connected with the cause he shall discover truth. And so he turns once more upon the forms, and uses other tests. He puts them through augmented changes for experiment. He boils, he burns, he dissipates, he fuses, he compounds them. His efforts often end in no discoveries, and yet they prove, at least, his firm conviction that the truth may be discovered through the outward changes, else why should he examine them? They prove, as well, his firm conviction that the truth cannot be attributed to that which is wholly in the outward changes, else why should he, in each experiment, try so hard to attain to that which has conditioned them?

Indeed, if the truth were wholly in outward shapes or changes, why would it not be patent to the eye of every one? To recognize it, what would be the need of more consideration than a single superficial glance? Yet all the world admit that truth is something that in any large degree is revealed alone to one with penetration, perseverance, and a more than ordinary measure of intelligence.

But to say that the truth for which these men are searching lies not wholly in the outward shape or change, is to make no more than a negation. Let us turn to the scientist and philosopher again, and find out positively, if we can, precisely what that is, in search of which each studies the appearances of nature. We need not linger long here. All recognize that no one is a scientist in reality who merely knows, no matter how extensively, the surface-facts with reference to shapes and changes. Before we can call him one, we must believe that he has looked beneath appearances, and through their agency has been led to apprehend, if not to comprehend, what in Chapter II. were termed the operations and the methods of the operations that have brought things to their present state. And is it not a fact that a man is acknowledged to rank high in science and philosophy in the degree alone in which he has been able to discover and to prove that certain of these methods operate identically beneath phenomena that in themselves are different? Have not Hegel, Spencer, and Darwin attained their eminence mainly because, in the opinion of their followers, they have had the penetration to detect some one of these methods whose operations can be illustrated by analogous occurrences in all the different departments and developments of nature? Some method of this kind, some principle of inevitable applicability, according to which each endeavors to explain the facts of nature,—in other words, to which each endeavors to show that these facts conform,—constitutes the basis of his scientific or philosophic system. This method is the thing to discover which the shapes and changes of the universe have been examined by him. This is that which, when discovered, he terms *the truth.*

That such is the case is exemplified by his treatment not only of the forms of nature, but of the statements of others representing what, before his time, they have learned from these forms. It is exemplified in his treatment even of verbal statements that he believes to be accurate. Take, for instance, because this is the best possible example to which one can refer, the way in which a Biblical scholar examines the text of the Scriptures even when he considers it to be inerrant. Is he satisfied to accept the surface-meaning of the text? Does he not rather search beneath it, just as we have found that scientists do when trying to discover the truth through the forms of matter? He doubts, he re-examines, and with any number of learned opinions weighed against his own decision, not infrequently, he ventures to uphold it. In doing this, he proves that he believes that the truth, though expressed in a form of thought, is not identical with the form itself, but underneath it.

Now, underneath a form of thought, what is it that must be considered before we can know the whole truth that is expressed? When wise men hear a statement, what is the chief criterion by which they test its credibility? Is it not the circumstances in which it is uttered, or to which it applies? And what are circumstances? Are they not things that stand around, that come before, beside, or after? To regard a thing in connection with its circumstances, what is this but to regard it as a something acted on, and thus as a something that is connected with other things that act—that is to say, as in itself a part of a process, as in itself a constituent element of an operation?

But an operation in its progress may pass through many different phases. At any given time, each of these phases in succession may represent the method operating through them all. If when the sun is on the horizon I affirm that in an hour it will be dark, I may speak truth or falsehood,—truth if it be evening, falsehood if it be morning. The truth or falsehood, which is not determined by a similarity or difference in the statements,—is it not determined by the degree in which the statement fits, or is true to methods as these really operate in nature? In nature it grows dark at eve, but not at dawn. Again, if I place a bud in the sunlight, it becomes a flower; but if I place a flower there, it withers. Therefore in making a statement concerning the effect of sunshine on the appearance of a bush, I must regard the period in the process of its growth. Once more, there is one method of operation in religious life. But if a patriarch in the early ages became religious, his impulse to duty might have prompted him to multiply the number of his wives (Deut. xxv., 5-9). A similar impulse in modern times prompts a Christian to content himself with one wife; and in making statements concerning the effects of religion on the lives of either of these men, one must regard the circumstances in which each is placed. These examples show that no one is fit to judge of the truth if devoid of sufficient insight—to say nothing of experience—to enable him to look beneath the formula. Precisely similar statements may be true or false even when applied to similar occurrences, if these be manifested in different circumstances of time or of place.

Nevertheless most men think that there is such a thing

as absolute truth. But where is it, and when do statements give expression to it? In the realm of nature, we have found the absolute to be suggested by a similar method indicated through all the different phases which the different forms assume; and we have found, too, that the philosopher discovers what he conceives to be the essence of the absolute so far alone as he discovers this method into which all differences fit, or to which they can all be manifested to be true. Why should not the same principle apply universally?

This question will be recognized by all as having a certain pertinence. But can the conception from which it springs stand the test of analysis? Appropriate as this conception may be when the term *truth* is used in an abstract and general sense, is it equally so when used in a concrete and specific sense? The answer to this question necessitates our taking up the second topic mentioned in the heading of this chapter, namely, the nature of truth as indicated by the terms by which men characterize it, in other words, as shown by the conditions to which men apply the word *truth*. Here, in order to make our survey of the subject as broad as possible, let us begin by noticing the use of the much more broadly applicable adjective *true*. Primarily, this adjective refers to that which conforms to something, or fits it. Nothing is true, except as it is true to some other appearance or conception with which it is compared. This meaning is evident, even when we use the term merely in contrast to the term *false*. When we say that a "door" is true, indicating that it is what it appears to be, that it is really a door, and not an imitation of one, we mean that it conforms, or is fitted, to that conception of a door which we have in imagination. In this use of the word *true*, one might think that we were merely comparing appearances with supposed appearances; but notice that we are also taking into consideration certain conditions underlying the appearances, which conditions cause the appearances, so to speak, to operate as they do upon the eye. The comparison is between the effect of a real door and the effect which some supposed door might have upon some supposed spectator.

This, in some of its applications, is not an uncommon use of the adjective. For instance, the sentence, "John is his true name," implies a comparison between the effect of a certain form upon us in calling to our thoughts or lips the word *John*, and the effect which his supposed form, if present, would have upon a supposed acquaintance.

But there are other possible ways of interpreting this phrase, "the door is true." It may mean that the door resembles in material, size, shape, color, or, perhaps, in only one of these regards, some other doors which are near it. In these cases, too, it is evident that the comparison is not between appearances except so far as they are considered effects produced by certain like methods of operation upon the eye. Or the phrase may mean that the door fits into its doorway, or conforms to the architectural design of the room or building in which it is seen; and, in this case, there may be involved no likeness whatever in the appearances as mere appearances. It is in the effects which certain principles controlling the construction of straight lines, angles, or curves have upon both the door and its framework, or upon the door and also upon the windows, cornices, or gables accompanying it.

The word *true*, therefore, does not imply necessarily a comparison between external forms or appearances.

which, upon different existences, or, possibly, in different spheres of existence,—one material and one mental,—have been operating to produce the appearances.

Truth is the substance of that of which *true* is the quality. As what is termed an *expression*, whether made in a form of words or of deeds, of literary art or of plastic art, cannot invariably conform in form or appearance to what is audible, visible, or tangible in the external world, *the truth* in such an expression cannot be said to be determined invariably by anything except the conformity of the method of the expression's operation upon the mind (whether influencing intelligence or emotion) to the method of operation (upon either the senses or the mind) indicated in existing external appearances or processes to which the expression refers. In such an expression, *the truth* or *a truth*, as the term is applied specifically, is determined by the conformity of the method of the expression's operation upon the mind to a particular method of operation to which a particular appearance is related. In a similar expression, *the truth*, as the term is applied generically, is determined by the conformity of the method of the expression's operation upon the mind to one method of operation in the universe to which one method all methods under particular appearances are supposed to be organically related. It is in this latter sense, to recall again what was said in Chapter II., that the truth can be said to be infinite, eternal, and absolute.

CHAPTER IV.

THE HIGHEST SIGNIFICANCE: THE NATURE OF TRUTH AS INDICATED BY THE METHODS IN LANGUAGE AND LIFE, THROUGH WHICH MEN EXPRESS IT.

Objections to the View Presented in the Third Chapter—Truth as Expressed in Language should not be Confounded with the Formula: Illustrated from Interpretations of the Bible—Its History Noteworthy for the Methods and Results of Life, etc., which the Events Exemplify—Its Prophecies Valuable for their Fulfilment not only, but Applicability to Laws Operating everywhere—Confirmation of this Principle of Interpretation of the Bible in its Explanations—Its Arguments—Its Injunctions—Real Meaning Lost when Truth is Supposed to be Conformed to Formulæ alone, and not also to Methods of Operation—Importance of Observing this Distinction—The Use of the Word *Truth* in the Bible—Illustrations—Truth as Expressed in Life—Truth to the Divine Spirit is Action in Conformity with the Divine Method—Truth is Perceived in the Process of Searching for it—Dangers of Supposing Progress or Change Inconsistent with Absoluteness in Truth: The Source both of Infidelity and Bigotry—Right Views of Truth as a Corrective of these—The Truth in Revealed and Natural Religion Lies in its Method—He who Recognizes this a Friend to both Progress and Permanence—Inferences from the View here Presented—A Few Forms in Space may Reveal Universal Methods—One Mind may Represent God—And One Life, if Full of Love—The Mission of the Friend—Comfort in this Suggestion—The Changes of a Few Moments in Time may Reveal Universal Methods—Child or Man, with Short or Long Life, may both have Experience of them.

BEFORE such conceptions as are here to be unfolded can commend themselves to all, it is necessary to show their conformity to what men accept and serve when the truth is received and obeyed by them. Otherwise, some may not perceive how, if not identical with a form of statement, as, for instance, in a creed or a dogma, the truth can influence thought or action to the degree in which it should. They may find fault with a theory which seems to weaken faith because lessening confidence in that on which spiritual life depends for guidance. In the present chapter an endeavor will be made to show that this theory does not have the effect thus attributed to it, but rather the opposite.

It seems to be a legitimate inference, from what was said in the third chapter, that, to be rightly influenced by a statement, we need to be influenced by something more than the statement itself. But the same inference may be drawn as a result of other considerations. For instance, if truth were identical with a formula presenting it, why would not one's wisdom be proportioned to his memory? But of course it is not. Again, why is candor necessary in order to attain success in an intellectual investigation, or charity in a religious one? How can wise philosophers or earnest theologians, convinced to the contrary, too, yield a conscientious toleration to the views of their opponents? With what reason can they, in their words as well as in their deeds, virtually act upon the hypothesis that truth may be expressed in statements diametrically opposed to those that they themselves make? How could one say of opposing statements, "Both may be true," unless intending to admit, and conscious that the one to whom the assertion is addressed will just as readily admit, that by the truth something is meant which is communicated through the statement, but is not by any means identical with it. Or, to apply the same thought where, in this connection, it will have the most significance, *i. e.*, to the statements of creeds or dogmas of which mention has just been made, what church is there that fails to recognize the necessity, where one is to be influenced, as he should be, by such statements, of that spiritual discernment of which the Apostle Paul speaks when, in 1 Cor. ii., 14, he says that "the natural man receiveth not the things of the Spirit of God, . . . because they are spiritually discerned"? What is spiritual discernment? Let us consider it for a little, and, that there may be no doubt as to its meaning, let us examine it where there is the least possible opportunity of admitting a difference between the phraseology and the meaning which the phraseology is intended to convey; let us apply it, that is, to the words of the Bible.

The greater portion, perhaps, of this book is composed of history and prophecy. Who imagines that the history in it is valuable chiefly on account of the events related considered merely as events? Is it not rather on account of the events considered as illustrative of principles, illustrative, *i. e.*, of the *methods* of the divine government, of the modes according to which spiritual laws *operate?* Do commentators or do preachers represent that the mere memory of the transactions recorded in the book is more important than the morals to be drawn from the transactions which, in the order of their occurrence, indicate the methods of the development of spiritual life everywhere? Are not the individuals and the nations mentioned in the book understood to be typical of all individuals and nations? Are not their experiences recognized to be intended to reveal primarily the methods in which doubt or faith and sin or righteousness in every age and country are either punished or rewarded? Is it not the revelation of these methods that renders possible a sermon based upon a story in the Bible? Is it not the possibility of our conforming our own lives to the methods, that renders it possible for us to be benefited by the truth derivable from the story? Certainly the last four questions can be answered in the affirmative. Indeed, it is to the wellnigh universal recognition that such an answer can be made, that we must ascribe the fact that, rightly or wrongly, the "higher criticism" of the last two decades has been able to persuade so many that the acknowledging that the evidence in the earlier part of the Bible of tendencies which, in unscientific ages lead men to draw what are wrongly supposed to be historic lessons from an indiscriminate use of traditions and legends that are not historic, need not lessen one's faith in the spiritual truth of the revelation itself,—any more than need the use of figures by David in his psalms, or of parables by Jesus in his discourses.

The same principle applies to the prophecy of the Bible. Of what special value to our time is it to be told that Tyre or Sidon *shall be* destroyed on account of wickedness? While comparing dates we learn, of course, that these denunciations of the cities came before the destruction of them; and our faith in prophecy may be strengthened by noticing the fact. Yet the sole value of passages of this kind does not rest in such an application of them; nor their chief value. Why do men to-day read and reread these same passages? Why does the clergyman preach about them? Is it not because it is felt that they have a significance for all time, as well as for the times in which they were uttered? Do not methods of operation evidenced in prophecy as well as in history repeat themselves? Although certain words used may have been uttered in denunciation of particular cities, and fulfilled with literal exactness as applied to them, may not the methods expressed in the words be applied to every town or country, in which existing evils may provoke similar violence? The world learned of the philosophy of history from Herder. The Church, if it had had but very little of its treasured "spiritual discernment," might have learned the same from Moses, and thus proved the prestige which the children of eternity ought to have over those of time.

Now let us turn from history and prophecy to those parts of the Bible in which the Scriptural reasons for the uses of both have been distinctly stated. How many times, and in how clear language, are we informed that certain persons and events are to be interpreted representatively! How many times that Abraham, Moses, Joshua, David, Jonah, are typical of the Christ! How many times that the flood, the exodus, the wandering in the wilderness, the lifting up of the serpent, are emblematical of a universal method operating everywhere, and through which man can be delivered from sin! How many times is the word Israel or Babylon employed, not with literal exactness, but to indicate, by way of metonymy, a class of people inclined to righteousness or to unrighteousness!

Those parts of the Bible which are not devoted to history or prophecy or explanations of their methods of imparting truth may be classified under the head either of arguments or of injunctions. Let us notice what we can learn from these. Through arguments, truth is demonstrated. Through injunctions, it is merely stated. How is truth demonstrated in the Bible? The Apostle Paul, whether writing to the Romans or to the Hebrews, argues thus: "Abraham believed God, and it was counted unto him for righteousness" (Rom. iv., 3). Through faith, Abel, Enoch, Noah, Abraham, and countless others "obtained a good report" (Heb. xi., 39). Therefore, if the Christian believe, his faith also shall be so counted, and he also shall obtain a good report. And again, all that priests and sacrifices of the former Testament accomplished, the Christ of whom they were symbolical has accomplished (Heb. x., 7). Therefore the Christian, different as are the forms of his religion, is saved according to the same method. But evidently arguments of this kind have no force whatever, except so far as it is recognized that the truth of religion consists less in conformity to the apparent *form*, than to the *method of operation* which this form exemplifies. Or let us recall the words of the Christ. We are told that he never spake without a parable (Mark iv., 34). How do parables present the truth? By means of a parallel instance. They illustrate a principle applicable to one phase of life, through pointing to the way in which it operates in another real or fancied phase. They indicate the working of a law in one department or development of nature, through instancing its operation in a corresponding department or development. And they have no force whatever; they suggest no arguments at all, except so far as mankind recognizes that there is a sense in which to find the one method operating in all different departments and developments of nature is to find the truth.

The words which caused the common people to affirm that the Master "spake as one having authority" (Matt. vii., 29) were almost invariably these statements of parallels. "Behold the fowls of the air," he said; " . . . your Heavenly Father feedeth them. Are ye not much better than they?" (Matt. vi., 26). "If ye, being evil, know how to give good gifts unto your children, how much more shall your Father which is in heaven give good things to them that ask him?" (Matt. vii., 11). "Ye shall know them by their fruits. Do men gather grapes of thorns, or figs of thistles?" (Matt. vii., 16). Such were the statements of the Christ; and not alone in his case, but from the time when he stood upon the shores of Galilee without one priest to place a hand upon his head and ordain him as a messenger of God, down to the present, in the cases of all men whom the people hear with gladness, as they throng the halls of all the sects, statements in the form of parables or parallels have had an influence beyond all others in proving to men the presence of a mind that has penetrated to the sources of truth, and can reveal it. Why? Because the masses have recognized the connection between the truth and a method of operation applicable universally.

From the arguments of the Bible let us turn now to its injunctions. How are these presented? If its arguments affirm conformity to like methods operating beneath different effects which are mentioned, its injunctions imply this conformity. They refer to one series of effects that necessarily suggests another. Indeed, one could almost assert that that which mainly causes the Scriptural precepts to be accepted by so many with the authority of absolute truth is this fact. They are precepts which it can be said that men of every age and place, the Hindoo and the Hottentot, the Englishman and the Egyptian, can recognize to be truthful. The more they search the book, too, the more they find in it passages which can apply to almost every series of their own experience and of their neighbors', and equally well to almost every series of events in the history of the human race and of the material world. Upon whatever ground a man may base his confidence in the Bible, the testimony of every thoughtful mind, the implication of every Scriptural discourse, the confession of every new convert, proves that a main source of Scriptural authority lies in the fact which Coleridge stated when he said, "It finds me." Here is a book which satisfies the wants of human souls, just as the earth about one satisfies the wants of human bodies. The force of the argument of Coleridge is derived from the inference that the Power which made man must have made the world, and that inasmuch as the precepts of the Bible accord with the laws which operate in the world they must accord with the purposes of this Power. It would be difficult to recall a single Biblical statement of a spiritual truth which cannot be illustrated by showing the application of the method which it indicates to the methods operating in the realms of intellect and of physics. For instance, take a passage like the following: "Quench not the Spirit" (1 Thess. v., 19). The analogy is obvious. Pour not water on fire. Extinguish not the life of one element by adding another hostile to it. Do not drive away spirituality by drawing in worldliness.

There are other cases in which the method indicated is less easy to recognize. In these we need to remember this,—that truths are simply finite, transient, and concrete embodiments of the truth which is infinite, eternal, and absolute; and that in order to perceive the latter in a given formula, we must distinguish it from what is merely finite, transient, and concrete. For example, take a statement like the following: "Believe on the Lord Jesus Christ and thou shalt be saved" (Acts xvi., 31). The truth that is to influence us in this is either in the concrete, transient formula, or in the absolute, eternal method of operation indicated by the formula. But if in the formula, we cannot reconcile the statement with such statements as the following, which also are in the Bible: "Abraham believed God"—without the words *Jesus Christ* added—

"and it was counted unto him for righteousness" (Rom. iv., 3); "In every nation he that feareth him, and worketh righteousness"—without mention of believing—"is accepted" (Acts x., 35); "These, having not the law" —without any reference even to a knowledge of Jesus Christ—"are a law unto themselves" (Rom. ii., 14). Accordingly we must conclude that the absolute, eternal truth in the phrase, "Believe in the Lord Jesus Christ, and thou shalt be saved," is less in the formula than in the *method* indicated by it. This method grows clear to a finite mind in the proportion in which it is translated into finite terms, or, better, is made definite. These two words, *Jesus Christ*, are intended to remind one of what that person said and did as *representing God*. To one who recalls the character of the representation, the words make the injunction well nigh infinitely clearer to comprehension. Yet these two words are definitive and not infinitive. The absolute and eternal truth which they make plainer is the necessity of faith in spiritual supervision, love, aid. In every phase of nature, all persons who are comparatively ignorant, weak, and sinful need to trust for guidance in the wise, the strong, and the loving, and for the highest guidance in the highest wisdom, strength, and love,—hence in God. To define this method of salvation by annexing *Jesus Christ* to the statement, communicates good tidings to the souls who otherwise would have vague notions of a God unseen; but it does not, save in a negative sense, communicate bad tidings to the souls who cannot, or who do not, know of the definition which makes the infinite truth more finite. Considered in relation to the context and with an accurate conception of the meaning of the words *believe, saved,* and *Jesus Christ,* the passage quoted expresses a truth fundamental to all religious character and charity. But divorced from its connection, no one can know that *believe* means more than intellectual assent, or *saved* more than mere comfort in this world, or *Jesus Christ* more than the being who is sending people to perdition in Michael Angelo's picture of the "Last Judgment."

Once more, not only in the history, prophecy, arguments, and injunctions of the Bible do we find that the truth which men are to accept and obey involves conformity to a *method of operation*, but also, and in the clearest light, in passages in which the sacred writers have employed the word *truth*. The Bible does indeed apply the term to language. "I tell you the truth," said Jesus (John xvi., 7). But it has already been pointed out that it is said that he never spake without a parable; and that all parables are founded on a recognition of the conformity of two or more events to the same method of operation. Moreover, not only did the Christ say, "I tell you the truth," he also said, "I am the truth" (John xiv., 6); and one cannot account for such a use of terms unless conceiving of the truth as something different from words, though of course it may also include them.

What did the Christ mean by the expression? What could he have meant except that he conceived of himself as the truth just as all nature is the truth,—conceived of himself as a representative of the character of the Creative Power? But how is character represented? Always, as shown at the end of Chapter II., through methods of operation. "What is truth?" asked Pilate of Jesus (John xviii., 38); and was answered—in not the words but the deeds of the Master—that one acts according to the methods of truth when long-suffering and self-sacrificing. "I am the way," said Jesus, "the truth, and the life" (John xiv.,

6). What is a way but a method? What is a life but a progress according to a method? The Apostle, looking down that way, enjoined upon his followers to "walk in love, even as Christ also hath loved us, and hath given himself for us an offering and a sacrifice to God" (Eph. v., 2). "For I rejoiced greatly," said John, "when the brethren came and testified of the truth that is in thee, even as thou walkest in the truth" (3 John 3); and again, "Let us not love in word, neither in tongue; but in deed and in truth" (1 John iii., 18). To walk "in the truth" and to love "in the truth" must mean to pursue a certain method. Again, when the Christ says, "Every one that is of the truth heareth my voice" (John xviii., 37), he must refer to every one whose feelings, thoughts, and deeds accord with his own,—to every one in active sympathy with his methods of life. The same idea is conveyed too in language like the following: "If any man will do his will, he shall know of the doctrine, whether it be of God, or whether I speak of myself" (John vii., 17); "Light is come into the world, and men loved darkness rather than light, because their deeds were evil" (John iii., 19); "Not every one that saith unto me, Lord, Lord, shall enter into the kingdom of heaven; but he that doeth the will of my Father which is in heaven" (Matt. vii., 21).

This thought introduces the last topic mentioned in the heading of the present chapter, namely, the nature of truth as shown by men's ways of expressing it not only in language, which we have already considered, but in life. In Chapter II. it was pointed out that, when a man observes the different phases assumed, say, by a tree, at different times, and considers also that these phases all appear in an object that continues to occupy the same space,—in other words, that all take place in the same tree,—then this fact not only makes the method of operation intelligible, but also causes the tree to manifest life.

We have noticed how closely the Bible connects life and truth. We can perceive now the reason for this. One's spiritual life, however vaguely that term may be used, is determined by one's truth to the spirit,—when we use the term *spirit* in the highest sense, by his truth to the *divine spirit*. Truth to the *divine spirit* is that which acts according to the divine method. In the case of a man, because the words *action* and *life* thus used mean the same, it is life according to the divine method. But if truth were supposed to be identical with the formula, where would be the suggestion in the term of the necessity of life? Why might not the truth be wholly possessed by being learned by rote? Why might it not be supposed to be expressed in its entirety in the formula of a preceding generation? And if so, why would not the theory tend to make men satisfied with what they have, and so to check all effort to obtain more? So far, however, as the truth is supposed to involve conformity to a method of operation, it is evident that no one can imagine himself to possess it wholly, except so far as it influences action, except so far as he lives it. It is this conception of the truth that enables us to perceive why the publican, who smites upon his breast and sighs out, "God be merciful to me a sinner," though he may not have fulfilled many a requirement of a formal law, should be commended rather than the Pharisee, though he may have left not one jot or tittle of this law unfulfilled. The publican yearns for higher conceptions and attainments. **He lives** according to true methods, and so has the **truth**. The Pharisee is content with what he possesses already. He does not live according to true methods He does not have the truth (Luke xviii., 10–14).

Let, then, the souls so often blamed because they look away from what they have, and search on every side of them for more, toil on! Their toil, though it may gain them little to be touched or seen, may yet develop life in them. Each sigh may force still farther from their breasts the poisonous breath of error, each aspiration draw still nearer them the inspiring air of heaven. There is so much more truth on the earth than mortals dream that there can be! When Lessing said, "Did the Almighty, holding truth in his right hand and search for truth in his left hand, tender me the one that I should prefer, I should ask for the search for truth"; when Malebranche affirmed, "If I held truth a captive in my hand, I would let it fly that I might once more chase it, and capture it," they spoke far more the wisdom of the heart than of the head. The truth held in one's hand? Can truth be handled—all of it? Is not often the effort of obtaining it, the method of discovering it, its most important factor? If this be so, it is through the desire for truth, and not in any sating of the desire, that it can be possessed. This is the reason why

> "There lives more faith in honest doubt,
> Believe me, than in half the creeds."
> *In Memoriam: Tennyson.*

To the spirit, progress is more acceptable than a precept, life than a tale that is told. Through struggle men experience development, and doubt that leads to struggle is a means of grace. The moment of the Christ's intensest doubt came just before the greatest victory of his faith. The cry, "My God, my God, why hast thou forsaken me?" (Matt. xxvii., 46), was the minor prelude preceding the triumphant cadence, "It is finished" (John xix., 30).

Even the very infallible unchangeableness of which dogmatism sometimes boasts may be in itself a ground for grave suspicion. Is it the sign of a living thing to stand unmoved for centuries amid the shifting seasons of the world's advance?—to fix the gaze of greatest admiration on the past?—to find the holiest ideal there, and to long for the superior sanctity that has been buried? Did ever painter yet depict one faintest realization of a living faith in which the face was not turned rather toward the future? What is the influence that sways the individual or the community whose aim is sought amid the smoke of centuries consumed? Remember Lot's wife! There is a civilization beautiful to look upon, which may be a monument of what? Of death—possibly of damnation. It is a question whether, without being crushed and killed, a living thing—and truth is surely this—can ever be confined for long in a single unchanged mould; whether a root having any life at all will not necessarily have enough of force to bend and crack and cast aside whatever urn of worldly manufacture may surround it. Has not every age had experience enough to be taught that previous ages held too firmly to the form, that changes in the form do not affect the substance of the truth? Why then should each new phase of truth be met with the same old folly of opposing it? Why should a theoretical misconception, as foolish as the child's that takes the mask for the man, cause all those mournful, yet quixotic, crusades that tend to persecution, if they do not end in martyrdom? In the world of nature, once at least in every year, the white snows melt upon the mountains; and the gleaming ice upon the streams is heaved up, rent apart, and swept away. Why, now and then, should not like changes be expected in the world of thought? Why should not men anticipate a breaking up and disappearing of formal aspects, however bright and beautiful, however appropriate and satisfactory they may have seemed in their own now long past season? But what men might expect and should expect, they will not; and when these changes come,—alas for those who base their confidence on forms alone! Like men who pitch their tents upon the shifting sands of a flooding stream, they find all things about them trembling, crackling, sinking; and in the sudden frenzy of bewilderment it often happens that the very voice most boastful of unwarranted credulity becomes most blatant of an equally unwarranted despair. "Truth is a form," says one. "Forms change. This fact is patent. Therefore truth must change. There can be no enduring ground of certainty; by consequence, no faith. At best, the truth consists merely in sincerity to personal conviction,"—and, arguing thus, he ends by having no convictions. "Truth," says another, "is immutable and eternal; it cannot change, and, therefore, forms should not. No change can be compatible with faith whose essence is submission to external standards. Accordingly the Church must hold to these implicitly, and, if it have occasion, must enforce them by the exercise of its authority,"—and, arguing thus, he ends by exercising, as if in its behalf, his own authority alone. The first man goes astray because he has perceived an operation changing the formula, but, while perceiving this, has failed to recognize that in the method of the operation lies the truth; the second goes astray because he has observed a method, but has looked upon a single aspect of it as a mould to which all future aspects are to be conformed. He does

whole souls were yearning for the knowledge of the godlike; those who held to our ideals so bright a love that we could never keep our thoughts from it; those in the sunshine of whose smiles truth, that no longer felt the wintry influence of frigid frowns, broke into buds upon our lips and flowered all round them in our blushes, —were they not the dearest messengers to teach our souls of God? "Every one that loveth . . . knoweth God." And was not this—the knowledge of God's self—the fond possession that made our blood so thrill in all our pulses, that made our souls tremble as if in ecstasy to shake off the robes of matter, nay, that made this old earth here itself a heaven? If we knew God, indeed, what further blessing could existence furnish us? And would not all the blessedness of such a state be owing to a mood which friendship had developed in us? "Every one that loveth . . . knoweth God."

There certainly is comfort to an earnest mind in conceiving that the truth, with all its infinite essence, may be learned through knowledge of some single phase of it; that a single world may teach us of the universe, a single man, of God; that we may find, though not in an exclusive sense, our heaven in our household, and our God himself in every friend—in the least of all his children who is hungry and is fed by us, and is thirsty and is given drink by us (Matt. xxv., 35–40).

The range of truth, however, by considerations such as these, is simplified, not only in the realms of space, but also in the realms of time. The experiences of life are granted us that we may learn the truth through them. How long must life be, ere we shall have learned it thoroughly? The insect that can flutter through its brief existence in a day can experience birth and growth and death as truly as the mastodon. A few words or a few deeds may reveal to us the character of friends. Through them we may learn their methods of believing, feeling, doing; through them we may learn the truth concerning them. A few words from the book of revelation, a few evolutions in the works of nature,—why may they not reveal to us, with equal certainty, the character of Him who is the eternal, the infinite, and the absolute?

When the Christ declared that every one of the truth would hear his voice, whom did he mean to mention? Only souls that could speak wisely of a long experience? Only the men whose feeble feet had travelled through the whole hard path of life, whose limbs were tottering on the borders of a grave from which, perhaps, they shrank in fear of an offended Deity? Did he not mean the little children also, who, perhaps, could not articulate a sound, whose limbs were tottering too, but not from heaviness, and who shrank too, but not from that sweet face which had gazed upon them through harsh crowds that would have kept them back from him? The eternal, the infinite, and the absolute truth,—think not that a mortal's share of it can be measured in the scales of time or space. "One day is with the Lord as a thousand years" (2 Pet. iii., 8). The soul of a little child that dies is riper than we think, perhaps. Some of the smallest in the graveyards have lived the truth in a deeper sense than those whom men call great. Are any of us certain that it would have been worse for us had we died early? Is there not much promise in a promise of perpetual youth? Are not the cherub faces crowded on the canvas of the artist a vague prophecy of some superior joyousness and beauty in the children who go forth to live as children evermore within the realms of spirit? How is it with mortals when they linger longer here? Let withering lips and deathlike countenances tell. We have our good things—Heaven forgive us that we call them good!—on earth. And is this wretched and distorted lie into which the earth has shaped so many of us, to speak and do and be ourselves forever? And if we be not satisfied with what this world can make of us, if we rebel against it, what comes then? To the Christ, who spake, and did, and was the truth, the world cried, "Crucify him! crucify him!" It is so with many still. For them to speak the truth is death to influence, to do the truth is death to position, and to be the truth,—this is to complete the aim of life. It is to be sacrificed, to die, and to live in spirit only. Yet this fate may not be without its compensations. In the last address of the Christ to his disciples—the same in which he prophesied his coming crucifixion—he also said, "These things have I spoken unto you, that my joy might remain in you, and that your joy might be full" (John xv., 11).

CHAPTER V.

SIGNIFICANCE, RELIGIOUS, SCIENTIFIC, AND ARTISTIC, AS RESPECTIVELY ATTRIBUTABLE TO MENTAL ACTION, PREDOMINANTLY SUBCONSCIOUS, CONSCIOUS, AND BLENDED.

Results Reached in the Foregoing Chapters—Mental and Material Conditions Preceding the Recognition of Truth—Religious, Scientific, and Artistic Conceptions—How they Differ—Religious or Spiritual Meaning—The Occult Side of the Mind—Proof of Subconscious Intellection in Memory, Fright, Fever—Hypnotism—Its Effects Allied to those of Art—Germs of Hypnotic Suggestion—Subconscious Philosophical and Mathematical Intellection—Resulting from Previous Conscious Action as in Skill—Not Resulting from Previous Conscious Action: Coburn, Mozart, Blind Tom—Subconscious Diagnosis of Disease at a Distance—Subconscious Apprehension of Distant Occurrences—Both in Space and in Time—Mind-Reading and Mediumship—Automatic Writing—The Truth and the Limitations of Spiritualism—Hudson's Theory—The Investigation of the Subject Justifiable.

IN all the methods indicated in Chapters III. and IV. of ascertaining, characterizing, and expressing the truth, we have been considering the relations between form and significance. But, as stated in Chapter I., this is precisely the question involved in the study of art. The transition in this chapter, therefore, from the general to the special applications of our subject is strictly logical. But before making this transition complete, and confining our attention to art alone, let us notice, for the purpose of getting clearly in mind what is meant by artistic truth, certain other phases of truth with which it is sometimes confounded and from which, for this reason, it needs to be separated.

The conclusion reached in Chapter IV., so far as it applies to significance in general, was that we fail to understand all that is meant by *the truth* embodied in a form, whether of substance or of statement, unless we take into consideration certain circumstances or conditions with which the form is really or ideally connected as one link in a chain of causes and effects—in other words, unless we observe the relations of the form to some *method of operation*. This conclusion at once suggests the question how far the links in the chain of causes and effects with which the form is connected are apprehensible; and if, in answer to this, we find that, in some cases, they are apprehensible only implicitly, because mainly mental and therefore inaudible or invisible; and, in other cases, very explicitly, because mainly material and therefore audible or visible, we cannot refrain from inferring that the significance, in each case, because differently derived, must be somewhat differently characterized and expressed. Moreover, if we find that artistic significance, which in particular we are now to consider, includes that which is apprehended both implicitly and explicitly, it will follow that, in order to understand all about this significance, we must study the results of apprehension according to each of these two methods.

The conditions thus suggested as possible will be shown presently to be actual. This fact explains the necessity of our making distinctions here between religious, scientific, and artistic significance. Every one admits that religion is concerned fundamentally with that which is supposed to be spiritual, with that which has to do with ideas and emotions pertaining to the mind and soul; that science is concerned fundamentally with that which is material, with that which has to do with phenomena and series of phenomena pertaining to the external natural world; whereas art, being concerned with that which is human, can exclude from consideration neither the spiritual nor the material, but must include both, having to do, on the one hand, with thoughts and emotions which belong to the realm of that which cannot be handled, heard, or seen, and, on the other, with natural phenomena which belong to the realm of that which can be. It is evident, therefore, that, to understand art, we must first understand something about each of the two spheres—that of religion and that of science—upon which art encroaches and whose effects it combines.

It will be recognized, moreover, that of the three—religion, science, and art—religion is the most nearly allied to the infinite, the eternal, and the absolute, which were considered in Chapter II., and therefore is that which we should naturally take up here first in order. This we shall do, applying each of the principles that will be unfolded in the chapters that follow to significance, first, in religion, after that in science, and finally in art. As a result, we shall find each phase of significance giving rise to what—because we lack a better word—we may term *conceptions* that are differently derived, characterized, and expressed. We shall find that they are derived, though not necessarily entirely developed, in religion, from what is termed the inner world, through the method known as *inspiration;* in science, from the outer world, through *investigation;* and in art, partly from the inner world and partly from the outer, which two are correlated in thought through *imagination.*

Again, we shall find that the conceptions are characterized in religion by *faith*, in science by *knowledge*, and in art by a combination of elements entering some into faith and some into knowledge, resulting in *ideality;* and finally, that the conceptions are expressed in religion through *spiritually influential suggestion;* in science through *logical formulation;* and in art through a combination of certain elements entering some into *suggestion* and some into *formulation*, resulting in *analogical representation.* These statements will enable the reader to understand the drift of the following chapters, as otherwise might not be possible, owing to the many ideas which must be considered in order to treat the subject in all its bearings.

The line of thought unfolded in Chapters I. and II. has prepared us to recognize that what we mean by significance is a subjective mental experience attributable to some objective excitation. Religious significance may be said to be an experience of this kind which is due to spiritual excitation; or which, in connection with any form of excitation, conveys a spiritual import. But what is spiritual import? It is something that is acknowledged to exist, not only by Christians, but by Mohammedans, Mormons, Buddhists, Hindoos, and, in fact, by all who admit that there are any distinctively occult sources of truth. It is something that is believed to be conveyed from a region which for all men during most of the time, and for most men during all the time, is entirely hidden from consciousness. It is believed that from this region, in certain circumstances, vague emotions and thoughts not only, but definite facts and words, can come to the mind. But if this region exist, there must be characteristics connecting the mind with influences coming from it, characteristics rendering possible thoughts and emotions affected not only in a normal way, as through the eyes or ears or any other senses, but also in a way that may be termed supernormal, and is sometimes termed supernatural.

If there be such characteristics of mind, we can account, philosophically, for religious and, so far as allied to religious, for artistic *inspiration*, as it is termed. Otherwise, we cannot. Are there such characteristics? There certainly are. There is a hidden, occult sphere of the mind, of the operations of which we are ordinarily unconscious, and of the results of which we know only so far as they influence another sphere of which we are ordinarily conscious. So different, in fact, are the operations in these two spheres, often engaged, as we shall find, in carrying on at the same time two different processes of thought (see page 71), that they have been termed—though, of course, not with scientific exactness, as the reader will understand whenever suggestions of this are made hereafter—two minds, namely, the conscious and the subconscious, which latter term is used to indicate a mind of some of the results of which we are conscious, but of the processes of which we are unconscious. It is noteworthy, too, that, even in the physical frame, there are indications of duality in the constitution of the mind. Not only are there two separate lobes in the brain, each apparently containing a separate set of mental organs, but there are two systems of nerves connecting the brain with the rest of the body. It has not been proved that, of the two brains, one is the seat of conscious and the other of subconscious action; but this has been proved of the two sets of nerves. Those of the cerebrospinal system, which move the hands, limbs, and the facial and vocal organs, are controlled by conscious action; those of the sympathetic system, which move the circulatory and digestive organs, are controlled by subconscious action. To complete the correspondence, as preparatory to observing the way in which the conscious and the subconscious spheres often work conjointly, it is well to notice, also, that there are certain movements, like winking and breathing, which can be carried on both consciously and subconsciously.

In considering these two spheres of mental activity and the relations between them, it is unnecessary to dwell upon the sphere of which we are conscious. But it is important, for a proper realization of all the bearings of the two forms of intellect and of the harmonizing of them in art, to develop, for a little, certain facts and inferences with reference to the subconscious sphere. The facts with which we are most familiar are afforded, perhaps, by memory. The mind is constantly recalling experiences of which it has been so thoroughly oblivious that they have been supposed to have been lost. But equally conclusive evidences of the same subconscious possibility may be furnished by other mental processes. When trains of thought are conducting to conclusions with the rapidity of lightning, what is the mind doing but making use of stores not only, but of methods that are not outside of it but in it, and yet are hidden so deeply in it as to be beyond the reach of any conscious control? In normal mental action we are only partly aware of the extent and importance of these stores, and may be startled to hear it stated that, probably, nothing whatever that a man has ever seen, heard, touched, tasted, smelled, or, by the slightest practice, developed into the suggestion of a habit, is lost, but remains indelibly impressed upon the intellect and character. Nevertheless such seems to be the case. Captain Frederick Marryat, author of "The Adventures of a Naval Officer," relates that at one time he jumped into the sea to save a sailor's life, and, on rising, found himself in the midst of blood, giving evidence of the presence of a shark. Between that moment and the moment almost immediately following, when he was rescued, he re-experienced, according to his story, about everything that he had ever done or said or thought. Coleridge states, in his "Biographia Literaria," that in a German village near Göttingen a young woman, twenty-five years of age, who could neither read nor write, was seized with a fever. While in this state she kept constantly repeating Latin, Greek, and Hebrew. The Roman Catholic priest of the village declared her to be possessed of a devil. But her physician, being of a scientific turn, traced back her history. He found that she had once been a servant in the house of a Protestant pastor. This man had been in the habit, while walking up and down in a passage into which the kitchen opened, of reading in a loud voice Latin, Greek, and rabbinical Hebrew. Many of the very phrases, which the physician had taken down in writing at her bedside, were found in the rabbinical books in this man's library.

Results analogous to these,—occasioned, as will be noticed, in the one case by fright and in the other by fever,—may be produced by hypnotism. That hypnotism exists as a fact no one informed with reference to the subject now thinks of denying. An influence that can cause a patient to have a tooth pulled or a limb amputated without experiencing conscious pain is a reality. An influence, not induced by another, but self-induced by nervous excitement, which can cause our Southern negroes in revival meetings to fall down as if dead, and fail to feel pins vigorously stuck into them, as the author has seen the experiment tried, is a reality. This much being conceded to hypnotic influence, as several references must be made to it hereafter, it is well, at the outset, to say that there is every reason for supposing that the immediate effect of this influence, like that of fright and of fever, is physical, and not, as is sometimes supposed, mental. It may be described as a method of putting the conscious body and, through it, the conscious mind to sleep. When this has been done, the subconscious mind may be made to wake up, and to take charge of the body's organs of expression. But there is no proof that hypnotism does any more than furnish an opportunity, availing itself of which the subconscious mind can exercise its influence in a way normal to itself, yet not ordinarily observed because hidden behind the activities of the conscious mind.

It is well to notice, too, that hypnotism, involving as it does a kind of skill which may be acquired, partakes of the nature not of religion but of art (see Chapter XV.). Formerly, and in some cases to-day, the hypnotizer caused a disk to revolve before the eyes of his subject or made passes before them with his hands. But now many experts, especially if dealing with one who has often been subjected to their influence, can induce the state by a single glance or word. In the former case, it is evident that the physical result is artificially produced by a series of regularly recurring effects; and even in the latter case we can see how this may be true, inasmuch as it would be in accordance with what we know of the vibratory nature of nervous excitation. But notice, now, that in any series of regularly recurring effects, we have an analogy to the effects produced in art by rhythm and proportion; and not only to these, but, as science has shown, to the effects produced by all sounds and colors when they are æsthetically pleasing in themselves, or when they are blended with others so as to form harmony. (See Chapters XII. and XIII. of "Art in Theory," also the parts treating of this subject in "Rhythm and Harmony in Poetry and Music," and in " Proportion and Harmony of Line and Color.") In connection with such series of regularly recurring physical effects, which are characteristic of all classes of art-forms, these forms are supposed to suggest significance. But it is in connection with just such series of regularly recurring physical effects that hypnotism is sometimes induced. Moreover, whether induced thus or not, the influence over thought and emotion exerted in connection with hypnotism is invariably exerted over the subconscious mind and is also a result, as we shall find by-and-by, of suggestion. Now, as applied to art, we are trying to find that in the mind which develops the significance which is suggested through forms. Is it not logical to find it in this subconscious region, in which hypnotism proves that suggestions are, in all cases, naturally developed, and are in some, if not in all cases, developed in connection with regularly recurring physical effects influencing the conscious mind in a way exactly analogous to the effects produced by the forms of arts.

The germs of thought from which the conceptions of the hypnotic patient are developed are often very elementary in character. Subjects possessing no oratorical gifts, for instance, are told to personate some famous public speaker, and at once they set out, and, with apparent ease, deliver addresses closely resembling not only in phraseology but in method some speech of this man which they have previously heard or read, though only in an extremely superficial and heedless way. The author knows of a reasonably authenticated instance, being personally acquainted with all the parties concerned, in which—though in the presence, indeed, of one who knew the Italian language, which fact may have influenced the result—a man who knew nothing of this language, when hypnotized by another, who also knew nothing of it, was made to sing, with correct Italian words and pronunciation, a song which the subject had heard but once and this years before.

This subconscious action of the mind, of which we are speaking, is not confined, however, to memory. If it were, the results could all be allied to the ordinary phenomena of recollection, of which it would merely be an unusual development. Similar action is evident in connection with logical and mathematical processes, and even with those involving skill, which would appear, at first thought, especially dependent upon conscious direction. Von Hartmann, in his "Philosophy of the Unconscious," as translated by W. C. Coupland, quotes this passage from Jessen's "Psychology": "When we reflect on anything with the whole force of our mind, we may fall into a state of entire unconsciousness, in which we not only forget the outer world, but also know nothing at all of ourselves and the thoughts passing within us. After a shorter or longer time, we then suddenly awake as from a dream, and usually at the same moment the result of our meditation appears clearly and distinctly in consciousness without our knowing how we have reached it. Also, in less severe meditation, there occur moments in which a perfect vacancy of thought is combined with a consciousness of our own mental effort, to which, in the next moment, a more vivid stream of thought succeeds. Certainly, some practice is required to combine serious reflection with simultaneous self-observation, as the endeavor to observe thoughts in their origin and their succession may easily produce disturbances of thinking and arrest the evolution of our thoughts. Repeated attempts, however, put us in a position clearly to perceive that, in fact, in every arduous reflection, a constant inner pulsation or a constant changing ebb and flow of thoughts, as it were, takes place—a moment in which all thoughts disappear from consciousness, and only the consciousness of an inner mental strain remains, and a moment in which the thoughts stream in, in greater fulness, and distinctly emerge into consciousness. The lower the ebb, the stronger the succeeding flood is wont to be; the stronger the previous inner tension, the stronger and livelier the contents of the emerging thoughts." Whether or not the reader has ever been able to detect these two processes in his own thinking, he will at least recognize that others have done so; and it is in logical accordance with the inferences derived from the existence of both processes that certain scholars have maintained that by fixing their attention, in the evening just before retiring for the night, upon some subject,—whether details to be committed to memory or problems to be solved,—they could find their work very much furthered, if not wholly completed, in the morning. It is said that the astronomer Kepler used to practise upon this theory.

The fact of the existence, side by side in the mind, of action both subconscious and conscious, is much more easy to prove than most of us are aware. How often have we heard a friend unconsciously hum, or even sing aloud in perfect time and tune, a song, while all his conscious energies were directed toward the accomplishment of a task entirely different in character! We are all more or less familiar too with the conditions under which a conscious action or series of actions may be made to become unconscious. Every one who has acquired skill in any department knows that it is a result of practice continued until the mind has become enabled to superintend a large number of details without having any of them clearly in consciousness. Every musician, for instance, is aware that after repeating a composition on the piano the execution may become so familiar that his fingers will play it automatically, as it were, while his thoughts are very intently fixed upon something else, possibly upon the general expression of the music, possibly upon something having nothing to do with music in any form.

When the subconscious action of the mind takes place in connection with logical, mathematical, or musical processes which a man has learned and mastered, we may always attribute it, as we do recollection, to previous conscious action. But there are cases in which previous conscious action has had nothing to do with the subconscious action. In these we begin to have suggested a difference, which will be brought out clearly hereafter, between religious and artistic inspiration. As illustrating what is meant, take first the cases of lightning calculators, as they are termed—many of them mere children, who have hardly mastered reading and writing, much less arithmetic. In a way apparently unknown to themselves, they are able to solve the most intricate mathematical problem almost as rapidly as it can be read to them. Zerah Coburn was but eight years old when exhibited before audiences of the foremost mathematicians of his time. Here, according to the English "Annual Register" of 1812, are two of the questions asked him, and answered before the numbers could be written down: "What is the square root of 106,929?" "What is the cube root of 268,336,125?" Or take, again, the cases of musicians able to execute apparently the most difficult compositions without having gone through any previous study or practice. Mozart was only three years old when he began to play in public concerts, and when only eight years old he had composed a symphony for a full orchestra. He was, however, the son of a musician, and his facility might be attributed to some extent to his surroundings or to heredity. But neither of these reasons can in any way account for the performances of others. There was, for instance, in our own country, Blind Tom, as he was called. He was an exceptionally ignorant negro, yet he could remember and execute, apparently, anything that was played but once before him, and, without a moment's hesitation, he could sometimes add to it variations as successful as the average of those resulting from long hours of labor on the part of educated musicians.

In these cases, the ultimate results of subconscious action are not essentially different from what might be expected if the facility were acquired through practice directed by conscious effort. It is possible to conceive of thoroughly educated mathematicians and musicians who, after long experience, might produce effects exactly similar to those that have just been mentioned. We can only say of these latter effects that in them the subconscious facility was not acquired through conscious effort *as a fact*. But now, going a step farther, we shall find that there are cases in which it could not have been acquired thus *as a possibility*. We shall find that the subconscious mind is sometimes influenced by conditions or occurrences with which it could not have become acquainted through the eyes or ears, or by any method through which the conscious mind obtains or develops knowledge or thought. The following is an illustration of such a case: Some years ago, my friend, Professor John W. Churchill of Andover Theological Seminary, in order to try an experiment, took the names and addresses of two persons in Boston, of whom he knew nothing, except that they were patients of a physician of his acquaintance. With these addresses in his possession he called upon a certain Dr. Tucker, residing in Brooklyn, N. Y. This Dr. Tucker, a graduate of the Harvard Medical School, claimed to have discovered in himself, soon after beginning to practise, a peculiar supernormal gift. My friend wished to test it. "Can you prescribe," he asked, "for a person now in Boston?" "I think so," said the physician. "Have you his address?" My friend read one of the addresses that he had brought. "I will go," said the physician, "and see the patient." Then, placing his hand on his brow, he began to talk something like this: "Number —, Blank Street. Yes, I see—red brick house—two storeys—bay window on the first floor. I enter—a winding stairway. The patient is in the second-storey front room—a lady—blonde—blue eyes—rather stout—about thirty-five years old—is troubled," etc., describing her symptoms and ending with a diagnosis and prescription. After attending to this patient, the physician went through a similar process with reference to the other. My friend handed a copy of what had been said, as taken down by the Brooklyn physician's stenographer, to the physician in Boston. "Everything here," said this physician, "is as accurate as it would be if the one who dictated it had come here by rail, visited the houses, and heard the patients describe their own symptoms." In olden times—possibly in some places in our own time—a physician whose mind could act in this way would be considered to be under the influence of divine inspiration. But Dr. Tucker is clearly not so. The ability to work "signs and wonders" of this kind does not necessarily guarantee the truth of the words uttered by the workers of them. The author knows of at least one patient—a son of the Rev. Dr. J. M. Ludlow, of Orange, N. J.—with reference to whom the subconscious diagnosis of this physician, though agreeing with that of other eminent physicians consulted, was shown by a post-mortem examination to have been unmistakably erroneous. Yet a previous description, supernormally given, of the symptoms and appearance of the patient had been as accurate as in the cases mentioned above.

In these cases the conscious mind seems to have been able to direct the course of the subconscious mind, causing it, apparently, to move from Brooklyn to Boston. Here is another case in which no such control was exercised. Yet the conditions at a distance were just as accurately perceived. Notice, too, how thoroughly the circumstances justify such a use as is made in "Macbeth" of the appearance of Banquo's ghost. The story was related to the author by an eye-witness, General Kargé, a prominent officer in our war of secession, and, for twenty years or more, a professor in Princeton College. He told the story as one of the reasons leading to an abandonment, on his part, of wholly materialistic views of life, into which he had fallen in early manhood. He said that during the war of secession, while recruiting in New York City for the cavalry, he was on Fourteenth Street opposite the Academy of Music, taking supper in the rooms of an Austrian military engineer who also was in the service of our government. This Austrian had a son, a graduate of the military school of Hanover, Germany, who, some months before this, with his father's connivance, had eloped from that place with the daughter of a Jewish banker, whose consent to her marriage could not be obtained. According to Jewish customs, the banker, after his daughter's flight, had gone through a ceremony in his synagogue excommunicating and anathematizing her for marrying against his will and outside her race. Very naturally this ceremony had had a serious effect upon the daughter's mind. At the time of the occurrence about to be related, the Jewess was presiding at the table at which the engineer and the author's friend were seated, her husband being absent. Suddenly, her hand, which happened to be holding a cup of tea, and her whole frame began to quiver, then, with a frightened look upon her face, she shrieked out in German, "My father is dead! My father is dead!" and fell senseless to the floor. A physician was summoned, but the lady, though partially restored, did not, for a long time at least, recover her reason. Soon after the physician had arrived, the Austrian engineer and the author's friend, in talking over the circumstances, decided to take down the exact time of the day. They did so, and three weeks later—telegraphic communication between Europe and America had not then been established—they received information that the banker had died in Germany at virtually the same hour at which the events just described had taken place in New York.

Exactly what was the form assumed by the impressions conveyed to this Jewess, the author's friend never ascertained. It never was feasible to do so, owing to the state of her mind. But that sometimes in such cases persons are seen, and at other times words are heard, seems abundantly proved. Certain reports made to the English Society of Psychical Research, published by Meyers and Gurney in a volume entitled "Phantasms of the Living," contain accounts of something like six hundred experiences of the same general character, all occurring in our own times, and confirmed by the testimony of at least two persons. Many of these persons, too, who all give their names and addresses, are widely known. One remarkable feature of such occurrences is that, in an occult way, they make known not only that which is distant in space, but sometimes also future in time, nothing, perhaps, being better authenticated than the experience which certain persons have of premonitions. Nor is there much reason to doubt that, in rare cases, the remote future [1] even is foreseen with

[1] When studying this subject, several years ago, the author used to hear quite a number of predictions, but the conclusion reached by him was that in no circumstances was it worth while to anticipate either trouble or success on the supposition that the predictions might be fulfilled. Almost all of them were proved to be mere fabrications of fraud or fancy. But now and then, with just sufficient frequency to throw doubt upon the result's being due to mere coincidence, such a prediction would be fulfilled, and with marvellous accuracy. For instance, an English psychometrist, consulted without premeditation because of a sign seen on a door,—a man who, as a psychometrist (see note on page 120), might, of course, have merely perceived distant property occultly, and, as any man might upon seeing it normally, have made a guess with reference to its prospective value,—described a house, of the existence of which the author was conscious of knowing nothing. The house was said to be a thousand miles or so away from where they were, and in a certain State where the author had never spent more than a week, the name of which State was given. The house was described so that its identity and surroundings were unmistakable, such terms being used as "near standing water," and—to quote from memory two phrases that seem to have been omitted from the notes written immediately after the interview—"unpainted," and "two storeys and a tower." It was stated that, on account of visiting a place in sight of this house, the author would obtain a sufficient sum of money to become independent. Two

visitor, "and was told so-and-so about it." Indeed, the writer, in experimenting once with an extremely successful mind-reader, found that certain words and questions written upon concealed papers could be read more accurately when the one who wrote them did not concentrate his thought upon them, but, in a general way, thought of something else.

Connected with this ability of the mind, through its subconscious powers, to receive communications from outside itself are some very interesting developments. The Rev. William Stanton Moses (M.A. Oxon.) states that while his hand was automatically writing his "Psychography," he spent his time in reading Plato. It is frequently supposed that such statements are due to self-deception or falsehood, and that all automatic writing on the part of "spiritual mediums" is fraudulent. In some cases this may be so (see page 82). But in other cases it is not. The author is well acquainted with a Presbyterian Doctor of Divinity, in exceptionally good standing, who himself, with other members of his family, practised automatic writing, till the results became so inexplicably accurate as literally to frighten them and they desisted. The author is acquainted with another person into whose mind come the words of essays concerning subjects of which, sometimes, the person writing them knows nothing when the essays begin. The sentences in these essays are involved, and their meanings difficult to determine. But after being written down, the one whose hand has transcribed them studies them, exactly as one would an old English text, and then translates them into plain English and publishes them—usually in religious weeklies. This person is a "Spiritualist," the reader may think. Not at all; but, at the time when these things were told, had never attended a "spiritualist" séance, and was strongly opposed to any one's doing it. Then an untrustworthy enthusiast, the reader may think. Not at all, again; but was the president of a society with ramifications all over the country, among the officers and members of which were clergymen and others whose names were household words in exceptionally conservative Christian denominations.

Indeed, any of us who may succeed in gaining the confidence of those about us will be amazed to find how many have had individual experiences of such a nature as to confirm the general trustworthiness of all the statements that have been made here with reference to the occult action of the mind. "You knew my son James," said a well-known Episcopal bishop to a friend of the author. "The night that he died, a thousand miles away from home, he came back, and we saw him." After making every allowance possible for mistakes in judgment, for mere hallucinations, and for coincidences, there remains a mass of evidence in rejecting which a man shows more credulity with reference to material limitations than he shows with reference to immaterial possibilities in accepting.[1] There are, however, two good reasons why people generally refrain from telling of such experiences in promiscuous society. Both reasons probably are at the root

---

[1] An exhaustive enumeration and description of treatises dealing with the occult will be found in Chapter XVIII., as also in the Bibliographical Index of "Demon Possession and Allied Themes," written by J. L. Nevius, D.D., for forty years a Presbyterian missionary to the Chinese, and published by the Fleming H. Revell Company of Chicago, 1894. Few are aware how thoroughly and scientifically this whole subject has been studied, or how extensive and valuable is the literature that treats of it. Dr. Nevius, it may be said, acknowledges communications from spirits; but from evil spirits only, dividing into good and evil those that the "modern spiritualist" would divide into more and less advanced orders.

of the theory of some of the Theosophists that a man should not tell of them in any society; and one reason certainly justifies the Hebraic laws against consulting soothsayers or practising sorcery. The first reason is that when one talks of such experiences to those who have no confidence in his keenness and judgment, he is in danger of making a fool of himself. The second is that when he talks of the same to those who have confidence in him, he is in danger of making fools of them. If they be led to believe in any man, to the extent of following his advice, who practises an occult art, this man has it in his power to ruin them; and the more of an adept he is, the more he has it in his power to do this. The records of the police courts of every large city reveal that many a "professional" fortune-teller, clairvoyant, medium, is merely a paid agent, leading the credulous into speculation, and even, occasionally, into vice. The slight facility in mind-reading which enables one to give his visitors' names and vaguely tell half a dozen incidents of their past lives is only a net spread in which the more easily to entrap some man into buying stock in a certain mine that has no value, or some woman into seeking employment in certain houses where virtue receives no consideration. Even a "professional" who intends no harm may be indolent or self-indulgent, or, at least, loath, for a few dimes, to undergo the nervous exhaustion frequently incident upon a genuine practice of his "gift." The author himself, upon placing his hand on the heart of one man when in this abnormal state, found it beating at the rate of about two hundred strokes a minute. No wonder if the "medium" thus affected preferred ordinarily, as was said of him, to practise sleight of hand, accompanied by tales conjured from his own normal imagination. Other "mediums," again, who have no wish to deceive, are so constituted, physically, that the very hypnotic susceptibility enabling them to give reports from the subconscious mind forces them to report, more than anything else, that which is in the thought and wish of their visitor. Others still,—and this is a very frequent result,—with the most honest intentions, seem unable to distinguish what the subconscious mind, supposed to be sent on its journey, sees or hears, from what the conscious mind imagines it possible to see or hear. Of course, to follow implicitly the advice of either of these last two classes would be about as wise as to follow that of an insane person. Finally, there are others who, though they can clearly distinguish the action of the subconscious mind, mistake its significance, and, as in the case mentioned on page 75, give advice that is erroneous.

Thomas J. Hudson, in "The Law of Psychic Phenomena," attributes all occult manifestations to the subconscious mind, acting either independently or as influenced by the conscious or unconscious thoughts or feelings of others. Modern "spiritualists" do not believe that this theory can account for all the facts. Owing to communications apparently received from some person who has passed away, and who only, as is alleged, could know of occurrences that are mentioned, they attribute many of the phenomena of which we have been speaking to the influence of spirits. But suppose that one accept this theory —what then? Does it change, in the least, the conditions pointed out in the last paragraph? May not communications coming through a genuine medium be just as untrustworthy as they would be if coming through one whose "gift" was owing to some phase of what is termed mere hypnotism? Are not many statements

CHAPTER VI.

SIGNIFICANCE AS ATTRIBUTABLE TO MENTAL ACTION: RELIGIOUS CONCEPTIONS HAVING THEIR SOURCE IN INSPIRATION.

Subconscious and Conscious Influences Found in all Intellection, but the Main Source of it Different in Religion, Science, and Art—Making it in Each Different in Kind—Origin of Religious Conceptions Concerning a Future State of Rewards and Punishments—Often Attributed to Natural Causes—Should be Attributed to Influences from Nature's Occult Side—Shown in Susceptibility of the Primitive, Uneducated Man to Such Influences—Instinct and Reason—Instinctive and Reflective as Correlated to Subconscious and Conscious Intellection—Result of Subconscious Intellection Allied to the Teachings of Nature and Religion—To the Mental Action of Animals—Of Negroes, Indians, and those Subject to Hallucinations, with Inferences therefrom—Like Inferences with Reference to the Origin of Religion Drawn from Primitive Religious Customs—With the Growth of Intelligence Physical Occult Manifestations are Considered Less Important than Verbal—But the Verbal Continue to be Associated with Subconscious Intellection—Truth Obtainable from this Depends on Suggestion Developed in it—Truth of the Suggestion Depends on Conscious as well as Subconscious Intellection Exercised by Some One—The Conscious Mind Modifies Everything Received from the Subconscious, Making it not Less Inspired, but More Intelligent—This the Condition in Inspired Writings—Intellectual Progress Resulting from this Form of Inspired Influence.

IN Chapter V. attention was directed to the two different spheres of mental action,—the subconscious and the conscious; especially to the former, for the reason that it is generally less understood. It was intimated that from this, *i. e.*, the subconscious, is derived, though not necessarily entirely developed, the religious phase of significance that may be said to have its source in *inspiration;* from the conscious the scientific phase that may be said to have its source in *investigation;* and from both together the artistic phase that may be said to have its source in *imagination.* The phrase, "derived, though not necessarily entirely developed," is important in order to express the exact truth. As shown on page 65, the range of a man's physical possibilities includes results attributable both to subconscious and to conscious activity; and it is logical to infer that the same is true of his mental possibilities. In other words, it is logical to infer that the results of both forms of activity are to be found in all departments of intellection. In religion, those mental possibilities of thought and emotion which are first influenced from without may be supposed, for reasons given in Chapter V., to be in the subconscious region, the results of which dominate over results—which nevertheless, as we shall find hereafter, must interpret them—in the conscious region; in science, the mental possibilities first influenced are in the conscious region, and its results dominate over results—which nevertheless, as we shall find hereafter, must intuitively judge of them—in the subconscious region; and in art, both the mental possibilities first influenced and the dominance may be either in the subconscious region, which is the religious requirement, or in the conscious region, which is the scientific; but whether in the one or in the other, no results ever become artistic except when, as in skill, there is a harmonious blending of influences traceable to both regions. Let it be understood, therefore, that while, for theoretical purposes, we are now to analyze and separate the actions of the subconscious region from those of the conscious, this is not because conceptions in either religion, science, or art are supposed to be determined by either phase of intellection exclusively. As will become evident hereafter, a clear recognition of the constant interaction between both phases will enable us to avoid many not uncommon errors.

The fact that artistic significance is derived from the same mental sphere, in part, as that of religion, and, in part, as that of science, modifies all the accompanying conditions of art to such extent as to make it virtually different in kind from either of the other two. A religious conception cannot become artistic until imagination has presented it in a form which manifests an observation of external appearances and an information with reference to them as accurate, in some regards, as are those of science. Nor can a scientific conception become artistic before imagination has haloed it about with suggestions as inspired, in some regards, as are those of religion. It is evident, too, as already intimated on page 63, that in order to understand either the range or the limitations of art, we must begin by understanding both that which allies it to these two other departments, and also that which differentiates it from them.

Turning to the first department, it will be recognized that religious conceptions are influenced not alone by the spiritual, but also, more or less, by the material. Material surroundings are capable of, at least, illustrating religious conceptions, and of being used, by way of reference, in communicating them. Nevertheless, the degree of the dependence of religion upon such surroundings is very much less than that of art. In order to realize this, let us try to get a clear understanding of exactly what is the degree of this dependence,—of exactly what is the source to which we can mainly attribute the phenomena of religion. Possibly every reader of this volume has heard even the fundamental belief in existence after death attributed to some one religious system, as, for instance, to the revelations recorded in the Hebrew and Christian Scriptures. Yet every observant traveller or historian knows that this belief is practically universal, as proved not only by that which is usually taught, but by such practices as the placing with the dead of their weapons and clothing, as among the aboriginal Americans, Australians, and Africans ; or the worshipping of the dead, and, at stated seasons, scores of years after their burial, the spreading of tables before their graves, as among the East Indians, Japanese, and Chinese; as well as by what is indicated upon the monuments and taken for granted in the literature of ancient Assyria, Egypt, Greece, and Rome. Indeed, it is simply a fact that among the people of Asia to-day there are more customs and ceremonies suggesting a belief in a life after death than there are among the Christians of Europe and America ; and there are more references to such a life in the literature of ancient Greece and Rome than in that of Judea. Every school-boy who has studied classic mythology can recall descriptions of Elyseum and Hades in the writings of the former peoples ; but our most learned commentators have failed to find more than a very few references to any such belief throughout the entire Old Testament. Nor among non-Christian people is there any failure to believe in future states of rewards and punishments. These also are described, or taken for granted, by the classic writers, and are just as thoroughly taught by the Buddhists and other religionists of the Orient as by ourselves.

Now, how did such beliefs originate ? The theory held

a few years ago attributed them, except among the Hebrews, to the imagination. It was said that they were gradually developed in human experience, at times when it was affected by such results as the rustling of trees in dark woods, or the dashing of waves on lonely shores—results arousing the mind to superstition, while they worked upon the sources of apprehension and conscience. Even more specific beliefs with reference to the personality of the gods, and their relations to men, were supposed to be derived through natural methods of development—some of them, for instance, through the same as those causing the formation of language. Take, for example, such an argument as this: When men had no word for the sun, they would naturally call it the father of the day, or—for a similar reason—call the earth a mother; and owing to this usage of words they would, after a time, come to associate real fatherhood with the one, or motherhood with the other, and finally to imagine each to have a personality, and thus to worship the sun or the earth as a god. Max Müller, in the fourth of his lectures on "The Science of Religion," gives a modification of this view, although still attributing the origin of religion to imagination, by saying that when the primitive man, feeling his incompleteness and need of dependence, and wanting something like a father in heaven, chose the name *sky* to express his conception of it, he "did not mean . . . that the visible sky was all he wanted. . . . But when that name had to be used with the young and the aged, with silly children and doting grandmothers, it was impossible to preserve it from being misunderstood. The first step downwards would be to look upon the sky as the abode of that being which was called by the same name. . . . Lastly, many things that were true of the visible sky would be told of its divine namesake, and legends would spring up destroying every trace of the deity that once was hidden beneath that ambiguous name."

There is one important defect common to all these explanations. This is that they fail to go to the bottom of the subject. They fail to show us why winds, waves, or skies, in combination with darkness, loneliness, or weakness, should cause a man to associate noise, force, or height with the influence of spirits; or to show us why particular uses of language or applications of it to things on earth or in heaven should suggest this influence. We attribute certain noises in our houses to the shutting of a door, to the draft of a furnace, or to the gnawing of mice. But why do we do this? Because we have had experience, or others have had experience of which they have told us, of similar noises that could be traced to these sources. This is that which occasions and justifies our inferences. Just so, experiences of his own or of others such as are related on page 76 would justify superstitious inferences on the part of the primitive man. Otherwise, though he might attribute certain sounds heard to birds or animals, he would scarcely think of attributing them to spirits. Take into a forest a child who has never been taught that there are ghosts, and you will have a hard time convincing him that any sound that he hears is produced by a being impossible to see. Only, therefore, as we consider the capability of the mind's being actually influenced at certain times from the hidden or occult side of nature do we seem to have a thoroughly satisfactory reason for the universal prevalence of superstitious beliefs.

That this is the true reason appears probable, moreover, in view of the fact that any consciousness whatever of being influenced through subconscious intellection is more likely to be experienced by a primitive, uneducated man than by an educated one. Education gives one control over his mental resources. It causes him to understand himself, as we say, or to be conscious of himself. This control, once established as a habit, inclines him to hold in check the promptings of the subconscious mind, so that its effects shall manifest themselves either not at all, or only indirectly, by coalescing with those of the conscious mind. When this is the condition, as often in art-production, the suggestions and imaginings due to subconscious intellection cannot easily be distinguished from the results of conscious intellection. The educated man, looking at his subconscious nature, as he does, through a glass darkly, always seems to see the texture of the material veil hanging in front of it. With the uneducated man, however, it is different. Influences exerted through the subconscious mind often appeal to him directly. Indeed, there are reasons for believing that when we go lower down than the uneducated man, we find these influences appealing even to the animal. There are reasons for believing that they are allied to all manifestations of intelligence which, in the absence of a predominating mental control, such as has just been said to characterize the educated man, we attribute to instinct.

Mr. Henry R. Marshall, in his "Instinct and Reason," defines instinct, which, in another place, he shows to be largely hereditary, as "the force within us which tends to make us act under certain conditions as all others who are of the same type, which leads us to undertake typical reactions," as, for instance, without conscious thought, to ward off with our hand a stone that seems moving toward our head. *Reason*, he defines as "the force which tends to make us vary from such typical reactions," as, for instance, not to ward off the stone when we have learned that it is fastened to a string and cannot reach our head. From this conception it seems logical to associate the action of instinct with any mental manifestation which is not the result of reason. But we found in Chapter V. that the range of mental action which is not the result of *conscious* reason is exceedingly large. It includes such subconscious mental action as seems to correspond both to that which is due to instinct, as in the case of conscience, and also to that which is due to reason, as in cases of lightning calculators and automatic writers. Whether this be owing to the fact that the subconscious mind parallels the conscious in possessing both an instinct and a reason of its own, or to the fact that everything that we attribute to instinct is really a result of subconscious reasoning, which we fail to recognize, merely because it is in the hidden region, the practical result is the same. All that we cannot consciously attribute to reason, whether it be due to instinct because hereditary, or to automatic physical or mental action because acquired by practice, or to subconscious reason acting behind every instinctive movement, as some suppose instinct to act behind all the movements of the lower animals,—all this we may call, because, as distinguished from rational, it seems to be such, *instinctive* —a word which differs from *instinct* in being an adjective signifying an effect which has the quality or appearance of that which results from instinct. It is in this sense that the word is used in this series of volumes. As contrasted with *instinctive*, the word *reflective* is also used, in the sense partly of responsive, as distinguished from spontaneous, which is suggested by instinctive, and partly the opposite of that indicated by such promptings. He does this because of his higher human possibilities, because of the preponderating and often counteracting influence that can be exerted by his conscious and reflective powers as influenced by his physical surroundings.

> Shades of the prison-house begin to close
>   Upon the growing Boy,
> But he beholds the light, and whence it flows,
>   He sees it in his joy;
> The Youth, who daily farther from the east
> Must travel, still is Nature's Priest
>   And by the vision splendid
>   Is on his way attended;
> At length the Man perceives it die away,
> And fade into the light of common day.
>
>   *Ode—Intimations of Immortality:* Wordsworth.

It is sometimes represented that the story in the third chapter of Genesis cannot be made to accord with the theory of development—much less with that of evolution. But it might be argued with some truth that it is exactly the kind of story that can be made to accord with this theory. What but a mental condition very close to that of an animal could be characterized by a lack of "knowledge of good and evil," a lack of experiencing temptation coming from without—from the lower physical side of life as represented in the serpent—and of such a nature as to conflict with the promptings coming from within? Only an animal can be true to every condition of his being, and obey these latter promptings only, and these *unconsciously*. A man, to be true to every condition of his being, must obey them indeed, but consciously and rationally, and in such a way as to make them conform to the good as contrasted with the evil of which the play of cause and effect in the outward material world has taught him. A very important reason for holding this opinion was given on page 85, and other reasons will be given hereafter. At present, our business is to make sure of the facts on which the opinion is based.

It has been said that there are grounds for supposing that the animals are influenced through methods corresponding to those according to which men are influenced through the subconscious mind. That this is so may be made to appear while we notice how the animals may be supposed to communicate with one another. Of course they are obliged to communicate without formulating thought in words or gestures, because they have neither articulating organs nor hands. But, though incapable of formulating thought, are they incapable of having it? If so, why does a dog wag his tail and ears and growl in his sleep? Is he not dreaming? But if he can dream, he must be capable of processes of thought. Yet how can he have processes of thought, without using words or gestures? How, but precisely as a man can—by seeing in imagination series of pictures? A man, when thirsty, thinks not only of the word *thirst*, but he has a vision of a tumbler or a spring. If he wish to communicate his feeling to another, he may use the word *thirsty;* and this other also, if understanding the word, will have a similar vision. But notice that the essential, indispensable factor is not the word, but the vision that is caused in the listener's mind. The word is convenient, and, if a feeling be at all complex, it is extremely important, in order to convey distinctness and discrimination of meaning. But the essential thing is to cause the vision. Now a dog certainly remembers what he has seen. If so, he can probably recall it, but to recall it, he must have a vision of it. If he himself have a vision of it, ability to transmit conceptions in an occult way will enable him to convey a similar vision to another dog's brain. Is it possible that this is the way in which animals communicate? Why is it not? Any one who will have the patience to watch them will notice that they often communicate without making a single sound or movement. Who has never seen two dogs or birds, at some distance from one another, start at exactly the same moment for the same place? Moreover, there is evidence that they are often influenced by men in this occult way. How is it that a snake is charmed, or a horse broken — or guided, for that matter? The next time that the reader is riding a horse, and comes to four corners, let him try to turn him in the direction chosen without using the reins, *i. e.*, by merely thinking. This can sometimes be done. A dog of which the author knows was in the habit of bounding up into a bedroom every morning, and drinking water poured out from a pail that had been standing there over night. One day, there was a discussion in his presence with reference to the unhealthiness of drinking water that had been uncovered for as many hours as this. From that time, no effort could get the dog to continue his former morning practice. It is hardly conceivable that he should have understood the subtle distinctions of words, and the bearings of the discussion, as men would have done. But it is conceivable that he should have been influenced by the concentration of the thoughts of the family—with or without the indication of the fact in their countenances—upon this particular water as something that one should not drink.

Nor, apparently, can animals be influenced thus by the thoughts of one who is merely near at hand. Dr. C. N. Pierce, of Philadelphia, once told the author about a dog whose master frequently goes to Europe. The moment the steamer bearing the master home reaches New York, his family, living sixty miles away, are made acquainted with the fact by the movements of this dog. The intellection in this case seems to be exactly similar to that of an old negress once known by the author. She would now and then announce by name to her mistress the coming arrival of a guest, who would reach the house from one to five hours later. This faculty of the negress, which could be paralleled by many other illustrations of the mind's being influenced from the subconscious side, perhaps even by that instinct which keeps the Indian from being lost amid dense, untrodden forests, manifests itself among members of the colored race in other ways. It is well known by Southern clergymen that, almost invariably, in describing their conversions, these people tell of perceiving figures and scenes which they take to be supernatural; and in such language that it seems scarcely possible to suppose the effects to be merely such as white men attribute to the imagination. Among the Indians, too, similar visions, if not common in this day, were, at one time, supposed by some tribes to be necessary to the formation of character. In Northern Michigan their young men, before being permitted the full prerogatives of manhood, were sent into the woods, and made to rest in hammocks swung among the trees, and to fast — the identical method pursued by Swedenborg—until they had had more or less of what in our day would be termed psychic experience. Of course, it is possible that every experience of this sort may be a mere hallucination, in the sense in which people generally, and not philosophers, use this term; *i. e.*, a result of imagination wrought upon by an abnormal, if not a diseased, condition of the physical nerves. But what of that? It does not lessen the force of the argument that has been presented. The argument is that such experiences come to certain persons now, and have come to others in the past; and that they are now, and have been, attributed to causes that are not material, normal, or natural, but supposedly the opposite,—spiritual, supernormal, or supernatural; and that this fact, especially in view of the far greater number of psychic experiences among primitive, uneducated people, sufficiently accounts for the origin of primitive beliefs in the supernatural, or—what is the same thing—for primitive religion.

Primitive religious customs, too, strengthen this general argument. Among the aborigines of America, Africa, and Australia, who, in historic times at least, have had no chance to imitate one another, there are two distinct forms in which spiritual communications are supposed to be imparted through the seer, or medicine-man, whatever he may be called. According to one form, this man goes into a dark place—sometimes a hut entirely shut in by poles —and those who consult him are said to hear utterances, and, less frequently, to see living figures emerging which are different from his own. According to the other form, while visible to all, he seems to be taken possession of by some influence that often makes him numb to physical sensation, and that always makes him talk or act in a manner apparently foreign to his own character.[1] The Assyrians, Egyptians, Greeks, and Romans seem to have given

[1] It is well known that, in our own time and country, there are conditions resembling this, into which certain persons fall, owing to their temperament or state of health, or to some hypnotic influence, as we may term it, consciously or unconsciously exerted upon them by others. In these conditions the body, while apparently put to sleep, seems to be made the direct instrument of the subconscious mind—either of the subject himself, according to

a ceremonial development to these primitive methods of receiving supposed spiritual communications. Most of the Egyptian temples contained rooms absolutely dark; and an old Assyrian séance is probably described with accuracy in the account in the twenty-eighth chapter of 1 Samuel of the visit of Samuel to Saul in the cave of the witch of Endor. Many references are made by the classic writers to the mysteries, especially the Eleusinian, as

the hypnotic theory, or of some other being, if we accept the trance-theory. The result is that, while in this condition, these persons sometimes manifest a degree of mental culture and force of which in their conscious moods they give no indications.

A telegram from San Francisco, published in most of the newspapers of January 21, 1897, contained the following : " A shock-headed boy of fifteen, whose school days have been limited to three short years, and whose life has been passed chiefly in a little country town in Washington, delivered a lecture here last night upon the 'Different Religious Systems of the World, Now and in the Past.' Charles Anderson is the boy's name. He was born in Cowlitz County, in 1882, and lived there until two months ago. When lecturing, the boy's language and manners seemed to belong to some gray-haired old patriarch, and many of his hearers pronounced the discourse a deep and learned dissertation. And yet his conversation reveals a woeful lack of education and he can scarcely read. Charles says he has been able to produce his condition at will, and though unable to foretell his subject, he is able to remember a little of his discourse after the trance, but not enough to render him any more intelligent in his everyday life."

The author himself has heard from the lips of a woman, apparently incapable even of understanding the subject discussed, what was virtually—though never purporting to be it, nor recognized to be it, so far as he knows, by any one but himself—the cosmic system of ancient Gnosticism, together with the main propositions of the Platonic germ which this seems to have developed,—all presented with a wealth of illustration, information, and eloquence which he does not hesitate to say he has never heard equalled by any unpremeditated effort on the part of any mind working normally. That the whole discussion was foreign to the woman's natural ability, range of thought, and, apparently, belief, was proved by frequent conversations with her when in her normal moods ; and that what was said in the abnormal moods was unpremeditated was proved by frequent questions that guided the

solving questions with reference to the future. Were they a continuation of the dark séances of the African woods and the Egyptian temples?—or only a ritualistic or representative continuation of these? As for the actions in the open daylight of those supposed to be possessed by a spirit, it is hardly necessary to point out that these must have been very similar to the actions of the Indian fakirs and of the Mohammedan dervishes, while all of the

course of her presentation, in which never, on different occasions, was the same phraseology or method of illustration exactly repeated. However, what was said in this way—though it was all upon an elevated plane—was not taken by the author for indisputable truth. Why not? Partly because it was impossible for any one to determine its source. It might have come from a hypnotic reading of that which was stored unconsciously in the mind of the investigator, though this seemed improbable, inasmuch as analogous deliverances of the same general tenor were made in his absence. It might have come from that which was stored in the subconsciousness of the woman herself, though this, too, seemed improbable, inasmuch as she would scarcely have been interested sufficiently in such lines of thought even to have read of them. It might have come from that which had been stored consciously or subconsciously, in the mind of some ancestor, or of some living person at a distance, or even been subconsciously read from some book. Or it might have come, as the woman herself supposed, from some spirit; yet, even so, this spirit might have been—to say the least—insufficiently informed to warrant confidence in the truth of the things uttered. Only two satisfactory conclusions could be drawn from the circumstances. First, the same as that which will be argued on pages 122 to 127, namely, that whatever may be uttered in this supernormal way must be judged precisely as it would be if uttered in a normal way;—that is, by its conformity to previous information, and to the results of intuitive insight and logical inference. The other conclusion reached was this: that here, presented to eyes and ears, in the nineteenth century, was something that legitimately suggested the origin not only of Platonism and Gnosticism, but of much of that imaginatively weird cosmogony of the ancients which has ordinarily been attributed to merely the Oriental imagination, and even of Polytheism as developed among such civilized people as the ancient Egyptians, Greeks, and Romans. These ancient people had minds as intellectual and logical as our own; and one may be sure that they had some good reasons for their beliefs. (See

methods indicated are apparently repeated in "modern spiritualism."

Now, let us notice another important fact. It is this: in the degree in which, among any people, the intellect becomes developed, they come to pay less heed to mere physical phenomena—*i. e.*, to abnormal sights and sounds, contortions of the body, mysterious rappings, or workings of wonders—than to verbal communications, sometimes accompanying and sometimes not accompanying these, which communications, because verbal, appeal more exclusively to the intellect. Is not this exactly what we should expect? A man, according to the degree of

Pliny's rational discussion of spectres in his letter to Sura, B. 7; xxvii.) Almost all commentators agree that the words of Paul in Col. ii., 18, "Let no man beguile you of your reward in a voluntary humility and worshipping of angels, intruding into those things which he hath not seen," refer to Gnosticism, and to angel-worship in it. Why, therefore, has not one come upon the original thing who—in connection with psychical phenomena and physical transformations which, if related, would not be credited by any one who had not seen something similar—has heard this system taught at regular intervals to people, some of them of decided intelligence, who believed themselves to be in the presence of a very superior spirit? Even supposing these people to have been completely deluded, why could not others, in similar circumstances, have been similarly deluded in ancient times? And if so, notice the inference not only with reference to Gnosticism but to Polytheism: how long would it have been before this superior spirit would have had followers; and after the "medium" through whom the utterances were received had passed away, how long would it have been before these followers would have conveyed to others, with all the suggestions with which imagination would naturally augment the original facts, a traditional belief in this spirit that had once talked to them? And what would a belief in this superior spirit and its teachings be, but a belief in what the Greeks meant by the term god,—not the Supreme Being, but a superior being, the existence of whom might or might not (from some of the literature of the Greeks we may judge that it did not) interfere with their acknowledging One supreme being. Does not this line of thought present a far more natural and justifiable theory through which to account for Polytheism than is usually advocated?

his mental development, demands particulars. He is not satisfied with such general conceptions concerning the existence of life beyond the visible as alone can be suggested through physical phenomena. He craves to hear everything described in words. He desires to understand, and, for this reason, to have a religion that will appeal with the authority not only of the subconscious mind but of the conscious mind,—in fact, with the authority of the whole rational being. Accordingly, in Greece and Rome we find religious truth attributed mainly to the utterances of oracles and Sibyls; and in India and Eastern Asia, as well as among the Hebrews, Mohammedans, and Christians, attributed to sacred writings.

It must be borne in mind, however, that even these writings are generally supposed to involve an exercise of subconscious intellection. Their authors have been almost universally represented as subject to influences exerted through the subconscious mind in other ways. As we all know, this is claimed to have been true of many of the writers of the Christian Scriptures; and not only of them, but of Mohammed and Joseph Smith; and it is Kant, the philosopher, who is authority for the trustworthiness of the same claim as made by Swedenborg, the latter, when in Denmark, having, according to Kant's testimony, accurately described to him at the time of their occurrence, certain events—a fire, for instance—taking place in Stockholm.[1] So much as to the general connection between what are termed sacred writings and the

---

[1] A similar claim is made also by the essayist mentioned on page 80. It is said that, some years before the essays there described began to be written, this person, who had been for many years an invalid, felt one day a chill coming on, and, at the same moment, began to describe a supposed scene outside the window,—an Oriental pasture-ground and a shepherd who apparently took possession of this person's body, which, rendered perfectly

other methods in which effects coming from or through subconscious agency manifest themselves.

Just here, to most readers, some extremely important questions will be suggested. These concern the degree of truth that may be supposed to be derived through the methods that have been described. Granted that to these methods certain features of primitive religion may be rightly attributed, how far may the substance of that which is thus received be supposed to be trustworthy; and by what means may any man or set of men determine its trustworthiness? These are questions very difficult to answer. How difficult, no one can fail to perceive who will recall the conditions determining the substance of communications thus received, as indicated on page 69. It may be said that those acquainted with the phenomena of hypnotism, and, therefore, with the operations of the subconscious mind as disclosed—though not originated—by hypnotic influences, believe themselves to have reasons for holding that all processes of memory and logic are developed in it with flawless consistency. When, for instance, a hypnotized patient is told that he is George Washington, or a lightning calculator is given

rigid, fell to the floor. The attendant, instead of being allowed to tender assistance, was urged to take a pen and write as dictated. What was dictated was a prediction, which came true, that, from that hour, there should be no more sickness, and that, in time, something of practical importance to the world, which subsequent events have caused to be associated with these essays, should be revealed through the agency of the invalid. As, too, in the cases of Mohammed, Swedenborg, and Smith, this person does not assume to have been influenced to supplant Christianity, but merely to interpret and develop certain phases of it. The whole story, which reads like a leaf torn from a life of a Joan of Arc, the author himself has heard from the lips both of the person receiving these communications and—unless in this one regard his memory fail him—of the person to whom the first communication was dictated.

a problem to solve, or a trance-speaker is made to improvise an oration or a poem, the result never seems to fail. It is like that which might come from a perfectly constructed automatic machine. When, however, from the method of development, we turn to ask what the germ is that is thus developed, we find that this depends, in every case, upon a suggestion given by the hypnotizer. The same subconscious mind, when given suggestions entirely antagonistic in meaning, will develop each of them with equal consistency. But if this be so, why does it not follow that, in case the suggestion be untrue, and the premise therefore false, the entire result of the subconscious mental action will be false? This certainly does follow. A hypnotized man, if told that he is a bird, will act in one way; then, if told immediately afterwards that he is a fish, he will act in another way, and each way will conform to his own conceptions of the mode of procedure of the being suggested. An insane man who supposes himself to be suffering from an injury inflicted by a friend, or to be a king or an animal, acts exactly as he might act had he been permanently hypnotized. He can often remember and argue certain points with great accuracy, but he applies his ability to the development of a false premise.

Now how, in a case of hypnotism or insanity, is the truth or falsity of the premise upon which the subconscious powers are working to be determined? How but by the conscious action of the mind?—of the conscious thinking of the subject, if we can restore him to his normal rational condition, or, if not, of the conscious thinking of others surrounding him, whose judgment must decide upon the premise submitted? Evidently, so far as concerns the hypnotic or insane patient, it is because, for the time being, his consciousness is not working, that he is a victim of groundless imaginings? Now how is it with reference to one who is in a trance-condition? Is not his consciousness too in a condition in which it is not working? And if so, what inference must we draw? Before answering this question let us recall that many attribute all inspiration to trance-conditions or to hypnotic conditions, which, in many of their manifestations, cannot be distinguished from trance-conditions. In addition to this, let us also recall that in certain countries, as in India and in parts of Southern Europe, the insane or idiotic, for the very reason that they manifest few results of conscious intellection, are supposed to be peculiarly gifted in the direction of inspiration ; and also that, in some philosophic books, insanity is allied to the subconscious intellection which is manifested in the artistic inspiration of genius. What, upon recalling all these facts, are we to conclude ? Undoubtedly, that insanity, hypnotism, trance-conditions, and artistic and religious inspiration, all involve, to some extent, the same form of mental action. But we need not go beyond this, and conclude that all the results of this form of mental action are similarly conditioned or are equally untrustworthy. The exact fact seems to be that their trustworthiness in each case depends upon the premise or suggestion which forms the germ from which the conscious result of the subconscious process is developed,—which, by the way, is a very strong argument, as the merest tyro in logic can recognize, for the importance of having external religious standards of belief conforming as nearly as possible to such as are absolutely true. To the insane, surrounding circumstances acting upon diseased nerves give the suggestion. To the hypnotized, the hypnotizer gives it. To the one in a trance, the persons consulting him—*i. e.*, for whom he goes into the trance—may give it. Even though consciously they may give nothing, nevertheless, they may give it in the form of general impressions, conveyed from their subconscious mental tendencies. It is this fact, indeed, that affords whatever warrant there may be for the claim of the "spiritualists" that those who consult a "medium" with the intention of finding fraud are almost certain to find it. In such cases the "medium" is the one hypnotized, and they are the hypnotizers who furnish the suggestion. In fulfilment of the same principle, those believing strongly in Catholicism usually hear, when consulting a clairvoyant, no doctrines radically inconsistent with their general belief; or if they be Quakers, none radically inconsistent with the opinions of Penn;[1] or, if they have a different experience, this fact usually furnishes good evidence that, at heart, they themselves are not in sympathy with their creed. Of course, they may be to blame for this; but in the degree in which the creed is erroneous, they must be commended; for the fact shows that they are more in sympathy with truth in general than with any particular form in which they have hitherto received it. Indeed, in case a mind has ever been wrongly instructed, it is only in the degree in which it is absolutely unbiased that it can

---

[1] This is not to say that they may not occasionally hear statements which they will find hard to reconcile with their beliefs; but only that, if so, they will be left to recognize the discrepancy for themselves. As bearing upon this general subject, Alfred Russel Wallace in his "Miracles and Modern Spiritualism," pages 218 to 220, says that conflicting sectarian dogmas are sometimes proclaimed through the agency of "mediums"; but he claims that these are never given except avowedly as the opinions of some individual spirit, and that, notwithstanding them, the legitimate inferences concerning the future life so far as it is actually described are in all cases, as coming from all "mediums," virtually the same.

obtain from one in a trance-condition anything resembling absolute truth.

What has been said leads inevitably to the conclusion that whatever is received through subconscious agency is liable to be more or less modified by thoughts and feelings in some conscious mind. This conscious mind may be either that of the person who is thus influenced, or inspired, as we say, by or through his own subconscious intellection; or it may be the mind of another who, through the combined results of conscious and subconscious processes, may be supposed to be furnishing external suggestions to the inspired person. If the conscious mind be that of the inspired person himself, the trustworthiness of the premise which he develops will depend upon his own intellectual and spiritual attainments and character. Nothing has been more clearly proved than the fact thus stated. In the degree in which a man becomes wise, the promptings of his conscience, for instance, which furnish one phase in which sub-intellection manifests itself, coincide with the deductions of rational judgment and inference. Another interesting fact is, that in the degree in which there is this coincidence, *i. e.*, in the degree in which the deductions—always logical, as has been said—of subconscious intellection are exactly paralleled by those of conscious intellection,—in this degree the mind itself becomes oblivious of any distinction between conscious and subconscious processes. It is a man not of high but of low intellectual and spiritual attainments who is constantly thinking and therefore talking about duty and conscience; that is to say, duty and conscience as such present their claims most strongly to the mind that is most strongly prompted to disregard them. The wise and good desire what is wise and good, and in pursuing them are hardly conscious that they have a conscience. So with the educated and refined as contrasted with their opposites. As a rule, only Indians or Negroes, at least the comparatively uncultivated, recognize a clear distinction between the results in their own minds of conscious and of subconscious intellection. In the degree in which a man's mentality is of a high order, or has been highly developed, he ceases to talk in an insane, trancelike, or even absent-minded way. At every stage, he seems instinctively to hold in check and to direct the course of subconscious logic by considerations that are in conformity with fact and common sense. This is probably one reason why the ancient Hebrews were forbidden to consult with familiar spirits or necromancers (Deut. xviii., 10, 11), as well as why it is said, in 1 Cor. xiv., 32, that "the spirits of the prophets are subject to the prophets."

Now notice that the prophet to whom the spirits are likely to be most subject is, as a rule, a writer. For he, as a rule, is a thinker, and therefore a man who, however unconsciously his mind may work at times, is always more or less under the influence of suggestions from the conscious region, even if merely because he is always accustomed, before his words are committed to script, to review and correct them. This is true even when he is not completely aware that he is thus reviewing them. Perhaps it is not too much to say that no thoroughly cultivated man will ever, whatever may be the sources of his inspiration, allow his thoughts to leave him before they have been filtered through **the clarifying criticism of conscious intellection.** For this reason, sacred literature is more conformed to the rational results of mental action than is any other form of religious influence.

Is not this fact sufficient to explain the remarkable intellectual and spiritual progress which begins to characterize the people of all countries just as soon as they begin to hold the theory that religious truth can be wholly or chiefly communicated through sacred writings? A peculiarity of the Hebrew religion was a belief in the authority of a traditional written law; and the people were forbidden to consult familiar spirits (Deut. xviii., 10, 11) or to hearken to diviners (Jer. xxvii., 9), who, but for these traditional Scriptures, would probably have been the chief agents of religious instruction. The result of following the injunctions of a written law, rather than of leaders like these, was a cautious, reflective, calculating habit of mind which two thousand centuries have not sufficed to eradicate from the character of the race. The same characteristics have been developed, too, among Protestant Christian nations, causing them, in this regard, to present a sharp contrast to the other Christian nations, with whom a written word is not so exclusively authoritative. A similar characteristic is evident also among the people of China and Japan, who are guided by the writings of Confucius, as contrasted with the inhabitants of Central Asia and of Africa, where sacred books have less influence than have fakirs and other supposed religious wonder-workers.

CHAPTER VII.

SIGNIFICANCE AS ATTRIBUTABLE TO MENTAL ACTION: RELIGIOUS CONCEPTIONS HAVING THEIR SOURCE IN INSPIRATION; ARTISTIC IN IMAGINATION.

Form of Inspiration partly Dependent on the Human Mind as Developed by Environments of Place and Time—This Theory Explains the Gradual Development of Truth in the Revealed Scriptures—Also the Necessity for Spiritual Discernment: no Form is an Adequate and Complete Expression of the Spiritual—Tracing all Inspired Writing to or through the Same Subconscious Mental Processes Need not Impair Authority or Authenticity of the Scriptures—Nor Need the Attributing of Signs and Wonders to Sources not Divine—Conformity of this View to the Theories of Modern Biblical Criticism—The Three Tests of the Truth in the Scriptures: Conformity to Previous Information—To Results of Intuitive Insight—To Results of Logical Inference—Different Views of Scriptural Inspiration Conformable to the Theory here Presented—Bearings of this Subject upon Artistic Sympathy, the Zeit-Geist, Imagination—Differences between Inspiration and Imagination—Failure to Recognize the Differences Detrimental to Both Religion and Art—Influence of Recognizing it upon Opinions Concerning Religion—Concerning Art—Nevertheless Art Lessens Materialism and Traditionalism, and Aids Religion, but is not a Substitute for it—Religion an Aid to Art.

A CANDID mind must admit that from what was said at the end of the chapter just closed,—even from the passage quoted from 1 Cor. xiv., 32, "The spirits of the prophets are subject to the prophets,"—it is a legitimate logical inference that the form of an inspired communication must depend to some extent upon the character of the minds through which and to which it is made; moreover, that this form must be affected by both conscious and subconscious intellection in these minds. The reason for this is that the results of conscious observation of external objects and events are constantly being stored and developed in the subconscious region, and furnishing mind with its material. The conditions, therefore, seem to indicate that what may be termed the formulation of inspiration is always somewhat modified by human agency, because developed under the influence of suggestions coming both from the mind of the inspired person and, sympathetically, from the minds of those to whom his communications are given. In other words, it seems to be necessary to admit the effect upon inspiration of environment, under which term we may include both the individual and the general thought of one's own age, and not only of this, but of former ages, of which the thought of one's own age is a result.

In these conditions we seem to find a needed explanation for those who argue—with however much or little reason it is outside the province of this essay to decide—that the earlier books of the Bible manifest in places the influences of comparatively low domestic, social, ethical, ecclesiastical, and, as applied especially to accuracy, scientific and historic standards. We can attribute such facts—if we have not the ability or data to prove that they are not facts—to the environments of him through whom the religious influences were communicated. It seems, too, as if this were a more satisfactory explanation of what is called "the development of truth" in the Old and New Testaments, than is the theory that ascribes it to some plan of the Almighty such as, if carried out by a man, would involve—as some think—a form of deception. Rather than to foster such an impression, and to seem to

impairs a belief in the authenticity and authority of any sacred writings, if it does not entirely deprive the world of any trustworthy standards of faith and practice. Let us consider, for a little, whether this opinion is justifiable. To begin with, is it not a fact that the vast majority of those who reject the teachings of the Bible, do so because at heart materialists? And are they not materialists largely because they fail to recognize that there is any subconscious, or hidden, mental nature, or any consequent possibility of its being influenced from a spiritual or hidden source? Did they realize these facts, and, therefore, the fact that the method of receiving truth represented in the Scriptures is not out of analogy with things that, with reasonable frequency, fall to the lot of human experience in other directions, might not the chief cause of their doubts be removed? And if this cause were removed, might not the acceptance of the plausibility of the general fact of inspiration preserve for the theologian a large number of arguments otherwise not available with which to substantiate important subordinate propositions?

But, says, perhaps, the objector, the view that has been presented implies that the mind acts according to the same method when coming into possession both of that which is religiously true, and of that which is religiously false; and this view tends to lessen the relative esteem in which one should regard the former. At first thought, this inference is natural, perhaps, but will it stand the test of reflection? To say that, in both cases, the method of receiving the truth is the same, is not to say that the truth itself is the same. Because we receive information about both cold stone and red-hot iron through the same sense of touch, it does not follow that the things felt are the same, or affect us similarly. What we are trying to show is that there is a method of becoming acquainted with objective influences that does not necessitate communication through one of the five physical senses. To acknowledge the existence of this method, does not involve acknowledging the equal trustworthiness of all things communicated through the method. It does not involve ranking every mind-reader or "medium" with the great prophets. The partial analogies that may be perceived between the influence exerted by Christianity and by hypnotism do not involve rating the two as the same. But they do involve a recognition of the use of similar mental possibilities in both cases. They do involve this very logical conclusion of common sense,—that only in the degree in which men realize that there is some method of influencing them through an objective appeal of which they become conscious not from without but from within, can they realize that the kingdom of God—though there may be much there besides this—is, as stated in Luke xvii., 21, within them.

But this line of argument, the objector may say again, involves an admission that not only revealed words, but "signs and wonders" that accompany and attest the authority of these words, are common to all religions; and are not necessarily fraudulent in inferior religions. Yes; but is this admission dangerous? Is it not more dangerous to hold an opposite theory? Would you have people accept as true what a man says, merely because he works what seem to be miracles? Magicians, hypnotizers, mind-readers, clairvoyants, fortune-tellers, all do this, and some of them who can tell with remarkable accuracy numbers of things that one has done in the past, as well as what is going on at a distance, frequently make statements that are utterly untrustworthy when referring to the most ordinary occurrences. What would be the result if the words of such were taken for the eternal, the infinite, and the absolute truth? Many of us refuse to follow the ecclesiastical guidance of Joseph Smith, the founder of the Mormon faith. Yet much of his influence is attributable to the fact that he was a successful reader of experience, character, and thought through a "peep-stone." Which theory would conventional Christians have had a right to consider the more dangerous to the regions visited by him,—that which denies the existence of a method of mental action like his unless one is divinely inspired, or that which admits its existence even where there is no divine inspiration?

It seems as if here, at least, the writers of the Bible were right. They do not deny that the witch of Endor, or Simon Magus, could produce genuinely supernormal results. They admit that the wise men and the sorcerers of Egypt "did *in like manner* with their enchantments" to Moses (Ex. vii., 11). But truth is not therefore attributed to the utterances of such characters. There is a clear intimation that, though "signs and wonders" may legitimately call attention to a religious leader, there are better ways through which to assure oneself of the truth of his utterances. "Blessed are they," said Jesus, "that hear the word of God, and keep it. An evil generation . . . seek a sign" (Luke xi., 28, 29). "Believe not every spirit," even though it be a spirit, says John, "but try the spirits whether they are of God" (1 John iv., 1).

Waiving for a little the question most directly suggested by these last quotations, it may be well at this place to point out that the conception of inspiration and its relationships which is here being presented not only conforms to the statements of the Christian Scriptures, but affords a strictly logical method of reconciling that higher form of inspiration which is found in them, with the theories of the most advanced Biblical criticism. These theories one need not himself accept in order to recognize the importance, in view of the many who have accepted them, of showing that they do not necessitate a rejection of the authoritative character of the writings to which they apply. One reason why they are sometimes supposed to necessitate this, is that, according to them, many of the books of the Bible, instead of being, as was formerly supposed, consecutive and original, were compiled from different writings existing previously to the time when they were arranged as at present. It is held, moreover, that these previous writings were not only of Hebraic origin, as indicated in such passages as Joshua x., 13, "Is not this written in the book of Jasher?" or as 1 Kings xi., 41, "And the rest of the acts of Solomon and all that he did, and his wisdom, are they not written in the book of the acts of Solomon?" but that they were often of Gentile origin. The first two chapters of the book of Genesis, for instance, are said to contain two separate accounts of the creation, in the first of which the word used for God is invariably the Hebraic equivalent for Elohim, a plural title for the Almighty adopted by the Hebrews from other languages, and in the second is invariably the Hebraic equivalent for Jehovah, the peculiar title of the God of the Jews. The first of these accounts, too, is said to have been discovered among the ancient Chaldean records, though mixed there with many childish legends and polytheistic explanations. It is claimed that the compiler of the book of Genesis reproduced this account, leaving out the legends, or at least those from which important spiritual lessons could not be drawn (see page 42), and making the explanations monotheistic. Can such a claim be reconciled with a theory of inspiration that shall continue to render these books authoritative? Evidently, according to the view presented in this chapter, it can be. For, in the first place, according to this view, inspiration may exist among any people. The general order of creation may have been perceived by some Chaldean seer—possibly later, with the same result, by a Hebraic—in the manner suggested in the note at the bottom of this page[1]; and if so, there would be truth in the general outlines. But, in the second

[1] William Denton, who was at one time the State Geologist of Massachusetts, in his book entitled "The Soul of Things," gives accounts of hundreds of experiments in what he calls psychometry. In this the subconscious mind seems to derive a suggestion from a material object, and to be influenced to make explorations into its past in a manner somewhat analogous to that in which the mind of the physician mentioned on page 74 explores the distant. Prof. Denton found certain persons to be what he termed "sensitives." Into the hands of these he would place a particular object without letting them see it; and they would then describe it and give its history. For instance, he would put lava into the hands of a child ignorant of its character, and this child would describe the whole process of its formation from a volcano. The author of this book has placed letters in the hands of persons of this kind, who, without opening them, have not only determined their contents, but have accurately described the characters of their writers and the localities from which the letters were sent. One of these persons is said to have described in this manner the experience of a nail, all the way from the mine, whence its iron was taken, through its voyages in a battleship to a sea-fight. It seems useless to argue any question with one who denies that a knowledge of the existence of such methods of mental action, does not materially assist the mind in conceiving how the series of pictures in the first chapter of Genesis, describing successive stages in the creation of the world, which no man could ever have seen, might have been composed. Nor does it lessen, but increase a true conception of divine inspiration, to find some way, as in this case, of making its possibilities more comprehensible. When the divine mind works through human agency, it is not only appropriate for us, but incumbent upon us as rational beings, to try to ascertain the methods of this agency.

place, according to this view, wherever inspiration exists, the conscious thinking of the seer or interpreter is apt to modify it. This fact may account for any number of additions, mythological or polytheistic, made to the inspired matter either by the Chaldean seers themselves, or by the priests who handed down their utterances. But the same fact may also account for the omission of myths, and the substitution of the monotheistic theory, on the part of the Hebraic compilers. We all know that certain minds, when a complicated mixture of fact and fiction is presented to them, manifest peculiar facility in separating the one from the other, and bringing to light the truth. Most of us feel, too, if we do not know, that such minds reach their conclusions through work that is not done wholly in the region of consciousness. They reach them intuitively, as we say, which is the same as to attribute them in part to the mental processes that are hidden. If, in the selection and arrangement of written records, these mental processes took place in the mind of one in thorough sympathy with the Source of all truth, and while developing suggestions derived from this Source, why might not the result conform completely to that which is demanded in inspiration? Why should there be any greater difficulty in ascribing inspiration to the selection and arrangement of prehistoric matter, as in the book of Genesis, than of historic matter, as in the books of the Kings? And, once more, going back to the main proposition advanced in this chapter, why should we not suppose that, in this prehistoric matter itself, there should be certain results of inspiration which, when selected and arranged by the inspired compiler, would have just as much authority as could be assigned to original documents? It is outside the province of this essay to discuss the degree of verity underlying the theories of the modern Biblical critic as contrasted with those of his more conservative opponents; but it is not outside of the province of any essay that attempts to get down to the bottom of any subject to show, if possible, that the hypothesis presented is broad enough to cover all the surface on which any theory can be honestly and consistently constructed—hence the excuse for this paragraph.

Now let us return to the suggestions derivable from the quotations at the end of the paragraph on page 118. These suggestions we shall find important, especially in view of what some may consider the too great concessions just made to the claims of modern Biblical critics. Broadly interpreted, the expressions, "Blessed are they that hear the word of God and keep it," "An evil generation . . . seek a sign," and "Believe not every spirit," even though it be a spirit, "but try the spirits whether they be of God," can have but one meaning; and this is that men should test a statement, even though coming from an acknowledged spiritual source, precisely as they would a statement coming from any other source. And how would they test this? Mainly, it may be said, in three ways: by its conformity to the results in consciousness,—first, of previous information; second, of intuitive insight, and, third, of logical inference, as determined according to the laws of evidence and of argument. In the Scriptures, all three methods are recognized as legitimate. Here is what is said of the first of them: "Search the scriptures" (John v., 39). "We ought to give . . . heed to the things that we have heard" (Heb. ii., 1). "To the law . . . if they speak not according to this word" (Is. viii., 20). "Let that therefore abide in you which ye have heard from the beginning" (1 John ii., 24). "Though . . . an angel (Gal. i., 8), "preach any other gospel unto you than that which we have preached unto you, let him be accursed." The general principle underlying such injunctions is almost self-evident. It is this: The individual has time to discover and develop comparatively little; he must avail himself of that which, through revelation or reflection, has been attained by others who may be considered to have been, on the whole, accurate in their observations, honest in their convictions, candid in their representations, and wise in their conclusions. In a general way, this may be said to necessitate every one's having what may be termed intellectual charity. Exercised toward the beliefs of his ancestors, and in an ecclesiastical direction, this charity might make a man a churchman, and zealous in training the young in the tenets of his church; but, at the same time, exercised toward the beliefs of strangers or of adherents of other sects or religions, the two methods of testing truth yet to be considered would, of themselves, cause him to recognize mental rights to a sufficient extent to keep him from being a bigot. But some may ask how, if we apply the first test, can we also apply the second and third tests; in other words, how can one let that "abide" in him which he has "heard from the beginning," and yet, while doing this, not surrender his individual exercise of intuitive insight, or logical inference? In this way, as it seems: According to what was said on page 66, that which is received from without the mind, when left to take its natural course,—*i. e.*, when left to influence one's spirit in the way in which nature has provided that the spirit should be influenced,—sinks into the region of unconsciousness. Here, digested, so to speak, by the mind, and incorporated into its working organism, the importations from without become a part of the subconscious material, giving inevitable bias to each subconscious prompting. For this reason they may be said to be constantly operative in the mind. But they are not operative in any such way as to interfere with the conscious freedom of the mind, whether exercised in forming judgments or in drawing conclusions. In Chapter IX., it will be shown that a man of faith is one who is governed by his subjective promptings, and, in this sense, by that which has been "heard from the beginning," and which gives bias to these; but, at the same time, it will be shown that he must exercise the conscious powers of his mind fully as much as others who have no faith. His mind works differently from theirs solely in being "not disobedient unto the heavenly vision" (Acts xxvi., 19), in giving not only due, but chief consideration to the spiritual side of life—to motives that come from the realm within, from the ideal; whereas the others do not give these the chief consideration, being influenced almost exclusively from the material side of life, from that which is outward and real. The great religious leaders—Augustine and Savonarola not only, but Jesus as well—have been characterized not by any neglect of the results of intuitive insight or of logical inference, but by a conscientious endeavor to subordinate and conform these to that which has been "heard from the beginning." They have sought to develop this latter, and not to destroy it. They have been conservative as well as progressive. They have tried to graft the new upon the old, and thus to reform rather than to revolutionize. If we grasp this conception of the subject, we shall perceive that an application of the test that we have been considering need not interfere with an application of the tests that are to follow. The most conscientious and conservative mind, when working normally, can be governed by that which has "been heard from the beginning," and yet be influenced not by precept but by principle, and, being so, can carry this latter out not according to the letter but according to the spirit, and therefore so as not in any sense to make the "word of God," communicated in any other way, "of none effect through" mere "tradition" (Mark vii., 13).

This last quotation may well introduce the second test of truth mentioned on page 122, namely, that afforded by the conformity of results to those of intuitive insight. "Blessed are they," said Jesus (Luke xi., 28), "that hear the word of God and keep it," *i. e.*, without any other evidence. "An evil generation . . . seek a sign" (Luke xi., 29); and the method of the apostles is said to have been "by manifestation of the truth commending" themselves "to every man's conscience" (2 Cor. iv., 2). The idea here seems to be that truth can be determined at times by its own inherent quality. Indeed, for other reasons, one might almost be justified in holding a theory that a mind working normally should recognize the difference between truth and error as inevitably as a tongue recognizes the difference between the sweet and the bitter. Of course, the trustworthiness of this theory can never be fully tested, because, as a fact, the mind seldom or never does work normally. Consciously or unconsciously, it is constantly under the influence of false standards of thought and action, causing false conceptions of what causes truth to be of authority, and mistaken endeavors to make the information freshly presented conform to falsehood already accepted. Notwithstanding this, it is probably a fact that absolute truth is attained mainly in the degree in which men who lead the world to the appreciation and application of new phases of the truth, as well as the followers of such men, are largely inclined to judge of it intuitively; and that no other method, if conscientiously applied, can so well preserve men in times of either religious decline or progress from too great retrogression on the one hand or precipitancy on the other.

The third test of truth was said to be conformity to the results of logical inference or reasoning. "Let us reason together," says Isaiah in Is. i., 18, and give a "reasonable service," urges Paul in Rom. xii., 1. A result may be rendered reasonable in many different ways,—chiefly, perhaps, by being made to fulfil the laws of argument or of evidence, as applied either to the substance of an utterance, or to the character of its utterer, as manifested in either words or actions. "Believe me," said Jesus to Philip, ". . . or else believe me for the very work's sake" (John xiv., 11). But to whatever this test of logical inference may be applied, it is a test which the mind is always ready to assume that it has a right to apply. Who ever heard a sermon in the most bigoted of sects the whole object of which was not to show the accordance of some statement in a text with not only the previous information of the audience concerning its subject or other subjects, and with the intuitive promptings of conscience, but also with conclusions logically deducible from an examination of testimony and argument? But if we may judge of truth according to these last two tests, some one may ask what are we to do with inspired statements to which neither test can be applied, with statements concerning matters beyond the reach of human insight or reasoning, with statements which have to be accepted upon faith? The answer is that one holding the theory just presented would have to accept such statements for the same reason that causes any one else to accept them.

The strongest argument in favor of them, is that the matters to which such statements refer form a part of a general system of belief and that a system which can be proved to be true as a whole, must be true in its parts; and the force of this argument cannot be lessened by applying to such statements as are submitted to proof, arguments which, while differing from those ordinarily presented, are really more conclusive.

The three tests just indicated, when applied to scriptural truth, will prove it abundantly able of itself to maintain any authority that it may need. Let us pass on now to notice—as a legitimate inference from this whole discussion—that subconscious intellection may be manifested in many more ways than when revealing immediate divine instrumentality. Some may attribute all conceptions thus received to the action merely of the subconscious mind of the utterer making suggestions to his conscious mind; and some may attribute them to the action, either conscious or subconscious, of the minds of others influencing the utterer's subconscious mind and, through it, his conscious mind. Evidently neither of these views conceives of the religious as anything beyond the possibility of the artistic. That which does separate the two is the attributing of certain manifestations of subconscious influence to a power higher than that of man. Nor do all who attribute them to this, agree as to the source from which they come. Some hold that they come from spirits who formerly inhabited the earth; others that they come from intelligencies of a different order from those that have lived on the earth; and others that they come immediately from the Deity. The first is the view of the modern "spiritualists"; the second the view of many, both "spiritualists" and Christians, especially

Catholics, and the third is the view of the orthodox Protestants. The Bible, in mentioning the reappearance of Moses and Elias (Matt. xvii., 3), and the appearances of angels of God (Acts xxvii., 23), as well as of the Lord (Jer. xxxi., 3), and of God (2 Chron. i., 7) seems to sanction all three views. Even this fact, however, though acknowledged, does not reconcile the conservative Christian to " spiritualism." Because of the passage in Rev. xxii., 18, " For I testify unto every man that heareth the words of the prophecy of this book, If any man shall add unto these things God shall add unto him the plagues that are written in this Book," which passage is taken to refer not merely to the Book of the Revelation, but to the whole Scriptures, he maintains that all that can be appropriately termed revelation has ceased. To account, however, for cases in which new doctrines have apparently been proclaimed, some Episcopalians and all Roman Catholics hold that the officials of the church, individually, or assembled in lawful councils, are divinely guided to interpret the truth " once delivered "; and certain of the latter church that the Pope is peculiarly inspired to develop this truth even to the extent, in connection with the councils of the church, of giving it unforetokened meanings. The inspired authority to develop the truth, thus attributed to the Pope and councils, is paralleled by a somewhat similar authority attributed by Mohammedans, Mormons, and Swedenborgians to their respective religious leaders. With these differences in theological opinion, except as showing that all the views can be made to accord with the view that has been advanced here, the present essay has nothing to do. But it has much to do, as will be brought out hereafter, with the acceptance of the general theory of the influence of subconscious mental action. Most of the reasons why this is so, can be satisfactorily indicated at only a later stage of our discussion. But some of them may be recognized now.

For instance, those who practise subconscious "gifts," whether as mind-readers, clairvoyants, psychometrists, or under other names, are always dwelling upon the necessity, in order to success, of an unimpeded interflow of "currents" between their own minds and the minds for whom they exercise their "gifts." What does this mean, so far as it refers to any condition actually existing, except what is meant when we speak of the necessity in the artist of "sympathy"? Or, again, what is it to be affected by the "*zeit geist*," the "spirit of the times," of which we so often hear? What is it to be "the spokesman of one's age"? What is it to be able, in the particular individualizations of art, to express the universal? What is it to be able, while depicting the phases of the present, to foretell the unfoldings of the future? All these things, every one admits to be characteristic of the great artist. But what are they all, except manifestations of the possession of a subconscious mind, delicately suspectable to influences exerted by other minds surrounding one, and moving forward with him,—possibly, as in cases of prevision, already borne beyond him?

Finally, what is the very substance of the art-product which we term a work of imagination? What is it but a result, the general outlines of which are taken from real objects or events in the external world, yet the significant substance of which is built out of the well-nigh infinite variety of material which has been stored in the subconscious mind? And when we consider the forgotten experiences that have invariably been brought to light, in order to be combined into the result, we have no difficulty in recognizing that art is not nature, but nature as mirrored in the mind,—mainly in the subconscious rather than in the conscious,—a fact which will be perceived to be true both of the simplest elementary exercise of comparison in which a single thing perceived reminds one of another single thing previously perceived, and equally true also of that more complex and most difficult exercise of constructive imagination in which a composite series of things perceived reminds one of another composite series previously perceived.

Such facts indicate that, in many regards, the mind works similarly in religion and in art. Indeed, the mere fact that both involve an exercise of subconscious action, is enough to explain why their results should blend so as frequently to be indistinguishable. But it does not follow that they are therefore always so. A spirit that had never had experience of an external world of sight or sound might be inspired. But such a spirit could not express thought through referring to the scenes of this world. A man may be inspired in uttering the general injunction, "Bless them that persecute you." But words in this form give no evidence of perceiving—or, because recalling, of being conscious of perceiving—external forms, and, at the same time, of conjuring in the mind similar forms, and of thus thinking through formulating mental images, as one does in an exercise of what we term imagination. Of course, inspiration is often—perhaps generally—accompanied by imagination, as in the mind of the writer of the descriptions in the Book of the Revelation. Imagination, too, is often accompanied by manifestations of inspiration, as in the writings of the poets,—in such a line, for instance, as this, from Milton's Sonnet on his Blindness:

> They also serve who only stand and wait.

The results of the two, however, in such cases, though they may be almost indistinguishable, differ both in their nature and in their sources,—as much as the waters in a spring differ from the pictures reflected on its surface. Inspiration is of the depths. It has to do with that which comes from within. Imagination is of the surface. It has to do with that which is mirrored from without. In religion the predominating relationship is to a source beyond human control; in art, a source within human control is of equal importance.

A failure to recognize this difference is detrimental not only to religion, lowering its character and weakening its authority, but also—what is of more importance for ourselves in this connection—is detrimental to art. Those who confound religious with what is termed artistic inspiration, will almost necessarily estimate musicians, actors, poets, orators, and even sculptors, painters and architects by the unconscious facility which they manifest in conception and execution. But, though owing to the pliability of his conscious nature to subconscious influence, the artist does, in certain moods, manifest this facility, it is not too much to say that no product of genius has ever, even in such moods, sustained itself on a high, artistic level, except as a result of much previous study and practice (see Chapter XII.) which has developed skill; nor, even then, has work thus produced been able to satisfy the highest demands of art, unless it has been very carefully and consciously revised. This is a fact essential to recognize, but very difficult to get into the minds either of the young who wish to become artists, or of the general public, or even of critics upon whom both artists and the public depend for instruction,

It is easy to see how this difference between the working of the mind in religion and in art, should affect the opinions of men with reference to both. It undoubtedly explains the reason why many reject as religiously untrustworthy any communications from the subconscious mind, induced through any methods at all resembling hypnotism—as do some that are used in "spiritualism"—which methods, as already indicated on page 68, are allied to those of art. The fact explains, too, why many, even of those who believe that revelation is no longer imparted through inspiration, nevertheless feel inclined to judge of the trustworthiness of those who interpret the traditional doctrines, by the degree of the unconsciousness manifested by the minds of these interpreters, while at their work "The Friends" are, by no means, the only sect who hold that only such thought is inspired as springs to the lips without previous conscious preparation. Do not some Presbyterians still have a subtle belief in the inspiration of the answer in the Westminster Catechism to the question, What is God? because composed of the first few unpremeditated words of a prayer, that ended a discussion in which no one had been able to think out a satisfactory definition? Are there not many intelligent people who have in them a little of the same feeling that made the old Seventh-day-Baptist ministers, after reaching their pulpits, open their Bibles and take the first text to which a casual undirected finger would point? We have probably all heard of one of their sermons—on Cant. ii: 12. "The voice of the turtle is heard in our land," "Brethren, you know the turtle ain't got no voice. But on a summer evenin' as you 're a walkin' a nigh the pools, you hear the turtles a droppin' off the logs into the water. The voice of the turtle is the sound of a droppin' into the water, the sound of a baptism, the sound of a joinin' of the church—That's the sound of the good time comin'." In general, it may be said that most men's conception of a distinctively religious teacher, to say nothing of a prophet, excludes anything supposed to call particular attention to his own conscious intellection, or even to his own intellect. He may possess, and add to his influence by possessing, accuracy of observation, breadth of information, and brilliancy of style, but it is felt that the value of his work does not depend mainly upon them. He is supposed to be guided to his utterance by an agency above him, which can, occasionally, make the words of an ignorant fisherman or a weak child as enlightening and uplifting as those coming from the lips of the most learned scholar and skilful advocate.

Notice, however, that just the opposite is true in the case of art. For success in it, accuracy of observation is essential, because the artist derives from nature not only his suggestions, but the very form of the image which he must use in indicating them. So with reference to breadth of information. When the results of subconscious mental action must be represented through the results of conscious observation, information obtained through this latter is indispensable. Again, too, because supposed, in a degree not true of a religious leader, to work out his conceptions according to conscious mental methods, it is felt that the artist must have more than a usual amount of mental ability. In fact, it is felt that there is, and should be, an immense difference between the motive underlying the effect produced by the preacher and by the actor. The actor we admire, as we do every artist, on account of a manifestation of acquired facility in holding the mirror of the subconscious as also of the conscious mind up to nature so that each mind shall work with apparent spontaneity as regards both impression and expression; and no matter how much he may reveal of the results of subconscious action, he is either supposed to have attained these results through lofty flights of his own self-impelled imagination, or else, if presumed to have received them precisely as prophets receive religious truth, to have rendered them effective through acquired skill, by means of which he has been enabled to give them form.

There is much religious truth in "Paradise Lost," for instance, but there might have been just as much of this in a poorly written prose work. What makes Milton's religious truth artistic, is its poetic embodiment; and the poetry is just as artistic, so far as concerns this alone, in places in which there is no suggestion of religion.

It would be a mistake, however, to suppose that, because not directly an aid to religion, art is not indirectly so, and this even where strictly confined to its own sphere. In ages like our own, when men rely chiefly upon the guidance of the conscious mind, it is extremely difficult for them to be brought to realize that there is any trustworthy guidance attributable to the action of the subconscious mind. Those in this state may be divided into two classes. One class of them holds that many years ago this inspirational form of guidance prevailed, but that now it does not. They believe in inspiration that was, but not in inspiration that is. They prize highly that which was once received in this way. But, so far as concerns a similar method of receiving the truth now, their own spiritual instincts are not allowed to guide them even to the extent—which might involve no great changes of opinion—of interpreting the spirit of the old according to the form of the new. The result is what is termed traditionalism; and it is needless to argue that the tendency of this is to cause the mind to hold on to that which has formerly been conceived, and to hold on so firmly as often to be prejudicial to development, and even to activity, of thought. The other class maintains that there never was, and never can be anything worth regarding in this inspirational form of guidance. They deem nothing trustworthy except that which results solely from the action of the conscious mind. This leads to what is termed materialism; and, so far as it has its perfect work, it is still more deadening to effort and ideality than is traditionalism.

Now, considered in relation to either of these two classes, notice how important is any agency that can lift people who have no theories admitting the possibility of inspiration, into a practical realization of it. This is what art does. Through the results of the subconscious mind, coalescing, as we shall find by-and-by, with those of the conscious mind, it everywhere surrounds the material with the halo of the spiritual, causing the minds that will not even acknowledge the existence of the latter, to enter upon a practical experience of it in ideas, and to accept, when appearing in the guise of imagination, what they would reject if presented in its own lineaments. So in an age like our own, art may do a large part of the work peculiar to religion. The artist though not a seer always has within him the possibility of being the seer's assistant. No wonder therefore that those not versed in making discriminations should identify the poets with the prophets. Perhaps the majority of all expressions to which we attribute inspiration are, in their form, poetical; and as shown in Chapters II., and IV., there is no truth so exalted, so infinite, eternal, absolute, that the artist, by reproducing the forms about him, cannot suggest it to imagination; nor any truth so spiritual and unfamiliar, or capable of being realized in only so remote a future, that he cannot present this truth in forms in which many minds, however prejudiced and material their tendencies, will not be glad to welcome it.

But a man would mistake if for these reasons he were to suppose that art can be an entire substitute for religion. It can no more be this in that which has to do with inspiration than it can be a substitute for science in that which has to do with investigation. In an age in which there is little scientific accuracy, there is little artistic accuracy; and in an age in which there is little religious inspiration there is little artistic. The subconscious mind works, as we shall find in Chapter XI., in accordance with suggestion. The stimulus of religious suggestion is needed by art in order to attain the loftiest heights of imaginative effort. Of course this suggestion can be experienced in the degree only in which there is a certain practical belief in the relation of subconscious to conscious mental action, even if there be not a clear theoretical understanding of it. This fact is a sufficient excuse for the somewhat lengthened discussion that has here been given to this subject.

CHAPTER VIII.

SIGNIFICANCE AS ATTRIBUTABLE TO MENTAL ACTION: SCIENTIFIC CONCEPTIONS HAVING THEIR SOURCE IN INVESTIGATION; ARTISTIC IN IMAGINATION.

Results of Scientific Investigation to be Contrasted with those of Artistic Imagination—Quotation from Huxley Showing Scientific as Contrasted with Religious View-Point—Is equally far from View-Point of Art—The Difference in View-Point is Owing to a Difference between a Desire to Investigate and to Imagine—Scientific Interest is in Preceding Conditions, Artistic in Conditioned Effects—The Detailing of Results of Investigation is Inartistic in Literature—Quotations from Gay—From Scott—Expression of Results of Imagination from Tennyson—Of Investigation from West—Of Imagination from Homer—Criticism upon an Explanation of a Quotation from Shakespeare—This Distinction of Universal Applicability—Thought in Modern Art Different in Range from Ancient—Justification for Introduction of Philosophy and Science in Art—Scientific Investigation Overlooks Nothing: Artistic Imagination Regards only the Prominent and Emphatic — Scientific Comparison is a Result of Thorough Study: Artistic Is not—Yet Being a Result of Sub-Intellection, in an Instructed Mind, it may be Accurate—Scientific Conclusions are Corrected at every Stage by Results of Investigation: Artistic are not—Inferences therefrom against and in Favor of the Artist—Science can not Cross the Border of the Unseen: Art can—Art Connects Religion and Science—Artist must be Something of a Scientist.

ARTISTIC conceptions have been said to be derived equally from the inner spiritual world, which is the chief source of influence in religion, and of which one learns through inspiration; and from the outer material world, which is the chief source of influence in science, and of which one learns through investigation; in other words, it has been said that they are traceable neither to inspiration alone nor to investigation, but to imagination. The ways in which the results of imagination contrast with those of inspiration have been considered in the preceding chapter. In this, we are to consider the ways in which they contrast with those of investigation.

It would be difficult to find both the fact of this contrast, and the reason for it, brought out more forcibly than in the following quotation from the review of Darwin's "Origin of Species" in Professor T. H. Huxley's "Lay Sermons, Addresses, and Reviews": "What," asks he, "is the history of every science, but the history of the elimination of the notion of creative or other interferences with the natural order of the phenomena, which are the subject-matter of that science? When astronomy was young, the 'morning stars sang together for joy' and the planets were guided in their courses by celestial hands. Now the harmony of the stars has resolved itself into gravitation according to the inverse squares of the distances, and the orbits of the planets are deducible from the laws of the forces which allow a school-boy's stone to break a window. The lightning was the angel of the Lord; but it has pleased Providence in these modern times that science should make it the humble messenger of man, and we know that every flash that shimmers about the horizon on a summer's evening is determined by ascertainable conditions, and that its direction and brightness might, if our knowledge of these were great enough, have been calculated."

This statement is very far—as some would argue, inexcusably far—from the view-point of religion. But it is equally far from that of art. Professor Huxley is criticising the poetry rather than the prose of the Bible. Nor could any amount of scientific discovery ever cause an artistic mind to cease to employ or to enjoy the poetry thus employed. Notice the following:

> Moon and stars
> Keep their most solemn vigils, when the clouds
> Watch also, shifting peaceably their place
> Like bands of ministering Spirits, or when they lie,
> As if some Protean art the change had wrought,
> In listless quiet o'er the ethereal deep
> Scattered, a Cyclades of various shapes
> And all degrees of beauty. O ye Lightnings!
> Ye are their perilous offspring; and the Sun
> . . . . .
> Loves his own glory in their looks, and showers
> Upon that unsubstantial brotherhood
> Visions with all but beatific light
> Enriched!
>
> *To the Clouds: Wordsworth.*

Scores of passages containing expressions similar in kind to this might be quoted from almost every poet, ancient or modern, religious or irreligious, ignorant of scientific truth or acquainted with it. They certainly indicate a very different way of looking upon nature from that suggested in the quotation on page 138. But this difference cannot be explained, as Professor Huxley certainly intimates that it might be, by saying that the scientist is intelligent and rational, while the poet is ignorant and superstitious. The explanation must be found in the fact that each is influenced by a different motive. The scientist is moved to investigate, and the poet to imagine. Investigation, as we shall find, necessitates an analysis and, following this, a comparison and a presentation in detail of all the conditions preceding or underlying appearances, whereas imagination does not necessitate an analysis, but merely a comparison and a representation, general in its nature, of appearances alone, either accepted as wholes, or regarded as composed of only their more perceptible parts. To descend into particulars, notice, first, that in observing the lightning, the scientist cares comparatively little about its merely outward aspects. He is interested in it less because of being awed or terrified by it, than because of indications that it gives of the conditions preceding it, of the "natural order of the phenomena" which lead to it. On the contrary, that which attracts the imagination of the artist affects necessarily the mind more or less as an image does. But an image is an appearance which has an interest in itself, wholly aside from any indication which it may give of an order or conjunction of phenomena occasioning it.

This difference between the interest awakened, on the one hand, by conditions that are preceding or underlying, and, on the other hand, by those that are present and apparent, will be found to separate universally the scientific from the artistic. In looking at a human body, a mere scientist—an ordinary physician, for instance—cares for its contour so far only as it may assist him to an understanding of the arrangements and workings of the different internal organs and their functions. But the sculptor or painter cares for the contour in itself. He studies the anatomy of the organs or movements of the muscles mainly for the purpose of observing and understanding better the external appearance. So in examining a piano, all of us, when considering the experiments resulting in its invention and the methods underlying its construction, think of it as a result of science. But we refer to the completed effects of these, whether of its appearances or of its sounds, as results of art. The same is true as applied to such a comparatively unsubstantial product as a sonata. We may speak of the method of its composition and presentation as being scientific; but when we refer to their resultant effects, we invariably use the term artistic.

This distinction has an important bearing upon the question of the subject-matter which should be presented in a work of art. The artist is supposed to be giving expression to a result not mainly of analysis but of perception. If, therefore, his product seem to be due to the former rather than to the latter, he appears to be working in the realm of science, rather than of art; if he be giving us literature, to be writing prose, not poetry. Notice the evidences of investigation in the following, and that they furnish one among other reasons for its prosaic effects:

> You must not every worm promiscuous use ;
> Judgment will tell the proper bait to choose :
> The worm that draws a long immoderate size
> The trout abhors, and the rank morsel flies :
> And, if too small, the naked fraud 's in sight,
> And fear forbids, while hunger does invite.
> Those baits will best reward the fisher's pains,
> Whose polished tails a shining yellow stains ;
> Cleanse them from filth, to give a tempting gloss ;
> Cherish the sullied reptile race with moss ;
> Amid the verdant bed they twine, they toil,
> And from their bodies wipe their native soil.
> *Rural Sports :   John Gay.*

Sir Walter Scott too in this next description from "Guy Mannering," i., 4, is repeatedly inserting the reasons which he has discovered for certain appearances. The general effect therefore is that of scientific rather than of poetic prose.

The landscape showed a pleasing alternation of hill and dale, intersected by a river which was in some places visible, and hidden in others—where it rolled betwixt deep and wooded banks. The spire of a church and the appearance of some houses indicated the situation of a village where the stream had its junction with the ocean. The vales seemed well cultivated, the little enclosures into which they were divided skirting the bottom of the hills, and sometimes carrying their lines of straggling hedgerows a little way up the ascent. Above these were green pastures tenanted chiefly by herds of black cattle, then the staple commodity of the country, whose distant low gave no unpleasing animation to the landscape. The remoter hills were of a sterner character, etc.

This next quotation, however, is strictly poetical:

> In the afternoon they came unto a land
> In which it seemed always afternoon.
> All round the coast, the languid air did swoon,
> Breathing like one that hath a weary dream.
> Full-faced above the valley stood the moon ;
> And like a downward smoke the slender stream
> Along the cliff to fall and pause and fall did seem.
> *The Lotus Eaters: Tennyson.*

The following verse, though intended for poetry, is rendered prosaic by constant mention of the conditions preceding those perceived, conditions possible to know only as a result of investigation.

> Then shall my youthful sons, to wisdom led
> By fair examples and ingenuous praise,
> With willing feet the paths of duty tread,
> Through the world's intricate or rugged ways
> Conducted by religion's sacred rays,
> Whose soul-invigorating influence
> Shall purge their minds from all impure allays
> Of sordid selfishness and brutal sense ;
> And swell the ennobled heart with blest benevolence.

LANGUAGE OF INVESTIGATION AND IMAGINATION. 143

> Fired with the idea of her future fame,
> She rose majestic from her lowly stead,
> While from her vivid eyes a sparkling flame
> Out-beaming with unwonted light o'erspread
> That monumental pile, and, as her head
> To every front she turned, discovered round
> The venerable forms of heroes dead,
> Who, for their various merits erst renowned
> In this bright fane of glory shrines of honor found.
> *Education: Gilbert West.*

In contrast to this, notice how the writer of this next passage leaves us in ignorance of all conditioning causes, except so far as, by describing mere appearances, he can suggest them.

> The counsel did not please
> Atrides Agamemnon; he dismissed
> The priest with scorn, and added threatening words:
> "Old man, let me not find thee loitering here
> Beside the roomy ships, or coming back
> Hereafter, lest the fillet thou dost bear
> And sceptre of thy god protect thee not.
> This maiden I release not till old age
> Shall overtake her in my Argive home,
> Far from her native country, where her hand
> Shall throw the shuttle and shall dress my couch.
> Go, chafe me not, if thou wouldst safely go."
> He spake; the agèd man in fear obeyed
> The mandate, and in silence walked apart
> Along the many-sounding ocean-side.
> *Homer's Iliad, I.: Bryant's Translation.*

In the song in Shakespeare's "Twelfth Night," act 2, sc. 4, are the words:

> Come away, come away, Death,
> And in sad cypress let me be laid.

With scarcely an exception, the hypercritics of Shakespeare explain this allusion to the cypress in the same way as does Knight in his note upon it. He says: "There is doubt whether a coffin of cypress-wood or a shroud of cypress be here meant." It does not seem to have occurred to these critics that, as poetry is an art, and poetic language the language of perception, the expression is more likely to refer to the appearance of the cemeteries in which the dead are laid away. Universally, in southern Europe, these cemeteries are filled, and in such ways as to be recognized at great distances, with what, owing to the principle of association, may be termed "sad" rows of cypress trees. When the reference is ascribed to the conditions preceding coffins or shrouds rather than to the apparent effects—i. e., rather than to these dark rows of cypress trees casting their thick shadows over the cemeteries—the expression of the poet is interpreted as if it were scientific rather than artistic.

But the question may arise whether the distinction thus indicated is of universal applicability. It may be asked, does not the artist also, like the scientist, regard, at times, the occasioning conditions preceding appearances, does he not at times reproduce " the natural order of the phenomena which," as Professor Huxley asserts, " are the subject-matter" of science? For instance, in this very passage, quoted from Wordsworth,

> O ye Lightnings!
> Ye are their perilous offspring,

are not the phenomena both of clouds and of lightnings—both of the conditioning causes and of the conditioned effects—perceived and mentioned in their natural order of sequence? Of course, one must answer that they are: and yet pure science never would have used the words, "O ye Lightnings!" or "offspring." The former indicates primary attention given to the phenomena; and so does the latter, for it indicates that the natural order of the phenomena is not perceived or presented for the sake of its natural order, as would be the case in science, but for the sake of the appearance of the order. The familiar fact of the lightning's issuing from the clouds is likened to the equally familiar fact that children issue from their parents. If the truth that lightnings spring from clouds needed demonstration, the demonstration would be scientific. But inasmuch as this truth can be revealed to glances extended only to surface-appearances, the perception of it, whether it be manifested in one isolated form or in a process of formation, involves no more than the view of the artist. The same must be true, too, of any fact, even though necessitating scientific discovery, the moment that it becomes so well known as no longer to need demonstration.

This is one reason why the range of thought in modern art differs essentially from that in ancient. The following from Tennyson contains the very essence of poetry; yet it could not have been written before science had demonstrated the existence of certain uniform laws of development:

> Flower in the crannied wall,
> I pluck you out of the crannies,
> Hold you here, root and all, in my hand,
> Little flower—but if I could understand
> What you are, root and all, and all in all,
> I should know what God and man is.
> *Flower in the Crannied Wall: Tennyson.*

The same could be said of Wordsworth's

> To me the meanest flower that blows, can give
> Thoughts that do often lie too deep for tears.
> *Intimations of Immortality: Wordsworth.*

is brought out alone, we recognize its truth the more from its being singly presented." All this is the same as to say that art derives its conceptions from the effective features of objects, sometimes from only one of them, but, if from more, in all cases, from those which are the most prominently perceptible.

Now we are prepared to consider the most important of the distinctions between investigation and imagination. It is that the result of the comparison which follows the analysis of science is really obtained from sources very different from the result of the comparison between an object and its image, or between the image of one object and of another, which is perhaps the most prominent condition which we associate with the term imagination. When the scientist has analyzed thoroughly, and found out approximately, all the conditions preceding one phenomenon, and afterwards all those preceding another phenomenon, then and then only does he compare the two phenomena together and make a scientific statement that they are alike, and conclude that, therefore, they have a like scientific significance. But the artist can make such a comparison and statement as a result not of study but of a merely superficial glance that has recognized that two things are alike in perhaps only one regard. For instance, to make a scientific statement with reference to lightnings and clouds, one would be obliged to show many intervening conditions between the two. These conditions the artist may skip. Merely because the clouds precede lightnings, in the order of time, as parents precede their offspring, he can say:

> O ye Lightnings!
> Ye are their perilous offspring.

The words would be equally artistic, too, did they

mention only one or two other of many apparent effects possible to a thunder shower, as those of the wind and rain on the ruffled streams, or on the swaying trees, or on the flying dust, sleet, or clouds. Any of these particulars, the artist may notice or skip, dwelling only upon features that are emphatically perceptible. Nor is there any denying that the same superficiality and inaccuracy may characterize all the work of imagination, even when employed, as it sometimes is, as an aid to science. Even then it is employed only because the scientist has not yet had time or opportunity to investigate—by which we mean to trace out carefully, and discover beyond dispute —whatever conditions may have intervened between the observed effect and its supposed causes.

It must not be inferred, however, that, for the reason just stated, these differences between the action of the mind in investigation and in imagination indicate that the latter method of intellection is without warrant and irrational. It is sometimes so; in the play of fancy, it may be intentionally so; in uninstructed minds it may be unintentionally so; but in very intelligent minds it is seldom so. It will suffice our present purpose, however, to say that it is not always so. Were this the case, we should be forced to forego any claim that art might make to express the truth; or that criticism might offer to control the methods of such expression. But it is not the case—and this is the important matter that we have been approaching, and which connects our present subject with all that was said in Chapters VI. and VII.—it is not the case because the difference between the conceptions derived from imagination and from investigation is owing chiefly to the degree in which the source of the former is in subconscious intellection and of the latter in conscious; and it has been found, contrary to that which is suggested in the passage quoted from Huxley on page 138, that both forms of intellect are legitimate and even necessary, in case all the resources of mind are to be brought to bear upon a subject. It has been shown, too, and will be made clearer on pages 211 to 213, that the mind frequently apprehends and develops truth according to the subconscious methods, just as rationally as it comprehends and unfolds it according to the conscious methods. Indeed, any one can prove the fact for himself by merely recalling how often he asserts, after an imaginative inference, that he has had reasons for it; and how, by searching for these reasons, he succeeds in finding them. He retraces his course along the subconscious pathway between his present conclusion and his last conscious thought, and, gradually, one by one, the intervening logical steps emerge into consciousness. That they do so indicates that, although his mind has jumped the steps, or, at least, been unconscious of taking them, nevertheless it has really given subconscious consideration to every one of them.

To offset what has just been said, however, another important difference between the processes of thought in investigation and in imagination needs to be noticed. It is this: At every stage of the conscious and reflective method employed in investigation, the results unfolded in thought are modified and corrected by the results of observation. But the subconscious methods of imagination start, as was pointed out on page 106, with some single suggestion to consciousness, and carry this out, according to subconscious processes alone, which, though often manifesting, as stated on page 105, the results of faultless memory and flawless logic, may, nevertheless, owing to their lack of regard for additional testimony from the outside, lead astray. Now, joining this statement to what has just been said, we can surmise a reason for several acknowledged facts with reference to imaginative minds. One is that they are often not practical. How should they be so when, during the interval in which the subconscious and it alone is at work, they have a tendency to be oblivious of the teaching of observation? Another fact is that they are frequently able to perceive and to express, as another cannot, that which may be considered the absolute truth. Why should they not be able to do this,—independent, as they are, in a peculiar sense, of the immediate influence exerted by concrete material conditions? A third fact is that they are frequently able to manifest prescience, if not actually to prophesy. Why should they not do this again? Everything in the world undoubtedly develops logically—which is only another way of saying that it develops rationally. Why should not a mind with keen powers of observation, and ability to take in a condition exactly as it is, be able, when under exclusive, unimpeded control of the subconscious logical processes, to argue out this condition to its conclusions exactly as they will be when its forces have developed logically that which is in them? A fourth fact, very closely connected with this, is that this same subconscious logical process may often argue out a legitimate result of scientific investigation, and therefore assist in the strictly scientific discovery of that toward which the investigation is directed. Suppose that one should ask why investigation analyzes rock and soil, or water and air, in order to detect a common element behind both? Would not the answer be because imagination has already surmised some resemblance between their manifestations? Or suppose that he should ask why science investigates the laws of construction, and invents such a product, say, as a steam-engine, a church-organ, or a bicycle? Would not the answer be because the mind has imagined the possibility of such a product?

A fifth fact is the one chiefly suggested in Chapter VII., namely, that these imaginative minds are the ones most closely allied to those of the great teachers of religion in their ability to apprehend and to make others apprehend the existence of causes which, as distinguished from those that can be made to appear, may be termed unseen or spiritual. One has to consider the subject for only a moment to recognize that science, in its work of investigating "the natural order of phenomena," of tracing backward the steps of development from one manifestation of nature to another, can never get beyond or behind that which has the possibility of appearing. But this is the same as to say that it can never get beyond the material universe. If it could it would cease to be science, for this, as has been shown, deals with the natural order or sequence of appearances; and all the work of investigation is based upon the idea that behind every ascertained appearance something else can be made to appear. Besides this, were it otherwise, the journey, step by step, through nature back to the supernatural, involves the passage over a realm of such infinite extent that no finite mind could take it. In contrast to these conditions, notice that the artistic method from its tendency to disregard many of the phenomena, and to skip intervening steps, and to jump to conclusions, leads one not invariably but readily to surmise an occasioning cause which does not and cannot be made to appear. If the poet's thought be directed towards nature, it can easily pass beyond and behind the material universe. As Wordsworth says:

> I have learned
> To look on nature not as in the hour
> Of thoughtless youth, but hearing oftentimes
> The still, sad music of humanity,
> Nor harsh nor grating, though of ample power
> To chasten and subdue. And I have felt
> A presence that disturbs me with the joy
> Of elevated thoughts ; a sense sublime
> Of something far more deeply interfused,
> Whose dwelling is the light of setting suns,
> And the round ocean and the living air,
> And the blue sky, and in the mind of man ;
> A motion and a spirit that impels
> All thinking things, all objects of all thought,
> And rolls through all things.
>
> *Lines Composed a Few Miles above Tintern Abbey.*

This in an expression not of investigation but of imagination, not of science but of art. Science, as has been said, cannot pass the boundaries of the material universe as revealed to consciousness. It could not do so without getting beyond the sphere in which its methods of comprehending, reflecting, and reasoning naturally work. Art, however, surmises, almost of necessity, an occasioning force behind these appearances. Like assimilates with like. The subconscious self within, through its subconscious steps of logic, subjectively draws near to that of which it cannot be objectively conscious. It is not only scriptural but philosophical to suppose that only the unseen spirit can hear the still small voice, and hold communion with an unseen, spiritual sovereign.

This thought will enable us to perceive clearly in what sense, as applied to imagination, it is true, as stated on page 63, that art encroaches upon the realms both of religion and of science, providing, as it were, a bridge connecting the two. As brought out in Chapter VII., the results of imagination and of inspiration are often indistinguishable. We have found in this chapter that the same is frequently true of the results of imagination and of investigation. Let imagination surmise a resemblance between the elements entering into rock and soil, or water and air, or the possibility of constructing a steam-engine, a church-organ, or a bicycle,—and after science, with slow and cautious steps, has caught up with this surmisal, does there not seem to have been some ground for it,—some positive knowledge preceding it? What is this but to say that there had been some steps of investigation before the leap of imagination, which latter, like the jump of the boy after his run, is, in part at least, a result of the momentum derived from the impetus of the former. Accordingly, we see how the two tendencies react on one another. Imagination is a forerunner of investigation; and investigation furnishes an impetus to imagination.

For this reason a great thinker, whether a poet or a philosopher, although he will incline to the one method or to the other, according to the bent of his genius, must not be wholly deficient in the qualities that go to make up either. Nor, so far as education can atone for deficiency, will his education be complete until he has cultivated the powers that go to make up both. Goethe was a student of science; and his poetry owes much to his scientific studies. Dante and Milton were scientific in their poetry, and Plato and Spinoza were poetic in their philosophies. As Sir Wm. Hamilton says, in the thirty-third of his "Lectures on Metaphysics": "A vigorous power of representation is as indispensable a condition of success in the abstract sciences as in the poetical and plastic arts; and it may accordingly be reasonably doubted whether Aristotle or Homer were possessed of the more powerful imagination."

CHAPTER IX.

SIGNIFICANCE AS ATTRIBUTABLE TO MENTAL ACTION: RELIGIOUS CONCEPTIONS CHARACTERIZED BY FAITH; ARTISTIC BY IDEALITY.

Connection of Thought—Faith, like Conscience, Related to Subconscious Control—Manifested in Practice as well as in Opinion—Thus Interpreted, Faith Allows for Possibilities of Difference Owing to Degrees and Kinds of Intelligence—Artistic Conceptions—These are Characterized by Ideality—Faith and Ideality usually Go together, and Tend to Develop one another—Art as an Expression of Religious Faith Fails both as Art and as Religion; Art Does the most Good when Attending to its own Business.

WE have found that religious, scientific, and artistic conceptions are mainly traceable, respectively, to *inspiration*, having its chief source in subconscious intellection, to *investigation*, having its chief source in conscious intellection, and to *imagination*, having its source about equally in both forms of intellection. We are now to notice, as intimated on page 64, that, as each of these phases of conception reveals itself in the mind, the religious, which results when the mind is dominated by subconscious rather than by conscious influence, is characterized by *faith;* the scientific, which results when the mind is dominated by conscious rather than by subconscious influence, is characterized by *knowledge;* and the artistic, which results when there is a comparatively equal blending of subconscious and of conscious influence, is characterized by *ideality*.

To consider, first, that which is characterized by *faith*, the Scriptures tell us, in Heb. xi., 1, that faith is "the evidence of things not seen," and the faith that we term religious is exactly characterized by this, *i. e.*, by an evidence in consciousness, augmented by all the comprehension of the particular subject-matter of which the conscious mind is capable, of an influence beyond or below the reach of consciousness, of an influence which, though manifested in its results, is not in itself perceptible. At first thought, the reader may be inclined to think that, while there may be in faith evidences of impulses, whims, moods that actuate some people, there is no evidence of what may be termed the dominance of subconscious intellection as described in Chapters V. to VII. But let him reflect a little. Did he ever ask himself what is the real significance of that word which he uses so often, —*conscience?* Everybody, of course, knows what the sensations are to which the word refers. He has felt them. But what is the explanation of this particular term? What was in the mind—occultly and unconsciously, perhaps, as in the case of so many other words when first used—of the man, or set of men, who originated the term? What is the connection between conscience and consciousness? What is conscience a consciousness of? When thus interrogated, one can scarcely avoid recognizing that it is a consciousness of a tendency in the direction of feeling, thought, or action; and that the particular direction indicated is a resultant of many factors—not merely of what religious people term spirit, and physiologists temperament, but, in connection with these, of an incalculable number of hereditary traits, of acquired habits, of social and educational influences, and of experiences, intellectual and emotional, that have been both reasoned out and suffered out,—a resultant, in fact, of the very things, and of all of them taken together, that form the contents of that part of the mind which men term the subconscious. The Christ, in speaking in Luke xv., 17, of the turning-point in the life of the prodigal son, says that "he came to himself." This is the exact language in which almost every one describes the way in which a man who has been insane, intoxicated, or asleep gets out of this state into one that is normal and rational. What the Christ evidently meant was that at this time the prodigal came to a consciousness of his own mind and life, especially in their higher spiritual relations,—to a consciousness, therefore, of those promptings of the better rational or spiritual subconscious self which ought to be supreme in every one. It is because of bringing one to a consciousness of these that conscience imparts a feeling of obligation. The fact alone of coming to consciousness in the sense just indicated might not make a man of faith, much less a man of Christian faith. Faith is determined not by the mere recognition but by the enthronement of these spiritual promptings; and Christian faith by the enthronement of them as a result of the spiritual influence of the Christ. At the same time, a recognition of these promptings in any form must tend to make one correct his conscious by his subconscious intellection, and thus tend in the direction of faith. It has to be confessed, however, that not even when this tendency has had its perfect work can the most complete faith, any more than what we term conscientiousness, wholly rid a man of folly and fault. Faith cannot do it, because it cannot make one cease to express his thoughts and feelings through his conscious mind and body, the one comparatively

This understanding of the word "ideals" will suggest, at once, the intermediate position (see page 155) already said to be occupied by ideality, between faith upon the one hand and knowledge upon the other hand. Take, for instance, the tendencies of instinct, the promptings of conscience, the motives to activity, which on page 159 were said to be at the basis of faith; or take later developments of these, as, in time, they come to be embodied in theological dogmas or creeds,—all these can make a man no more than an enthusiast, or a fanatic, unless he have those qualities of mind which we term practical? But what is it to be practical? What, but to have the ability to accommodate one's speech and action to existing emergencies, *i. e.*, to surrounding material conditions, to facts as discovered by investigation, and comprehended within the sphere of what we term *knowledge?* Only as that which takes its rise in the realm of spirit is correlated by a man to that which is in the realm of matter, so as to find expression through it, can he do all for men that an artist, a genius, or merely a man of culture should do. This is true as applied to him, not only as a thinker, but as a teacher and leader of others who would think. No one can cause either himself or his neighbor to apprehend the full import of spiritual conditions, whose imagination is not able to perceive the correspondences between them and material conditions. He cannot fully recognize the religious connection between mercy and salvation, or faith and love, unless he can illustrate them by analogues of the same in secular connections. He cannot fully realize the relations between God and man, unless he can see these relations, or can cause them to be seen, imaged in the relations between man and man, especially between the

Great Master and man. Indeed, religion cannot become in the highest sense rational, intelligent, enlightening, unless it be led not merely by ideas but by what we have termed ideals: and ideals are always earthly vessels with heavenly contents; outlines modelled on the lower world, filled in with light and color from the upper; figures of the actual transfigured by the potential.

Now we begin to perceive the best of reasons why science, as pointed out in Chapter VIII., cares primarily for the "natural order of the phenomena" preceding an appearance, or for what are usually termed the occasioning causes, whereas art accepts the phenomenal, being seemingly satisfied with the merely apparent effect. It is because science is concerned with knowledge; and one cannot have knowledge without some comprehension of preceding material conditions. But art is concerned with ideals; and ideals, however much or little one may know of a preceding condition, are not material. They are mental. Circumstances and our very nature prevent all of us from learning about more than a few objects and from experiencing more than a few phases of life. Nevertheless, we all desire to possess the results that would ensue, provided such were not the case. Therefore the boy who cannot have the experience surmises what might be the experience of a sailor or a general; and the man in the same condition surmises what might be the experience of a fairy or a saint. As Shakespeare says:

> The poet's eye in a fine frenzy rolling
> Doth glance from heaven to earth, from earth to heaven,
> And, as imagination bodies forth
> The forms of things unknown, the poet's pen
> Turns them to shapes and gives to airy nothing
> A local habitation and a name.
> *A Midsummer Night's Dream, v., 1.*

Or, if Shakespeare belonged to an unscientific age, let us see what a poet of our own age has to say on the same subject:

> We strolled along
> By the still borders of the misty lake,
> Repeating favorite verses with one voice,
> Or conning more, as happy as the birds
> That round us chanted. Well might we be glad,
> Lifted above the ground by airy fancies
> More bright than madness or the dreams of wine;
> And, though full oft the objects of our love
> Were false, and in their splendor overwrought,
> Yet was there surely then no vulgar power
> Working within us,—nothing less, in truth,
> Than that most noble attribute of man,
> Though yet untutored and inordinate,
> That wish for something loftier, more adorned,
> Than is the common aspect, daily garb,
> Of human life. What wonder then if sounds
> Of exultation echoed through the groves;
> For images and sentiments and words
> And everything encountered or pursued
> In that delicious world of poesy
> Kept holiday, a never-ending show,
> With music, incense, festival, and flowers!
>
> . . . . . .
>
> Visionary power
> Attends the motions of the viewless winds,
> Embodied in the mystery of words;
> There darkness makes abode, and all the host
> Of shadowy things work endless changes,—there,
> As in a mansion like their proper home
> Even forms and substances are circumfused
> By that transparent veil with light divine,
> And through the turnings intricate of verse
> Present themselves as objects recognized
> In flashes, and with glory not their own.
> *The Prelude, v.: Wordsworth.*

Between the man who has the conception of the things surrounding him that is represented in this passage and the man who has not, there is the widest possible difference. The former, to quote from Wordsworth again, is characterized by

>   ——a mind
> That feeds upon infinity, that broods
> Over the dark abyss, intent to hear
> Its voices issuing forth to silent light
> In one continuous stream ; a mind sustained
> By recognitions of transcendent power,
> In sense conducting to ideal form.
> *The Prelude, xiv. : Wordsworth.*

The latter—the man of no ideality—passes through life in the condition described in *Peter Bell*:

> He travelled here, he travelled there ;—
> But not the value of a hair
> Was heart or head the better.
>
> He roved among the vales and streams,
> In the green wood and hollow dell.
> They were his dwellings night and day,
> But Nature ne'er could find the way
> Into the heart of Peter Bell.
>
> In vain through every changeful year
> Did Nature lead him as before :
> A primrose by the river's brim
> A yellow primrose was to him,
> And it was nothing more.
> *Peter Bell : Wordsworth.*

These differences between the man with ideality and without it are supposed by some to be important mainly because affecting the mind in the direction of religion. But they are equally important because affecting it in the direction of science. Consider for a moment the fundamental method in science—Why, when brought face to face with appearances of matter or of mind, does the scientist analyze the different effects in each; why does he trace them backward, step by step, to their ultimate elements, and, when these have been found, and often not till then, compare the first appearances with others in which the effects of the same elements are visible? Is there any better answer to this than that of Sir William Hamilton in one of his "Lectures on Metaphysics"? "The mind," he says, "cannot conceive that anything that begins to be is anything more than a new modification of pre-existent elements; it is unable to view any individual thing as other than a link in the mighty chain of being; and every isolated object is viewed by it only as a fragment which to be known must be known in connection with the whole of which it constitutes a part." In other words, according to this philosopher, the answer to our question is that science proceeds as it does because it has a conception of a whole which has appeared in parts, or, as philosophers say, a conception of an ideal substance, or an ideal of a substance, which has the possibility of appearing in effects, though it does not itself appear. But what is the nature of this ideal, and whence is it obtained? Its nature is the same as that of an ideal in art, and it is obtained, just as is an ideal in art,—through the imagination. To show this, let us take a very elementary conception, and trace it to a condition in which it passes into what we term a general law or, as explained in Chapter II., a general truth of science.

If one have been so circumstanced that he has never known of more than one death, he may say, "A man appeared for a little while and then vanished." This is not an expression of imagination, it is the statement of a fact ; and, so far as it goes, of a result of investigation. But after the observation of many deaths, he may make the statement general. He may say, " A man appeareth for a little while and then vanisheth." Here is a result of investigation which has had added to it a result of imagination. The general statement is made because the lives of many persons have been observed, and have all manifested the tendency indicated. Again, joining to his observations of men an observation of a single material appearance, one may say : " Man is a vapor ; he appeareth for a little while and then vanisheth." Here we have a still clearer result of imagination : we have two factors of a comparison both indicated, namely, man and vapor. Once more, observing a similar tendency not alone in men and in vapor, but in many other things, one may make his statement universal. He may say : " All life is a vapor " ; " The things that are seen are temporal " ; " This life 's a dream, an empty show." But notice that just as soon as he makes his statement universal, even though his surmisal be based upon such wide observations of life and its methods that his words have almost the accuracy of scientific conclusions, nevertheless, he has gone outside the realm of investigation into that of imagination. It is impossible that one should investigate all the objects, events, or experiences to which a universal law can apply. He can associate it with all of them only so far as he can conceive of them as being imaged in the few of which he knows. He can make the law universal only so far as his mind has accepted an ideal of the whole world, framed upon the particular world with which he is acquainted.

There is a difference, indeed, in the way in which science and art carry out this principle,—science never ceasing to investigate so long as investigation is possible, whereas art, as we have found, is often satisfied to do no investigating whatever. But in the end the same principle is operative in both. It is the effect upon our minds, the ideal which is formed in these, which furnishes the stimulus of effort whether in poetry or philosophy. The scientist may be given a conception of no more than a universal material substance, the methods of the operations of which, when ascertained, furnish the conditions of universal laws, or truths. Nevertheless this conception is a purely mental effect, derived from nature, in just as true a sense as is the less indirect and more immediate conception of significance behind material nature which is awakened in the mind of the artist. Other things, undoubtedly causing many exceptions to the general rule, being taken into consideration, it cannot be disputed that the mind most likely to be stimulated to the methods of science, as accounted for in the passage quoted from Hamilton on page 170—in other words, the mind most likely to be influenced by the general conception of unity of substance, is the mind most likely to be influenced also by that conception of unity of significance which resolves itself into the ideal of one

> Spirit that impels
> All thinking things, all objects of all thought,
> And rolls through all things.
>
> *Lines Composed a Few Miles above Tintern Abbey : Wordsworth.*

All that was said at the end of Chapter VIII. with reference to both the limitations and the possibilities of the imaginative mind, on the one hand, and of the investigative, on the other, necessarily applies, in general principle, to those more concrete results of each, respectively, which we have in ideality and in knowledge. Of course, there is no necessity that the same line of thought should be repeated here.

CHAPTER XI.

SIGNIFICANCE AS ATTRIBUTABLE TO MENTAL ACTION: RELIGIOUS CONCEPTIONS TENDING TO EXPRESSION THROUGH SPIRITUALLY INFLUENTIAL SUGGESTION; ARTISTIC THROUGH ANALOGICAL REPRESENTATION.

Subconscious, Conscious, and Blended Intellection, as respectively Tending to Spiritual Suggestion, Logical Formulation, and Analogical Representation—Inference from Hypnotism concerning Connection between Influencing Subconscious Intellection and Giving Suggestions—How Religion, as Distinguished from Science and Art, Influences Feeling, Thought, and Conviction Suggestively, Shown from the Methods of Jesus—From the Nature of what, Coming from the Subconscious Region and Having to Do with the Unseen World, cannot be Formulated—This True as Applied to the Imaginative Phraseology of Art—More True as Applied to the Inspired Phraseology of Religion: Dogmas Not True Scientifically—Nor many Statements in Scripture—Importance of this View—How Religion Suggestively Influences Life, Conduct, and Character—Illustrated from the Analogy of Freedom of Action under Hypnotic Control—Conversion—Religious Methods Rendered more Apprehensible by the Analogy between them and Methods of Hypnotism—The Law of Self-sacrifice—The Christ, Creation, Future Life—Why Suggestive Influence is Necessary to Stimulate Spiritual Life—It is the only Spiritual Influence upon the Mind in Harmony with that of External Nature—Difference between Suggestive Expression in Religion and Representative in Art—Art Benefits, even religiously, in the Degree in which it Confines itself to Representation, Shown in Poetry—In Sculpture and Painting.

WHAT has been said of the derivation and character of that which constitutes the subject-matter of religion, of science, and of art, renders it inevitable that the respective expressional results of each should be different. Conceptions determined, as in religion, by the vague promptings of subconscious intellection, inspired in their origin and infinite in their reach, and in this sense spiritually influential, must be more or less indefinite. An indefinite conception, if communicated in such a way as to preserve its character, cannot be expressed in a definite form;—that is, it cannot be formulated, it must be suggested. Religion, therefore, may be said to tend to expression through *spiritually influential suggestion*. Conceptions determined, as in science, by all the conditioning causes and the relations between them that can be apprehended by conscious intellection, must be more or less definite; and if communicated in such a way as to preserve their character, they must be expressed in a definite form, and, so far as they have to do with causes and effects, in a logical form. Science, therefore, may be said to tend to expression through *logical formulation*. How now is it with art? Its conceptions have been said to partake of the nature partly of those of religion and partly of those of science. They must, therefore, be partly indefinite and partly definite; and their expression, therefore, must partake of the nature partly of suggestion and partly of formulation. An indefinite suggestion is imparted through definite formulation according to the method not of logic, but of analogy; and a formulation of that which cannot be definitely communicated, but only indefinitely suggested, cannot be said to be presented, but only represented. These are the reasons for maintaining, as will be done in this chapter, that an artistic conception tends to expression through *analogical representation*.

The use of the phrase, *spiritually influential suggestion*, will probably remind the reader that, on page 106, suggestion was said to be the one influence universally employed in hypnotism, which itself may be said to be the only scientific method yet discovered of attaining control over the processes of the subconscious mind. But what is the object of religion, or of the expression of any religious conception, except this very thing; namely, to attain control over the subconscious, or spiritual nature. There is, too, as has been already shown and is soon to be shown still more clearly, an indisputable and inevitable connection between suggestion and faith. Indeed, Thomas J. Hudson, in "The Law of Psychic Phenomena," considers the strongest argument in favor of the inspired mission of Jesus to be afforded by the fact that eighteen hundred years before scientists had discovered this connection the Christ had proclaimed it. Why this view is worthy of attention will be indicated in a moment. At present let us notice the two directions in which suggestion, if used as a method of influence, naturally manifests itself:—first, in the character of the words that it causes to be uttered and, second, in the character of the deeds that it causes to be done.

In considering the first of these we are forced to recognize that the statement that suggestion is the method of expression which is the most religious in its nature and effects carries with it the conclusion that, in itself, a creed is not religious but scientific, for it does more than suggest the truth, it formulates it; and that a ceremonial is not religious but artistic, for it does more than suggest the truth, it represents it. Nor will the statement allow all to hold, without modification, certain views that they may have with reference to the methods of accepting the phraseology of the Scriptures. These objections, however, are not insurmountable. The scientific, artistic, or literary, added to that which exerts a religious influence, need not necessarily destroy it. In such a case, to recognize that each can affect the religious nature only indirectly through understanding, emotion, or imagination, might be a help rather than a hindrance. To go immediately to the most indisputable source of inspiration and faith of which we know, take the words of that Master who spake " as never man spake." So far were his words from being like those of a philosopher formulating a system, or of a leader dictating action, that hardly two associations of men since his time have been completely agreed as to exactly what form either of belief or of organization most accurately represents Christianity as he proclaimed it, his apparent theory being that, if men came to take into their natures, as a living force, the inspiration derived from the suggestions that he gave them—from such a suggestion, for instance, as that they were sons of God—then that, both as individuals and as members of his corporate church, they could safely be left, in applying the suggestion, to exercise the "liberty" with which he had made them "free" (Gal. v., 1). Now if such were true of the words of Jesus, why should it not be true of the words of other inspired prophets? Have any of them been more truly inspired than he was?

This argument from example may be confirmed by one based upon the nature of the conception which in religion is communicated. Significance obtained, as it mainly is in science and largely is in art, through the conscious action of the mind, may be imparted with definiteness and accuracy to an extent not true of that which has been obtained mainly or wholly through subconscious action. When we speak of scientific truth as applied to a statement, we mean something that formulates the mind's conscious knowledge of every essential detail entering into the general result; we mean something that manifests no defective work of observation or of memory. When we speak of religious or even of artistic truth, of truth that is either inspirational or imaginative, it is often impossible that we should mean this; for we are speaking of something that involves certain contributions from the mind's hidden sphere of action, and because this reveals to us no form that can be perceived or even distinctly conceived, they cannot be formulated. They can be merely represented or suggested. Take the following:

> Why man he doth bestride the narrow world
> Like a Colossus; and we petty men
> Walk under his huge legs, and peep about
> To find ourselves dishonorable graves.
>
> *Julius Cæsar*, i., 2 : *Shakespeare.*

Scientifically considered, hardly one word of this is true. No man who ever lived could bestride the world like a Colossus, or have any grown man not a dwarf walk under his legs. Yet the statement is not false, because the words mean merely that certain spiritual or mental relations existing between the man and us, which relations cannot be seen, are the same as those that might exist between the height that might be supposed to be seen in a Colossus and in a petty man, and that, therefore, these forms that might be seen can *represent* or *suggest* these unseen relations. Or take another illustration:

> True hope is swift, and flies with swallows' wings,
> Kings it makes gods, and meaner creatures kings.
>
> *Richard III*, v. 2 : *Idem.*

This again is not literally or scientifically true, but only by way of *suggestion*. Hope never had swallows' wings; and it takes a good deal more than it to make kings gods, or meaner creatures kings.

If a principle like this apply to the phraseology of art, it must apply still more to that of religion. Notwithstanding the many ecclesiastical controversies concerning the doctrine of "eternal generation," which phrase itself furnishes a fitting commentary upon the results of extreme literalism, the fundamental conceptions with which this doctrine started, and which are accepted by most Christians, are not in a scientific or literal sense true. It is not in any such sense true that God is a father, or Jesus a son of God, or an elder brother of Christians, or that the latter are children of Abraham. Whatever truth may be in these words is in the existence of a relationship in the unseen, spiritual world, which may *suggest*, or be *suggested* by, the relationship of father, son, brother, and children as it exists in a visible and material world.

According to the same analogy, when we are informed in the Scriptures that "The Lord spake unto Moses," or unto some other prophet, and we are told the words spoken, how can one hold that we are justified either in affirming or denying that the term *spake* refers to words heard? Why need it indicate more than an influence exerted in an unseen, spiritual sphere *suggestive* of that which, in the material sphere, would be exerted through the use of language? We are acquainted with this method of understanding a statement, even when applied to like conditions in two different spheres that are both material. A mother explains to her child that the mother-bird pushes the young birds out of her nest and *tells* them to fly; or she explains her feelings, when the child does wrong, by saying that she is *angry*. In both cases, she says what, scientifically considered, is false; yet it is strictly true—in *spirit*, as we say. And how else can we suppose the Scriptures to be true? If thus interpreted,—*i. e.*, considered to be true merely in spirit—we can explain the most of their apparent discrepancies. We can explain why, for instance, we are told in Ex. xi., 1, 2, that, just before the Israelites were to leave Egypt forever, "The Lord said unto Moses" . . . "Speak now in the ears of the people, and let every man borrow of his neighbor and every woman of her neighbor, jewels of silver and jewels of gold"; and yet are told in Ex. xii., 35, that "the children of Israel did according to the words of Moses, and they borrowed," etc. If scientific accuracy had been the object here, we should have been informed, in both cases, either that the Lord originated the idea or that Moses originated it. As it stands, we may choose either horn of the dilemma. Doing this, when we come to consider the far greater discrepancy indicated between what we conceive to be the character of God and the advice to do evil that good may come, we may conclude that these passages, interpreted in a literary, and not a literal sense, mean no more than that Moses was inspirationally impressed with the conception that he should lead the people out of Egypt, and obtain funds for the purpose in the best way that he could, in which circumstances the natural promptings of a descendant of Jacob as well as of an enslaved race impelled him into advising the subterfuge of the false pretence of borrowing. So with the words of David and the works of Joshua. The accounts of these picture to us minds inspirationally impressed with the importance of suppressing and ending unrighteousness and idolatry. If these minds carry out the despotic and military prompting of their age, though uttering imprecatory psalms and committing wholesale slaughter, such manifestations, though suggesting the feelings and methods of the Lord, do not necessarily express them with scientific accuracy. Notice again what is said on page 113.

When we think of all the iniquity and cruelty in family, society, and state which have resulted from the extreme literalism of the officials of ecclesiastical organizations, we cannot avoid feeling that the interpretations of the Scriptures rendered possible by considering religious expressions mainly suggestive, as just indicated, may be as much in the interest of philanthropy as of philosophy. Nevertheless, it is not supposed that all will accept these methods of interpretation. Some are so constituted that they imagine that inspired words cannot be true unless they are true literally. There are some, too, who think the same of poetry. But, as was intimated a moment ago, they are not the ones who understand poetry the best or get the most truth out of it.

Now let us consider the second direction in which suggestion, if used as a method of influence, naturally manifests itself, namely, in the character of the deeds that it causes to be done. Mr. Hudson, in "The Law of Psychic Phenomena," mentioned a moment ago, attempts to show that the result of suggestion exerted upon the subconscious mind in hypnotism is in exact accord with that produced by the central doctrine of Christianity, namely, salvation through faith. So too, one may add here, is the freedom with which, after the suggestion has been accepted by the mind, the subject is left to carry it out. He is told "You are Abraham Lincoln," perhaps, and, if, exercising a form of faith that involves a voluntary yielding of his own will, he believes the words that are told him, he becomes to his own conception what the hypnotizer suggests. Yet the hypnotizer suggests this in only a very general way, and watches, with as much interest as any one else, to see what will be the result of his subject's conception of Mr. Lincoln's character. In like manner, according to the Christian theory, when Jesus told men that they were sons of God they became these by believing in him and in his words and voluntarily yielding their wills to him; but at the same time he merely suggested a conception which they were left free to carry out in their own ways. He did not for either individuals or communities formulate creeds or dictate actions. His followers were "called to liberty." (Gal. v., 13. Notice again, too, what was said on page 160.) If one wonder how his suggestions could permanently change character, even ordinary hypnotism, which is not a divine but merely a human agency subordinating the conscious nature in such ways as to allow the subconscious mind to be influenced directly, may indicate how this should be the case.

Observe the following from an article by Dr. R. Osgood Mason on "The Educational Uses of Hypnotism" from the "North American Review" for October, 1896. "In the summer of 1884," he says, "there was at the Salpêtrière, a young woman of a deplorable type—a criminal lunatic, filthy in habits and violent in demeanor, and with a lifelong history of impurity and theft. M. Auguste Voisin, one of the physicians of the hospital staff, undertook to hypnotize her at a time when she could be kept quiet only by the straight-jacket and the continuous douche to the head. She would not look at the operator, but raved and spat upon him. M. Voisin, however, kept his face close to hers, and followed her eyes wherever she moved them. In ten minutes she was asleep, and in five minutes more she passed into the sleep-walking or somnambulistic state, and began to talk incoherently. This treatment being repeated on many successive days, she gradually became sane when in the hypnotic condition, though she still raved when awake. At length she came to obey in her waking hours commands impressed upon her in her trance—trivial matters, such as to sweep her room,—then suggestions involving marked changes in her behavior; finally, in the hypnotic state, she voluntarily expressed regret for her past life, and, of her own accord, made good resolutions for the future, which she carried out when awake, and the improvement in her conduct was permanent. Two years later M. Voisin wrote that she was a nurse in a Paris hospital, and that her conduct was irreproachable."

There are several other of our religious conceptions that a recognition of these analogies between religious and hypnotic influence may render more explicable. Take, for instance, the conception of the necessity for the incarnation and atonement of Jesus. As a rule, even such a degree of confidence as must antedate the influence of a hypnotizer, must depend upon his subject's belief not only in his ability but in his good will and kindly interest. But what can afford the highest evidence of these?—what but love? And how does love manifest itself? In this world it is simply a universal law that love, from that of a friend to that of a mother, manifests itself in self-sacrifice, and the degree of it in the degree of self-sacrifice. "Greater love hath no man than this, that a man lay down his life for his friend" (John xv., 13). Take again the conception of the spiritual unity of the Christ with God, as well as the associated conception of which the church, with its literalism (when applied exclusively, as all literalism must be, to only a single application of the general principle involved) is in danger of losing sight,—the conception of the spiritual unity of all believers with God, the conception expressed in the prayer of Jesus, in John xvii., 21, "That they all may be one; as thou, Father, art in me and I in thee, that they also may be one in us":— what in human experience can cause us to conceive of the possibility of spiritual unity existing at the same time with separate personality, as well as an understanding of the ascertained fact that a hypnotizer can actually control the mind of his patient, and yet, as in the case in which he tells him that he is Abraham Lincoln, can allow him virtual freedom of both thought and action; allow him, that is, to develop his own conception of Mr. Lincoln's character?[1] Again, take the statement in the opening of the Bible, that the world was created in six days, and the corresponding statements in Is. xxxiv., 4, and Rev. vi., 14, that the heavens shall finally be rolled together as a scroll. It may be said with truth that there is only one possible explanation in accordance with which such statements can be shown to be analogous to anything supposable in human experience. A hypnotizer can make a dozen or

---

[1] The fact that a subject, though hypnotized and thus caused mentally to develop a false premise (see page 106), nevertheless usually continues to give expression to his own idiosyncrasies—a man, for instance, to manifest his sense of dignity, and a woman her sense of modesty—is important. It shows not only the groundlessness of much of the fiction which ascribes the commission of crime to hypnotic influence, but also a reason for supposing that the agent of expression, however elsewise influenced, is, in the last analysis, the subconscious *self*, and so for supposing also, so far as the conditions throw light upon life as it will be when wholly free from the body, that *selfhood*, individuality of character, will continue in the future state.

more men all agree in conceiving of themselves as being in a place wholly different from that in which they were a moment before. What is to prevent millions of thinking creatures from being made to perceive a world created out of nothing, and kept in this condition for generations and then being made as suddenly to see this world disappear? Nothing except a lack in the universe of power able to exert a broader and longer influence of exactly the same kind as can be exerted by a man. Similar considerations may show us why it is rational to suppose that the future life of the individual should be wholly determined by his present life, not only spiritually considered but intellectually. In the results of hypnotism, we have a picture of what the mind does when its own physical powers are not dominant over it. What does it do? It goes on, till the hypnotizer interferes, developing the last premises presented to it. It perceives in itself and in its visible surroundings whatever the hypnotizer suggests to be within one or about one. It experiences the literal, as well as poetic, truth of what Milton says:

> The mind is its own place, and in itself
> Can make a heaven of hell, a hell of heaven.
> *Paradise Lost*, 1.

Let the suggestion embody a belief in the Fatherhood of God and the brotherhood of souls,—what could prevent the mind's continuing, after being freed from the body, to live on forever in the same belief? "To-day," said Jesus to the penitent thief upon the cross—"to-day shalt thou be with me in Paradise" (Luke xxiii., 43). Who shall say that it is not strictly in accordance with the laws of this world as well as of the next that this promise should be fulfilled? Again, subconscious intellection, when its activities are once started, develops, as we have found, with perfect recollective, logical, and illustrative consistency that which previous conscious experience has stored. Now so far as what is thus developed has its germs in previous experience, so far is it not logical to conclude that spiritual life in the next world must continue to unfold from ideals formed in this world? and, if so, have we not a provision for future limitation? But if, at the same time, the mind subconsciously through memory, logic, and imagination can develop its stores in ways practically infinite, then, in connection with limitation, have we not also a provision for infinite expansion? And if we can answer these three questions in the affirmative, can we not perceive more clearly than otherwise one reason why life in this world should be one of probation and acquirement, but in the next world one of fruition and rest? And can we not perceive also a true sense in which the exercise of creative genius may be—not alone figuratively as some suppose but—literally divine? It certainly is so, if the divine or heavenly life be a life of perpetual imaginative creation developed out of the experiences obtained on earth. Besides this, too, if subconscious minds be able to have intercourse with one another, what is to prevent the discoveries, inventions, and conceptions of every age, which must necessarily be confined to a material plane, from being a help to those who have gone before and who are now upon a spiritual plane? If nothing can prevent this, then we may understand why a patriarch of old could be pronounced blessed owing to the character and achievements of his descendants, and why the presence of a cloud of witnesses on high (Heb. xii., 1) should be used as an inducement to one who cares little for anything except the opportunity of helping others.

Notice now that there are the best of reasons why spiritual influence should be supposed to be exerted in the suggestive way that has been indicated. In what way except through the endeavor to understand suggestions, and to embody them in definite mental and material forms, can spiritual life develop? Even by divinity itself could it be developed according to any other method? A fully formulated, dictatorial control relieves a man of the necessity of thinking. A suggestive control obliges him to think. Oblige him to do this, where both he and others have liberty, and no matter how unwisely he may, at first, carry out suggestions, a right tendency thus started will ultimately attain complete righteousness; a little leaven, after a time, after many generations, perhaps, will finally leaven the whole lump. It is probably because of a recognition of this principle that the apostle Paul, in 2 Cor. iii., 6, speaks of himself and his fellow workers as being "ministers of the new testament; not of the letter but of the spirit; for the letter killeth, but the spirit giveth life." The letter killeth, probably, not only because the theory of literalism, so conscientiously advocated, has been the death of any belief in the Scriptures whatever, on the part of large numbers who—debarred from a theory which might explain—cannot fully ignore what to them seem to be their discrepancies; but also because the truth, when considered only in itself, so far as it is supposed to be identical with a form or a formula (see page 50), fails to stimulate to activity, and so to spiritual life. To-day, as in the days of Adam and Eve, knowledge of good and evil, so far as it is accompanied by a desire for nothing beyond this, tends to spiritual death. The curse of bigotry and priestcraft lies not alone in the fact that by false forms and traditions they make void the truth, but that they make it void by true forms and traditions so far as they exalt these to undue importance; so far as they point to forms logical to thought or attractive to the eye, and say "Know these, or do these, and thou shalt live." If the church be paradise on earth, this latter Eden may have its tempter as surely as the former one. When a man is told that he can attain all that mind or soul can need through accepting some dogma, performing some ceremony, undertaking some service, what can be the result but to counteract the tendency to faith in that which is unseen? On earth the soul should walk by faith, because this leaves all about one an infinite margin that stimulates desire; and only through desire for surer, purer, better things can intellect be developed or spirit sanctified.

Such a view of divine influence as thus exerted in the invisible realm is the only one in harmony with the same as exerted in visible nature. This gives a brook rocks to rise above and ledges to dash upon, that, farther on, through their agency its volume and speed may be increased. So, also, nature gives a man personal foes to rise above, and financial woes to dash upon, that, farther on, through their agency his wisdom and energy may be increased. Amid material obstacles, the man who tries to save his life by flying from the conflicts granted to experience may lose it; but the man who pushes forward, though he lose his life, may find it. Amid spiritual obstacles, the soul that has the faith to move is vivified with health; the one that is content to lie and sleep and dream, whoever or whatever may give the authority to do so, is only stiffened into death. Toward this alone does any organization, which by ceremonies or by creeds can check a tendency to effort, lure its deluded devotees ; and all the more so if it call itself a church.

Now let us notice the difference between *spiritually influential suggestion* in religion, and *analogical representation* in art, though a full explanation of what is meant by the term *analogical* must be left to the chapter following. The difference between the expressional result in religion and in art corresponds of course to that already noticed between *inspiration* and *imagination*, and also between *faith* and *ideality*. Artistic as well as religious significance has a suggestive influence. But in religion, the nucleus of this influence, as in the directions of the hypnotizer, or in the injunction "Follow me," may often be conveyed in an expression indicating no result whatever of imagination or ideality, and therefore none of art. Neither is an expression that is artistic, even when designed to be religious, invariably religious. This fact follows from the nature of that to which men trace religion and art. They feel it to be inappropriate to express conceptions intended to exert only spiritual influence in ways that involve such conscious observation and use of material surroundings as are necessary in artistic representative imitations. For this reason religious suggestions, even when they happen to be communicated as are those of art,—*i. e.*, indirectly and through forms,—are generally acknowledged to have a religious effect in inverse ratio to their representative effect. A Christian man through his conduct, and a church through its services, may represent the Christian life, but the moment that the representative element in either is emphasized, the moment that it is brought to our attention that the man's actions, attitudes, or facial and vocal expressions are assumed for the purpose of representing, he suggests to us a Pharisee, if not a hypocrite. With art it is the opposite. Its object is to represent; and the actor upon the stage, or the imitator of real life as delineated in the drama or the novel, or depicted in the picture or the statue, awakens our approval in the exact degree of the unmistakably representative character of his performance.

In Chapter IX., when speaking of ideality, it was shown that the more strictly the artist confines himself to his legitimate work, the more successful will this be both in itself and in its influence for good upon work in associated departments. Notice here, in analogy with what was said there, that, in every age, art in the exact degree in which it has confined itself to its own sphere of suggestion through analogical representation has been, for this reason alone, of incalculable benefit to the development of religious truth. It can be said, almost without qualification, that in all times of extreme traditionalism and unenlightenment art has proved the only agency that, without offending ignorance and superstition, has been able to counterbalance their influence. It has done this by using the forms of nature, and contenting itself with the truth as represented in them. Guised in familiar aspects, appealing to the mind by ways of suggestion which leaves the imagination free to surmise or deduce whatever inference it may please, the thoughts expressed in art do not, as a rule, repel even the most prejudiced, or excite their opposition. A man in Italy, in the thirteenth century, would have been sent to the stake if he had made a plain statement to the effect that a pope could be kept in hell, or a pagan admitted to paradise. Yet when Dante pictured both conditions in his great poem, how many questioned his orthodoxy? The mask is a fitting symbol for the poet, not only because the classic actors wore one in presenting tragedies and comedies, but because the poet himself appears in one whenever he writes objectively or dramatically — indeed, one could almost say, whenever he writes artistically. Words and deeds that would provoke disesteem and persecution, if employed by a philosopher or an essayist, can be made to fit the characters or situations represented in a poem or a novel, and never raise a protest.

So with the themes of painting and of sculpture. What a rebuke to the bigotry and the cruelty of the Middle Ages are the countless products of the arts of those periods, pleading constantly to the eye against the savage customs of the times for the sweet but little-practised virtues of justice and charity! Within our own century, too, notwithstanding the traditions of society, the state, and the church, which have often exerted all their powers to uphold and perpetuate slavery, aristocracy, and sectarianism, recall how the modern novel chiefly, but assisted largely by the modern picture, has not only changed the whole trend of the world's thought with reference to these systems, but has contributed, more, perhaps, than any other single cause, to the practical reorganization of them, in accordance with the dictates of enlightened intelligence.

CHAPTER XII.

SIGNIFICANCE AS ATTRIBUTABLE TO MENTAL ACTION: SCIENTIFIC CONCEPTIONS TENDING TO EXPRESSION THROUGH LOGICAL FORMULATION; ARTISTIC, THROUGH ANALOGICAL REPRESENTATION.

Introduction—Formulation rather than Representation Necessitated by the Sources of Scientific Expression—By its Nature—By its Results: Science Presents Thought Logically; Art, Analogically—This Latter Fact Renders Form Essential in Art—Also Significance, which is the Basis of the Analogy Expressed through the Forms—Difference between that which Looks like and which also Operates like—To Bring out the Latter Involves a Higher Effort of Imagination—Because Making Art in the Highest Sense Natural: Illustrated in the Novel, Drama, Ballad, Descriptive Poetry—In these such Comparisons as are not Based on Analogies Taken from Nature are not Indicative of High Imaginative Gifts—The Same Principles Apply to Conceptions of Poems as Wholes—To the Use of Separate Words—Same Principle Illustrated in Music—When both Artistic and Natural—Illustrated in Painting and Sculpture—Further Explanations—In Architecture—That Art should Represent Analogies through Forms not Inconsistent with its Representing Beauty—Relative Use in Art of Natural Beauty and of Ugliness—Representative Expression a Limitation to Art; yet the Reason why its Products Have such Enduring and Universal Influence.

LET us now consider what was meant on page 175 when it was said that the conceptions of science result in expression through *logical formulation*. While doing so, we shall be able to indicate, more clearly than in the preceding chapter, what was meant when it was said that the conceptions of art, as contrasted with those of science, result in expression through *analogical representation*.

The distinctions about to be made thrust themselves upon our notice whether we consider the source, the character, or the results of the scientific as contrasted with the artistic. The conceptions of science are due, as we have found, to an investigation, so far as possible, of every condition preceding an apprehended phenomenon. Of course, what is thus obtained can be imparted to others just as it is, only so far as every factor entering into the knowledge communicated has been given expression in the outward form of communication, or, as we may say, has been *formulated*. On the contrary, the imagination of art draws its ideas and constructs its ideals of a whole class of phenomena from observing a few conditions only, which are the more apparent ones and are taken as *representative* of all of them. It is evident that what is thus obtained can be imparted to others just as it is experienced in the mind, only so far as these same few conditions can be given expression in the outward form in such ways as to exert on the minds of others the same *representative* effects.

Again, we have found that a conception of science differs from one of art in character. Many of the agencies which must be considered in order to have a knowledge of all the intervening links of influence necessary to a complete unfolding of scientific knowledge, cannot be connected in thought with any formal appearance. We may know that some force, say chemic or electric, has operated, and we may indicate the fact in a formula, and, in this sense, formulate it. But a scientific formulation—mathematic or geometric, for instance—usually indicates the interdependence of the conditions for which it stands without conveying the slightest conception of their appearances. In the ideality which, as shown in Chapter X., characterizes art, this is not so; the imagination conforms the ideas to the outlines of certain known objects, events, or experiences. Artistic conceptions are therefore necessarily connected in thought with form, *i. e.*, with a visible or audible effect which is referred to, or is imitated, in order to express them, as, in such cases, they must be expressed, by way of *representation.*

Finally—the fact most pertinent to the line of thought in the present chapter—the results communicated in science and in art are different. In science they appeal to the understanding and reason, and to do this they must show the connection between each occasioning condition and its conditioned effect. The expression therefore must be, as has been said, *logical,*—sufficiently so, at least, to be indicative of logical sequences in the development of that of which it conveys information. On the contrary, an expression may be artistic, and this in the highest degree, without being at all logical, at least in the sense of being indicative of logical sequences. Imagination, as shown in Chapter VIII., is accustomed to jump the steps of logic. Yet often, as we have found, through subconscious intellection, it reaches exactly the same conclusions as are reached by investigation. How does imagination do this? Through arguing not logically but analogically. The term analogy is derived from two Greek words, ἀνά, signifying *thereon*, and λόγος, signifying *a word.* The conception underlying the term, therefore, seems to be that a natural appearance, *i. e.*, a form to which the term is applied, has the effect of a *word;*—that it is a part of that whole of nature which is frequently called the "unwritten word." Moreover, analogy implies, beyond this, that some one natural appearance or form has been compared with at least one other, which is found to furnish a *word thereon*, or a word *in addition*, so that the two or more appearances taken together can be considered as words of the same meaning or significance. It is an argument from an analogy between not two but many—in fact, as many as possible—different appearances, that causes the conception of the unity of nature mentioned on page 172, or of the unity of meaning in art as expressed in the following used by Carlyle in his essay on "The State of German Literature":

> As all Nature's thousand changes
> But one changeless God proclaim,
> So in Art's wide kingdoms ranges
> One sole meaning still the same.

An argument from analogy is always derived from a few forms that are representative, on the one hand, of a whole series of forms, and are representative, on the other hand, of a certain mental significance that is expressible through forms alone, and is actually expressed through the particular forms thus used. Now notice that if a man wish to communicate with the greatest possible accuracy the effect upon his own mind of an analogical argument, he will not impart it, as in religion, through a spiritually suggestive statement, or, as in science, through a logically formulated statement. To do either would merely direct thought and emotion into channels of activity leading, in the one case, into faith or fidelity, or, in the other, into knowledge or learning. His object is neither, but to give others an experience exactly like his own, *i. e.*, an experience of that association of ideas with forms which, on page 161, is termed *ideality*. How can he accomplish this object? How better than by adopting the same method through which nature has influenced his own mind? How better than by himself using, for the purpose, forms appealing to imagination? How better than, with a full sense of the method through which natural forms have influenced his own thought or emotion, by reproducing them in such ways as to reveal the analogies, and, through them, the laws and principles of nature which they have seemed to him to illustrate? How better than through what is meant here by *analogical representation?*

This last paragraph suggests a fact which must never be overlooked when considering the use made in art of the forms of nature. This is the fact that just as truly as the suggestions of religion, or the formulæ of science, these forms are meant to appeal to the *mind*. It is for this reason that it is important that they should illustrate analogies. An analogy, as has been said, implies a resemblance not between forms so much as between the significance expressed through the forms. But that there may be this resemblance, and a resemblance that it is worth while for art to represent, the significance in the forms used must have been, preliminary to the comparison, rightly interpreted. Analogy proceeds upon the supposition that every form of nature illustrates, in some way, a principle, a law, a truth, and that this is confirmed by an illustration of the same principle in another form. In estimating the degree of success therefore, with which imagination, ideality, and representation, as manifested in art, give expression to significance, we must learn to take a comprehensive view of the subject. Analogy includes likeness both in the external forms and in the internal methods of formation, and in the forms chiefly because they exemplify the like methods.

That a man recognizes this latter phase of resemblance is one of his surest ways of proving that he understands art in its entirety. Every schoolboy believes himself to be a literary genius in the degree in which, in details of form, he can use comparisons as in similes and metaphors; and the first thing of which the most ignorant peasant thinks, when brought face to face with a work of painting or sculpture, is whether, in details of form, it bears comparison with the natural object which it represents. But that which occurs neither to the schoolboy, nor to the peasant, nor to the majority of people in any condition, is to draw a distinction between a merely superficial and an organic comparison; between that which looks like and that which operates like. In the following, for instance, the resemblance is superficial:—

> And far in the hazy distance
> Of that lovely night in June,
> The blaze of the flaming furnace
> Gleamed redder than the moon.
> *The Bridge: Longfellow.*

But in this the resemblance is in the operation:

> And like those waters rushing
> Among the wooden piers,
> A flood of thoughts came o'er me
> That filled my eyes with tears.
> *Idem.*

Now in contrast to both of the above, notice the following:

> Not from the grand old masters,
> Not from the bards sublime,
> Whose distant footsteps echo
> Through the corridors of time.
> *The Day is Done: Idem.*

In this last, the appearance of different epochs through which we mark the stretch of time is compared to that of corridors in a hall; and, together with this, the movement of thought in the mind, as reported in the poetry of each period, is compared to the footsteps of persons moving in the corridors. Hence a resemblance is indicated both in appearance and in operation, and for this reason we probably all feel that, as contrasted with the former quotations, this last involves a higher effort of the imagination. In Chapter III. it was shown that what we term the truth of nature can be known only so far as, through its forms, its methods of operation are made known. The same principle must apply to whatever forms may be supposed to represent nature. A work of art completes our ideal of that which should characterize an image of nature, in the degree only in which it is a *word in addition*, in the sense of being something that both suggests nature in appearance and, at the same time, exemplifies the laws that operate in nature. We term the work one of creative imagination mainly because, in both form and significance, in the way in which it appeals to both the physical senses and to the whole mind, it seems to be a continuation of the work of creation.

Indeed, whenever we term a product of art "natural," and argue that, because it is so, it is artistically effective, we include in the term "natural" a conception both of form and of conditions which precede and determine form. For instance, we all recognize that the events portrayed in a drama or a novel are effective in the degree in which they are natural to the conditions that lead up to them, *i. e.*, to the causes occasioning them. We deem them so in the degree in which the author seems simply to transfer to an ideal world, amid ideal surroundings and events, the same developments of love and hate, of joy and suffering, which would be experienced by real persons placed in like circumstances. The simplest ballad is effective in the degree in which it portrays the experience of some members of the human family after a method so accordant with the course of nature that the reader feels that it would be the experience of all its members of similar temperament if similarly circumstanced. Descriptive poetry is effective chiefly in the degree in which it suggests the operations of the general laws of nature through the outlines of the special forms which it delineates. It produces the highest effects; it becomes sublime alone in the degree in which, like some of the poetry of Wordsworth, it suggests resemblances between the methods of the material universe and the operations of the mind.

On the contrary, no mere collecting, no mere crowding of comparisons, can add real effectiveness to a composition if these fail to indicate analogies existing in the nature of things. Sometimes similar operations are pointed out in objects, one of which does not exist in nature. Thus, in the following the mind is likened to a machine:

> And now I see with eye serene
> The very pulse of the machine,
> A Being breathing thoughtful breath,
> A Traveller between life and death.
> *She was a Phantom of Delight : Wordsworth.*

And in this a man and a woman are likened to a bow and its cord :

> As unto the bow the cord is,
> So unto the man is woman;
> Though she bends him, she obeys him,
> Though she draws him, yet she follows,
> Useless each without the other.
> *Hiawatha*, x. : *Longfellow.*

Do any of us fail to recognize the lack of poetic effectiveness in comparisons like these? How different are they from any one of the comparisons in the verses at the end of the paragraph following this!

The analogies of poetry may be expressed either in the general theme or in the special details that constitute the style. The "Divine Comedy" of Dante and the "Paradise Lost" of Milton represent, according to the analogies of earthly experience, spiritual life as a whole; but the tendency to think analogically is no more apparent in the general plots of these poems than in their shortest terms and phrases. It might not be too much to say that every word that one ever uses has truth and beauty and history embodied in it. In its first conception, either its sound or its sense, or, if compound, its structure, is analogous, in a sphere of form, to some experience of consciousness, or to relations between different experiences of consciousness in a sphere of thought. Analogies too, expressed thus in the earliest words of the natural man, are still perceptible in every language, and are recognized as essential in causing style to be artistic. Notice the italicized words in the following; and also the relations between the different italicized words in the same phrases:

> That all the *jarring notes* of life
> Seem *blending* in a psalm,
> And all the *angles* of its strife
> *Slow-rounding* into calm.
>
> *My Psalm: Whittier.*

> I like the people,
> But do not like to *stage* me to their eyes.
>
> *Measure for Measure, i., 1: Shakespeare.*

> *Fasten* your ear on my advisings.
>
> *iii., 1: Idem.*

> No marvel though you *bite* so sharp at reasons,
> You are so *empty* of them.
> > *Troilus and Cressida*, ii., 2 : *Idem.*

> My reformation, *glittering* o'er my fault,
> Shall show more goodly and attract more eyes
> Than that which hath no foil to set it off.
> > 1 *Henry IV.*, i., 2 : *Idem.*

> How *sharp* the point of this remembrance is !
> > *Tempest*, iv., 1 : *Idem.*

> To teach the *young* Idea how to *shoot.*
> > *The Seasons, Spring :* Thomson.

> The *toiling* pleasure *sickens* into pain.
> > *The Deserted Village :* Goldsmith.

If we turn now from poetry to music, we shall find that in this art, too, effectiveness, so far as this depends upon naturalness, is determined by truth to the analogies of nature. Indeed, it is not possible for the majority of our music to be true to nature in any other sense. Nature furnishes art with sounds produced by moving objects, as vibrating reeds or cords, and by the accents of men and animals; but in no respect is a work of music a literal imitation of these. Nevertheless, when listening to the expression of naïve flirtation in such a ballad as "Comin' thro' the Rye," or of despairing love in one like "When Sparrows Build," or of reminiscences of woods and streams such as are recalled in the pastoral symphonies of Beethoven or Handel, or in the bird-music in Wagner's Siegfried, we all feel like exclaiming, "How natural!" Evidently the phrase implies no more than that the same tendencies which control the audible expression of certain conditions in nature are present as controlling elements in the sounds of art; in other words, that the tones operate according to such a mode that their effects upon the mind are analogous to the effects of nature.

An illustration of this truth may be derived from the manner in which the papal choir in the Sistine Chapel at Rome were formerly accustomed to introduce the Christmas carols and also the Miserere of Holy Week. Each was preceded by a refrain chanted through long hours until one's whole ear—in fact, one's whole being—was thoroughly exhausted by the monotony of it. At last, just as one seemed wearied to the point of leaving the chapel, the choir would break into the glorious chords that had been so long expected. From the effect, everybody recognized this method of introducing the music to be thoroughly artistic. Few, perhaps, had the discrimination to perceive that it was so because thoroughly natural. In nature, it is often the contrast between the confusion occasioned by the struggle and bustle of ordinary life and the satisfaction suggested by finding harmony and sweetness in the world of sound, that causes the chief enjoyment to be derived from music. Even those who have no ear for the art recognize the peculiarly soothing influence of the notes of birds and insects at evening—above all, of the voices of friends in the family circle, supplanting the business-din of the day. Who has not sat for hours, charmed by the sweet accents of one whose thoughts and person, aside from this one characteristic, had no attraction for him? And who has not been irritated himself, and seen others almost kept in discord, by the unmusical, discordant tones of some one, in other respects by no means unamiable or unworthy? With good reason does Longfellow say:

> Then read from the treasured volume
>   The poem of thy choice,
> And lend to the rhyme of the poet
>   The beauty of thy voice.
>
> And the night shall be filled with **music**,
>   And the cares that infest the day
> Shall fold their tents like the Arabs
>   And as silently steal away.
>   *The Day is Done: Longfellow.*

It is mainly, too, by the contrast afforded between a realm known only to the soul and one apprehended only by the senses; by the transition from the subjectivity of dreaming to the objectivity of listening, that such transcendent sweetness is sometimes imparted to the serenade at midnight, and also to the songs of the birds at daybreak.

Even in the more imitative arts of painting and sculpture, this principle will be found to hold good. If we apply the term "natural" to the products of one of these arts, we do not mean to praise it solely for its photographic qualities. The portrait and the bust, which reproduce the forms of nature most perfectly, are not necessarily entitled to the highest rank; and when they are entitled to it, like the works of Titian or Velasquez, they rank thus not merely on account of the accuracy of their imitation, but also because, in addition to this, they have the quality to which Sir Joshua Reynolds referred when he snapped his fingers, saying of a work, "It wants *that*." No matter, at present, what this quality is. The subject has been discussed at length in Chapters IV. to VIII. of "Art in Theory." Just now, it is enough for us to recognize that the value of a portrait or a bust does not depend alone upon its accuracy as a copy. Nor, even were this the case, could "natural," as the term is used, be applied to it with any more propriety than to a picture of the Madonna, whom Raphael never saw; or to a landscape of scenes in Greece which Rottmann never beheld; or to a statue of the struggles of a Laocoön, which existed only in the brain of a Virgil.

We are told that when Pheidias was competing for a colossal statue of Minerva, the Athenians who saw his work before it had been raised upon its pedestal declared its features to be distorted and ugly, whereas those of the product of his rival, Alcamenes, appeared to be full of symmetry and beauty. But after both works had been lifted to their appropriate places, and were examined from the intended point of view, this decision of the people was reversed. Then the Minerva of Pheidias alone exhibited the effects that all desired. It did this because Pheidias had recognized that it was necessary to do more than copy accurately the appearances of nature; that it was necessary to consider certain conditions preceding these appearances. When we say that a work of painting or sculpture is "natural," we include the conception of its fulfilling the same conditions as are fulfilled in the works of nature; in other words, the conception that the effects produced upon the senses and mind are analogous to those produced by the imitated appearances.

That a similar principle applies in architecture hardly needs stating. The forms in a building, unless works of sculpture, are artistic less on account of an imitation of nature—even of the structures of the primitive natural man,—than because they are constructed so as to operate according to the methods or analogies of nature—so as to shed the snow, to keep out the water, to ward off the wind, as well as to operate æsthetically upon the eye, in the way of effects of light, shade, color, bulk, balance, proportion, and symmetry, according to the analogies of appearances which in nature are recognized to be beautiful.

This last word suggests a thought which ought, perhaps, to be added. So much has been said here about analogy as underlying the use of representative form in art, that some may fancy that too little emphasis has been given to the element of beauty, which is generally considered to be of paramount æsthetic importance. But no inference detrimental to the importance of beauty need follow legitimately upon the line of thought just unfolded. Our standards of beauty, concerning which the reader may consult Chapters X. to XIV. of "Art in Theory," are derived primarily from certain forms of nature, which, because attractive and charming in themselves, cause men to like to look at them and to think about them. Accordingly, if a man wish to produce forms of art which men will like to look at and to think about, it is merely a dictate of policy, and, if he be an artist, it is generally a dictate of preference, for him to select these forms for his models; and in the degree in which he reproduces them, or any effects analogous to theirs, his product will have beauty. What is to prevent his selecting them because, viewed in one aspect, they are beautiful; and yet also selecting them because, viewed in another aspect, they, as well as all other natural forms, are analogical? Certainly there is no conflict between the conception that beauty is of paramount æsthetic importance, and the conception that the effects obtained through the use of beauty should be analogical.

Nor need it be supposed that what has been said endorses the mistaken view that any subject which is "natural" is legitimate for artistic treatment. The truth seems to be that ugliness, simply because it is repulsive, is not legitimate in art except so far as, by way of contrast, as in the case of shadows which throw that which they surround into brighter relief, the ugliness enhances the beauty to which it is kept in manifest subordination. What the particular phases of this beauty shall be must be determined, of course, by the taste of the artist. But their effectiveness will depend upon his powers of observation and his study of the analogies of nature. Beauty is never so attractive as when it appears in the dignity attaching to the creative proportions there; truth is never so operative as when it manifests the sanction of the laws of the Creator that are there embodied.

Evidently the general conclusion to be drawn from the line of thought unfolded in this chapter corresponds to that which was drawn at the ends of Chapters IX. and XI. The fact that the conceptions of art, as distinguished from those of religion and of science, cannot communicate significance except through the use of analogically representative forms, involves a limitation, which, like all limitations is, in one sense, a source of weakness. But, in another sense, it is a source of strength, and a source of this in the exact degree in which its limitations are clearly recognized and no effort is made to transgress them. What but a consciousness of these limitations has caused all our great artists, when desiring to make their presentations of truth accord with the degree of knowledge or the phase of thought of their own period or country, to content themselves, in place of discussing and explaining conditions, with merely describing their appearances? But notice that it is precisely because they have contented themselves with this, that progress in knowledge and thought, which is constantly rendering obsolete the results presented in science, in philosophy, and even in systems of religion, does not interfere with the enduring influence of works of art. In these works, certain appearances of nature, material or human, have been selected for reproduction. Through unique combinations of these, the significance behind them has been brought out more uniquely, yet the inferences which are drawn from them, so far as art is strictly and solely representative, can be drawn with as little arbitrary bias as from nature itself. Art of this character can appeal to the intelligence and the sympathy of all audiences of all periods. Its significance can be perceived and felt wherever men have eyes or ears, for its products continue always to be what they were when first conceived,—faithful images of the real life by which humanity is constantly surrounded.

CHAPTER XIII.

ARTISTIC SIGNIFICANCE AS ATTRIBUTABLE TO BODILY ACTION, AND HAVING ITS SOURCE SUBJECTIVELY IN TEMPERAMENT, OBJECTIVELY IN TRAINING.

Connection between the Thought in this and in Preceding Chapters—Subjective and Objective Relationships of Expression—Instinctive, Reflective and Emotive Sources of Mental Effects—Conscious Reflective and Investigative Mental Action Slow—Subconscious Intuitive and Imaginative Action Rapid—The Two Actions do not Differ as Thought and Feeling, but as Unexcited and Voluntary from Excited and Involuntary Thought—The Artistic Involves Much Emotion—The Exciting Cause, being Permanent in Some, is Due to Temperament—Difference between Scientific and Artistic Temperament largely one of Degree—Some necessarily Excluded from the Sphere of Art, Some Included in it—Effects of Education and Practice—They Develop Mental through Physical Nature—Even Develop Possibilities of Genius—Illustrations—Connection between Results of Artistic Inspiration and of Skill—Inspiration, or Unhindered Expression of Subconscious Intellection, Helped by Cultivation of Expression and Memory—Even by Scientific Study—Broad Culture not Injurious to the Æsthetic Possibilities—Here as elsewhere Labor the Measure of Worth—Nothing Necessary in Religion or Science Fails to be an Aid to Art.

IN the preceding six chapters we have been considering how far significance may be attributed to subconscious and to conscious intellection, and the differences between the conceptions that may be classed as religious, scientific, and artistic. We have found the last to be imaginative, ideal, and analogically representative,—conceptions, therefore, that always tend to embodiment, in what in art is termed form (see page 1). This fact is acknowledged so universally that no one thinks of objecting to applying to the higher arts, as is so frequently done, the phrase " arts of expression," which term *expression*, as will be recognized, indicates always the general result when a man's invisible or inaudible thoughts or emotions are represented visibly or audibly in deeds or tones. As thus understood, expression involves effects produced both by the mind, which is the source of the conception embodied, and by the body—the voice, hands, whatever they may be, that constitute the agencies through which the conception is made to pass into form. It is evident, therefore, that we shall not have considered all the sources to which artistic significance is attributable until we shall have noticed certain effects which, though mental, are due nevertheless to the connection of the mind with a physical body, which body, too, must exert an influence upon physical surroundings,—until we shall have noticed, in other words, effects which are due to a *human mind* which must influence *humanity*. So far as the mind is human, the thoughts and emotions expressed in art must be conditioned by certain physical considerations which may be termed *subjective*, because affecting the mind when originating art's *subject-matter*. So far as this mind must influence humanity, these thoughts and emotions must be conditioned by certain physical considerations which may be termed *objective*, because due to what the body is and does when the mind in it becomes an *object* which the art-work, after being produced, must influence.

What has been said will sufficiently explain the subdivisions into *subjective* and *objective*, of each of the more general divisions of this part of our subject as treated in this and the two following chapters. These more general divisions themselves correspond to the three used

if we can, the conditions which, in the artist, occasion the emotion which in turn occasions a manifestation in expression of the results of subconscious mental action. What gives rise to this emotion? If it were experienced only now and then, it might be accounted for by circumstances to which one was accidentally subjected. The works of the lesser or occasional artists are produced amid excitement which at intervals avails in all to paralyze the logical powers and to stimulate the analogical. But when, as in the greater artists, such phases of emotion are the rule and not the exception; when they are constant, when the man by nature is subjected to them and habitually views things in an artistic light, and that, too, although not greatly influenced by external causes, then the experience must be attributed mainly to *temperament*.

This is a word which, as will be noticed, does not refer merely to physique, but to a certain kind of mental action which naturally accompanies a certain kind of physique. A blending of effects, some of which are physical, as in instinctive action, and some of which are mental, as in reflective action, was said on page 210 to underlie emotive action. But the proportions of this blending are what determine the different kinds of temperament. It must be temperament, therefore, that determines the characteristic emotive condition. It is important to notice, too, that this blending manifested in temperament has not at all the same result as the exclusively physical qualities tending, when not blended with intellection, to passion and sensuality. If this fact were recognized, not so many of our critics would express conceptions about artists which are on a par with those which presuppose all religionists to be too ascetic ranters or too æsthetic ritualists. Susceptibility to intellectual and spiritual excitation very often entirely supplants that which responds to the merely physical appeal; whereas susceptibility responding only or mainly to the latter frequently causes practical grossness and actual indulgence to deaden entirely the artistic possibilities. It is true, of course, that a man characterized by what may be termed an excess of force in one department is apt to be characterized by the same in another department; that one who has force of mind is apt to have force of body also. But this is no more true than that one who has force of mind is apt by means of it to subordinate the body, and thus to cause the two to work together to the advantage of both. To return, however, to the main thought in this paragraph, the story of Pygmalion who fell in love with his own statue of Galatea is merely an artistic embodiment of the conception of the naturally emotive susceptibility of the true artist. It is doubtful if one of these ever lived who lacked the tendency developed in the tale. It is doubtful if one without the capacity for falling thoroughly in love with his own product could ever be an artist. God made men, as we are told, in His own image, and the highest manliness results when His spirit becomes incarnated in them. So the artist forms art in his own image; his works reflect his thought or feeling; and the highest excellence follows only in the degree in which his soul has found complete embodiment in them.

If what has been said be true—and who can deny it?—we have reached at last an ultimate fact beyond which analysis cannot go. It is the ground on which was based that old expression: "The poet is born and not made." Lest, however, we exaggerate the differences between men as thus suggested, let us try to ascertain precisely what that temperament is which may be rightly termed artistic.

From what has been said already, we must infer that, primarily, it is one that is quick in apprehending effects of nature in both their isolations and relations, as also in making comparisons between these effects, and in drawing surmisals from them. All children, because their brains are active, are artistic in their tendencies. The very essence of artistic imitation is mimicry; and what child is entirely destitute of this? Very nearly all the young pass through a dramatic age, in which they flower into poetry; and whether the blossoms soon fade or bloom perennially depends mainly upon the permanence within them of the characteristics thus manifested. When men arrive at maturity, the artistic mind, as distinguished from the scientific, continues to form theories before it reasons them out, and to imagine truth before it investigates. If one naturally of an artistic temperament ever does reach results that are scientific, this term "scientific" cannot be applied to the movements of his mind preparatory to these. Instead of advancing step by step toward his end, he first jumps to his conclusions, and then turns backward to discover the intervening steps. Very difficult, too, as a rule, is his task in bringing these to the light. Through the mist-hung marshes which the wings of his imagination have borne him across, he must flounder on foot, picking his pathway painfully until he reach his starting-point. Yet if he do not do this, his own explanations of what he has accomplished will be more apt to entitle him to rank as a visionary among idealists than as a guide among practical thinkers. Notice, nevertheless, that the method of mental action just described is that which is most allied to the method which the world usually attributes to genius. A genius perceives a specific effect in nature, and surmises thence a truth or principle which is generic (see Chapter III). Newton is said to have surmised the law of gravitation from the sight of a single apple falling from a tree, and almost every one who has invented any kind of a machine has conceived of it as a whole before he has tried to construct its separate parts. As everywhere else, therefore, the difference indicated here between the artistic and the scientific mind is one of degree and not of kind. The artist works almost exclusively according to the method just indicated, so the world supposes that he must be a genius necessarily. The scientific man has very much to do besides surmising and inventing; so the world confines the title genius to the few scientific minds pre-eminent in doing these latter.

However, though the difference between the actions of the artistic and of the scientific minds is one of degree, in the extreme developments of the two it virtually becomes one of kind. All men have emotion. All may be strongly moved, and, in such circumstances, the minds of all may be subject to that subconscious action which is one source of imagination. But when we try to answer the question,—To what extent may one as compared with another be subject to this? we find the difference between men almost world-wide. We must conclude, therefore, that large numbers are by nature excluded from the sphere of action of the artist. They are too cautious, too much under the control of consciousness, or, as we say, self-consciousness, to give themselves up to the abandon of subconscious mental activity. It is not only great orators who lose themselves in their subjects before they become eloquent. Sculptors, painters, and musicians have a similar experience. "If you think how you are to write," said Mozart, " you will never write anything worth hearing. I write because I cannot help it." Viewed in this light, we may trace to the power that Shakespeare and Goethe had of objectifying and so of forgetting themselves, not only the effects but the causes also of their greatness. It might be almost said that faith in the results of that which is beyond the sphere of consciousness enables one to reach the æsthetic paradise no less than the heavenly. Especially in these intensely practical times of factories and furnaces, what but the ability to preserve one's relationship with something hidden, with some ideal that cannot be smelt or touched, with something real though in realms of mystery,—what but this can keep the soul in a region where results of art are possible? And if some by nature be excluded from the sphere of action of the artist, it must be equally true that some by nature are included in it. And, now and then, their products may evince this fact. From the realm of their nativity they can be banished wholly neither by the deadening effects of practical life, nor by the lack of the quickening influences of æsthetic education.

At the same time it is easy for us to exaggerate unduly these natural differences between men. It is easy for us to suppose that we have discovered them when we have discovered nothing. Very often, that for which we are in search, though latently present, has merely not been brought to the light. It is easy for us, therefore, to ignore the methods through which whatever artistic possibilities one may possess may be cultivated. This thought suggests the other subject to be treated in this chapter, namely, artistic significance as traceable, objectively, to *training*. In order to unfold this subject logically, it will be best to start with a conception of the influence upon mental action of education in general. From this conception the transition will be easy to that of the particular effect upon education produced by training. The word education is composed of the two Latin words, *e*, meaning *from* or *out of*, and *ducere*, meaning *to lead*. But why should to educate mean to *lead from* or *out of?* Is it possible to ask this question without having suggested what was said on page 66? It was there noticed that all that we consciously experience through the agency either of the physical senses or of psychological intellection passes into the mind's regions of subconsciousness. Here, though much appears to be lost, probably nothing actually is lost; it always remains. This seems to be abundantly proved by the results of abnormal excitation, as in fright, fever, hypnotism, and in well authenticated cases of what are termed trance-conditions. It seems to be proved, too, that the recollective, illustrative, and argumentative powers of the subconscious mind, as related to any given premise, which premise, as stated on page 106, may or may not be trustworthy, works with flawless precision. If this be so, the problem of education has to do not with the methods of obtaining information from without, so much as of bringing back to consciousness information already stored within, so as to be able to use it for oneself and for others. The mind that is best able to bring this back to consciousness at the right times and places, is the best educated.

Now on what does the ability of the mind to do this depend? There is reason to suppose that it depends largely upon the quality and comparative strength of the physical brain through which one does his work. It is said that the brains of Daniel Webster and of Amos Lawrence, a successful merchant of Boston, both of whom died about the same time, were compared, and were found to be of very nearly the same size and weight, but the convolutions in the brain of **Webster** were found to be more numerous. That is to say, his brain was of finer physical fibre. Some brains are apparently of such coarse fibre that almost everything that passes toward the depth of subconsciousness goes through them as through a sieve. They hold and keep conscious control of very little. That the ability of the mind depends upon the physical strength of the brain, may be shown in another way. Give a small child a message to deliver, and he will bring it up to consciousness with difficulty, hesitating between almost every word. " My mother—wishes—wishes—me to—to—my mother wishes me to—present—to present—her compliments—her compliments to you—and to say," etc. But the same child after a year or two, when older and stronger physically, will experience little of this difficulty, and, after attaining manhood, none whatever, even though the communication to be recalled be a thousand times more complex. Yet wait again a few years, and the same man, when approaching the period of second childhood, merely because of the weakening of the physical powers, will again experience difficulty, even when the message is extremely simple. To a few it may seem humiliating to be obliged to acknowledge that the intellectual superiority in which some of us pride ourselves may be determined at all by conditions having to do merely with physique; but as long as we remain men, such must be the case.

It is not, however, merely the passage of time and its influence upon growth that in youth can strengthen and in old age can weaken our physical powers. The same effects may be produced by *training*, especially by that form of it which we give to ourselves through *practice*. We know this to be true as applied to our hands and voices. Why should it not be true as applied to our brains? But notice that if it be true as applied to these, and, if all that was said in the last paragraph be also true, then *training* can do much more for artistic development than some suppose. It can produce facility not only in outward expression, giving the singer, orator, or actor a flexible voice or a graceful body, or the musician, painter, or sculptor dexterity in the use of fingers, brush, or chisel. It can produce facility in the methods of inward preparation for expression, enabling the mind to draw at will from the subconscious resources that which is the subject-matter of artistic invention and inspiration.

It is true, of course, that no amount of practice can enable some to become artists, and that, in exceptional cases or upon extraordinary occasions, some may produce genuine works of art who have practised little; but, as a rule, practice is indispensable if one wish to attain the characteristics supposed to be possessed habitually by the great artists. We find this fact illustrated almost universally. Of course, there are a few exceptional cases like that of Mozart, mentioned on page 73. He was giving concerts when he was three years old, and had composed an overture for an entire orchestra when he was eight. For him, notwithstanding the instruction that he received when he was older, practice does not seem to have been absolutely indispensable. And it was not so, say some, because he was a genius. But let us think a moment. Might he not have been a genius, and also have been obliged to cultivate his powers? Was not Beethoven a genius? Yet when he was three years old he knew nothing, so far as we are aware, of music; and very little when he was eight. But after he had practised many hours a day for ten or fifteen years, he could do as well as Mozart could in early manhood ; and, not only so, but a few years later he could do better than Mozart ever could. Not a few to-day consider Beethoven the greater genius of the two. Yet the genius of the one owed comparatively little, as some would say almost nothing, to practice, while that of the other, but for it, might never have been revealed at all.

Exactly what was it that practice had thus done for Beethoven? Had it imparted to him merely information concerning the methods of fingering the keys of instruments so as to prevent interference and secure facility, or concerning the methods of printing music, and of arranging notes, one after another or together, so as to produce effects of melody or harmony? More than this, certainly. He could have learned all these things without practice, and after having learned them, if he had done no more, they never could have made him an artist. What practice had done was this: it had given his fingers muscular flexibility, enabling them to sound upon an instrument whatever notes a composition demanded. But besides this, practice had given the brain controlling his fingers what also we might term flexibility; and it had given the mind, too, lodged in his brain, a mental habit of using the right fingers in the right places, and all the fingers in the right orders of succession. Beyond this, it had enabled his mind to comprehend in a single glance large groups of notes on a printed staff and, no matter how numerous and complex, to send his knowledge of them through the nerves, and transfer them to sound with precision and yet with the rapidity of lightning. Moreover, all this, which, when he began, had involved the slow and painful process of consciously thinking of each note on a printed staff, and of each corresponding key on an instrument, practice had enabled him to do at last unconsciously at the same time that all his conscious powers were employed in giving expression to the general effect.

Now what is true of music is true of every art. There was Demosthenes. We all know that, when he first ventured before an audience, his stammering articulation, interrupted respiration, ungraceful gestures, and ill-arranged periods brought upon him general ridicule. What was it necessary for him to do in order to speak artistically? To think, every time that he came before the public, of his articulation, respiration, gestures, and periods? Had he pursued this course, he never could have waxed eloquent, because he never could have entered into his theme with unconscious abandon. What he did, was to withdraw altogether from the public until, by a course of persistent practice, he had cultivated habits of clear articulation, regular respiration, graceful gesturing, and rhetorical phraseology. Only after he had acquired these traits could he exhibit them as the perfect results of art, yet as the instinctive and unconscious expression of the free play of his thought. Nor must it be supposed that the results in his case, or in that of any other man practising similarly, were confined, or could be confined, to such as can be manifested merely in external style or form. Practice reaches the whole range of artistic possibilities. A boy, in learning to read or to compose in writing, is conscious of every letter, syllable, epithet, phrase, or metaphor, but, after sufficient practice, he can not only peruse but produce all these in line after line and page after page, with absolute unconsciousness of details, or even of effort. Many find the strongest indication of what they term the inspired genius of Henry Ward Beecher in his marvellous illustrative ability, in his imaginative facility in arguing from analogy. He himself, in his "Yale Lectures," says that not only did he practise elocution "incessantly for three years," but that, while in later life it was as easy for him to illustrate as to breathe, he did not have this power to any such extent in his early manhood, but cultivated it.

The truth is that everybody has within himself these subconscious powers of mind, which operate of themselves, like an automatic machine, as we may say, producing approximately perfect results of recollection, illustration, and—as developed from the premise submitted—of logic. The problem of education is how to cultivate the conscious powers so that they shall become pliant to the touch of subconscious influence; and thus be enabled to manifest its effects. The problem of expressional art is how to cultivate the conscious agencies of expression so that they shall respond without interference to the promptings of the subconscious agencies. The musician has always practically solved this problem when he is pouring his whole soul into his music, unconscious of anything but the emotional effect that he desires to produce upon the souls of his hearers. The sculptor and the painter have always solved it when they are projecting into line or color, unconscious of being hampered by any thought of technique, that image which keen observation of the outer world has impressed upon their conceptions. The poet has always solved it when he has lost himself in his theme, unconscious of anything except that to which Milton refers in "Paradise Lost," ix., when he says that it

> —dictates to me slumbering, or inspires
> Easy my unpremeditated verse.

But, now, this method, of which we remain unconscious, through which thoughts and emotions pass from the subconscious sphere of mind, through the conscious, and out of it again into the details of form, is the result of what most men mean when they use the term artistic inspiration. Yet notice that it is often, too, even in cases of the most indisputable genius, a result, in part at least, of skill acquired by *practice*.

This is a fact which justifies many opinions which at first thought seem inconsistent, if not illogical; as for instance, those of the "spiritualists" and Quakers to the effect that their "inspirational" speakers preach better after they have become accustomed to preaching. To admit the truth of this opinion is not to admit that all could become accustomed to it. By temperament many are constitutionally unqualified to give any utterance to instinctive promptings, to throw themselves with abandon into anything; but, granted this power, it is often the accuracy, breadth, and largeness of the cultivation received that determine the truth, comprehensiveness, and greatness of the result. A wholly uncultivated man may produce a perfect stanza or sketch; but usually not a long poem or a painting.

The truth seems to be that, although there is the wide separation between the conscious and the subconscious powers that has been indicated in this volume, the mind as a whole is one, and almost any method of cultivating one part of it involves cultivating other parts. What forms of mental action can seem more widely separated than those of memory and of imagination? Who does not recognize the point in Sheridan's remark about an opponent

—Fox, was it not?—that he relied upon his memory for his wit, and upon his imagination for his facts? And yet there is some truth in what E. S. Dallas says in "The Gay Science," that "it is not so much to a trained invention as to a trained memory that the poet who seeks for variety must chiefly trust; and it will be found that all great poets, all great artists, all great inventors, are men of great memory—their unconscious memory being even greater than that of which they are conscious. These unconscious memories, stirring we know not what within us, fill some men with a sense of the mystery of life, and shed on all things visible the hues of poetry,—that 'light' which, according to Wordsworth, 'never was on sea or land.' Other men they enrich with visions of what they fancy they have never seen. In a moment, at a single jet, the picture is in the mind's eye, complete to a pin's head, with all the perfectness of imaginative work. One blow, one flash, is all we are conscious of; no fumbling, no patching up, no retouching; we are unconscious of the automatic energy within us until its work is achieved, and the effect is not to be resisted. We have the finished result; of the process we know nothing. We enjoy the one and we stand in awe of the other. We endow these extraordinary memories with divine honors. 'Ye are as gods,' we say to the poets. And thus far, at least, we can see a deeper wisdom in the doctrine of the Greeks that the Muses were all daughters of Mnemosyne."

What is thus suggested by Mr. Dallas with reference to the influence of the cultivation of memory upon imaginative results, or—what is the same thing—upon the analogical significance which an artist is enabled to embody or express in his works, might be affirmed in principle of the cultivation of almost any other of the mental powers. Take, for instance, the discipline derived from the practice of the scientific method of investigation. Not only need this involve no injury to the powers of imagination—it may often be of great help to them. So effective is it in enabling a man to bring the results of subconscious intellection into consciousness as in some instances to create almost a new sense. Sailors do not always need to study their charts in order to avoid the shoals about them; nor foresters the direction of the sun or compass in order to find their pathways home. With more accuracy of meaning than some of us think possible, deaf men sometimes talk of hearing, and blind men of seeing. Some years since, Dr. Chadbourne, afterwards president of Williams College, with some others, was lost in a fog at sundown on a spur of Greylock Mountain in Massachusetts. In that condition, by a mere accident, he brushed his hand against what seemed to the others but an ordinary bush, yet it was really the only specimen of the kind in the neighborhood; and instantly he told the party where they were. In all such cases, sight, hearing, and touch act intuitively as a result, not of nature, but of practice, and of practice, too, in scientific pursuits. In fulfilment of the same principle, a general on a battlefield is enabled to detect at a glance the key of a position. He does so in part, of course, on account of that natural aptitude of mind which we attribute to genius,—by an exercise of ability precisely akin to that of the artist when he selects the viewpoint of a picture, or of a poet when he chooses the formative idea of a lyric. Yet, for all this, neither general, nor artist, nor poet can, as a rule, reach the most desirable conclusions, formed though they may be instinctively, save as a result of experience derived from previous practice.

Accordingly we see how, even when there is no intention of developing the kind of mental action dependent upon the subconscious powers, the development of this is associated necessarily with that dependent upon the conscious powers. There is less danger, therefore, than is sometimes supposed, that scientific pursuits will diminish the facility of one's imagination. There is always a possibility, of course, that a single mode of thinking, if pursued exclusively, will predominate in the mind; but if two modes be pursued together, and especially if one be pursued for the direct purpose of giving efficiency to the other, this aim will cause both to be kept in use, and counterbalance the possibility. As a fact, we find few instances in history in which a liberal education, properly subordinated, has proved an injury to the æsthetic nature. Milton wrote little poetry until he had finished his political work. Goethe and Schiller both profited much from the discriminating scientific criticism to which, as appears in their correspondence, they were accustomed to submit their productions; at all events, they achieved their greatest successes subsequent to it. And with criticism playing all about his horizon, like lightnings from every quarter of the heavens, who shall calculate how much of the splendor of Shakespeare is attributable to this by-play among the circle of dramatists by whom he was surrounded? With new forms rising still like other Venuses above the miasmas of the old Campagna, who shall estimate how much the excellence of the Italian artists has been owing to the opportunities afforded in historic Rome for critical study?

Enough, at all events, we know, to conclude that the results of art have not disproved that universal principle according to which the degree of labor, mediate or immediate, generally measures the degree of worth. A bountiful exuberance of imagination usually accompanies abounding information. The analogies of art are usually most natural to the mood that meditates most upon nature. Truth, comprehensiveness, and greatness, manifested in artistic products, are usually crystallizations of the accuracy, breadth, and largeness of the formative thought occasioning them.

It would be difficult, in fact, to discover a single element necessary to success in religious or scientific endeavor which, if held in due subordination, is really not available in the realm of art. Religion is an aid to it because, to interpret the truth of nature in all its depth and breadth of pureness and of charity, one must have a spirit capable of being often drawn into sympathy with that which is purest and best in nature. Such a spirit has been possessed by all the greatest artists: by men like Raphael, Angelo, Beethoven, Mendelssohn, Shakespeare, Dickens, Dante, Schiller, Goethe. Do not deem the latter an exception. As Jean Paul Richter says of him, "He is a healthy nature. The moral compass is firm in him. The needle may waver, but it returns to its place again." And to a thinking man it must appear in the highest sense necessary that with any pre-eminent artist the first condition of success should be the fact that his own spirit, especially in those involuntary moods which we have found to be the fountains of artistic inspiration, should be in sympathy with the Creative life,—with the Spirit behind the material universe. And science, too, is an aid to art; and in the same category with science we must place all those phases of life which are appropriate subjects of investigation, everything that can enlighten man with reference to the laws of nature or of mind, or to the histories of either, so that one's surmisals of the truth suggested shall be accurate and trustworthy. Indeed, the resources that may be utilized in art are practically infinite. No man can observe so much as to see any facts outside the limits of its sphere. No man can reflect so much as to arrive at any thoughts beyond its possibilities of suggestion. No man can be so much as not to have mind and spirit lifted to greater heights through its inspiration.

CHAPTER XIV.

ARTISTIC SIGNIFICANCE AS ATTRIBUTABLE TO BODILY ACTION, AND CHARACTERIZED SUBJECTIVELY BY A PERSONAL EFFECT, OBJECTIVELY BY A SYMPATHETIC.

Connection between the Thought in this and the Preceding Chapter—The Surmisals of Art those of One Individual, the Artist—Should Have a Personal Effect—A Prose Description that Lacks this: Scott—A Poetic: Crabbe—A Poetic that Exhibits it: Byron—A Prose: Dickens—The Latter Descriptions Show the Effects of an Intervening Human Mind—As Personality is most Apparent in Unconscious Action, to Represent these Effects does not Interfere with consciously Representing Nature—The Personality of Artistic Effects is Recognized in the Universal Proneness to Attribute to Artistic Genius Originality and Eccentricity—Personality of Effect always Appeals to Others through Awakening Sympathy for or against—So the Arts are the Humanities—Illustrations of Artistic Appeal to the Sympathies—Explanation of the Passages—The Principle Involved—Why Artists Seem often Interested in Technique rather than in Significance—Individuality of Effect not Inconsistent with an Appeal to Universal Interest—Yet the Artist must Have a Peculiar Temperament to Fulfil both Requirements—Genius Has a Temperament Congenial to Nature and Man—German Words Corresponding to Genius, Genial, and Geniality—Brilliancy—Art Humanizes Nature according to the Sentiments of One, yet Accords with the Sentiments of All.

AS a result of the second of the questions discussed in Chapters VII. to XII., the conclusion was reached that, so far as attributable to mental action, the conceptions of art, as distinguished from those of religion and of science, are characterized by *ideality*. Corresponding to this result both in order and in substance of thought, let us try to determine now by what a conception of art, or, to use a more general term, the significance of art, so far as it may be attributable to bodily action, is characterized. The answer will be found to be this: *subjectively*, by an individual, or *personal* effect, what might be almost termed an idiosyncratic bias; and *objectively*, closely related to the former and because of it, by a *sympathetic* effect which, in the circumstances, is necessary in order to cause the artist's conception to become the possession of others.

It was shown in the preceding chapter that the artist is one who, owing to temperament or training, is able, to an exceptional extent, to manifest in speech or action the results of his subconscious intellection. What does he obtain through this form of intellection? Surmisals, which, sometimes, as was shown in Chapter II., correspond to the absolute truth. Nevertheless, even if they do, he obtains this truth in those forms only in which his own temperament, as influenced by his training, is able to interpret and, according to the method indicated on page 165, to frame into an ideal the scenes or sounds that suggest the truth. And what does he communicate? Nothing again but his own surmisals, interpretations, or ideals. Moreover, if he be a genuine artist, producing nothing but effects which represent those of nature, he communicates his surmisals in such forms only as cause others, as a result of their own imaginings, to make similar surmisals. The artist therefore interprets nature according to his own temperament, and causes others to interpret it as he does. This evidently secures a very different result than follows in the case of either religion or science. Their truth, no matter what may be the temperament or training of the original proclaimer or discoverer, becomes the property of

CHAPTER XV.

ARTISTIC SIGNIFICANCE AS ATTRIBUTABLE TO BODILY ACTION, AND TENDING SUBJECTIVELY TO THE POSSESSION OF CULTURE, OBJECTIVELY TO THE EXPRESSION OF SENTIMENT.

Connection between Thought in this and in the Preceding Chapter—Culture: its Relation to Training—Its Development through Art-Study—Sentiment as Defined by Kames and Schiller—Is Characteristic of Artistic Expression—The Tendency of the Distinctively Artistic to Express and Awaken Sentiment is a Test by which to Distinguish it from the Religious Influencing Conduct and the Scientific Imparting Information—Inartistic Examples from Pollok and Wordsworth—But it must not be Supposed that Sentiment itself cannot be Religious or Scientific—Examples from Tennyson and Shakespeare — Milton's Expressions of Religious Faith in Form of Sentiment—Of Information to Awaken Sentiment—Criticism of these Passages—Mistake of Supposing that not to Use the Religious and Scientific except for Sentiment Means the same as not to Use them at all—Great Artists have Manifested a Desire to Promote Religion, Morality, and Learning—Quotations from Shakespeare Evincing this—Shakespeare's, Dante's, Milton's, and Wordsworth's Affirmation of this Desire—The Great Poets Men of Education—Same Facts Exemplified in the Products of the Great Musicians, Painters, and Sculptors—No Inconsistency between the View Presented in this Chapter and that which Deems Pleasure the Aim of Art—Sentiment Meets all Demands of this Theory and Fulfils them better.

CORRESPONDING in order and substance of thought to the third of the questions discussed when treating in Chapters VII. to XII. of conceptions in religion, science, and art, let us notice now the general result of significance so far as attributable, as it is in all the arts, to bodily action. We shall find this result to be, so far as it is *subjective*, the possession, within the mind, of what is termed *culture*, and, so far as it is objective, the expression of what is termed *sentiment*.

That the subjective result is culture, follows from the difference indicated on page 224 between that which the mind is supposed to receive through information and through training. Is it not almost entirely to the effects of the latter that we apply the term culture? When we say that a man has cultivated himself, whether referring to his voice or hands, as in elocution; to his ears or fingers, as in music; or to his logical or imaginative powers, as in oratory, we mean more than that he has merely received information. If he had received this only, we should not use the word that we do. We mean that he has acquired what he possesses through *practice*. And as practice, of the kind which can be consciously undertaken through the agency of the bodily voice, hands, or brain (see pages 220 to 232), is indispensable to the obtaining of efficiency in artistic invention or expression, the conclusion is inevitable that what we have termed the subjective result of this practice should be culture.

Or consider the subject in another light. What, according to the conceptions of men in general, is a man of culture? Does not the following describe him? He is one who has been educated in the sense of having been trained; who has not only a brain but a working brain; who is prepared therefore to deal not only with information but with suggestion; a man whose aims in study—to express his condition in terms to accord with the general thought presented in this volume—have regarded duly both the conscious and the subconscious powers of mind; a man whose memory is able to recall from his own experience and that of others, from history current and past, from books and life, the scores and hundreds of associated facts and fancies teeming about, and through, and beyond the immediate object of consideration; a man whose sphere of thought belongs, therefore, not to the small but to the great, not to the single but to the universal; a man whose whole nature is open to the currents of tendency moving in upon him from all directions, and is prepared both to apprehend and to comprehend, to appreciate and to appropriate whatever truth may loom from any quarter. Now to attain these results, one influence in this world seems to be particularly effective. This is the influence of art. A scientific specialist with any amount of learning, if it be merely learning, may not give any suggestion of what is meant by culture. A man may study science all his life, and never do it—which fact is the one irrefutable argument against an entirely scientific course in our universities. But it is impossible for one to be a student of art—a dabbler is not meant now, but a student—and not begin to have some culture, and this for the simple reason that he is obliged—a statement which cannot be made so absolutely with reference to any other department of study—to experience some of the results of *practice*. It will be found, too, that the degree of his culture will often depend upon the degree of the thoroughness with which he has studied some art in some of its phases. Nor is it too much to say that a broad and deep view of life can never be obtained except as a result of such a conception of all its relations as are apprehensible through both conscious and subconscious intellection in the forms in which they invariably appeal, whether he know it or not, to the great artist. Of course, in saying this, one must not be understood as denying that high culture may also include, even necessitate, much that is not in itself distinctively artistic. Nor must one be understood as holding that the effect of culture is limited to that which is direct and specific. When one develops by practice his illustrative, logical, or any other powers, he does much more for himself often than he supposes. It is probably not possible to cultivate the mind in one direction without cultivating it, more or less, in all directions. Besides this, the term culture is itself very broad in meaning. It refers just as frequently to the general condition of the intellectual atmosphere as affected by the light and heat at the place where the fire has been kindled in the mind, as it does to that which furnishes the material for its kindling.

Now let us turn to the objective result of artistic significance so far as influenced by bodily action. This has been said to be an expression of *sentiment*—a result, like that noticed in the case of culture, following upon what has already been unfolded. In Chapter XIII. it was shown that it is because of emotions succeeding one another too rapidly to permit one's preceptions or expressions to flow wholly in the channels of conscious thought that the artist's mind works imaginatively with reference to the forms of nature, and causes the minds of others to work similarly with reference to the forms of art which are made similar to those of nature. In other words, the imaginative ideality embodied in art is due to thought as prompted by emotion. But this is exactly what Lord Kames in his "Elements of Criticism" says that sentiment is, namely, "thought prompted by passion or by feeling." Schiller, too, in one of his letters to Goethe, expresses the same conception. "It is a want of the poetic nature, not to say of the human mind generally," he says, "to bear around it as little as possible that is void, to appropriate to itself, through feeling, as much as is going on, to look for the bottom of all appearances, and to require everywhere a whole of humanity. Is the object as individual empty and in a poetic view without import? Then the combining faculty will make a trial with it, and take hold of it by its symbolical aids, and thus out of it make a language for humanity. Always, however, is the sentimental—in a good sense—an effect of the poetic endeavor."

A slight attempt to recall the foremost trait of expression distinguishing any man who has given himself to the study and production of art will verify by facts this conclusion of Schiller. Is it not true that artists and poets, and often even mere admirers of music, painting, sculpture, or poetry, are persons given above all things to sentiment? Can we not perceive this sometimes in their very gaits and gestures, in the involuntary waverings of their lips, in the unconscious bewilderment of their eyes? Does not the very sight of them often make us feel that they are men who have been exhilarated, if not intoxicated, by drinking in thoughts that brim above the commonplace; that they are men whose moods are loyal to an all-pervading sovereignty of soul? Can we not often detect, behind all that they do or say, the spiritual force of unseen ideality, the unselfishness of non-material purpose, the virtue of involuntary industry, the enthusiasm that revels amid dim twilights of inquiry and starry midnights of aspiration? How different is their mien from that of those who manifest none of their vaguer, softer qualities, but pride themselves upon the fact that they are sharp! And, verily, too often they are sharp, their very visages whittled to a point like snow-plows on a wintry track that always draw attention downward and cleave through paths that chill. The brightness of their eyes is that of diamonds that are only used to cut, the summons of their voices that of trumpets that are ever blowing of their own sufficiency. No radiance of a spiritual light that streams from inward visions, is haloed from the one. No call toward a sphere too subtle to be heralded by aught except " the still small voice," is echoed from the other. What is lacking in the methods of mental action of men like these, as everyone who knows the highest possibilities of art can testify, is the kind of culture secured by practice, which leads to the conception within and the expression without of sentiment—not sentimentality, which is its caricature, and an effect not based upon facts; but vigorous manly sentiment, something rooted deep in common sense but yet not common; rather its uncommon development when the material branch and leaf, grown upward, burst into that which sheds the fragrance of the spirit's flower.

The fact that artistic significance, for the reasons that have been given, tends to sentiment, both in the artist himself and in the one to whom his product sympathetically appeals, affords a very efficient test by which to distinguish the use of significance in art from its use in religion, which in Chapter XI. we found to be aimed toward influencing conduct; and also from its use in science, which in Chapter XII. we found to be aimed toward imparting information. The following, for instance, is intended chiefly to influence conduct. For this reason, though arranged in the form of poetry, it cannot be said to be poetic:

On what pretense soe'er
Of right inherited, or else acquired;

> Of loss or profit, or what plea you name,
> To buy and sell, to barter, whip, and hold
> In chains a being of celestial make—
> Of kindred form, of kindred faculties;
> Of kindred feelings, passions, thoughts, desires,
> Born free and heir of an immortal hope:—
> Thought villainous, absurd, detestable!
> Unworthy to be harbored in a fiend!
> And only overreached in wickedness
> By that, birth too of earthly liberty,
> Which aimed to make a reasonable man
> By legislation think, and by the sword
> Believe.
>
> *The Course of Time, iv. : Pollok.*

This again is not poetic, because it is intended mainly to impart information:

> The discipline of slavery is unknown
> Among us,—hence the more do we require
> The discipline of virtue; order else
> Cannot subsist, nor confidence, nor peace.
> Thus duties rising out of good possessed,
> And prudent caution needful to avert
> Impending evil, equally require
> That the whole people should be taught and trained.
>
> *The Excursion, ix. : Wordsworth.*

Passages like these show that much that is called art is not art. But one must be careful not to draw the inference that, therefore, the mere presence in a composition of thoughts that in their nature are religious or scientific is sufficient to render it inartistic. The principle that we are unfolding applies to the subject-matter of an expression so far only as concerns the use to which it is put. A hortatory use, showing a predominant desire to influence conduct, or a didactic use, showing a predominant desire to impart information,—this is that which violates the principle. But an imaginative use, showing only a desire to give form to sentiment, may make almost any kind of subject-matter artistic. There is nothing inartistic, for instance, in the passage in which Tennyson causes the dying Sir Bedevere to say:

> If thou shouldst never see my face again,
> Pray for my soul. More things are wrought by prayer
> Than this world dreams of. Wherefore let thy voice
> Rise like a fountain for me, night and day.
> For what are men better than sheep or goats
> That nourish a blind life within the brain,
> If, knowing God, they lift not hands of prayer
> Both for themselves and those who call them friend?
> For so the whole round world is every way
> Bound by gold chains about the feet of God.
> *Morte d'Arthur : Tennyson.*

All this is natural for a pious man when dying. Therefore, for a poet to represent him as saying it, is artistic. The same may be affirmed of Shakespeare's representing the English King as urging his followers:

> To chase these pagans in those holy fields,
> Over whose acres walk'd those blessed feet
> Which, fourteen hundred years ago, were nailed
> For our advantage on the bitter cross.
> *1 Henry IV., i., 1 : Shakespeare.*

In Milton there are many passages enunciating dogma and imparting information. But as bearing upon his rank as a poet, it is important to notice the *forms* in which he usually endeavors to present these. Observe, in the following, how the words in the second line, "proceed, and up to him return," suggest an imaginative play of thought as prompted by emotion. Observe also, following this, the same effect in the explanations surmised of hidden mysteries through representing them in the imagined forms of a world that is not hidden. And observe, finally, the image in the last lines. It is evident that the passage, as a whole, though, in a sense, it may influence conduct and impart information, does not convey an impression of being primarily intended for either of these ends, but to awaken thought and feeling which, though religious, partake of the nature of sentiment.

> O Adam, one Almighty is, from whom
> All things proceed, and up to him return,
> If not depraved from good, created all
> Such to perfection, one first matter all,
> Indu'd with various forms, various degrees
> Of substance, and, in things that live, of life :
> But more refined, more spirituous and pure,
> As nearer to him placed, or, nearer tending,
> Each in their several active spheres assigned,
> Till body up to spirit works in bounds
> Proportioned to each kind. So from the root
> Springs lighter the green stalk, from whence the leaves
> More aery, last the bright consummate flower
> Spirits odorous breathes.
>
> *Paradise Lost, v. : Milton.*

This next quotation reads like a scientific enumeration designed to impart information; yet is this its design? Is it not rather to convey an impression of the extent of the territory over which the Christ was offered sovereignty; and therefore to cause what might be termed a sentimental appreciation of the greatness of his temptation, and of his resistance to it?

> To this high mountain top, the tempter brought
> Our Saviour and new train of words began.
> . . . Here thou beholdest
> Assyria and her empire's ancient bounds,
> Araxes and the Caspian lake, thence on
> As far as Indus east, Euphrates west,

> And oft beyond ; to south the Persian bay,
> And inaccessible the Arabian drought :
> Here Niniva of length within her wall,
> Several days' journey, built by Ninus old,
> Of that first golden monarchy the seat,
> And seat of Salmanassar, whose success
> Israel in long captivity still mourns ;
> There Babylon, the wonder of all tongues,
> As ancient, but rebuilt by him who twice
> Judah and all thy father David's house
> Led captive, and Jerusalem laid waste,
> Till Cyrus set them free ; Persepolis,
> His city, there thou seest, and Bactra there ;
> Ecbatana her structure vast there shows,
> And Hecatomylos, her hundred gates ;
> There Susa by Choaspe's amber stream,
> The drink of none but kings ; of later fame
> Built by Emathian, or by Parthian hands,
> The great Seleucia, Nisibis, and there
> Artaxata, Terodon, Ctesiphon,
> Turning with easy eye thou may'st behold.
>
> *Paradise Regained, iii. : Milton.*

All this and more that follows certainly detracts from the effect of movement in the poetry, the necessity for which will be indicated in Chapter XXV. But the passage cannot be condemned on the ground merely of imparting information. This is evidently not its principal motive. At the same time, a short, sharp enumeration as in the following—an enumeration not materially impeding the movement—would have been more artistically effective :

> Now were all transformed
> Alike to serpents, all as accessories
> To his bold riot : dreadful was the din
> Of hissing through the hall, thick swarming now
> With complicated monsters, head and tail,
> Scorpion, and asp, and amphisbæna dire,

> Cerastes horn'd, hydrus, and ellops drear,
> And dipsas ; not so thick swarmed once the soil
> Bedropped with blood of Gorgon, or the isle
> Ophiusa.
>
> *Paradise Lost, x. : Milton.*

Very often passages like this merely add to the impressiveness of the picture conjured before the imagination, and are distinctly within the limits of an appeal to sentiment. For this reason, though having much to do both with influencing conduct and imparting information, they are legitimate to art, because subordinated to its aims. This is a fact important to recognize. Indeed, the failure to recognize it is one of the artistic mistakes of our own age ; and is doing more than any other, perhaps, to prevent art from attaining the rank due to it, as a great instrumentality for the betterment of humanity. In the criticisms in our papers—often, owing to an affectation of æsthetic knowledge, in our religious papers,—one finds an almost universal tendency to discount, and for this reason solely, poetry, painting, and statuary that give any marked evidence of being the product of an earnest, ethical, or religious nature. One reason—though, of course, not by any means the sole reason—why certain of our greater as well as minor pessimistic poets, whose influence is anything but inspiring, are so lavishly praised, is because they give so few indications of having such a nature; and it is certain that many critics of the drama would think twice before imperilling their reputation by objecting to a really artistically constructed play merely because of its immoral tendency. Yet what can be more thoroughly unphilosophical than to gauge artistic ability and taste by an absence of those traits which, in ordinary life, give a man not only character but common sense?

Nevertheless this is not the conception which some of the prevailing views of art convey to the ordinary mind. "Do I appreciate art?—do my daughters appreciate art?" said once a fashionably dressed woman of Chicago in the author's presence: "Formerly they did n't; but now, you know, we have been to Europe, and got used to the undressed statues and pictures there." And in this woman's estimation this fact was not an incidental, but the essential condition of artistic appreciation. Nor was the remark a joke. It was made seriously, more seriously, possibly, than the excuse given in a New York police court by "Little Egypt" for the lack of drapery about her in a public performance. The excuse was that she did it "in the interests of art." Possibly, however, she was in earnest. But, if so, it is well enough for others to bear in mind that art has also other interests; that opinions of this sort, if human nature continue to be what it has been, are very likely to lead, one of these days, to a Puritan revival, in which, as in the times of Cromwell, inoffensive as well as offensive art-works will be converted, as speedily as possible, into the natural, not to say chaotic, condition in which the Creator may be supposed to have originally left their constituent elements.

This contingency aside, however, the absurdity of the conception that the sentiment of art cannot be in its nature religious, ethical, or even scientific, in the sense of manifesting learning, can be proved by the slightest review of history. Probably no art-product has ever continued to influence ages succeeding its own, except in the degree in which it has shown itself to be the work of a man deeply interested, as a matter of sentiment at least, in religious, moral, social, or intellectual problems, and in their effects upon humanity. The oldest music that we have is all of it religious. So, when it is not merely ethical, is the oldest poetry. This is true not only of that which is in the Bible, and the Vedas of India, but in the Iliad, the Æneid, and in all the greatest tragedies of the Greeks. So is much of the best of modern poetry also,—that of Dante, Racine, Spenser, Milton, Wordsworth, Schiller, and Shakespeare. Very nearly as large a proportion of quotations having to do with the right conduct of life can be taken from this last poet as from the Bible itself. Nor are they brought into his plays incidentally, though they are brought in artistically, *i. e.*, in such ways as to aid in the representation of the characters depicted. Yet even to aid in this, they are often so unnecessary as to prove that their author is intentionally availing himself of an opportunity to introduce thought of a distinctly religious or moral tendency. Notice again the quotation on page 258. And now notice these:

> Renowned for their deeds as far from home,
> (For Christian service and true chivalry,)
> As is the sepulchre in stubborn Jewry,
> Of the world's ransom, blessed Mary's son.
> *Richard II.*, *ii.*, *1.*

> I feel within me
> A peace above all earthly dignities,
> A still and quiet conscience.
> *Henry VIII.*, *iii.*, *2.*

> What stronger breast-plate than a heart untainted?
> Thrice is he armed that hath his quarrel just;
> And he but naked, though locked up in steel,
> Whose conscience with injustice is corrupted.
> *2 Henry VI.*, *iii.*, *2.*

And, over and over again, he stops almost to preach against certain vices, as, for instance, intemperance:

O that men should put an enemy into their mouths to steal away their brains!—that we should with joy, revel, pleasure, and applause, transform ourselves into beasts!—*Othello, ii., 3.*

Every inordinate cup is unblessed, and the ingredient is a devil.—*Idem.*

O monstrous beast! how like a swine he lies!
—— *Taming the Shrew, Int. i.*

What's a drunken man like, fool? Like a drowned man, a fool, and a madman; one draught above heat makes him a fool; the second mads him; and a third drowns him.—*Twelfth Night, i., 5.*

And the old man Adam, in a part said to have been often acted by the poet himself, goes out of his way to explain why he has preserved his strength to old age. He says:

> Though I look old, yet I am strong and lusty:
> For in my youth I never did apply
> Hot and rebellious liquors to my blood;
> Nor did with unbashful forehead woo
> The means of weakness and debility;
> Therefore my age is as a lusty winter,
> Frosty but kindly. Let me go with you;
> I'll do the service of a younger man.
> *As You Like It, ii., 3.*

How a modern æsthete would score a modern poet who should manifest no more knowledge of the limits of the æsthetic than to "lug into" his verse such manifestations of interest in religion and ethics! "From time to time," says Oscar Wilde, only uttering what many a critic of our day is ready to repeat after him, "the world cries out against some charming artistic poet because, to use its hackneyed and silly phrase, he has 'nothing to say.' But if he had something to say, he would probably say it, and the result would be tedious. It is just because he has no new message that he can do beautiful work." "If the poet," says the French critic Baudelaire, "has pursued a moral aim, he has diminished his poetic power, and it is not imprudent to wager that his work will be bad. Poetry has not truth for its object, it has only itself." Has it? Here are a few other opinions on this subject:

> Spend'st thou thy fury on some worthless song,
> Darkening thy power to lend base subjects light?
> Return, forgetful muse, and straight redeem
> In gentle numbers time so idly spent.
> *Sonnet C: Shakespeare.*

> Yet, to discourse of what there good befel,
> All else will I relate discovered there.
> *Inferno, i: Dante.*

> That to the height of this great argument,
> I may assert eternal Providence
> And justify the ways of God to men.
> *Paradise Lost, i: Milton.*

> My best and favorite aspiration, mounts
> With yearning toward some philosophic song
> Of Truth that cherishes our daily life.
> *Prelude, Introduction: Wordsworth.*

And what poets rank higher than these?

The same fact is true as regards introducing into verse matter imparting information. Notwithstanding the criticism upon the quotation from Milton given on page 259, there is no doubt that the evidences of learning in any poem, though, of course, they should always be artistically introduced, increase its value. That this is so may be recognized upon recalling the Iliad, the Æneid, the Divine Comedy, and even the plays of Schiller, Goethe, and Shakespeare. One fact closely connected with this subject seems important, because it is frequently overlooked and not seldom misrepresented. This is the fact that the greatest poets of all times have been educated men, many of them men of great learning. Those of Greece, Rome, Italy, Spain, France, Germany, have all illustrated this fact. So have the poets of England and America, the only seeming exceptions being Shakespeare and Burns. But this much is known of the Shakespeare of Stratford. His father was a Bailiff of the town; and the school of the town was, in his time, one of the few of the King's schools, ranking with Eton and Winchester. Even if afterwards it could be said of him that he knew "little Latin and less Greek," this very phrase shows that he had received the rudiments of a very thorough education, and a bright boy, by the time he was nineteen, at which age Shakespeare is said to have left Stratford, might with such advantages have learned as much for that period as for our own period the ordinary college student learns with his; especially if Shakespeare in his last year at Stratford studied law, as is said. Burns, too, though the son of a peasant, was the son of a well-read man; and was himself a close student of books, and especially of verse as an art.

Not much space is needed in which to show that the same recognition by the world of the value of that which makes for the betterment of humanity is exemplified in the welcome which it gives to products of all the other arts. Think how large a proportion of the painters, sculptors, and architects whose names are remembered have painted altar-pieces, or decorated chapels, or modelled statues of gods or heroes, or erected temples, cathedrals, or mosques! And then think how small a proportion of those who have never done work of this character are remembered. Is there one who has attained the highest rank? If so, it is not Pheidias, nor Praxiteles, nor Raphael, nor Titian, nor Rubens, nor Angelo, nor Brunelleschi.

Who is it? Undoubtedly, here and there, one, in more recent times. But there are not a sufficient number in any age to prove that a religious, ethical, or distinctly scientific phase of sentiment is prejudicial to artistic success. What is prejudicial to this is the supposition that poetry or any art can be at its best when the mind that produces it is devoid of moral purpose or mental information. The highest result, as art is, of human intelligence and skill, it cannot be produced when only part of the highest possibilities of manhood are engaged upon it. It needs all the resources that a man can command, as well as all the facility that he can acquire through the education that enables him to command them.

The theory that considers the objective result of the artistic tendency, so far as it is affected by physical conditions such as temperament and personality, to be sentiment, experienced within and communicated to others, is not materially imperilled by the arguments advanced by those who claim that its aim is pleasure. Mr. Dallas in his "Gay Science" holds this theory, and moulds all contradictory facts to fit it. If some one remind him that the drama often gives pain, his theory tells him that pain is only one development of pleasure; if another argue that the highest art, the grandest poem or picture, gives less enjoyment than the current novel or than the caricature at which we laugh until we cry, then his theory tells him that we cannot measure pleasure by our consciousness of it. Nay, he even argues that the highest pleasure is annihilation,—identical with the anticipated hell of the Second Adventist.

There scarcely seems to be occasion for a theory leading to inferences like these. If the phases of expression which we find in art, and which depend on such con-

roundings; and, in the degree in which this significance is, in the highest sense, scientific, it involves an extremely accurate reproduction of these. *Artistic-artistic* significance is that which is the most nearly conformable to the results of *imagination*, and imagination is conditioned partly by *inspiration*, and partly by *investigation*. The artistic-artistic tendency, therefore, is conditioned by a combination of the two other tendencies.

All three are termed *tendencies*, because they refer to the significance, or subject-matter of art, as it manifests itself during the process of passing into form, *i. e.*, to significance when existing not in and for itself but when moving *toward*, *into*, and *through* outward representation. In Chapter III. of "Art in Theory," significance—often termed subject-matter—and form were said to be the two factors entering into what we mean by expression, and the necessity was pointed out of ascribing due importance to each. In strict accordance with this general thought, let us notice, now, how the different emphasis given to significance or to form manifests itself in the expression of the three tendencies that we are to consider. We shall find the three respectively giving rise to three different classes of expressional results. These are apparently produced, in the first class, from *behind* the form; in the second, *in* the form; and in the third, *through*, *with*, or *by* the form. As related to the mind, from which it is derived, *religious-artistic* expression, which is that of the first class, seems to be the most *instinctive*, the most spontaneous, the most free from any conscious endeavor to limit or fit the subject-matter to the form of representation. *Scientific-artistic* expression, which is that of the second class, seems to be the most *reflective*, the most calculating, the most under the influence of that which would accurately measure the subject-matter and accommodate it to the form. But in *artistic-artistic* expression, which is that of the third class, the *instinctive* seems to have been influenced by the *reflective*, and yet to have also controlled it, causing the subject-matter *instinctively*, as it were, to force its way through the limitations *reflectively* given to the form, and—so to speak—to transfigure it. This condition accords with what was brought out on page 210 of Chapter XIII., where it was said that the distinctively artistic is neither solely *instinctive* nor solely *reflective*, but a result of the blending of the two, and, therefore, is what may be termed *emotive*. Again, *religious-artistic* expression, as it emphasizes the source of significance, or the thing signified, *i. e.*, the subject-matter, may be characterized as *subjective ; scientific-artistic* expression, as it emphasizes the relations between the thing signified and the form signifying, may be termed *relative ;* and *artistic-artistic* expression, as it emphasizes the *form* signifying, *i. e.*, the object toward which the use of the significance is directed, may be characterized as *objective*. Once more, the first tendency, in conforming the representation to the idea within, naturally gives expression to that which is known as *idealism ;* the second, in conforming the representation to the real conditions without, naturally gives expression to *realism ;* and the third, in conforming the representation to the blending of these two other tendencies, naturally gives expression to that *idealized realism* which is the chief quality, as will be shown presently, of the *dramatic*, when a contrast is indicated between it and the *epic*. What has been said thus far may be summarized thus; and some may be interested in noticing here the same terms and arrangements of them as are used on page 243 of " Art in Theory ":

Significance in Representative Form according as its Tendency is

Religious,		Instinctive,		Subjective,		Idealism,
Scientific,	is, in derivation,	Reflective,	in character,	Relative,	and is Expressed in	Realism,
or		or		or		or
Artistic		Emotive		Objective		Idealized Realism.

These respective tendencies thus distinguished will enable us to classify, and, sufficiently for our purpose, to define certain terms with which every one is more or less familiar. The first three of these terms, all of which seem to be determined chiefly by the relation of the result to the *religious* or spiritual tendency, because they are mainly attributable to the source or subject-matter of the expression, are the *good*, allied to the religious; the *true*, allied to the scientific; and the *beautiful*, allied to the artistic. The second three, all of which seem to be determined chiefly by the relation of the result to the *scientific* tendency, because they are mainly attributable to the nature of the expression when the subject-matter comes in contact with form, are the *sublime*, allied to the religious; the *picturesque*, allied to the scientific; and the *brilliant*, allied to the artistic. The third three terms, all of which seem to be determined chiefly by the relation of the effect to the *artistic* tendency, because they are mainly attributable to the expressional result when the subject-matter has passed through the form and is exerting an influence on the man who contemplates it, are the *grand*, allied to the religious; the *simple*—called thus because not elaborated or changed essentially from the condition in which it is presented in nature—which is allied to the scientific; and the *striking*, allied to the artistic. A summary of these terms is in the chart on page 311.

Before all the possibilities of these last three effects can be understood, it is necessary to consider them as modified by the fact, brought out in Chapter XV., that art is the expression not merely of thought, but of sentiment, which is thought under the influence of emotion. Therefore the *grand*, the *simple*, and the *striking* must not be considered as mere intellectual conceptions, but as tendencies susceptible of being modified by different degrees and kinds of emotion. Emotion, as we know, may be *serious*, as when one is conscious of dealing with matters of importance ; or *playful*, as when he is not conscious of this; and, in either case, the emotion may affect one pleasurably or not pleasurably. If the three forms of expression, while continuing to manifest *serious* emotions, be affected in the direction of the non-pleasurable, they are turned respectively into the *horrible*, the *pathetic*, and the *violent ;* if, instead of manifesting serious emotions, they manifest, in ways to be indicated in Chapter XVII., *playful* influences, then, in the direction of the pleasurable, the three become, respectively, the *burlesque*, the *ludicrous*, and the *ridiculous*, etc. ; or, if affected in the direction of the non-pleasurable, they have the effect of *caricature*, of *satire*, and of *sarcasm*.

Now let us try to understand the differing conditions that lead to these different results. What was said on page 274 with reference to the first three terms need detain us only a moment. None will have difficulty in recognizing the reason why the subject-matter of religious-artistic expression should be termed distinctively *the good ;* or why the subject-matter of scientific-artistic expression, which is concerned chiefly in causing the forms of art to be accurate representations of the forms or laws of nature, should be termed distinctively *the true ;* or why the subject-matter of artistic-artistic expression, as the very term artistic indicates, should be termed distinctively *the beautiful*. In speaking of artistic beauty, Prof. H. N. Day, whose analysis, in his "Science of Æsthetics," differs in other regards from the one presented here, says: "It contrasts itself at once with those two kinds of beauty named, one of which, looking more at the idea,"—corresponding therefore to what has been termed here the religious-artistic tendency,—"we have called ideal beauty; the other, looking more at the matter in which the revelation is effected,"—corresponding to what has here been called the scientific-artistic tendency,—"we have called material beauty."

Now let us examine the terms that are applicable to the character of the expression where it comes in contact with form. It has been said that the religious-artistic tendency is that which is most spiritual and intangible, the most nearly allied to the infinite, eternal, and absolute essence or force lying behind material forms supposed to embody it. A moment's reflection will show us that this same tendency can always be affirmed of an expression which we term *sublime*. The sublime conveys an impression of a conception too disproportionately large to be distinctly embodied in a material form or even to be entirely grasped by human apprehension. Here, for instance, is Milton's celebrated description of Satan, so often used as an illustration of this sentiment:

>   He above the rest,
> In shape and gesture proudly eminent,
> Stood like a tower ; his form had not yet lost
> All her original brightness, nor appeared
> Less than arch-angel ruined, and the excess
> Of glory obscured ; as when the sun, new risen,
> Looks through the horizontal misty air,

> Shorn of his beams ; or from behind the moon
> In dim eclipse disastrous twilight sheds
> On half the nations ; and with fear of change
> Perplexes monarchs.
>
> *Pardise Lost, i.*

This is sublimity. And the whole character of Satan as portrayed by Milton is sublime; it is so, for one reason, because vague and intangible. In sublimity, says Burke, in his "Essay on the Sublime and Beautiful": "The mind is hurried out of itself by a crowd of great and confused images, which affect because they are crowded and confused; for separate them, and you lose much of the greatness; and join them, and you infallibly lose the clearness."

The same vagueness is characteristic of Michael Angelo's picture of "The Last Judgment," as well as of his statue of "Moses," whose colossal proportions and divine brow are suggestive of far more spiritual breadth of force than can fitly be contracted within the limits of a human figure. Kant, in his "Critique of Judgment," says that the effect of the sublime is owing to "the inability of our imagination to grasp the totality of certain natural grandeur,"—a difficulty which will exactly explain the impression conveyed by the following:

> Hast thou a charm to stay the morning star
> In his steep course ? So long he seems to pause
> On thy bald awful head, O sovereign Blanc !
> The Arve and Arveiron at thy base
> Rave ceaselessly, but thou, most awful Form !
> Risest from forth thy silent sea of pines,
> How silently ! Around thee and above,
> Deep is the air and dark, substantial, black,
> An ebon mass. Methinks thou piercest it,
> As with a wedge ! But when I look again,
> It is thine own calm home, thy crystal shrine,

> Thy habitation from eternity!
> O dread and silent Mount! I gazed upon thee,
> Till thou, still present to the bodily sense,
> Didst vanish from my thought; entranced in prayer,
> I worshipped the Invisible alone.
> *Hymn before Dawn in the Vale of Chamouni: Coleridge.*

Jouffroy, in his "Cours d'Esthétique," distinguishes the sublime from the agreeable. He says that in the latter, the pleasure is "less grand, but pure; in the sublime, more lively, but mixed"; and what he means by mixed, he explains by stating that, connected with it, is an impression of fear (see page 287), of inferiority, of humiliation, and an idea or hope of infinity. Chaignet, in his "Les Principes de la Science du Beau," terms the sublime "the highest degree of energy or of grandeur of æsthetic ideas revealed in objects." The sublimity in the following would correspond to the requirements of both Jouffroy and Chaignet:

> If thou dost slander her and torture me,
> Never pray more; abandon all remorse;
> On horror's head horrors accumulate,
> Do deeds to make heaven weep, all earth amazed,
> For nothing canst thou to damnation add
> Greater than that.
> *Othello, iii., 3: Shakespeare.*

> Arise, black vengeance, from thy hollow cell!
> Yield up, O love, thy crown and hearted throne
> To tyrannous hate! swell bosom with thy fraught,
> For 't is of aspic's tongues!
> *Idem.*

Burke, in his "Sublime and Beautiful," like Kant in his "Critique of Judgment," makes the sublime differ from the beautiful by terming the latter a mode of pleasure, and the former a mode of pain. "Astonishment," he says, Pt. II., Sec. 1, "is the effect of the sublime in its highest degree; the inferior effects are admiration, reverence, and respect." He then shows the relation of sublimity to such elements as terror, obscurity, power, vastness, and infinity. "A clear idea," he affirms, Pt. II., Sec. 5, "is another name for a little idea. There is a passage in the Book of Job amazingly sublime, and this sublimity is principally due to the terrible uncertainty of the thing described: 'In thoughts from the visions of the night, when deep sleep falleth upon men, fear came upon me and trembling which made all my bones to shake. Then a spirit passed before my face. The hair of my flesh stood up. It stood still, but I could not discern the form thereof: an image was before mine eyes; there was silence; and I heard a voice, saying, Shall mortal man be more just than God?'" (Job iv: 13-17.) "We are first prepared with the utmost solemnity," Burke goes on to say, "for the vision; we are first terrified before we are let even into the obscure cause of our emotion; but when this grand cause of terror makes its appearance, what is it? Is it not wrapped up in the shades of its own incomprehensible darkness, more awful, more striking, more terrible, than the liveliest description, than the clearest painting, could possibly represent it?"

In his "Lectures on Metaphysics," Sir William Hamilton, following in the footsteps of Burke, says: "Our feeling of sublimity is a mingled one of pleasure and pain—of pleasure in the consciousness of the strong energy, of pain in the consciousness that this energy is vain. But as the amount of pleasure in the sublime is greater than the amount of pain, it follows that the free energy that it elicits must be greater than the free energy that it repels. . . . Sublimity . . . requires magnitude as its condition; and the formless is not infrequently sublime." "In this species of beauty," says Professor Day, in his "Science of Æsthetics," "the idea asserts its superiority over form, spirit over matter; the idea overmasters the form, breaks through it, as it were, and stands forth in the majesty of its own divine unparticipating nature. It is that kind which is familiarly recognized as the sublime." "Duration, magnitude, any beautiful expression which enlarges and overpowers the mind in its apprehension, may become sublime," says Bascom, in his "Science of Beauty." After these quotations, few will doubt, as soon as they understand what is meant in this chapter by the religious-artistic tendency of expression, that this is the tendency giving rise to the effect of *sublimity*.

When the subject of artistic conception becomes entirely comprehensible and tangible, it passes to the method of expression which has been termed scientific-artistic. Science deals with facts as they are; and the scientific tendency in art represents thoughts, sights, or events with literal fidelity. It does not labor to rearrange them so as to make them conform to some ideal standard either in the mind or out of it. When we come to consider historic or realistic art, many illustrations of this tendency will be given. The ancient ballads, as well as modern poetry, are full of them; so also are historic paintings and sculpture and even architecture and music. At present, it is only necessary to say that all these products manifest more or less of what is termed the *picturesque*. Concerning this quality, Sir William Hamilton in his "Lectures on Metaphysics" says: "Variety, even apart from unity, is pleasing; and if the mind be made content to expatiate freely and easily in this variety without attempting painfully to reduce it to unity, it will derive no inconsiderable pleasure from the exertion of its powers. Now the picturesque object is precisely of such a character."

The following, for instance, is picturesque; and if it were represented in a painting, or in architecture, as it might easily be, it would, of course, furnish an illustration of the picturesque in these arts also :

> And me that morning Walter showed the house,
> Greek, set with busts ; from vases in the hall
> Flowers of all heavens, and lovelier than their names,
> Grew side by side ; and on the pavement lay
> Carved stones of the abbey-ruin in the park,
> Huge Ammonites, and the first bones of Time.
> And on the tables every clime and age
> Jumbled together; celts and calumets
> Claymore and snow-shoe, toys in lava, fans
> Of sandal, amber, ancient rosaries,
> Laborious Orient ivory, sphere in sphere,
> The cursed Malayan crease, and battle-clubs
> From the isles of palm ; and higher on the walls,
> Betwixt the monstrous horns of elk and deer,
> His own forefathers' arms and armor hung.
> *The Princess : Tennyson.*

The following, too, is picturesque, but less decidedly so than is the preceding; because one feels, all the way through, that the artist is trying to give *form* to the variety which he describes and to do this by bringing all things into harmony, or, what is the same thing, into unity with the sentiment controlling his own spirit. The tendency of this passage therefore is in the direction of what we shall presently find to be characteristic of the brilliant.

> All the land in flowery squares,
> Beneath a broad and equal blowing wind,
> Smelt of the coming summer, as one large cloud
> Drew downward ; but all else of heaven was pure
> Up to the sun, and May from verge to verge,
> And May with me from head to heel. And now,

> As tho' 't were yesterday, as tho' it were
> The hour just flown, that morn with all its sound,
> (For those old Mays had thrice the life of these)
> Rings in mine ears. The steer forgot to graze,
> And, where the hedgerow cuts the pathway, stood,
> Leaning his horns into the neighbor field,
> And lowing to his fellows. From the woods
> Came voices of the well contented doves.
> The lark could scarce get out his notes for joy,
> But shook his song together as he neared
> His happy home the ground.
> *The Gardener's Daughter: Tennyson.*

When the subject of conception comes to be expressed in form the artistic impulse is sometimes so strong as virtually to transfigure the form. This condition gives rise to the *brilliant*. In the *sublime*, that which is represented seems too large or grand for the form; in the *picturesque*, it seems exactly reproduced in the form; in the *brilliant*, it seems enhanced in value by the form. The effect in the last case is like that of placing a lens before a picture, or what this effect might be if the lens were a precious jewel. The brilliant is characterized therefore by the opposite of vagueness, *i. e.*, by luminosity, by a luminosity, too, which gives not only light, shade, and color, but outlines also that often seem greatly magnified. Of course, in the brilliant, the subject-matter may be of importance, but this is not necessary. The following passages all derive their artistic value from subordinate considerations added to the principal subject-matter in order to enhance the brilliancy of the presentation:

> I saw young Harry,—with his beaver on,
> His cuisses on his thighs, gallantly arm'd,—
> Rise from the ground like feather'd Mercury,
> And vaulted with such ease into his seat,
> As if an angel dropp'd down from the clouds,

> To turn and wind a fiery Pegasus,
> And witch the world with noble horsemanship.
>> 1 *Henry IV.*, iv., 1 : *Shakespeare.*

> The fiery Tybalt with his sword prepared ;
> Which, as he breathed defiance to my ears,
> He swung about his head, and cut the winds,
> Who, nothing hurt withal, hissed him in scorn.
>> *Romeo and Juliet*, i., *1 : Idem.*

> O my soul's joy !
> If after every tempest come such calms,
> May the winds blow till they have wakened death !
> And let the laboring bark climb hills of seas
> Olympus high, and duck again as low
> As hell 's from heaven !
>> *Othello*, ii., *1 : Idem.*

Or take the following description of scenery which it will be profitable to contrast with the examples of the picturesque quoted above, especially with the last of them in connection with what was said about it :

> And what is so rare as a day in June ?
>   Then, if ever, come perfect days ;
> Then heaven tries the earth if it be in tune,
>   And over it softly her warm ear lays :
> Whether we look or whether we listen,
> We hear life murmur or see it glisten ;
> Every clod feels a stir of might,
>   An instinct within it that reaches and towers,
> And, groping blindly about it for light,
>   Climbs to a soul in grass and flowers ;
> The flush of life may well be seen
>   Thrilling back over hills and valleys ;
> The cowslip startles in meadows green,
>   The butter-cup catches the sun in its chalice,
> And there 's never a leaf or a blade too mean
>   To be some happy creature's palace ;
> The little bird sits at his door in the sun,
>   Atilt like a blossom among the leaves,

> And lets his illumined being o'errun
>   With the deluge of summer it receives;
> His mate feels the eggs beneath her wings,
> And the heart in her dumb breast flutters and sings;
> He sings to the wide world and she to her nest,—
> In the nice ear of Nature which song is the best?
>
> *The Vision of Sir Launfal: J. R. Lowell.*

It will be remembered that Kant, Burke, and Hamilton make a distinction between the sublime and the beautiful. "The beautiful has reference to the form of an object," says the latter, "whereas the formless is not infrequently sublime." It is in accordance with this idea that the sublime has just been termed a development of the religious-artistic tendency rather than of the artistic-artistic, where we must place the brilliant. At the same time, it is important to notice that the classification that is made here is less one of division than of development. Every preceding division is more or less inclusive of that which follows. The *good*, for instance, the subjective impulse, not only precedes but includes the *true;* and the *true*, the *beautiful;* and the *beautiful*, the *sublime*, etc.

But, at the same time, the distinctive effect of beauty, *i. e.*, of beauty when least influenced by considerations drawn from goodness and truth, is *brilliancy*. It is by the term *brilliant* that the excellence of a poem or an oration that manifests the least possible influence of motives drawn from goodness or truth, and yet is artistically beautiful, is best characterized. When we say that a poet or an orator is distinctively *brilliant*, we indicate that, while he may have those qualities fitted to obtain success in the realm of beauty, he may lack others that render one good and truthful; and for the same reason we imply—and those who hear us infer—that his productions are seldom distinctively sublime or grand. They are simply, so far as he gives accurate expression to his own character, brilliant and striking.

By classifying the *brilliant* rather than the *beautiful* as the objective tendency of the same impulse that, subjectively considered, causes the *sublime*, one escapes from such a criticism as is made, for instance, by Chaignet in his "Les Principes de la Science du Beau" upon the inclination manifested by most writers to separate the sublime altogether from the beautiful. "On the contrary," he argues, as has been done in this chapter, "the sublime is only one department or phase of the beautiful; otherwise there would be no place at all for the sublime in art, inasmuch as art is no more nor no less than the expression of beauty." To this he might have added that probably no instance can be cited, from either art or nature, in which a sublime effect is produced otherwise than in connection with beauty. Of course, beauty is impossible without form; and Sir William Hamilton, as just quoted, says "the formless is not infrequently sublime." But this statement is not true, except as applied to conception; and what gives us this conception is the suggestion of formlessness conveyed through some form which is constantly representing itself as inadequate to do justice to the subject-matter. Chaignet instances, too, a very striking illustration of the close connection between the sublime and the beautiful, in three successive quotations. One is from Jouffroy. In this, in order to show the difference between the effects of two works of art, the writer says that, in gazing at the Apollo, you recognize that you experience the pleasure of the beautiful; whereas in gazing at the Laocoön, "you experience the emotions of the sublime." The next quotation is from Lessing, who declares in his "Laocoön" that one experiences the sensation of beauty in that statue; and the third is from Winckelmann, who says in his "History of Ancient Art" that one experiences the sensation of the sublime in the face of the Apollo. When doctors disagree thus, there must be a good reason for it. "Therefore," argues Chaignet, "the sublime is not different from the beautiful, only one department of it."

While saying this, however, Chaignet seems to fail to tell us completely what the sublime is. According to the classifications of this chapter, it will be seen that it is a result of the beautiful when the influence of this is most combined with that of the invisible, spiritual force behind the form—*i. e.*, of the force that is sovereign over our religious nature and our conscience, and whose distinctive authority is exercised when it impels one to the good. It is interesting to notice how closely this deduction, though differently derived, corresponds to that of Kant when, in his "Critique of Judgment," he dwells upon a connection between a man's capacity for appreciating the sublime and his susceptibility to influence exerted through the moral feelings.

The impression of a force too nearly allied to what is infinite, eternal, and absolute to be entirely embodied in a material form necessarily carries with it, as intimated on page 278, an effect of the *grand*. This is so evident that we pass at once from it to an effect correspondingly produced by the *picturesque*. In this, as we have found, the subject-matter is not too great for the expression. The scenes in nature are left very much as one finds them. Of course, the consequent effect neither impresses us like the sublime, nor moves us like the brilliant. It merely furnishes enjoyment akin to that which comes from the simplicity of nature itself. Therefore it has been termed here the *simple*. See illustrations on page 288. Once more, the artistic-artistic tendency, or the *brilliant*, has an effect which, in distinction from the *grand* or the *simple*, we may term the *striking*. The *brilliant* not only attracts attention, it enforces it. In the *sublime*, which is *grand*, we have a repetition of spiritual force without an adequate medium; in the *picturesque*, which is *simple*, we have an equilibrium between the two; in the *brilliant*, which is *striking*, we have a medium that is almost more than adequate. We have a condition in which what was spiritual has found transfiguration, and what was immaterialized force has found weapons. Notice the illustrations of the striking on page 289, and how all the passages thrust a concrete picture before the imagination from the impression produced by which one cannot escape.

A very few words will serve to illustrate what was said of the modifications of *the grand, the simple*, and *the striking* when the emotion tends toward the non-pleasurable. In considering *the sublime*, we have already found many quotations, as on pages 278-9, which justify us in attributing to it the effects not only of *the grand* but of the form of the terrible which includes that conception of overwhelming size or strength which is the source of the feeling that we term *the horrible*. Notice again the quotations on page 278; also the following:

> What may this mean
> That thou, dread corse, again, in complete steel,
> Revisitest thus the glimpses of the moon,
> Making night hideous; and we, fools of nature,
> So horridly to shake our disposition
> With thoughts beyond the reaches of our souls?
> Say, why is this?
>
> *Hamlet, i., 4 : Shakespeare.*

> But that I am forbid
> To tell the secrets of my prison house,
> I could a tale unfold, whose lightest word
> Would harrow up thy soul ; freeze thy young blood,
> Make thy two eyes, like stars, start from their spheres,
> Thy knotted and combined locks to part,
> And each particular hair to stand on end,
> Like quills upon the fretful porcupine !
> Hamlet, i., 5 : Shakespeare.

When the expression represents what affects the emotions seriously and painfully, yet assumes a form that is almost scientifically true to the facts, and, in this sense, *picturesque* and *simple*, we have the *pathetic*. Its characteristic feature, as a mode of expression, is an apparent lack of art, of all attempt to exaggerate or to embellish, or to do anything that shall interfere with accuracy, and therefore with naturalness of effect. There is in it not the remotest suggestion either of the *sublime* or the *grand* or of the *brilliant* or the *striking*. The effect is the same as if the author were anxious to have us recognize that the facts themselves were of such importance as to need no effort of his own to increase it. Observe the phraseology in these :

> She dwelt among the untrodden ways
>   Beside the springs of Dove ;
> A maid whom there were none to praise,
>   And very few to love.
> . . . . .
> She lived unknown, and few could know
>   When Lucy ceased to be ;
> But she is in her grave, and O
>   The difference to me !
> The Lost Love : Wordsworth.

> Touch her not scornfully,
> Think of her mournfully,

THE VIOLENT.

Gently and humanly,—
Not of the stains of her ;
All that remains of her
Now is pure womanly.

. . . .

Alas ! for the rarity
Of Christian charity
Under the sun !
O it was pitiful !
Near a whole city full,
Home she had none.
The Bridge of Sighs : Hood.

If thou tellest the heavy story right,
Upon my soul, the hearers will shed tears ;
Yea, even my foes will shed fast falling tears,
And say,—Alas, it was a piteous deed !
3 Henry VI., i., 4 : Shakespeare.

Once more, when, instead of being overawed and stilled as in *horror*, one is stirred as in the *violent* to attack and conquer opposition, there is only one form of expression that can fitly represent his conditions. Notice it in the following—how every separate word flung out of the lips is fitted, by the very *brilliancy* of the language in a most literal sense, to *strike :*

The devil damn thee black, thou cream-faced loon !
Where gottest thou that goose-look ?
Macbeth, v., 3 : Shakespeare.

She-wolf of France, but worse than wolves of France,
Whose tongue more poisons than the adder's tooth,
How ill beseeming is it in thy sex
To triumph like an Amazonian trull
Upon their woes whom fortune captivates !
3 Henry VI. i., 4 : Idem

All the contagion of the south light on you.
You shames of Rome !   You herd of—   Boils and plagues

> Plaster you o'er ; that you may be abhorred
> Farther than seen, and one infect another
> Against the wind a mile !
>
> *Coriolanus, i., 4 : Idem.*

To these illustrations from poetry there need be added here no references to the other arts, partly because these will be given in other places, and partly because, so far as concerns the general principles involved, their applicability to each of these arts will be easily recognized. Whether manifested in music, painting, sculpture, or architecture, we all associate the *sublime*, the *grand*, and the *horrible* with more or less of the same sort of vagueness in rhythm, melody, harmony, color, or outline which in poetry has been shown to suggest something beyond the possibility of exact formulation. In the same art-elements too we associate the *picturesque*, the *simple*, and the *pathetic* with that which is normal in effect, often in the sense of being exactly imitated from nature ; and we associate the *brilliant*, the *striking*, and the *violent* with runs and chords in which each note, amid difficulties overcome by skill, rings out with exceptional distinctness ; with colors, the exact hues of which, amid similar difficulties, it is impossible to mistake ; and with outlines that, notwithstanding equal obstacles, stand out in correspondingly bold relief.

CHAPTER XVII.

ARTISTIC SIGNIFICANCE AS CHARACTERIZED BY THE SAME THREE TENDENCIES IN NON–SERIOUS CONDITIONS: THE BURLESQUE, THE LUDICROUS, AND THE RIDICULOUS, AS IN THE MOCK-HEROIC, PARODY, AND FARCE; THE GROTESQUE, THE DROLL, AND THE JOCULAR; TRAVESTY, HUMOR, AND WIT; CARICATURE, SATIRE, AND SARCASM.

Playful Conditions—Incongruity as in the Burlesque, the Ludicrous, and the Ridiculous—The Burlesque in the Mock-Heroic—In the Parody—In the Farce and Pun—The Ludicrous in the Grotesque—Another Example—In the Droll—In the Jocular—The Ludicrous in Travesty—In Humor and Wit—Humor Truthful, Wit Beautiful—Humor Picturesque, Wit Brilliant—Humor Simple, Wit Striking—The Ridiculous, as non-Pleasurable Play in Caricature—In Satire—In Sarcasm—Similar Developments of Incongruity in Music—In Painting, Sculpture, and Architecture.

ALL the forms of expression mentioned in the preceding chapter were supposed to be developed under the influence of serious emotive conditions, in which the mind is conscious of dealing with matters of importance. In this chapter, in accordance with the plan indicated on page 275, we are to consider the corresponding developments in connection with playful conditions. That which turns serious into playful effects is the different use made of the factors entering into them. The two chief factors in expression, as we have found, are the *subject-matter* and the *form*. A serious intention always manifests itself by making the two appear congruous. One of them may be emphasized more than the other, as the subject-matter is in the *sublime* and as the form is in the *brilliant;* but the subordination of the form, in the one case, merely makes us feel that a man is trying to express what no one can express fully; and the emphasis of the form in the other, that he is trying to make us realize what no one can realize fully. In neither case is there any suggestion of *incongruity* as an end in itself. Just the opposite is true of the playful. The incongruity in this is sometimes between the subject-matter and the form, and sometimes, as developed from this general condition, between different parts of both subject-matter and form. It is important to notice, too, that this incongruity is a result which, except by way of association, can be attributed to only the human being, never to God or to nature. It is inconceivable that natural forms should not fulfil those natural laws which cause them to represent, and all together to represent in an analogous way, the conceptions of the Creator. But with man it is different. The use that he makes of forms depends upon his own will, and the ability to represent what he chooses carries with it the ability to misrepresent. If, when he is supposed to be serious, he misrepresent intentionally, he deceives; if unintentionally, he blunders. But, in this last case, he sometimes may produce—as in the forms of expression colloquially termed *bulls*—the same effects as when he is not supposed to be serious. Among these effects we may detect three general tendencies, corresponding, respectively, to those already indicated among serious effects. These are in the *burlesque,* the *ludicrous,* and the *ridiculous.* In the *burlesque,* sport is made chiefly of the subject-matter which is travestied in a grossly incongruous form.

In the *ludicrous*, sport is made of either the subject-matter or the form, or of different parts of either, because they are incongruously associated. In the *ridiculous*, sport is made chiefly of the form which causes to appear incongruous the thing through which or the person through whom the subject-matter is expressed. As a rule, the *burlesque* makes us laugh *for*, the *ludicrous* makes us laugh *with*, and the *ridiculous* makes us laugh *at*, which fact furnishes a very good reason why the last often passes over into the region of non-pleasurable play.

A *burlesque* phase of the *sublime* and the *grand* may be said to be expressed in the form of the *mock-heroic;* the same phase of the *picturesque* and the *simple*, to be expressed in the *parody;* and of the *brilliant* and the *striking*, in the *farce*, closely connected with which, as we shall find, is the *pun*. In the *mock-heroic* the importance of the subject is not great, which fact is made clear by joining and likening the subject, as well as the heroes, to very insignificant matters; but, on the other hand, all the subjects mentioned are sometimes treated as if of very great importance. The subject of the following is the cutting off of a lock of hair; and the conjunction of " husbands and lap-dogs " will be recognized to be equally belittling to the one and enlarging to the other:

> The meeting points the sacred hair dissever
> From the fair head, forever and forever !
> Then flashed the living lightning from her eyes
> And screams of horror rend the affrighted skies ;
> Not louder shrieks to pitying heaven are cast
> When husbands or when lap-dogs breathe their last.
> *Rape of the Lock : Pope.*

The *parody* does not, like the *mock-heroic*, exaggerate the form when expressing through it incongruously inferior ideas, nor does it belittle the form. It exactly imitates some existing form, thus allying itself to the expression of *the true, the picturesque*, and *the simple*. Besides this, its effects are distributed over an entire sentence, paragraph, or composition ; and therefore are less single, sharp, *brilliant*, and *striking*, than are those of the *farce* or the *pun*. These facts, for reasons that will be given presently, connect the *parody* with *humor* rather than with *wit ;* e. g :—

>   Now shine the spires beneath the paly moon,
>   And through the cloisters peace and silence reign ;
>   Save where some fiddler scrapes a drowsy tune,
>   Or copious bowls inspire a jovial strain ;
>
>   Save that in yonder cobweb-mantled room,
>   Where sleeps a student in profound repose,
>   Oppressed with ale, wide echoes through the gloom
>   The droning music of his vocal nose.
>   *An Evening Contemplation in a College ;*
>   *written in the manner of Gray's " Elegy*
>   *in a Country Churchyard" : Duncombe.*

>   To print, or not to print—that is the question.
>   Whether 't is better in a trunk to bury
>   The quirks and crotchets of outrageous fancy,
>   Or send a well-wrote copy to the press,
>   And by disclosing, end them. . . . To print, to beam
>   From the same shelf with Pope, in calf well bound,
>   To sleep, perchance with Quarles—Ay, there's the rub.
>   *In the manner of Hamlet's Soliloquy :   Jago.*

The *farce*, together with the *pun*, which latter corresponds to individual sallies of *wit* in pure comedy, is always more or less dramatic in the sense of being dependent upon *brilliant* and *striking* effects. At the same time, the very remote resemblances usually suggested, and the ease with which habits of suggesting them may be acquired, render both methods of making sport of inferior comic rank unless, as in the following, the association of ideas or of sounds is particularly striking:

> His death, which happened in his berth,
>   At forty-odd befel ;
> They went and told the sexton, and
>   The sexton tolled the bell.
>   *Faithless Sally Brown: Hood.*

Of the three divisions of the *ludicrous* that we are about to make, it will be noticed that the first often borders closely upon the *burlesque* and the third upon the *ridiculous*. But, though the three sometimes overlap, there is a distinction between them. A thing may be *ludicrous* which suggests neither the *burlesque* nor the *ridiculous*. That phase of the *ludicrous* which is nearest to the *sublime* or the *grand* is the *grotesque*, as in *travesty;* that which is nearest to the *picturesque* or the *simple* is the *droll*, as in *humor;* and that which is nearest to the *brilliant* and the *striking* is the *jocular*, as in *wit*. Of course, according to the principle applied on page 284 to the *good*, the *true*, and the *beautiful*, etc., all of these characteristics are manifested more or less in all *ludicrous*, to say nothing of *burlesque* and *ridiculous*, products. At the same time, few will fail to perceive that a man may make fun, as in the *grotesque* or in *travesty*, and not possess a particle of that which is recognized as distinctively *droll* or *humorous* and that he may make fun in the way of both the *grotesque* and the *humorous*, and yet not be *jocular* or *witty*.

But, to be more specific, in the *sublime* and the *grand*, although a serious effort is made to represent the subject-matter, the importance of it is too great to be adequately represented in any form. In the *grotesque* it is not too great, otherwise it would not be a legitimate subject for the *ludicrous*, which, as Bain tells us in his " English Composition and Rhetoric," " is for the most part based on the degradation, direct or indirect, of some person or interest,—sometimes associated with power, dignity, or gravity. It is further requisite that the circumstances of this degradation should not be such as to produce any other strong emotion, as pity, anger, or fear." Here is a form of the *grotesque* which can hardly be distinguished from the *burlesque*. So far as it can be, it is merely because the burlesquing in it is slightly toned down.

> "The plaintiff, gentlemen," continued Serjeant Buzfuz, in a soft and melancholy voice, "the plaintiff is a widow; yes, gentlemen, a widow. The late Mr. Bardell, after enjoying for many years the esteem and confidence of his sovereign, as one of the guardians of his royal revenues, glided almost imperceptibly from the world, to seek elsewhere for that repose and peace which a custom-house can never afford." At the pathetic description of the decease of Mr. Bardell, who had been knocked on the head with a quart-pot in a public-house cellar, the learned Serjeant's voice faltered, and he proceeded with emotion: "Some time before his death he had stamped his likeness upon a little boy. With this little boy, the only pledge of her departed exciseman, Mrs. Bardell shrunk from the world, and courted the retirement and tranquillity of Goswell Street; and here she placed in her front parlor-window a placard bearing this inscription—'Apartments furnished for a single gentleman. Inquire within.' . . . Did it remain there long? No. The serpent was on the watch, the train was laid, the mine was preparing, the sapper and miner were at work. Before the bill had been in the parlor-window three days—three days, gentlemen—a Being erect upon two legs, and bearing all the outward semblance of a man, and not of a monster, knocked at the door of Mrs. Bardell's house."
>
> *The Pickwick Papers, xxxiii. : Dickens.*

But here is another form of the *grotesque*, which hardly suggests the *burlesque*. It is from Sydney Smith:

> "Mrs. Jackson called the other day, and spoke of the oppressive heat of last week. 'Heat, Madam,' I said, 'it was so dreadful that I found nothing

left for it but to take off my flesh and sit in my bones.' 'Take off your flesh and sit in your bones, Sir? O, Mr. Smith, how could you do that?' 'Nothing more easy, madam; come and see me next time.' But she ordered her carriage and evidently thought it a very unorthodox proceeding."

As contrasted with the above, the following, which we may term *droll*, illustrates the ludicrous analogue of the *true* and the *simple* rather than of the *good* and the *grand*. The incongruity in it is produced by the contrast between the subject of which most persons do not like to think, much less to speak, and the frank, transparent, and, when the song is sung, decidedly loud expression of it:

> Sad is the woman's lot who, year by year,
> Sees one by one her beauties disappear.
>
> . . . . . .
>
> Silvered is the raven hair,
>   Spreading is the parting straight,
> Mottled the complexion fair,
>   Halting is the youthful gait,
> Hollow is the laughter free,
>   Spectacled the limpid eye;
> Little will be left of me
>   In the coming by-and-by.
>
> Fading is the taper waist,
>   Shapeless grows the shapely limb,
> And, although severely laced,
>   Spreading is the figure trim;
> Stouter than I used to be,
>   Still more corpulent grow I,
> There will be too much of me
>   In the coming by-and-by.
>
> *Patience, ii. : Gilbert.*

By what, for the lack of a better word, has been termed the *jocular*, is meant very nearly what is expressed by the term *pure comedy*. It is a result when, through incongruity, say in situation, suggestion, or language, an otherwise serious thought or emotion is made ludicrous; *e. g.*:

> FIRST CLOWN. Come, my spade! There is no ancient gentlemen, but gardeners, ditchers, and grave-makers; they hold up Adam's profession.
> SECOND CLOWN. Was he a gentleman?
> FIRST CLOWN. He was the first that ever bore arms.
> SECOND CLOWN. Why, he had none.
> FIRST CLOWN. What, art a heathen? How dost thou understand the Scripture? The Scripture says Adam digged: could he dig without arms?
> *Hamlet, v., 1 : Shakespeare.*

> MRS. CROAKER. Nothing diverts me more than one of these fine old dressy things, who thinks to conceal her age by everywhere exposing her person . . . in the public gardens looking, for all the world, like one of the painted ruins of the place.
> HONEYWOOD. Every age has its admirers, ladies. While you, perhaps, are trading among the warmer climates of youth, there ought to be some to carry on a useful commerce in the frozen latitudes beyond fifty.
> MISS RICH. But, then, the mortification they must suffer before they can be fitted out for the traffic. I have seen one of them fret a whole morning at her hairdresser, when all the fault was in her face.
> HONEYWOOD. And yet I'll engage has carried that face at last to a very good market. This good-natured town, madam, has husbands, like spectacles, to fit every age from fifteen to fourscore.
> *The Good-Natured Man : Goldsmith.*

As was said on page 295, the *grotesque*, the *droll*, and the *jocular* respectively develop, in their more artistic forms, into *travesty*, *humor*, and *wit*. Here, in methods of expression perfectly legitimate for a subject warranting them, but grossly exaggerated for the subject treated, is a good example of *travesty:*

> There is no question that he [Adam] is actually buried in the grave which is pointed out as his—there can be none—because it has never yet been proven that that grave is not the grave in which he is buried. The tomb of Adam! How touching it was, here in the land of strangers far away from home, and friends, and all who cared for me, thus to discover the grave of a blood relation. True, a distant one, but still a relation. The

unerring instinct of nature thrilled its recognition. The fountain of my filial affection was stirred up to its profoundest depths, and I gave way to tumultuous emotion. I leaned upon a pillar and burst into tears.
Innocents Abroad, liii. : *Mark Twain (S. L. Clemens).*

Many attempts, usually by way of antithesis, have been made to distinguish *humor* and *wit*. In order to refer to these without needless repetition, the two will be considered here in the same antithetic manner. The former was said, on page 295, to be the result of the incongruous when produced in accordance with the scientific-artistic tendency that leads through the *true* to the *picturesque* and the *simple;* and the latter to be a result of the same when produced in accordance with the artistic-artistic tendency that leads through the *beautiful* to the *brilliant* and the *striking*. We shall find many distinctions that have been drawn between the two which will suggest the pedigree of each, as thus indicated. First, let us notice the connection of the one with the *true* and of the other with the *beautiful*. " The characteristic of humor," says a writer in the " British Quarterly," vol. lvi., p. 45, " is nature, that of wit is art." " Novelty," says Quackenbos in his " Course of Composition and Rhetoric," page 232, " is not essential to humor. Its truthfulness to nature prevents it from being tiresome. . . . Humor is not like wit, sudden and short-lived, a brilliant scintillation which flashes forth and is then lost in obscurity." " Humor," says Welsh, in his " Complete Rhetoric," page 259, " is immortal in its truthfulness to nature." " Wit," says Bardeen, in his " Complete Rhetoric," page 116, " may be wholly imaginative." " When wit," says Sydney Smith, in a " Lecture on Wit and Humor," " is combined with sense and information "—which implies that often it is not so combined—" it is then a beautiful and delightful part

termed *instinctive* and *subjective*, and indicated as manifesting *idealism*. Now add to this the further fact, brought out on pages 274 to 280 and 286, namely, that the same tendency leads to the expression of *the sublime* and *the grand;* and we have all the elements necessary to constitute what are usually recognized to be the characteristics of *epic* art, a well-known definition of which is that of Blair in his "Rhetoric," namely, "the illustrating of some great and general idea." This might be improved by saying that it is the illustrating of a great idea or spiritual principle, through forms typical of the general effect of its influence. This definition will be exemplfied from the different arts hereafter.

On the pages just mentioned, it was shown also that the scientific-artistic tendency emphasizes the relations between the thing signified and the form. In fulfilment of this condition, both subject-matter and form seem in it to be given, as far as possible, equal consideration, neither being subordinated to the other. But, of course, the practical effect is great accuracy in the delineation, all the details of natural appearance, in the order of succession and of interaction, being, in a sense not true in epic art, necessary to the desired result. This we find to be the condition in what may be called *realistic* art—the art not necessarily of that which is termed realism, but the art which has the same general tendency as realism, and may be defined as the delineating of material and mental effects in human or non-human life exactly as, on the surface, they appear to be. The term *historic* has sometimes been applied to this form of art, but it is narrower in its meaning, and accurately distinguishes only one subdivision of the form.

Once more, it has been shown that the artistic-artistic tendency emphasizes the "form signifying." This is the characteristic of *dramatic* art, which accepts the influence of the subject-matter only after this has taken possession of a particular medium of expression and transfigured it, producing thus a result, as will be noticed, exactly the opposite of the religious-artistic tendency. Instead of giving supremacy to the general and indefinite, of which the form is typical, the dramatic emphasizes the special and definite, thus enlarging the attractiveness and importance of the form itself, furnishing

>   —to airy nothing
>   A local habitation and a name.
>   *Midsummer Night's Dream*, v., *1*: Shakespeare.

In contrast to the epic and the realistic, the dramatic may be defined as the impersonating of individual characteristics as affected by considerations influencing them from within and from without. It will be noticed that the definition is broad enough to include dramatic effects as produced in and by not only human forms but also those that are non-human.

These definitions of the three main divisions of art-form differ in phraseology, but correspond in essentials to the same as recognized many times before. Thus Fuseli, in his third "Lecture on Painting," says that "in the epic, act and agent are subordinate to the maxim; and in pure history"—what has here been termed the realistic—"are mere organs of the fact; but the drama subordinates both fact and maxim to the agent, his character and passion." The distinction between the three and also their natural order of sequence, as related to one another, may be better understood, perhaps, through an illustration. Suppose that one feel moved to tell a story. That which first prompts him to do so is some thought, usually a general impression, which strikes him in connection with certain transactions that he has witnessed or heard; and because the impression remains, he tells the story in such a way as to convey to his hearers an impression similar to his own. His whole object in the recital, though he may not be conscious of it, is to make clear the impression, or, as we sometimes say, the *moral*, the *point* that has interested him, and so long as he does this, he cares little about accuracy in all the details. Now this is the condition requisite to the epic form of art, and, as all of us will probably recognize, this is the condition of the method most *instinctively* adopted by those who gain the reputation of being good story-tellers. Therefore it seems appropriate that the Greeks, taking their term from a word meaning story, should have named this form, *par excellence*, the epic, or story-style.

But there is another way in which one may recall the same transactions. After reflecting upon them a little, he may begin to analyze the different deeds or words of the persons implicated, and to ask himself, Why did this one do this or say that? These reflections will lead him to think more particularly of the details of the transactions and sayings, and of each of them in the order of its occurrence. When, after such a consideration, he comes to tell the story, although possibly he may not neglect to bring out that which at first seemed to him to be its "point," nevertheless this will appear subordinate to the accuracy with which he relates the details themselves and their interaction. In other words, his desire to be true to the facts in their order of sequence—*i. e.*, to the scientific-artistic tendency—will realize the condition requisite to what has been termed *realistic* art; and with reference to this, it is evident that while such a mode of recital may render a story far less interesting as a mere story, it will render it far more satisfactory to a consideration purely intellectual and analytic.

Once more, there is still a third way of telling the story. After analyzing the different words and deeds of the persons engaged in the transactions, a man may become conscious of forming definite conclusions with reference to the motives and characters of these persons, and, as a result of his conclusions, he may be joyous or otherwise, according to the degree in which the events have pleased or grieved him. At this stage, he will be prompted to express his pleasure or grief; *i. e.*, his emotions, and while doing so, in order to manifest his reasons and enforce their reasonableness on others, he will be led instinctively to imitate the expressions or appearances of the characters to whom he is referring. This, at last, gives us the condition requisite to *dramatic* art—from the word *dramo*, to act. In this form, the story is told, not with supreme reference to the *point* or *moral*, as in the *epic*, or to the *details* or *facts*, as in the *realistic*, but to the *effects* produced upon thought or feeling, and to the way in which they can be represented in *action*.

Just here it may be well to direct attention to a fact for which unnecessarily elaborate explanations have been given. In the history, not only of literature, but of almost all art, it has been noticed that, well-nigh invariably, the epic form is the first to manifest itself, and the dramatic the last. In the light of the illustrations just employed, it must be evident that this result is owing to the very nature of the epic as distinguished from the dramatic. As has been shown, the epic narrative is the first result of a superficial view. A man catches certain inferences from certain scenes, and then represents these scenes in such a way as to convey the same inferences to others. When a man, so to speak, is in the epic state, his mind is in the attitude of mere apprehension, curiosity, or wonder. Because, as a rule, the minds of children are necessarily in such an attitude, we find that the stories told by them are generally epic in character. Nor is it strange that the same form should prevail in the childhood of the race, before men acquire habits of scrutiny and analysis.

The dramatic form, on the contrary, is necessarily a later result of observation. No child resorts to mimicry except with reference to scenes with which he has become somewhat familiar. It is usually the mode in which he echoes an old opinion, or reiterates an old story. There is a reason, therefore, founded on the very nature of things, why a great dramatist like Shakespeare should appropriate old plots. There is still more reason why all the art of a later age should incline toward the dramatic. Indeed, it is a question whether an attempt to write in the epic form in modern times among people who have become accustomed to a large exertion of individual thought and feeling with reference to everything that they observe, has not some tendency in the direction of affectation unbecoming the dignity of art. Especially are we led to surmise this when we recall that the highest development of the epic has always been considered to be the heroic, and that the highest development of the heroic deals with gods and goddesses. Certainly these beings, to whom it was natural to refer in a superstitious age, are very unnatural personages to introduce into a poem of the nineteenth century. As a fact, few believe in them now, and to pretend to believe in them involves an attitude of mind not naturally expressive of the race's maturity. Not that the less mature form is not deserving of very great admiration. All of us capable of tenderness and sympathy regard with pleasurable interest and fascination the pranks and prattle of the children. But we should hardly fascinate the household, were we ourselves to imitate them. A different form of expression is appropriate to maturity.

The same principle is true in art. The "Inferno" and the "Paradise Lost" are great as epics; but they are inferior to the "Iliad"; and, proportionately, perhaps, as the world advances, productions that are epic in form will be less and less successful. This is not the same as to say that the epic is artistically inferior to either of the other two, or to claim that one of them, as Aristotle claimed of the dramatic, is superior. Take, for instance, the rank that may be assigned to each of them, owing to the nature of its subject-matter. As judged by this alone the epic should apparently rank highest. Taine, in his "Ideal in Art," as translated by J. Durand, points out that one way of determining the relative values of artistic products is by the degrees of importance of the character delineated. "All things in other respects being equal," he says, "according as the character set forth in a book is more or less important, that is to say more or less elementary and stable, this book becomes more or less beautiful, and you will see the layers of the moral strata communicate to the literary works which express them their proper degree of power and duration. . . . On the surface of man are grafted manners, ideas, a kind of character which lasts three or four years, such as that of fashion and the passing hour. . . . Below this we find a substratum of character a little more solid; it lasts twenty, thirty, and forty years, about the half of an historic period. . . . We have now reached the substratum of the third order, which is very vast and very deep. The characters composing it last a whole historic period, like the Middle Ages, the Renaissance, and the Classic period." Then he speaks of the characters of communities and of races. " Finally, at the lowest stage, are found the characters peculiar to every superior race capable of spontaneous civilization, that is to say, endowed with that aptitude for general ideas which is the appanage of man, and which leads him to found societies, religions, philosophies, and arts; similar dispositions subsist through all the differences of race; and the physiological diversities which master the rest do not succeed in affecting them. . . . The superior rank and the first importance belong to the most stable characters; and if these are more stable, it is that, being more elementary, they are present on a much larger surface and are swept away only by a greater revolution."

The truth of all this, so far as it goes, no one would dispute. To apply it to our present subject, it makes evident that of the three forms of art which have been mentioned, the epic, having for its purpose to give embodiment to general ideas, is much more apt to occupy that superior rank which belongs " to the most stable characters . . . present on a much larger surface," and " swept away only by a greater revolution." Nothing certainly can be more important or stable than the sublime and grand ideas to which the themes of the highest forms of epic art are allied. Their attractiveness, depending little upon transient, definite, and local conditions, may be felt lastingly and universally in a sense that is not necessarily true of realistic or dramatic products. These last may be capable of exciting greater interest in the particular age and country for which they are written, but because of the different phases of individual characters and customs peculiar to different periods and nations, their subject-matter is, on the whole, less likely than that of the epic to awaken general and permanent interest. This is especially true of the products of realistic art. Their subjects, because associated almost entirely with the local and the transient, are exceptionally restricted in range and durability of influence.

But the different values of artistic products, besides being determined by "the degrees of importance of the character delineated," may be determined, according to Taine, by the "beneficence of the character." "At the lowest step of all," he says, "are the types preferred by the literature of realism and by the comic drama; *i. e.*, simpletons and egotists, weak and inferior natures." . . . Next, "a family of powerful but incomplete types, and generally wanting in balance. Some passion, some faculty, some disposition or other of mind or of character is developed in them with enormous accretion, like a hypertrophied organ, at the expense of the rest, amidst all sorts of ravages and misfortunes. Such is the ordinary theme of dramatic and philosophic literature. . . . Advancing a step farther, we encounter complete personages, true heroes. We find many such in the dramatic and philosophic literature of which I have just spoken. . . . But creations truly ideal are fertile only in primitive and simple epochs."

These last quotations indicate their own moral. Whether we classify the products of art according to the degrees of the beneficence or to the degrees of the importance of the character, we arrive at the same result. So far as concerns the significance expressed in art, the epic has what we may term the greatest natural advantages. As indicated in the summary on page 311, of all subjects that can be treated, its are the most nearly allied to sublimity. Where they fall short of this, at all events they are generally grand and dignified ; and the persons who are described, whether in their repulsions or attractions, are, as a rule, heroic. But in realistic and dramatic art, a fitful sublimity or grandeur is soon exhausted, and instead of heroes we have merely heroism.

Yet from what has been said, let us not rush to the conclusion that, therefore, the epic is, in all regards, superior to all other forms of art. As related to the general subject-matter to be expressed, this form certainly possesses great advantages. But we must remember that the subject-matter, or theme, is only one requisite of art. A second feature is the form or body to be given to the theme ; and this, in all cases, is taken from the world of physical reality, as made prominent in the realistic. A third feature, too, is the way in which the form or body is made to conform to individual psychical or emotional requirements, as in the dramatic. Or, to change our phraseology, art involves beauty of expression ; and this, as brought out in Chapters X. to XV. of " Art in Theory," involves the fulfilment of requirements emphasizing sometimes the subject-matter, as in the epic ; sometimes the appearances of nature represented in the form, as in the realistic ; and sometimes the way in which the subject-matter has taken possession of the representative form, as in the dramatic. To take a department of art that fulfils in all regards only one of these requirements, and to say that it alone realizes the best that art can accomplish, is evidently unphilosophical. Yet we probably all know many who do this. Some, apparently thinking that nothing can have the highest excellence that was not originated in the past, assign superiority to the epic. Some, apparently hoping to convince people that the epic work of Homer, Dante, or Michael Angelo, or the dramatic work of Raphael, Shakespeare, or Goethe, is inferior to the work of their own age, if not to their own individual work, assign superiority to the realistic; and some, apparently imagining a far more exclusive interpretation of the words of the poet than he himself conceived when saying

All the world's a stage
And all the men and women merely players
—*As You Like It*, ii., 7: *Shakespeare*—

rank the dramatic highest. It certainly seems more discriminating to hold that, in certain circumstances, each of the three may be the most appropriate, and therefore the most successful; for there are times and ways in which each influences us differently. The epic artists, Michael Angelo and Milton, may inspire our admiration; but not as frequently as the realistic artists, Teniers and Burns, do they stir our sympathies; nor, as the dramatic artists, Raphael and Shakespeare, broaden our enthusiasms.

It is well, also, in drawing distinctions, to recognize that our classifications should not themselves be made too exclusive. It has been said that sublimity is a characteristic of the thought embodied in the epic, picturesqueness of that in the realistic, and brilliancy of that in the dramatic. But let it not be supposed that therefore any one of these forms of art contains merely one of these qualities. A great epic product must be sublime; a great realistic one, picturesque; a great dramatic one, brilliant; but in every epic product, especially in its lower forms, as, for instance, in the metrical romance, there is much that is picturesque and brilliant; and in every dramatic product, especially in its higher forms, as in tragedy, there is much that is sublime and picturesque.

Therefore, though the eternal, infinite, and absolute truth may be germane to the epic, there are instances in which both realistic and dramatic art may rise to it; and in art, as in life, a high result attained in spite of natural disadvantages, for this very reason, seems deserving of higher commendation. He who in the wisdom of mature life still retains the purity of childhood, seems doubly worthy of regard. Why should not the same be true of dramatic or realistic art, whenever either reveals the nobler range of thought peculiar to the epic?

Possibly, just here, some reader may be prompted to ask whether the distinctions between the epic, the realistic, and the dramatic that have been made in this chapter, are really necessary; whether they have, after all, any practical bearing. The answer will be found in "The Genesis of Art-Form," particularly in Chapters VIII. and IX., which unfold the importance in art of producing an impression of *unity*, especially through *congruity* between different parts of the thought and the treatment. An art-product that is neither distinctly epic, realistic, nor dramatic is lacking in definiteness of *form*, and is felt to be so, and, therefore, its effect is inartistic. Wholly satisfactory results can be attained by the artist in only the degree in which he recognizes clearly both the limitations and the possibilities that distinguish such divisions and subdivisions of art in general as are to be considered in the chapters following.

CHAPTER XIX.

THE EPIC, REALISTIC, AND DRAMATIC IN POETRY.

Epic, Realistic and Dramatic Subdivisions in All the Arts — Necessity of Certain New Terms for Some of These—Chart of—Definitions of the Epic Derived from Combining Previous Definitions — Its Symbolic Form — Allegoric Form — The Epic Proper — Realistic Poetry — Its Didactic Form—Wide Range of—Its Naturalistic Form—Treating of Natural Scenery—With not Sufficient Individualism to Awaken Sympathy—Yet Nature may be Made Human—Narrative Form of the Realistic and the Ballad—The Dramatic as Distinguished especially from the Epic—Its Subjective Form in the Lyric—How Differing from the Didactic—The Naturalistic Narrative—The Protactic, a New Term —But Needed and Applicable ; Illustrations—The Drama.

IT will avoid repetition and, in other regards, be equally satisfactory to consider in the different arts the various exemplifications of the Epic, the Realistic, and the Dramatic forms at the same time that we consider in the same arts certain subdivisions of these forms. The chart on page 325 will indicate what these subdivisions are.

At first glance, certain arrangements of the chart may seem fanciful; and all the more so, inasmuch as some of the terms employed are new. But this latter fact, as will be made clear presently, was unavoidable. For instance, in the art of poetry, which we shall consider first, the names of the different styles, still preserved in all our works upon the subject, have been handed down from a time anterior to the existence of some of the forms which are now the most popular, as Robert Browning's "The Ring and the Book," Mrs. Browning's, "Aurora Leigh,"

Tennyson's "Princess," Robert Bulwer Lytton's "Lucile," Byron's "Corsair," and a host of others too numerous to mention. Strictly speaking, these are neither epic, lyric, pastoral, elegiac, didactic, dramatic, descriptive, nor satiric. Great artists and great schools of artists originate new forms. Why should not critics designate these by new terms? Aside from this fact too, the ordinary terms, such as have just been quoted, exemplify no single principle of classification. What, for instance, is to hinder the dramatic from being satiric? the pastoral from being descriptive? or the elegiac from being didactic? One need not dwell upon these questions. Their answer is evident.

In order to show the general connection of the chart with the development of the thought in the chapters immediately preceding this, notice the following repetition of the summaries already given in them.

Significance in Representative Form according as its Tendency is

Religious		Instinctive		Subjective	and	Idealism
Scientific	is, in derivation	Reflective	in character	Relative	is	Realism or
or		or		or	expressed	
Artistic		Emotive		Objective	in	Idealized-realism

Religious-Artistic	Tendencies pass respectively into	the Good	the Sublime	the Grand	and into	Epic	Form
Scientific-Artistic		the True	the Picturesque	the Simple		Realistic or	
Artistic-Artistic		the Beautiful	the Brilliant	the Striking		Dramatic	

Let us turn now to the chart on page 325, and consider, first, the subdivisions in poetry of the *epic form*. "According to Aristotle," says Quackenbos in his "Rhetoric," "the plot of an epic must be important in itself and instructive in the reflections it suggests; must be

SUBDIVISIONS OF ART-FORMS

Tendency		POETRY	MUSIC	PAINTING	SCULPTURE	ARCHITECTURE
Epic	The Religious, Subjective, or Epic	Symbolic	Fantasia	Symbolic	Symbolic	Of Vaulted Support in Round Arches as in Byzantine
	Scientific, Relative, or Realistic	Allegoric	Fugue	Allegoric	Allegoric	Later Etruscan
	Artistic, Objective, or Dramatic	Typical Heroic or Epic Proper	Symphony	Typical Heroic or Epic Proper	Typical Heroic or Epic Proper	Romanesque
Realistic	Religious, Subjective, or Epic	Didactic	Of Accompaniment	Decorative	Architectural	Of Horizontal Support in Straight Lines as in Egyptian and Grecian
	Scientific, Relative, or Realistic	when also Naturalistic or Descriptive	when also Naturalistic	when also Naturalistic	when also Naturalistic	Roman and Renaissance
	Artistic, Objective, or Dramatic	Narrative	Analogic	Historic	Commemorative	Revived Grecian Romo-Grecian
Dramatic	Religious, Subjective, or Epic	Lyric	Song	Character	Character	Of Perpendicular Support in Straight Lines and Pointed Arches as in Arabesque
	Scientific, Relative, or Realistic	Protactic	Oratorio	Pantomimic	Pantomimic	Tudor
	Artistic, Objective, or Dramatic	The Drama	The Opera	Dramatic Proper	Dramatic Proper	Gothic

Each respectively develops the Subdivisions in each of these Arts filled with suitable incidents, as well as enlivened with a variety of characters and descriptions; and must retain throughout propriety of character and elevation of style." Besides this, Hart in his "Rhetoric" maintains that the "epic should have a hero." But a clearer idea of this form is conveyed in Long's "Art, its Laws, and the Reasons for Them." Quoting Blair's definition in his "Rhetoric" that it is the "illustrating of some great and general idea in verse," he goes on to say: "This we adopt as the best that we can find, as in the definition we discover the great characteristic difference between epic and dramatic writing, 'the tragedy of which,' says Mr. Blair, 'has for its object compassion, and the comedy of it ridicule.' The epic is further distinguished from the drama by the broad and liberal manner in which everything is conducted, by its admitting no discrimination of character, nothing, in short, that is individually characteristic, other than as that individual trait illustrates the leading idea of the poem, as exemplified in the parting scene between Hector and Andromache in the Iliad, a poem whose subject is 'War,'—it being there admitted, not to exhibit a phase of the character of Hector and Andromache, but because such scenes constitute a feature in all warlike operations. . . . No character is discriminated but where discrimination discovers a new look of war; no passion is raised but what is blown up by the breath of war, and as soon absorbed in its universal blaze. As in a conflagration we see turrets and spires and temples illuminated only to propagate the horrors of destruction, so through the stormy page of Homer we see his heroes and his heroines only by the light that blasts them." All this accords, as will be recognized, with what was said of the epic in Chapter XVIII., namely, that it is the illustrating of a great idea or spiritual principle through forms that are typical of the general nature of its influence. Without further comment, every one will recognize this characteristic in the heroic or epic proper, as exemplified in such poems as the "Iliad," "Æneid," and "Paradise Lost."

But before we take up the epic proper, let us consider the two other forms into which, in the chart on page 325, the epic is subdivided. The first of these, the most subjective form, is termed the *symbolic*. The following, for instance, reads as if intended to be an accurate description of what we all recognize to be a symbolic painting:

> The Register that up this order drew
> Is Time itself clad all in azure blue,
> Winged like an angel, shadowed with a veile,
> And Truth his daughter bearing up his traile,
> Nobly attended with a Lady kind,
> More quick and nimble than the swift foot hind.
> Within his mouth a lofty Trumpe did stand,
> And a sharp scythe or sickle in his hand.
> *The Glasse of Time: Thomas Peyton.*

This may properly be termed *symbolic* poetry; and, as most of us will recall, it characterizes many so-called epics, especially those whose writers affect what is called the classic style. It is, perhaps, impossible for it to predominate throughout a long product; but we find an immense amount of it not only in real epics, but in such as are merely didactic poems with epic passages, like Pollok's "Course of Time" and Peyton's "Glasse of Time." Besides this form of poetry, however, another, not at all classic in the sense just indicated, is also called symbolic. It is a form mainly used in France in an endeavor to express through words more than the words themselves express,—a perfectly proper endeavor except where it is supposed to be a sufficient excuse for hinting at all sorts and degrees of triviality through all sorts and degrees of vagueness,—in fact for violating the very first condition of poetic art, which is that it should be constructed of words and phrases, which are not mere sounds but sounds with definite meanings. The only justifiable symbolism constructed upon the principle which the French have in mind, is that which conveys, through a perfectly apprehended surface-meaning, a profounder meaning which is not upon the surface, as in the following representation of an idealist:

"Whom lovest thou best, enigmatical man, say, thy father, thy mother, thy sister, or thy brother?"
"I have neither father nor mother nor sister nor brother."
"Thy friends?"
"You use there a word whose sense has to this day remained unknown to me."
"Thy fatherland?"
"I know not in what latitude it is situated."
"Beauty?"
"I would fain love it, godlike and immortal."
"Gold?"
"I hate it as you hate God."
"Eh? What lovest thou then, extraordinary stranger?"
"I love the clouds . . . the clouds that pass . . . over there . . . the marvellous clouds."

The Stranger: Baudelaire, tr. by Stuart Merrill. From "*Pastels in Prose.*" Copyright *1890* by Harper & Brothers.

In English poetry, effects resembling this are uncommon, and, of course, difficult to find, which is a sufficient excuse for using the following. It appears to tell of a love experience, and, like the forms of a symbolic painting, the words are intelligible, if accepted as referring to this alone. But they mean more. They are symbolic of a universal law of human life, namely, that, to be successful, a man while following to some extent his own ideals, must also avail himself of his opportunities, and accommodate his ideals to them. But in the poem this general principle is suggested, not stated :

> She came ; and I who lingered there,
> I saw that she was very fair ;
> And, with my sighs that pride suppressed,
> There rose a trembling wish for rest.
>> But I, who had my own design
>> For destiny that should be mine,
>> I turned me to my task and wrought,
>> And so forgot the passing thought.
>
> She paused ; and I who questioned there,
> I heard she was as good as fair ;
> And in my soul a still small voice
> Enjoined me not to check my choice.
>> But I, who had my own design
>> For destiny that should be mine,
>> I bade the gentle guardian down,
>> And tried to think about renown.
>
> She left ; and I who wander fear
> There comes no more to see or hear ;
> Those walls that ward my Paradise
> Are very high, nor open twice.
>> And I, who had my own design
>> For destiny that should be mine,
>> Can only wait without the gate,
>> And sit and sigh—" Too late ! too late ! "
>
> *The Destiny-Maker: G. L. Raymond.*

The question is not whether this kind of poetry is symbolic, but whether it should be termed so by way of distinction. If, as brought out in Chapters X. and XI., all art should present arguments from analogy, verses like these, so far as the symbolic means the representing of the general through the special, do no more than all poetry should do, if of an artistic quality. Moreover, is there not a clear distinction between symbolizing a truth, as these verses do, through phraseology that is perfectly intelligible even if no symbolism be detected in it, and symbolizing the same through personifications like those of Time and Truth in the quotation on page 327,—personifications involving phraseology the very first meaning of which, as all recognize, is symbolic? And if so, are we not justified in confining the term symbolic to such cases; and in allowing the more subordinate and comparatively incidental symbolic method illustrated in the quotation on page 329 to be termed, in accordance with one or another of the principles to be unfolded hereafter, either realistic or lyric?

The next subdivision of epic poetry, the *allegoric*, is epic in the sense that in it, too, the general truth that is illustrated—and it is usually a religious or moral truth—aside from the details through which it is represented, is of primary importance. The "Faerie Queen" of Spenser, which is usually classed as a metrical romance, was designed, according to its author, "to fashion a gentleman or noble person in virtues and gentle discipline." In it, the twelve private moral virtues are represented in the persons of twelve knights, and their various adventures are designed to teach lessons with reference to these virtues. In the same sense, too, though humorous, "The Dunciad," by Pope, in which he depicted the fate of the literary dunces of his period, is an allegorical form of the epic.

Under the epic proper, besides the great poems mentioned on page 327, we may place Tennyson's "Idyls of the King." It should be said, however, that the idyls of Theocritus, which suggested the title, were less epic than realistic; and parts of them were also, to some extent, lyric. Like Tennyson's "Dora," they treat of simple stories of natural life. The "Idyls of the King," on the contrary, treat distinctively of heroes, living in a supernatural atmosphere, and by their conduct representing, in accordance with what was said on page 312, the influence, upon typical persons and events, of great ideas and spiritual principles. See the quotation from "Morte d'Arthur" on page 458. Therefore though, owing to the less emphasized unity of the plot, this poem perhaps must rank with the "Odyssey" of Homer rather than with his "Iliad," or with the "Æneid," the "Divine Comedy," or the "Paradise Lost," it must nevertheless be classed as epic.

Under the general head of *realistic* poetry one may include all that large class in which characters, scenes, or events are treated as if interesting chiefly on account of what they are seen to be in themselves without reference to the general idea which their appearances illustrate, as in the epic, or to the special characteristics which their actions manifest, as in the dramatic. Undoubtedly the realistic, in some of its forms, because so nearly allied to the scientific, is not supremely artistic. Nevertheless, it is the most common form of poetry, the works even of the greatest poets being full of passages exemplifying it.

The religious or subjective development of this form is found in what is known as the *didactic*. This term, applied to poetry that deals with what is true or real in principle as well as in illustration, is derived from a Greek word meaning to teach; and in the chart it is indicated that the didactic is not a legitimate form of poetry except when it is also *descriptive* in the sense of *naturalistic* or *narrative*, which conception is paralleled by indicating that except when also *naturalistic*, the *decorative* does not belong to the art of painting nor the *architectural* to the art of sculpture. This is the same as to indicate that the *didactic* is not a legitimate form of poetry, nor the *decorative* of painting, nor the *architectural* of sculpture, except so far as it is made so through an accompanying and distinctively artistic method of treatment. In poetry, for instance, it is the descriptive or narrative illustrations that make the didactic acceptable. Notice this fact as exemplified in these verses:

> Man, like the generous vine, supported lives;
> The strength he gains is from the embrace he gives.
>
> *Essay on Man, iii. : Pope.*

> The fiery soul abhorred in Catiline,
> In Decius charms, in Curtius is divine:
> The same ambition can destroy or save,
> And makes a patriot as it makes a knave.
>
> *Idem, ii.*

Again the following didactic lines—didactic because the lesson in them is indicated so clearly—exhibit as much imagination—but not art—as they might do if presented in an epic or dramatic form:

> Self-love but serves the virtuous mind to wake,
> As the small pebble stirs the peaceful lake;
> The centre moved, a circle straight succeeds,
> Another still, and still another spreads;
> Friend, parent, neighbor, first it will embrace;
> His country next, and next all human race;
> Wide and more wide, th' o'erflowings of the mind
> Take every creature in of every kind:
> Earth smiles around, with boundless bounty blest,
> And heaven beholds its image in his breast.
>
> *Essay on Man, iv.: Pope.*

The very wide range of didactic poetry includes most discoursive and meditative products, such as Horace's "Art of Poetry," Pope's "Essay on Man," Cowper's "Task,"

Young's "Night Thoughts," Campbell's "Pleasures of Hope," and Akenside's "Pleasures of the Imagination." In all of these the subject-matter seems intended to cause reflection and awaken thought according to the methods of logic fully as much as to cause perception and appeal to the sympathies according to the methods of analogy. In fact, one might almost hold that this poetry necessitates a scientific action of mind fully as much as an artistic. But though this be true of its subject-matter, the treatment is often poetically redeemed, as has just been exemplified, by the descriptions or narratives that illustrate the subject-matter.

Of the other developments of realistic poetry, we come first to that which in the chart is termed *naturalistic*. This term is preferred to *descriptive* (which sometimes includes the *narrative*), because *naturalistic* is not quite so indefinite in its meaning as applied to poetry, and, at the same time, can be applied to corresponding developments in the arts of sight. Of the naturalistic, we may make two divisions:—the one, of works that do not treat of the aspects of human life; and the other, of works that do. Some of the critics foreign to England have argued that compositions such as are particularly characteristic of that country—compositions which do not treat of human life but only of natural scenery—are not legitimate to the art of poetry. But this is going too far. Such poetry may not appeal strongly to the æsthetic tastes of all. But the reason for this may be the same that prevents much of the art of landscape-gardening, as developed in England, from appealing to all. Just why it is a fact would be difficult to determine, but it is a fact that to commune with nature exactly as it reveals itself seems more germane to the Anglo-Saxon mind than to any other. One seldom sees in England the clipping of trees into artificial shapes that one finds in the parks of the continent of Europe; nor, on the continent, such a degree of adaptation of roadways and walks to the lay of the land, as in England. At the same time the naturalistic tendency in poetry may be carried to inartistic extremes. Owing probably to a certain phase of influence exerted by Thomson, Wordsworth, and Tennyson, it is not too much to say that, frequently, among English-speaking people, the supreme test applied to new poetry is the degree of accuracy with which the words that are used depict the objects of nature to which they refer—*i. e.*, do approximately what a painter does when imitating in line and color. To do this undoubtedly involves an artistic use of language; but it does not involve, as some of these critics evidently suppose, the only nor even the most artistic use of it. In neither the Bible nor in Greek or Latin poetry is there much descriptive language of this kind. The most important element in rendering language artistic is that which makes it imaginative; and it becomes this through imaging in material form spiritual — by which is meant both intellectual and emotional—conceptions. Accurate descriptions of nature may make the material form of the image seem more natural, and therefore more artistically effective, and thus cause it to fulfil an important function as a means to an end. But they are not an end in themselves, as they evidently are supposed to be by the writer of the following:

> Fiercely the gaunt woods to the grim soil cling
> That bears for all fair fruits,
> Wan wild sparse flowers of windy and wintry spring
> Between the tortive serpent-shapen roots,
> Where through their dim growth hardly strikes and shoots
> And shews one gracious thing;

Hardly, to speak for summer one sweet word
Of summer's self scarce heard.
But higher the steep green sterile fields, thick-set
With flowerless hawthorn even to the upward verge
Whence the woods gathering watch new cliffs emerge
Higher than their highest of crowns that sea-winds fret,
Hold fast, for all that night or wind can say,
Some pale pure color yet,
Too dim for green and luminous for gray.
On the Cliffs : Swinburne.

For in no deeps of midmost inland May
More flower-bright flowers the hawthorn, or more sweet
Swells the wild gold of the earth for wandering feet ;
For on no northland way
Crowds the close whin-bloom closer, set like thee
With thorns about for fangs of sea-rock shown
Through blithe lips of the bitter brine to lea ;
Nor blithelier landward comes the sea-wind blown,
Nor blithelier leaps the land-wind back to sea.
The Garden of Cymodoce : Swinburne.

The interest in this form of poetry resembles too nearly that which one takes in a curio. The natural scene or object described is treated as the central point of attention, and about this the mind is made to work according to the method of the artisan rather than of the artist. In that highest form of art which we find in the humanities, the human mind is at the centre, and the natural objects described are made to revolve around it, and are kept subordinate to it. We are all familiar with this method as exemplified in such poems as Bryant's "Thanatopsis," Thomson's "Seasons," and Wordsworth's "Prelude" and "Excursion." It may be well, however, before directing attention to the illustration of the method in the following quotation, to say that the poetry of Wordsworth is exceedingly difficult to classify. The thought, though suggested by nature, shows a constant tendency to transcend its limitations as in the epic. In fact, we often feel like classing him with Milton. But, on the other hand, his ode entitled "Intimations of Immortality" and other of his shorter poems are distinctly lyrical. The main body of his work, however, seems to be about equally divided among all three forms — *i. e.*, the didactic, the naturalistic, and the narrative — of the realistic, *e. g.*:

> Earth hath not anything to show more fair;
> Dull would he be of soul who could pass by
> A sight so touching in its majesty:
> The city now doth like a garment wear
> The beauty of the morning; silent, bare.
> Ships, towers, domes, theatres, and temples lie
> Open unto the fields and to the sky,
> All bright and glittering in the smokeless air.
> Never did sun more beautifully steep
> In his first splendor, valley, rock, or hill;
> Ne'er saw I, never felt, a calm so deep!
> The river glideth at his own sweet will:
> Dear God! the very houses seem asleep;
> And all that mighty heart is lying still!
> *Sonnet on Westminster Bridge: Wordsworth.*

From what has been said, it follows necessarily that the objection mentioned on page 333 does not apply to that form of naturalistic art which treats of human life,—a fact which may be illustrated by recalling Goldsmith's "Deserted Village," Burns's "Cotter's Saturday Night," Byron's "Childe Harold," Campbell's "Gertrude of Wyoming," or Beattie's "Minstrel." Of course, too, the reason why such poems cannot be classed with the narrative form of the epic is because there is no single general idea underlying their plots which, as in the epic, is the determining cause of the whole and of which the different facts narrated are merely so many illustrations. On the contrary, the facts themselves often suggest the ideas, *e. g.*:

> From scenes like these old Scotia's grandeur springs,
>   That makes her loved at home, revered abroad :
> Princes and lords are but the breath of kings,
>   "An honest man's the noblest work of God."
> And certes in fair virtue's heavenly road,
>   The cottage leaves the palace far behind ;
> What is a lordling's pomp? — a cumbrous load,
>   Disguising oft the wretch of human kind,
>   Studied in arts of hell, in wickedness refined !
>
> *Cotter's Saturday Night: **Burns.***

Burns is essentially a realistic poet. Let us recognize him as such.

The last and most artistic form of realistic poetry is the *narrative*, including works like Chaucer's "Canterbury Tales" and Morris's "Earthly Paradise," as well as almost everything cast in the ancient form of the ballad. This latter form, by the way, is often misunderstood. Psychologically, it is the result of such interest in successive details that the writer has no inclination to stop in order to express his own opinions or feelings with reference to them. This mood gives simplicity to the style and consequent speed to the movement, and makes any expression at all which is strictly *subjective* rather than *relative*[1] in its character entirely out of place. Modern poetry, as developed by Keats and Byron and their followers, has seldom been characterized by this form of simplicity, and this is the reason why so few modern ballads are successful, notwithstanding the fact that attempts to write them are carried often to the extreme of artificiality. Even if a writer of the present does express the ballad spirit in the only style that would be natural to a narrator of the unromantic homespun period that he is representing, he is more than likely to be accused of writing doggerel, notwithstanding that almost every page contains lines like these:

---

[1] See page 273.

> God guided it and us, alas,
> But how he scorch'd our heaven to pass
>   His finger through the skies!
> *Our First Break with the British: G. L. Raymond.*

> And they forgot, we mountaineers,
>   High rangers, like the Swiss,
> Had learn'd to value freedom's world
>   By looking down on this!
>
> . . . .
>
> Too few were they to brave a fort
>   Well mann'd at every gun;
> Yet those who slight the light of stars
>   But seldom see their sun.
> *Ethan Allen: Idem.*

Other illustrations of the various forms of realistic poetry will be given in connection with what is to be said now of *dramatic* poetry.

"In our analysis of 'the epic,'" says Mr. Long, in his "Art, its Laws, and the Reasons for Them," "we stated that the business of both the epic poet and the epic painter was the illustrating of some great general idea, and that to this everything else was subordinate. On the other hand, the avowed object of both the dramatic writer and painter is to exhibit character, to develop the passions, to lay open the heart, and to excite in every bosom corresponding emotions. Whatever, therefore, by reflected self-love, inspires us with hope, fear, pity, terror, love, or mirth, is the legitimate sphere of both the dramatic poet and painter." It is in strict accordance with this that it has been said that the dramatic, in distinction from the epic, which is the illustrating of a great idea or spiritual principle through forms that are typical of the general nature of its influence, is the impersonating of individual character, as manifested in action excited both from within the mind and from without it.

The subjective form of the dramatic seems to be the *lyric*. This term is derived from the same word as the term *lyre*, and originally was applied to poetry composed to be accompanied by the lyre; and, as a fact, was usually accompanied by both music and dancing. In other words, it was composed to be used in a primitive form of acting. Hence it seems right to infer an organic connection between it and the drama. " Lyric poetry," says Chaignet, in his " Les Principes de la Science du Beau," " appears to us to be a subdivision of dramatic poetry; for it consists, as appears to us, eminently in action. The ode is the form which takes words to express a solitary action of a single actor, at least most frequently." In addition to this, Chaignet might have said that the lyric not only represents action—the epic does the same—but, like the soliloquy, it represents character, and character under excitement moving on from the expression of one emotion to that of another. It will be understood, of course, as was brought out in Chapter XIII., that emotion is expressed in all forms of art; but in the artistic-artistic phase of it represented in the dramatic form, the emotional effects are particularly emphasized. The term *lyric cry* is often used by critics. What does this indicate except a recognition that, in this form of poetry, the soul, as in the case of one crying out in excitement, is over-mastered by the impulse from within. Yet there is little suggestion that the thought or emotion, as in the epic condition, is absolutely too great to be adequately expressed. There is often a suggestion of the opposite. Judging of the persons who cry loudest, and of the circumstances in which they do so, it might be argued that this form of expression, as a rule, exaggerates the amount and quality of the experience; and this is the condition in dramatic art. Viewed with this in mind, any one who will examine a typical lyric will be interested in observing how few traces it manifests of either the *epic* or the *realistic*. In neither of the following, for example, are there any great ideas illustrated, as in the epic; nor many facts delineated in the order of their sequence and interdependence, as in the realistic. Nothing is mentioned except what is necessary in order to reveal to us how the poet's individual imagination has been affected by the suggestions received. Just as, through a few outlines, a good draughtsman gives us a conception of a whole form, so the lyric poet, through a few words, gives us a conception of a whole series of scenes or events. But in the lyric these few words do more than represent, as in realistic art, what exists or may be supposed to exist. They create something that without them would not exist. They give apprehensible form to impressions made upon thought and feeling; form too which is represented not merely in a few words and phrases, as illustrated on page 200, but in whole poems. In what sense this is true, will be found explained from one point of view in Chapter VI. of "The Genesis of Art-Form," and from another point of view in Chapter XXVI. of "Poetry as a Representative Art." At present it is enough for the reader to observe how entirely the æsthetic interest awakened by the following is an interest not in any great idea illustrated nor in successive events accurately detailed, but in the *form* which the writer has constructed in order, through it, to represent the particular character of the emotional *effects* which, owing to his own poetic sensibilities, he himself has, or may be supposed to have, experienced:

" O Mary, go and call the cattle home,
    And call the cattle home,
    And call the cattle home,
  Across the sands o' Dee ! "
The western wind was wild and dank wi' foam,
  And all alone went she.

The creeping tide came up along the sand,
    And o'er and o'er the sand,
    And round and round the sand,
  As far as eye could see ;
The blinding mist came down and hid the land :
  And never home came she.

" O is it weed, or fish, or floating hair—
    A tress o' golden hair,
    O' drownèd maiden's hair—
  Above the nets at sea?
Was never salmon yet that shone so fair,
  Among the stakes on Dee."

They rowed her in across the rolling foam—
    The cruel, crawling foam,
    The cruel, hungry foam—
  To her grave beside the sea ;
But still the boatmen hear her call the cattle home
  Across the sands o' Dee.

      O Mary, Go and Call the Cattle Home : Kingsley.

The sun had scattered each opal cloud,
  And the flowers had waked from their winter's rest,
The song of the skylark rang free and loud,
  And ah ! there were eggs in the swallow's nest !
And for joy of the spring that so sweet appears,
I sang with the singing of twenty years.

Out from the meadows there passed a maid,—
  How can I tell you why she was fair ?
To see was to love as she bent her head
  Over the brooklet that murmured there.
As I gazed, in an April of hopes and fears,
I dreamed with the dreaming of twenty years.

> Next,—for I saw her just once again,—
> Just once in that rare spring-tide,—
> I felt a heart-throb of vague sweet pain,
> For I noticed that some one was by her side !
> And I turned, with a passion of sudden tears,
> For they loved with the loving of twenty years.
> *Twenty Years : Trs. from the French of E. Barateau.*

There is no great liability of confounding the lyric with the epic; but there is of confounding the lyric with the realistic. The tendency may be best avoided perhaps by remembering that the lyric is always dramatic ; and that in the dramatic, as contrasted with the realistic, imagination is never itself subordinated to natural conditions or forms; it clothes itself in these forms, and makes them give expression to its own activities, — in fact, it makes the forms take on character, and often its own character. The following, for instance, is realistically didactic. It is an exhortation expressing a conscious subordination of thought and feeling to certain great realities of life:

> Not enjoyment, and not sorrow,
> Is our destined end or way ;
> But to act, that each to-morrow
> Find us farther than to-day.
> . . . .
> Trust no future, howe'er pleasant !
> Let the dead Past bury its dead !
> Act,—act in the living Present !
> Heart within, and God o'erhead !
> *A Psalm of Life : Longfellow.*

A similar thought expressed as follows is lyric. It is an exultant cry expressing conscious ability to subordinate certain realities of life to one's own thought and feeling :

> Not in vain the distance beacons. Forward, forward let us range.
> Let the great world spin forever down the ringing grooves of change.
> . . . .

O, I see the crescent promise of my spirit hath not set.
Ancient fonts of inspiration well through all my fancy yet.
Locksley Hall: Tennyson.

The following, devoid, as it is, of any suggestion of character, almost of any action that has affected character, is realistically descriptive of nature:

> Below me trees unnumbered rise,
> Beautiful in various dyes:
> The gloomy pine, the poplar blue,
> The yellow beech, the sable yew,
> . . . .
>
> And see the rivers how they run
> Through woods and meads, in shade and sun,
> Sometimes swift, and sometimes slow,—
> Wave succeeding wave, they go
> A various journey to the deep,
> Like human life to endless sleep.
> *Grongar Hill: John Dyer.*

Tennyson's "Farewell" illustrates a descriptive phase of the lyric. Instead of placing man and nature side by side, it reveals him expressing his own moods, through referring to nature:

> Flow down, cold rivulet, to the sea,
>   Thy tribute wave deliver;
> No more by thee my steps shall be
>   Forever and forever.
>
> A thousand suns will stream on thee,
>   A thousand moons will quiver,
> But not by thee my steps shall be
>   Forever and forever.
> *The Farewell: Tennyson.*

"The Cloud" does the same emphatically. It personifies nature, and puts a man's character inside of its activities:

I am the daughter of earth and water,
   And the nursling of the sky,
I pass through the pores of the ocean and shores,
   I change, but I cannot die.
For after the rain when with never a stain
   The pavilion of heaven is bare,
And the winds and sunbeams, with their convex gleams,
   Build up the blue dome of air,—
I silently laugh at my own cenotaph,
   And out of the caverns of rain,
Like a child from the womb, like a ghost from the tomb,
   I rise and unbuild it again.
The Cloud: Shelley.

Finally, let us look at the historic or narrative phase of the realistic, as exemplified in the ancient ballad:

The stout Earl of Northumberland
   A vow to God did make,
His pleasure in the Scottish woods
   Three summer's days to take.

The chiefest harts in Chevy-Chace
   To kill and bear away;
The tidings to Earl Douglas came,
   In Scotland where he lay.

Who sent Earl Percy present word
   He would prevent his sport;
The English Earl not fearing this,
   Did to the woods resort.
More Modern Ballad of Chevy-Chace: Percy's Reliques.

In contrast to this, each of the following gives a narrative still, but it is presented dramatically; in other words, for the purpose of representing the effects exerted upon or through the characters engaged in the transactions. The passages are therefore lyric:

'T was at the royal feast for Persia won
   By Philip's warlike son;

Aloft in awful state,
    The godlike hero sate
On his imperial throne.
        .   .   .   .

The lovely Thais, by his side,
Sate like a blooming Eastern bride
In flower of youth and beauty's pride.
    Happy, happy, happy pair,
        None but the brave,
        None but the brave,
    None but the brave deserve the fair!
        .   .   .   .

Timotheus, placed on high
    Amid the tuneful quire,
    With flying fingers touched the lyre;
The trembling notes ascend the sky,
    And heavenly joys inspire.
            Alexander's Feast: Dryden.

Half a league, half a league,
Half a league onward,
All in the valley of death
    Rode the six hundred.
" Forward, the light brigade!
Charge for the guns!" he said.
Into the valley of death,
    Rode the six hundred.
        The Charge of the Light Brigade: Tennyson.

The form of the dramatic which it seems proper to place half-way between the lyric and the dramatic proper, sustaining the same relation to each respectively as the *naturalistic* to the *didactic* on the one hand and to the *historic* on the other, is the *protactic*. This is a new term; but it is appropriate, and there is occasion for its use. The word has one meaning and one only. It was formerly applied to those who appeared in the introductions of the Greek plays, for the purpose of explaining the meanings of them. "Protactic persons in plays," says Webster, "are those who give a narrative or explanation of the piece." This is exactly what is done by the writers of the form of composition to which it is proposed to apply this term. They give a narrative or explanation of a distinctly dramatic series of passages representing actions through the words of the characters depicted. These poems are not, like Scott's "Lady of the Lake," and other merely narrative poems, novels in verse. They exemplify a form of literary art not extensively used previous to the last half-century; and it seems desirable to have a term which can distinguish them. As a rule, the basis for the dramatic unity of this style of poem is the fact that the narrator himself is a principal actor in the scenes described, which he relates in the first person, *e. g.*:

> Do you see this square old yellow book I toss
> I' the air and catch again, and twirl about
> By the crumpled vellum covers,—pure crude fact
> Secreted from man's life when hearts beat hard,
> And brains, high-blooded, ticked two centuries since?
> *The Ring and the Book: R. Browning.*

> Of writing many books there is no end;
> And I who have written much in prose and verse
> For others' uses, will write now for mine,—
> Will write my story for my better self, etc.
> *Aurora Leigh: E. B. Browning.*

> R-r-r, you brute, beast, and blackguard! cowardly scamp!
> I only wish I dared burn down the house
> And spoil your sniggering! O what, you're the man?
> You're satisfied at last! You've found out Sludge?
> We'll see that presently: my turn, sir, next!
> I too can tell my story; brute, do you hear?—
> You throttled your sainted mother, that old hag,
> In just such a fit of passion; no, it was . . .

> To get this house of hers, and many a note
> Like these . . . I'll pocket them, however, . . . five,
> Ten, fifteen . . . . ay, you gave her throat the twist,
> Or else you poisoned her! Confound the cuss!
>
> *Mr. Sludge, the Medium: R. Browning.*

The form of dramatic art termed the dramatic proper, or the drama, needs little mention here. We are all acquainted with its main characteristics. The different persons in it are usually represented precisely as in life, by their own utterances, and, as portrayed on the stage, by their own actions. These two facts are the fundamental ones on which are based all the other requirements. Nothing in word or deed is usually introduced which it is not supposable that a character represented would introduce in the circumstances, nor omitted, which it is not supposable that this character would omit. Moreover, as dramatic art is particularly representative of that which is emotionally effective (see page 339), and as the effective is the result, in all cases, of more or less action, the drama, to a greater extent than any other form of poetry, must represent action. To have every character on a stage stand still, while one is declaiming a passage like the following, is fatal to success:

> Why then, you Princes,
> Do you with cheeks abashed behold our works,
> And think them shames which are, indeed, naught else
> But the protractive trials of great Jove,
> To find persistive constancy in men?
> The fineness of which metal is not found
> In Fortune's love; for them, the bold and coward,
> The wise and fool, the artist and unread,
> The hard and soft, seem all affin'd and kin:
> But, in the wind and tempest of her frown,
> Distinction with a broad and powerful fan,
> Puffing at all, winnows the light away;

And what hath mass or matter by itself
Lies rich in virtue and unmingled.
Troilus and Cressida, i., 3: Shakespeare.

Far more effective are both words and deeds, when given a form like this:

> *Macduff.* Turn, hell hound, turn!
> *Macbeth.* Of all men else have I avoided thee:
> But get thee back; my soul is too much charged
> With blood of thine already.
> *Macd.* I have no words;
> My voice is in my sword: thou bloodier villain
> Than terms can give thee out. (*They fight.*)
> *Macb.* Thou losest labor;
> As easy may'st thou the intrenchant air
> With thy keen sword impress . . .
> Before my body
> I throw my warlike shield; lay on, Macduff;
> And damned be him that first cries "Hold, enough!"
> *Macbeth, v., 7: Idem.*

CHAPTER XX.

THE EPIC, REALISTIC, AND DRAMATIC, IN MUSIC AND PAINTING.

These Forms more Difficult to Determine in Music; yet Distinguishable—The Epic in Music—The Realistic—The Dramatic—The Three Forms in Painting—Quotations from Others—Epic Painting as Symbolic—As Allegoric—As Epic Proper, Heroic or Typical—The Epic in Landscapes—The Realistic, its High Rank in the Arts of Sight; as Decorative—As Naturalistic when Imitative—When Imaginative as in Figures or Landscapes—As Historic, and how Differing from the Dramatic—Quotations—Illustrations—The Dramatic as Character-Painting—As Pantomimic—As Dramatic Proper—Dramatic Landscape.

IN music some difficulties confront us,—not peculiar, however, to an endeavor to distinguish the particular phases of artistic form that we are now considering, but incident upon all endeavors to determine with definiteness any phases of expression represented in inarticulated sounds. A complete discussion of both the possibilities and the limitations of these sounds, will be found in the essay of this series entitled "Music as a Representative Art," which is printed in the volume entitled "Rhythm and Harmony in Poetry and Music." At present, it is only necessary to direct attention to certain general considerations suggesting in what sense it is appropriate to speak of music as epic, realistic, or dramatic. To take up, first, the *epic*, there is no doubt that certain musical compositions may be termed "illustrations of general ideas." What is meant by a musical idea is explained on pages 198 and 200 to

210 of "Art in Theory," and has been well expressed by Choron, the author of the " Introduction à l' Étude Générale et Raisonnée de la Musique." " In music " he says, " and in the arts in general, we call idea that which in more exact language we call thought. However that may be, the musical thought or idea is usually a passage of melody which presents itself to the mind of the composer with all its suitable accessories. We ought also to distinguish ideas into principal and secondary. The first are suited to form the basis or foundation of a composition; the others are applied to the development of the principal ideas." Now in certain varieties of music, it is easy to perceive the subordination of every special or secondary to some general or principal idea. We listen in a mood disposed rather to feel after this general idea than to rest contented with special separate effects. Perhaps one could say more appropriately, we attempt to feel the general idea through experiencing the separate effects. But this, and this alone, is the legitimate influence of epic art.

To separate epic music into departments of it corresponding to symbolic, allegoric, and heroic poetry, is difficult and not important. In a general way, however, it may be said that the capriccio and the *fantasia*, which are the least constrained by the rules of precise form, represent the most subjective tendency; that the complications, the constant departures yet returns to the same subject-matter of illustration as in the *fugue* and canon, are analogous to the movements of a metrical romance or allegory like " The Faerie Queen " of Spenser; and that the more elaborated developments and enlargements of the theme, as in the concerto, overture, and symphony, in cases where none of them are dramatic, correspond to the most objective or artistic epic tendency. Especially the *symphony*, with its illustrations of the influence in the realm of sound of grand and spiritual sequences of emotive conditions, seems to be the musical analogue of the heroic or highest form of the epic.

When we come to *realistic* music, subdivision is perhaps still more difficult. What best corresponds to the didactic in poetry, is apparently the music of *accompaniment*, when, as in many operas and oratorios, especially those of Haydn and Handel, it is naturalistic. As for the distinctively *naturalistic*, it need not be confined entirely to imitations of the jingling of sleigh-bells, the popping of champagne bottles, and the thunder of cannon such as abound in third-class concert halls. It characterizes, as in the dragon-scene from "Siegfried," a good deal of the music of Wagner, and adds much interest to the Pastoral Symphonies of both Beethoven and Handel. Finally the third form of realistic music is illustrated in products avowedly composed to represent successive series of sensations, as awakened in the mind by successive external scenes and experiences. This is the sort of music which, for lack of a better word, is termed in the chart *analogic*. It is well exemplified in the "Poème Sympathique of Liszt."[1]

Dramatic music may be said to include, first, corresponding to the lyric, the *song* in its various forms, whether of the ballad, the glee, the hymn, or the anthem; second, corresponding to the protactic in poetry, indeed resembling it very closely in its alternation of description in the recitative and of characterization in the aria, the *oratorio*; and third, of course, corresponding to the drama, the *opera*. It must not be supposed, however, that the words which usually accompany this form of music are necessary

[1] Upon this whole subject consult pp. 250–319 of "Rhythm and Harmony in Poetry and Music."

in order to render it dramatic. On account of them the music is often made what it is, and they often serve to interpret its meaning. But representing, as it does, the rise, development, conflict, victory, defeat, or decline of successive and different emotions, music contains in itself all the elements needed in order to depict—within, of course, its own limitations—the beginning, unfolding, and end of a completed play of passion. This was the theory of Wagner, and many of his compositions reveal as much of the dramatic in the interchange of notes and chords as in that of words and gestures. In the earliest composed overture of Tannhäuser, for instance, the conflict of theme with theme, and the final suppression of the one by the other, is as clearly indicated as if the sounds had bodies that we could see meeting and grappling, till, finally, the one was thrown and trampled by the other. So, too, where there is not conflict. The very tune of a song, when rightly composed, indicates the tenor of its sentiment, whether of love or of war, of melancholy or of exultation. All this, however, has been amply discussed in the essay on "Music as a Representative Art," published in the volume of this series entitled "Rhythm and Harmony in Poetry and Music."

Now let us turn to painting. As in the case of music, another volume of this series, namely, "Painting, Sculpture, and Architecture as Representative Arts," includes, though examined from another point of view, much that, were it not desirable to avoid repetition, might be introduced here. But, even omitting this, it is hoped that enough will be said to enable the reader to differentiate in all the arts of sight the three phases of artistic expression which we are now considering. When treating of painting, Opie, in the third of his "Lectures on Design," says that its subjects "are epic or sublime, dramatic or impassioned, historic or circumscribed by truth. The first astonishes, the second moves, the third informs." Notice again, too, the quotation from Fuseli on page 313. If for Opie's historic, we substitute the broader term realistic, which includes the historic, his analysis will accord exactly with that given in this book. Long, too, in his " Art, its Laws and the Reasons for Them," similarly distinguishes the three classes. In speaking of the epic painter he says : " His aim being equally "—with that of the epic poet—" to impress one general idea, is in like manner, dignified, sublime, and elevated,—dealing only in generals, excluding detail, admitting no minute discrimination of character, or introduction of varied pathos,—not aiming to develop the man, to exhibit the movements of the heart, as that would be dramatic,—not striving to present the portraiture of a fact, as that would be historic,—but causing all to blend in one great and leading idea, the visible agents that he employs are only the agents to force that idea on the mind and fancy."

First under epic painting, as under epic poetry, we may place the *symbolic*. This differs from the allegoric, in that it suggests no continuous story ; from the realistic, in that the figures draw attention to themselves less than to the ideas of which they are emblematic ; and from the dramatic, in that they represent traits of character that are typical rather than individual. Symbolic painting depicts groups, or single figures, which are of some interest in themselves, yet which cannot be wholly understood except as they are perceived to represent attributes or functions. Many paintings of this kind are among the decorations of the National Library at Washington, such as the " Government," " Peace and Prosperity," and

"Anarchy" of Vedder; and probably all of us are well acquainted, through engravings or photographs, with other examples, like the "Aurora"[1] and "Hope" of Guido; the "Justice," "Prudence," "Religion," and "Innocence" of Raphael; and the "Poetry," "Philosophy," "Science," and "Religion" of Kaulbach.

Next to the symbolic form of epic painting comes, as in poetry, the *allegoric*. This form frequently represents as present at one time and place either mythologic or historic personages belonging to different periods or countries. A phase of the form which is allied to the symbolic is exemplified in the great picture by Delaroche in the hall for the distribution of prizes in the School of Fine Arts in Paris. In this, the figure of Fame sits in the centre, crowning with laurel seventy figures, the great artists of every land and age, who are represented as standing or seated before her. Another phase of the form which is allied to the historic, is exemplified in the "School of Athens,"[2] by Raphael. In this we see, in addition to the great philosophers and artists of ancient Greece, Raphael himself and his master, Perugino. In Kaulbach's "Reformation," too, we see Copernicus, Shakespeare, Raphael, and their contemporaries, all in one church, in which Luther is holding up an open Bible. An objection to this form of painting, owing to the fact that it attempts to depict as appearing at one time a collection of persons or a series of events which in real life could be perceived only in succession or at different times, will be discussed on page 418 of this volume. At present,

---

[1] See Fig. 34, page 71 "Paint., Sculpt., and Arch. as Rep. Arts."

[2] See Fig. 156, page 249, also pages 201, 248, 249, 250, and 272, "Paint., Sculpt., and Arch. as Rep. Arts"; also Fig. 10, page 41, "Genesis of Art-Form."

it is enough to notice that all the personages thus grouped together could not be represented as appearing in one time and at one place except as imagination were supposed to be thinking of them in connection with some general idea illustrated by the lives and characters of all; and that this condition corresponds exactly to the requirement of the *epic* as indicated on page 312.

The most artistic form of epic painting is found, of course, in the *epic proper*, sometimes called the *heroic*, or, as it might be termed still more appropriately, the *typical;* and the name that stands first in this department of the art, is undoubtedly that of Michael Angelo, " in all of whose productions," says Long, in his " Art, its Laws and the Reasons for Them," "sublimity of conception and grandeur of form characterize everything." His great epic, indeed, *the* epic painting of the world, is in the series of paintings in the Sistine Chapel in Rome. Fuseli, in his third " Lecture on Painting," thus interprets them: " The veil of eternity is rent. Time, space, and matter teem in the creation of the elements and of earth. Life issues from God and adoration from man, in the creation of Adam and his mate. Transgression of the precept at the Tree of Knowledge proves the origin of evil, and of expulsion from immediate intercourse with God. The economy of justice and grace commences in the revolutions of the Deluge and the covenant made with Noah. The germs of social intercourse are traced in the subsequent scene between him and his sons. The awful synods of the prophets and sibyls are the heralds of the Redeemer, and the hosts of patriarchs are the pedigree of the Son of Man. The brazen serpent and the fall of Haman, the giant subdued by the stripling David, and the conqueror subdued by female weakness in

Judith, are types of his mysterious progress till Jonah pronounces him immortal; and the magnificence of the Last Judgment by showing the Saviour in the judge of men, sums up the whole and reunites the founder and the race." But though the greatest, Angelo is not the only epic painter. Such productions as Murillo's " Immaculate Conception," Correggio's " Holy Night,"[1] and, notwithstanding suggestions of the dramatic, Titian's " Assumption " all may be placed in the same category.

Before turning from epic painting, it seems necessary to guard against the supposition that the application of the principle underlying it is confined to the delineation of figures. That which causes an epic result is the method in which the conception is expressed. The epic artist has an intuition of a general idea, which, though suggested by natural forms, entirely transcends them, and, in representing it through the forms, he subordinates more or less his desire to imitate them, to his desire to have them illustrate his idea. Of course, this can be done in the painting of landscapes as well as of figures. As a fact, the conditions seem perfectly realized in such compositions as Ruysdael's " Jewish Cemetery,"[2] in which, in connection with the tombs, a ruined church tower, a tree swept bare of bark and leaves, and clouds torn into shreds—though with a glimmer of sunshine and a rainbow in the distance,—all blend, and, in a distinctively typical way, exemplify the effects of death and resurrection. So in Turner's " Decline of Carthage "[3] and Claude's " Evening,"[4] as well as in

---

[1] Fig. 70, page 215, " The Genesis of Art-Form."

[2] See Fig. 157, page 261; also pages 260–262 of "Paint., Sculpt., and Arch. as Rep. Arts."

[3] See Fig. 51, page 175, " The Genesis of Art-Form."

[4] See Fig. 40, page 119, " The Genesis of Art-Form "; also page 262 of " Paint., Sculpt., and Arch. as Rep. Arts."

many other of the works of all these painters, the human beings subordinately introduced, as also the natural and architectural forms, are made distinctively interpretive of one another by being made illustrative of the same general idea.

The character of representation in painting and sculpture causes these arts to be more naturally allied to reality than are poetry and music. Hence the *realistic* in the arts of sight ranks relatively higher than in the arts of sound. Of course, too, like epic painting, the realistic can be manifested both in landscapes and in figures. The most subjective phase of this form—that which corresponds to the didactic in poetry—is termed, in the chart, *decorative*, to which term is added, "when also *naturalistic*." By this is meant that the decorative is not to be ranked with the highest art except when it involves a use of pictures. It will be remembered that it was said on page 332 that in didactic poetry an otherwise argumentative and scientific theme may be rendered imaginative through a use of illustrations. It is the same with an otherwise scientifically constructed and decorated wall-space. The fundamental requirement of decorative painting is that it fit the place in which it is put. It might be supposed that so far as the place dominates the figures and colors of the limbs, drapery, flowers, or fruit depicted, this form of painting could not attain high rank. Yet at times it may do so, though in these cases it ceases to be merely decorative. Few finer specimens of epic or dramatic art exist than in the frescos of Michael Angelo and Raphael.

Next to decorative painting in the chart is placed the *naturalistic*. This includes, of course, what is termed "still life,"—*i. e.*, pictures of fruit, or flowers, or of dead fish, beasts, or birds. But besides this it includes imitative landscapes and figures of the kind of which, in the fourth of his "Lectures on Painting," Fuseli speaks,—" Landscapes entirely occupied with the tame delineation of a given spot, and enumeration of hill and dale, clumps of trees, shrubs, water, meadows, cottages, and houses, what are commonly called 'views.'—little more than topography." It includes also that kind of portrait which he terms "the remembrancer of insignificance, mere human resemblance, in attitude without action, features without meaning, dress without drapery, and situations without propriety . . . in which the aim of the artist and the sitter's wish are confined to external likenesses,—it is furniture."[1]

Realistic art, however, is not all merely imitative. While showing the most scrupulous fidelity to all the features of the scenes or faces depicted, it may contain so much in addition, in the way of the arrangements of form, drapery, color, and light, as to suggest, as powerfully as can almost any kind of painting, the effects of imagination and invention. But so long as the subjects of these paintings are predominantly "circumscribed by truth," as Fuseli expresses it, they furnish examples of realistic, rather than of epic or dramatic, art. In this division of realistic art, we may place most of the landscapes—and perhaps they are the majority of all of them—that are essentially photographic, in the sense of being exact reproductions; and we may place here also figures, especially portraits, that are not in any sense typical, or illustrative of general ideas, as in the epic, nor strongly representative of character, as in the dramatic. Perhaps the best exemplifications of this

[1] See illustration of "Light and Shade," Fig. 16, page 41, "Paint., Sculpt., and Arch. as Rep. Arts."

kind of art are found among the Dutch painters, like Denner, for instance, who apparently never lets a hair of a man's head escape his notice. Some of the work of Willems and Meissonier, however, seems almost equally accurate.

In the degree in which the realistic in painting suggests action, it may become *historic*, and, in certain circumstances, dramatic. The historic and dramatic differ thus: the former is intended to impress upon us the truth with reference to certain occurrences that have actually taken place or that, owing to what we know, may be believed to have taken place. The dramatic is intended to impress upon us the truth with reference to certain individuals, either historic or not, who are depicted as representing their own characters as excited either by their own moods or by the actions of others. Broadly considered, historic painting, like historic literature, may include much that is no more than an illustration of the customs and costumes of different nations. In its highest form, however, which is the highest form also of realistic art, it requires almost as much imagination and invention as epic or dramatic painting. In order to illustrate precisely what an historic painting is, Mr. Long, in his "Art, its Laws and the Reasons for Them," speaks of Sir Joshua Reynolds's "Portrait of Elliot," the British commander at Gibraltar in the year when it was attacked by the combined French and Spanish forces. "The painter's design was not simply to give a portrait of Mr. Elliot, but of General Elliot; not only that, but of the successful defender of Gibraltar upon that occasion. He has therefore represented him in his military costume, and holding in his hands a key, in symbolic allusion to the fact of that citadel being the key to the Mediterranean. In the distance may be seen the two squadrons at the moment of battle,[1] and behind him a cannon pointed downwards to show the loftiness of the fortress,—all which surroundings connect him with that transaction, and thus make the representation a good illustration of historic portraiture. But to define the class under consideration more particularly, it may be proper to state that the painter of pure history does not, like the dramatic painter, represent that which might be, but that which was or is."

Fuseli, in his third " Lecture on Painting," gives a still clearer description of historic art : " History strictly so called follows the drama; fiction now ceases, and invention consists only in selecting and fixing with dignity, precision, and sentiment the movements of reality. Suppose that the artist choose the death of Germanicus,—he is not to give us the highest images of general grief which impress the features of a people or a family at the death of a beloved chief or father, for this would be epic imagery ; we should have Achilles, Hector, Niobe. He is not to mix up character which observation and comparison have pointed out to him as the fittest to excite the gradations of sympathy ; not Admetus and Alceste, not Meleager and Atalante ; for this would be the drama. He is to give us the idea of a Roman dying amidst Romans, as tradition gave him, with all the real modifications of time and place which may serve unequivocally to discriminate that moment of grief from all others."

From what has been said, it will be evident that to distinguish historic from dramatic painting is in some cases extremely difficult. Nor can it be done at all except by first deciding what is the predominating motive that the

[1] See criticism on this statement in "Paint., Sculpt., and Arch. as Rep. Arts," p. 266.

picture exhibits. When we look, for instance, at some of
the products of the Dutch School, at a picture, say, of
Teniers,[1] or at some of the work of a painter like J. F.
Millet,[2] we find much that suggests the dramatic. But
when we seek for the predominating motive of the artist,
we recognize that it must have been to picture the life of
the peasant as he really saw it; and this leads us to class
his work as realistic. On the contrary, when we look at a
picture like Piloty's "Death of Wallenstein" or Gérôme's
"Pollice Verso"[3] it suggests, at first, only the historic;
yet the predominating motive of the artist was so evidently to portray character as affected by certain specific
emotions that, as in the case of Shakespeare's historical
plays, we can call the paintings historic in only the sense
of being historico-dramatic.

The object of *dramatic* painting is to reveal the effects
upon particular characters or temperaments of particular
occurrences or surroundings. As in dramatic poetry, so
in this kind of painting, all must be definite and vigorous,
if not *brilliant* and *striking*. We have placed first here
what may be called *character-painting*. The most typical
form of this seems to be exemplified in that popular phase
of art represented by "The Beggar Boys" of Murillo and
"The Newsboys" of J. G. Brown. But portraits, too, are
often so composed as to come strictly within this class.
All of us probably can recall the likenesses of wives,
daughters, or mistresses which Raphael, Rubens, and
Rembrandt were accustomed to produce in the guise of

[1] See "The Village Dance," by Teniers, Fig. 43, page 142, "The
Genesis of Art-Form."
[2] See "Leaving for Work," by J. F. Millet, Fig. 169, page 299,
"Paint., Sculpt., and Arch. as Rep. Arts."
[3] Fig. 8, page 31, *idem.*; also Fig. 26, page 81, "The Genesis of Art-
Form."

fictitious and sacred personages.[1] "In the Louvre," says Kugler, when speaking, in his "Handbuch der Kunstgeschichte," v., 8, of the portraits of Titian, "we find the Marchese del Guasto with his mistress, to whom Cupid, Flora, and Zephyr are bringing gifts." Of the portraits of Titian's daughter, Lavinia, he says: "One of the finest specimens is in the Berlin Museum. Here the beautiful and splendidly attired girl is holding up a plate of fruit." "Another" is "in the possession of Lord De Gray, where, instead of fruit, she is holding up a jewel-casket. A fourth is in the Madrid Gallery, but here it becomes an historical representation; it is the daughter of Herodias." No one needs to have explained why portraits like this can be said to be *portraits in character*. But the same may be affirmed also of many less ostensibly designed with this object in view,—portraits which, while omitting the costumes causing us to associate the persons represented with others who have certain individual traits, nevertheless preserve everything else that will emphasize these traits; portraits, for instance, like some of Sargent's,—the "Little Marjorie," or that of Mr. H. G. Marquand in the Metropolitan Museum of New York.

For the scientific or realistic phase of dramatic painting, no better word seems attainable than *pantomimic*. *Genre* is the term first suggested. But a *genre* painting that depicts common life without drawing attention particularly to character may be realistic, as is the painting of Teniers mentioned on the preceding page. When a *genre* picture or any other derives its chief interest from the fact that it represents an interchange of feeling, thought, or action between different characters, it affects us precisely as a

[1] See the Madonnas in Fig. 38, page 116, and Fig. 39, page 117, "The Genesis of Art-Form."

pantomime would on a stage. Why, therefore, should it not be called *pantomimic?* By what word could we better describe a painting like "The Summer Night" by Van Beers,[1] or better, say, "The Card Players" by Caravaggio?[2] In this latter, we see cards and money on a table. Seated on one side of this is a man with a dishonest face. On the other side, playing with him, is a man with an innocent face, evidently just the one to be made a dupe. Behind this last man, looking over his shoulder, stands a third, muffling his breath to prevent his presence from being detected, and holding up two fingers to let the first player know what cards are being played by the second. In the same way the panel-paintings by Alexander, in the National Library at Washington, termed "The Making of a Book," are dramatically pantomimic rather than realistically historic. The differences between them, by the way, and those of Vedder in the adjoining corridor, afford a good opportunity for contrasting the dramatic in this form with the epic in the form of the symbolic.

Even pantomimic painting usually necessitates some representation of the customs and costumes of periods and countries. For this reason, they must be, to some extent, historic as well as dramatic,—a fact which, when we consider the blending of the narrative and the dramatic in protactic poetry, will give us a reason for perceiving a certain correspondence between this form of poetry and pantomimic painting.

The *dramatic proper* in painting, as in poetry, sometimes differs from the historic in only the degree in which the historic features are subordinated. For instance,

[1] Fig. 161, page 273; see also pages 271 and 272, "Paint., Sculpt., and Arch. as Rep. Arts."
[2] Fig. 160, page 271, *idem*.

her Children," now in the British Museum in London, appear to be less dramatic than epic.

Until one has thought over the subject, architectural effects seem dependent upon the constructive elements of the form, as in curves, straight lines, and angles, to a far greater extent than do those of painting and sculpture. The latter arts represent figures, as of men, animals, and trees, which we are accustomed to accept from nature as wholes, without analysis of their parts. Nevertheless, we do analyze the parts whenever the figures produce an epic, a realistic, or a dramatic effect. This is a fact of which we may remain unconscious when looking at a picture or a statue, but not, if we are to be influenced by the effect, when looking at a building. For this reason, before going farther, it seems well to notice that the fact is really exemplified in all the arts of sight—exactly, indeed, as it has already been shown to be exemplified in all the arts of sound. Almost all the verses quoted in Chapters XVI. to XIX. were short extracts necessarily representing only certain parts of whole poems. No attention was there directed to this fact, because it was not necessary. We are always accustomed to judge of poetry or music by considering separate sentences or phrases. Besides this, as we employ sounds in language, it is comparatively easy for us to recognize that every intonation or articulation has its own significance. Of paintings or statues, however, we not only judge as wholes, as has been said, but — mainly for this very reason — we do not often, when considering them, associate a separate significance with each constituent element of the form. Nevertheless, that we may and often should do this, is shown by illustrations, more than enough to establish the general principle, in the volume of this series entitled "Painting, Sculpture, and Architecture as Representative Arts." At present, we are interested in the subject so far only as it has a bearing upon the representation, to some extent in painting and sculpture, but especially in architecture, of an epic, realistic, or dramatic effect.

In considering this subject, let us start by recalling that, as manifested in the conditions of the form, the *epic* is that which seems to have been least moulded to the subject-matter,—*i. e.*, to the thought, feeling, purpose, whatever it may be, that may be supposed to be underneath the form; that the *realistic* is that which seems to have been most exactly moulded to it; and the *dramatic* is that which seems to have been moulded to it, so to speak, in excess. Applying this principle to outlines, we shall find that, as a rule, an absence of material interference, which, in this case, would represent the moulding purpose —therefore a free, unimpeded expression of the forces underlying natural life, corresponding in this to the *epic* condition—tends to produce a predominance of curves. The eye itself is circular, and the field of vision which it views at any one moment always appears to be the same. So do the horizon and the zenith, and so, too, do most of the objects which they contain,—the heaving mountain, the rising smoke or vapor, the rolling wave, the gushing fountain, the rippling stream, the bubbles of its water, the pebbles of its channels, every plant with all of its developments, and every animal with all of its movements. Again we shall find that a presence of material interference when exactly fitted to mould nature to its own purposes — corresponding to the *realistic*, especially to this as developed from the scientific condition (see page 312)—is apt to result in straight lines and angles, *i. e.*, in rectangular forms. Boxes and buildings and the majority of the objects constructed by men have this shape; and, by way of association, the same shape, when we see it in the horizontal hill-top, or in the sharply perpendicular cliff or peak, causes us to think often, and to say, that it looks precisely as if a man had been at work levelling and blasting. Once more, we shall find that material interference when carried to excess—corresponding to the *dramatic* condition—leads to the presence, and in exaggerated conditions too, of all forms of outlines that have been mentioned, *i.e.*, curves, straight lines, and angles. It is the complication and irregularity arising from such combinations which, by calling attention to the effect produced rather than to that which has produced it, result in the *dramatic*. These may be comparatively slight in their influence, as in that which fascinates us in a curio; or they may be of grander import, as when the tree and bush are wreathed above the precipice, or as when the dome-like mountain and the rolling cloud lift above the sharp peak and the cloven crag, while far below them lies a flat plain or lake. But it is always in connection with such blendings of effects that the most exciting appeal is made, through the emotions, to the imagination. Notice, too, that at the basis of this phase of variety essential to dramatic effect, lies always a suggestion of force which has broken up the sort of development in nature which one may term normal,—force that seems exerted like that of the tempest when it tosses the wave to edges and points of spray, and tears the cloud to shreds, or like that of the volcano when it cleaves the mountain and levels the cliff, and is tracked everywhere by the results of cracking and crystallizing. The legitimate influences upon our minds of such appearances of violence are themselves violent, or, as we say, exciting.

They are influences, too, the characteristic effects of which might be suggested by what we have all experienced in the realm of touch. From this we have learned that while the rounded and regular surfaces are, as a rule, agreeable, the sharp and irregular pierce and cut ; that while the globules of the healing oils belong, as a rule, to the one class, those of the irritating salts belong to the other.

Now add to this observation with reference to the expression of outlines in material nature, another with reference to the expression of thoughts or emotions in the human form. Whenever these find vent under the predominating influence of a subjective or instinctive prompting, corresponding to the *epic ;* in other words, whenever, wholly from within, a man is inspired to rapture, enthusiasm, and eloquence, either of a joyous or serious character, then his gait, postures, gestures, and all the movements of his body, in the degree in which his sentiment is able to find unimpeded expression in his physical frame, will take the form of free, large, graceful curves. But whenever his thoughts or emotions find vent under a predominating influence of a relative or reflective prompting corresponding to the *realistic*—in other words, whenever he is actuated by a desire, conscientious, self-conscious, and therefore more or less constrained, to accommodate expression exactly to that which it is to express, then his form will be erect, and his gestures straight and stiff, and, so far as is necessary in order to make them straight, angular. And once more, whenever he is under a predominating influence of objective or emotive promptings, corresponding to the *dramatic*—in other words, whenever his chief impulse is to emphasize in the forms of expression that which in view of outward circumstances or consequences has stirred him profoundly, then the excitement or passion either joyous or grievous, in the degree in which it is effectively manifested, will double up his form, throw out his chin, bend violently his elbows, knees, and wrists, and make all his body a human representation of the same sort of varied irregularity already described in the forms of nature which have been said to represent the same tendency.

There are reasons, therefore, founded both upon the principle of association and upon methods of expression pertaining to the very nature of our body, why the three tendencies of form should find expression as has here been indicated. "We have renewedly to refer," says S. P. Long in his "Art, its Laws, and the Reasons for Them," "to the ancient Greek sculptures, in which a correspondence between the disposition of the figure and the sentiment of the subject will always be found, — the forms of virtue and of wisdom" — religious, as will be noticed — "being less varied than those of pleasure." Again he speaks of the "Minerva's position" as "being perpendicular, and her drapery descending in long uninterrupted lines . . . the plain, the simple, the dignified and the intellectual" — she was the Goddess of Wisdom — "being the sentiment." Charles Blanc, too, in his "Grammar of Painting and Engraving," speaks of "the horizontals, which express in nature the calmness of the sea, the majesty of the far-off horizon, the vegetable tranquillity of the strong resisting trees, the quietude of the globe, after the catastrophes that have upheaved it"; and again, in describing the lines in two dramatic paintings, he says: "Poussin torments and twists his in the pictures of 'Pyrrhus Saved,' and 'The Sabines'"[1]; and Barry also in his "Lectures of the Royal Academicians,"

---

[1] See Fig. 36, page 75, "Paint., Sculpt., and Arch. as Rep. Arts."

referring to the Laocoön,[1] one of the foremost existing specimens of dramatic sculpture,[1] says that "the convex lines predominate and the forms are angular."

Enough has been indicated now with reference to the artistic effects of mere outlines to show that it is reasonable to suppose that even an art like architecture, wholly dependent, as it is, upon these effects, should be able to manifest an *epic*, a *realistic*, and a *dramatic* tendency. It is true that the forms of this art are not usually classified according to this principle; and that its products, like those of poetry, are already divided into different styles, the names of which have been fixed for years, and are to-day as familiar to most of us as are household words. At the same time, the most superficial examination of what is meant by terms like Egyptian, Assyrian, Grecian, Reviewed Grecian, Moorish, Byzantine, Saracenic, Romanesque, Renaissance, Gothic, must convince us that, however these may serve the purpose of indicating chronological or national developments of the art, they are not the results of any philosophic principle of classification.

But in architecture is a classification based upon such a principle possible; and is there any sense in which architecture can be termed *epic, realistic*, or *dramatic ?* The moment that we ask these questions, a new difficulty confronts us. All these terms, as has been shown, imply the influence in architecture of significance as well as of form. But can it be said that in any way reasonably analogous to that exemplified in the other arts, architecture can manifest significance ? This is evidently the first question that must be asked here. Can it be answered satisfac-

---

[1] See Fig. 21, page 49, "Paint., Sculpt., and Arch. as Rep. Arts"; Fig. 75, page 226, "The Genesis of Art-Form."

torily? It can. The subject is fully discussed on pages 92 to 96 and 227 and 228 of "Art in Theory," as well as in Chapters XVII. to XIX. of "Painting, Sculpture, and Architecture as Representative Arts." In these places it is shown that the plan of a building may represent the general purpose for which it is designed, and also that each individual feature in it may represent some special constructive purpose. The plan, for instance, may indicate a theatre, or a temple; and each individual pillar, bracket, or beam may indicate the exact degree of support for which it is intended. In these regards, architecture fulfils the analogies of the other arts, in which the product as a whole has a general significance, and each individual note, word, line, or color, as related to each other factor of the same kind, has a special harmonic, grammatic, or proportional significance.

Bearing these facts in mind, it is easy enough to recognize that certain buildings may be suggestive of the subordination of the form to general or special constructive principles developed in it, and may thus, in the main, fulfil the conditions of *epic* art; that other buildings may be suggestive mainly of the exact adaptation of the constructive principles to the constructed material, suggestive, *i. e.*, of the correlation of the one to the other, and may thus fulfil, in the main, the conditions of *realistic*, in the sense of scientific, art; and that other buildings may be suggestive of the subordination of the constructive principles to the method of rendering the forms æsthetically effective, and thus fulfil, in the main, the conditions of *dramatic* art. This system of classification certainly seems satisfactory, whether judged by the standards of philosophy or of æsthetics; and that it is not adopted merely because a convenient way of making architectural developments conform to what in this book has been said of the other arts, may be shown by the following quotation from an article by Mr. E. A. Freeman in the "Fortnightly Review," entitled "The Origin and Growth of Romanesque Architecture." "To judge," he says, "from the popular disputes about Law Courts and the like, people in general group all forms of architecture under two heads. Architecture is supposed to be divided into two great styles, 'Grecian' and 'Gothic'; and it is thought a very good joke to call the admirers of the supposed styles respectively Greeks and Goths. It is not very easy to find out what people who talk in this way mean by the words which they use. The only sound classification of styles of architecture is that which arranges them according to their leading principles of construction. Of such principles, as far as we know at present, there are only three; more accurately speaking, there are only two, one of which again falls into two great subdivisions. The two great systems of construction are the entablature and the arch, and the arch, again, may be either round or pointed. We thus get three distinct forms of construction, the entablature, the round arch, and the pointed arch. And each of these principles of construction has been, in its own time and place, the animating principle of a style of architecture." Here then are three forms of architecture, and if one can show that they correspond in any way to the three forms already indicated as existing in all the other arts, he can have at least one authority sustaining the general truthfulness of the classification on page 325. Take, for instance, changing the order in which these styles are mentioned by Mr. Freeman, so as to make them conform to the method that has been adopted in the other arts,—take the architecture of the *round arch*, or, as it is termed in the chart on page 325, the architecture of *vaulted support*, this phrase being used because it seems the best both to differentiate this style from all others, and to apply to all features in which identical characteristics usually appear, namely in caps, gables, ceilings, roofs, and domes. Suppose that we ask of what this style is significant, in other words, for what it seems intended, of what it reminds us? There is but one answer. " It is the generic office of an arch," says Professor Bascom, in his " Science of Beauty," " to bear a burden. It is this very burden which consolidates and strengthens it, and enables the piers and abutments to endure its side thrusts." Whether perceived in the foundations of a bridge or of a building, in the capping of a window or of a porch, or forming, as it does, the whole contour of a dome, vaulted support, of which the round arch is typical, is always suggestive of the constructive principle exemplified in the form. But whatever is suggestive, and mainly suggestive, of this, manifests, according to what was said on page 311, the *epic* tendency. " A Romanesque church," says Mr. Freeman, referring to one phase of this style, " always seems to carry me nearer than any other building to the men who dwelt or worshipped within its walls." This is very nearly the same as if he had said "to carry my thoughts back to those who erected the building, and to their reasons for erecting it as they did "—in other words, to the building's conditioning antecedents.

But there are other features necessarily associated with this style, which also ally it to the *epic*. The *round arch* cannot be constructed of stone except as it is sprung from piers of great size and strength, and this—to go no farther—produces that effect of grandeur, which we have found to be characteristic of the epic in other arts. This effect is very noticeable in pure specimens of the style, as in the Suleymaniya Mosque[1] or in St. Sophia,[2] at Constantinople; but it is also made noticeable, as if their artists had recognized the necessity of an appearance of strength as a matter of artistic congruity, in buildings in which this style is blended with the Grecian, as in St. Peter's at Rome[3] and St. Isaac's at St. Petersburg.[4] The great blocks of stone that uphold all the arches, to say nothing of the domes of these buildings, are as different as possible from the innumerable shafts, slender in shape and minutely chiselled, which, massed together, support the pointed ceilings of a Gothic cathedral.[5] Not less noteworthy are the differences in the accentuation of the parts as separated from one another. No greater contrast could be afforded than that between the even fronts of Suleymaniya Mosque or St. Sophia,—even between the slight relief given to the pilasters of St. Peter's,—and the width of half the chancel characterizing the flying buttresses of the Gothic Notre Dame at Paris. Now all these kinds of effects, peculiar to the architecture of the round arch, are distinctively *epic*. Correggio's "Holy Night,"[6] Murillo's "Immaculate Conception," Michael Angelo's pictures in the Sistine Chapel, or his statues of "Moses" or of "Night and Day,"[7] are characterized by a size of parts and a vagueness of outline which, while producing effects of grandeur, often border on a disregard of those of nature. Neither in the paintings

[1] Fig. 30, page 86, "The Genesis of Art-Form."
[2] Fig. 42, page 123, *idem*; Fig. 40, page 80, "Paint., Sculpt., and Arch. as Rep. Arts."
[3] Fig. 23, page 78, "The Genesis of Art-Form."
[4] Fig. 12, page 35, "Paint., Sculpt., and Arch. as Rep. Arts."
[5] See Cologne Cathedral, Fig. 41, page 81, also Beverley Minster, Fig. 43, page 84, "Paint., Sculpt., and Arch. as Rep. Arts"; also Fig. 2, page 17, Fig. 78, page 235, and Fig. 79, page 236, "The Genesis of Art-Form."
[6] Fig. 70, page 215, "The Genesis of Art-Form."
[7] Fig. 170, page 301, "Paint., Sculpt., and Arch. as Rep. Arts."

nor in the statues is there anything to suggest the scrupulous regard for details that is apparent in so many Dutch pictures and Italian busts. Think how the faces of angels and cherubs in all the former paintings blend with one another and the clouds, making this epic art in a sense the forerunner of modern impressionism.

We come now to the architecture, as Mr. Freeman calls it, of the entablature, termed in the chart on page 325 that of *horizontal support*. This term, like that given to the style just considered, seems the one best adapted to differentiate it from all others. It may be applied, too, to all the features exhibiting the method, whether in the entablature itself, or in the caps, cornices, or even pediments, the sides of which are so nearly flat that they cannot be supposed to be supported either in the vaulted method of the style already considered, or in the perpendicular method of the style to be considered hereafter. That these statements are justified will be recognized at a glance by any one who will contrast examples of these different styles.[1] In typical architecture of *vaulted support*, there is often visible scarcely a single horizontal straight line, and never many of these lines, while in the architecture of *perpendicular support*, every other effect—even the thrust of the arches—is entirely subordinated to that of verticality. In speaking of the significance of what is termed the Greek style, " It is universally felt," says Mr. Freeman, " that the architecture of the entablature is the expression of *horizontal* extension." " The old predominance of horizontalism," says Prof. Wyatt, in his " Fine Art,"

[1] Compare Suleymaniya Mosque, Fig. 30, page 86, with Fig. 2, page 17, " The Genesis of Art-Form " ; St. Sophia, Fig. 40, page 80, or St. Mark's, Fig. 15, page 37, with the Theseum, Fig. 14, page 36, and also with Cologne Cathedral, Fig. 41, page 81, all in " Paint., Sculpt., and Arch. as Rep. Arts."

"has shown men thinking of themselves and running parallel with the soil, 'of the earth, earthy,' rather than breaking away from it." Could any language have been framed to express more accurately than do these words of Professor Wyatt that parallelism between conception and form which in this book has been said to characterize the realistic, or scientific-artistic, tendency? Or look at the subject in another light, this style, even where it does not reveal horizontal lines alone but vertical, and, as in the pediments, slanting, always manifests in an exceptional degree continuity, parallelism, and, as in the pediments, an exact conformity of equivalents, or balance. All these are effects that rarely impress us with a sense of underlying strength, as do the vast domes that rest above huge blocks of masonry in a style like that of St. Sophia [1]; or that appear artistically striking, as do the aspiring arches to which thousands of frailly constructed filaments in pillars and windows point in a style like that of Cologne Cathedral.[2] The flat caps and horizontal lines rather elicit our admiration for the perfect adaptation of the parts to one another and to the whole, and thus suggest mechanical accuracy, and the testing of every appearance by square and plummet. With good reason, therefore, can this style be considered as in the chart on page 325 a development of the realistic in the sense of scientific tendency. In some of the arts this tendency is supposed to be indicative of inferiority. But even if such a supposition were well founded, it would not follow that it could be justified when applied to architecture, simply because scientific and mechanical contrivance are more

[1] See Fig. 42, page 123, "The Genesis of Art-Form"; or Fig. 40, page 80, "Paint., Sculpt., and Arch. as Rep. Arts."
[2] See Fig. 2, page 17, "The Genesis of Art-Form"; or Fig. 41, page 81, "Paint., Sculpt., and Arch. as Rep. Arts."

legitimate in buildings than in poetry or painting. The classification here made, therefore, need not be supposed to deprive the Egyptian, Renaissance, or Greek architecture, in which this horizontalism predominates, of its artistic pre-eminence.

But this style of architecture is allied not only to the scientific tendency. The Greek form of it may be shown to be allied to the distinctively historic phase of this tendency. Mr. Freeman calls it the architecture of the entablature. But what is an entablature? It is that part connected with a column which is over the capital, including the architrave, frieze, and cornice. The entablature, therefore, is only the crowning feature of the column. It implies the column, and is a development in connection with it. But what is the column, or better, what does it mean? From the time when a rude stone was set up above the buried form of a great man of the desert, to say nothing of the Egyptian obelisk, what meaning has it had if not historic? For what has it been used, if not to commemorate persons or events? Accordingly, though the colonnade of the Greek temple was undoubtedly used in part, because these temples were modelled upon primitive roofs supported by poles,[1] why may it not also have been derived in part, especially as developed into its more elaborated forms, from a desire to commemorate? What was the entablature but the fitting crown of a collection of columns[2]; and where more appropriately than in it could be placed the statuary illustrating the events in which those to whose honor the temples were erected were supposed to have figured?

---

[1] See pages 374 to 377 of "Paint., Sculpt., and Arch. as Rep. Arts."

[2] Rows of like stone *lanterns*, high enough to be columns, may be seen in Japan to-day, all together commemorative of some one man,

The last of the three styles that we are considering is what Mr. Freeman terms the architecture of the pointed arch, but which, for reasons similar to those already given when speaking of the other styles, is termed in the chart on page 325 the architecture of *perpendicular support*. This phrase need not apply solely to perpendicular straight lines. It may apply to arches in case they be sharply pointed. As a fact, when practically developed, the style always does include arches in this form. Notice now that, so far as it does this, it necessarily includes all the forms entering into the two other styles. At the points of the arches, there are angles, and in other parts of them there are curves, while everywhere there are multitudes of straight lines, most of them perpendicular, as in the excessive parallelism in buttresses and pinnacles; but some lines are also horizontal. This combination of forms makes this third class of architecture both a blending and — if for no other reason, because contrast necessarily emphasizes — an emphasizing of the features entering into the two other classes, exactly as is the case with every third class throughout all the corresponding classifications attempted in this volume. Notice the statements on pages 62 and 271; and recall the arguments in Chapters V. to XII., showing that a combination of the requirements essential to religion and to science results in the artistic. When we consider, too, the architectural significance of the effects of mixed lines, such as have just been described, we shall find other reasons for allying this style with the distinctly artistic. It is evident, for instance, that the great verticality of the arch in a cathedral nave results from a desire to increase its apparent height. But why should this be increased? Why but to make the building as a work of art more æsthetically effective, which, as we have found, is the chief impelling reason for every dramatic development. Again, in itself considered, a roof with a pointed apex affords the most satisfactory kind of a water-shed, and, in this regard, it may be said to be an expression of the idea of protection. But in many parts of a building where, nevertheless, a pointed arch is used, as over windows and doors, it is not needed to afford protection in the same sense in which the round arch is needed in order to afford support. When therefore we perceive this pointed arch in such places, places in which it is needed, if at all, only slightly, we are forced to infer that it is used merely for the sake of its appearance,— in other words, for an artistic purpose, *i. e.*, in order to produce effects of harmony between different parts of the building. Thus, whether we consider the relation of the pointed arch to the roof, or to the cappings, we can perceive a sense in which it may be looked upon as a development of the distinctively artistic tendency. But this tendency is manifested not alone in the pointed arch, but also in the bewildering complexity of lines of other kinds that accompany this arch,— of spaces so enormous, yet so minutely elaborated, of outlines the strongest in architecture, yet broken into the most delicate subdivisions, many of them massed against the buttresses, yet others by themselves, drooping like feathers to form tracery, — effects which are sometimes augmented, too, as in the Arabesque and Venetian styles, by colors as varied as are the outlines. Could anything afford a better analogue to the *brilliant* and *striking* results of what we have termed the *dramatic* in painting and sculpture? "In a grand Gothic building," says Mr. Freeman, " the purely artistic effect is so perfect, so entrancing that it is hard to turn our thoughts from the art

THREE ARCHITECTURAL STYLES SUBDIVIDED. 385

to the building." Thus in all particulars do this writer's general conclusions, though differently derived, confirm the methods of classification that have been here suggested.

The subdivisions of these three radically different architectural styles are not important; nor, any more than in the case of music, can they be accurately determined, especially in view of the way in which the whole subject has been confused by the national or racial designations which have been given to the styles. In some cases, two or three of these terms indicate the same style; and, in other cases, one term applies to a combination of styles. In a very general way, however, it may be said that, of the styles that may rightly be considered the results of artistic study and intelligence, the Byzantine, as illustrated in St. Sophia,[1] Constantinople, exemplifies the most subjective or epic development of the epic tendency; that the later Etruscan,[2] showing us, as in the gate at Perugia and in the Cloaca Maxima at Rome, the Roman arch before the Greek entablature had been added to it, exemplifies the most scientific or realistic development of the epic; and that the Romanesque, especially the Venetian as in St. Mark's,[3] but also much of the later Romanesque of Italy[4] and of Germany and of the Norman of England, exemplifies the most objective or artistic development of the epic. In the same way, it

---

[1] Fig. 42, page 123, "The Genesis of Art-Form"; Fig. 40, page 80, "Paint., Sculpt., and Arch. as Rep. Arts."

[2] Producing a result approximately like that in Fig. 30, page 86, and Fig. 11, page 47, "The Genesis of Art-Form."

[3] Fig. 31, page 88, *idem*; Fig. 15, page 37, "Paint., Sculpt., and Arch. as Rep. Arts."

[4] See Cathedral of Sienna, Fig. 97, page 292, "The Genesis of Art-Form"; also Fig. 84, page 240, *idem*.

25

may be said that the Greek style,[1] with its slight tendency to elevation in its inclining pediments, exemplifies the most subjective or epic development of the realistic tendency; that the Egyptian style[2] exemplifies its most scientific development; and that the Roman style,[3] including the Renaissance[4]— *i. e.*, flat caps and cornices surmounted by round arches — and also the Revived Grecian, or, as it is better termed, the Romo-Grecian,[5] *i. e.*, the entablature surmounted by the dome — on account of their combinations of forms, if of nothing else, — represent the most objective or dramatic development of the realistic; while the Mohammedan or Moorish style, to which Rosengarten, in his "Architectural Styles," ascribes " free vent to overwrought fancy and eccentric tone, in conjunction with spectacular display," may be said to exemplify, as in the Taj-Mahal,[6] and especially as in the Arabesque forms of the Alhambra,[7] the most subjective or epic development of the dramatic; the non-ecclesiastical[8] or so-called Tudor Gothic, its scientific or relative development; and

---

[1] Temple of Theseus, Fig. 14, page 36, "Paint., Sculpt., and Arch. as Rep. Arts"; The Acropolis, Fig. 1, page 15, "The Genesis of Art-Form."

[2] Temple at Ipsambool, Fig. 227, page 394, "Paint., Sculpt., and Arch. as Rep. Arts."

[3] Court of Honor, Fig. 203, page 365, "Paint., Sculpt., and Arch. as Rep. Arts."

[4] Fig. 173, page 319; Fig. 196, page 349; and Fig. 201, page 361, "Paint., Sculpt., and Arch. as Rep. Arts."

[5] St. Isaac's, Fig. 12, page 35, "Paint., Sculpt., and Arch. as Rep. Arts"; also St. Peter's, Fig. 23, page 78, "The Genesis of Art-Form."

[6] Fig. 3, page 19, "The Genesis of Art-Form."

[7] Fig. 96, page 290, *idem*.

[8] Fig. 198, page 351, also Fig. 206, page 369, Fig. 13, page 36, "Paint., Sculpt., and Arch. as Rep. Arts"; Fig. 22, page 78, "The Genesis of Art-Form."

the so-called pointed Gothic[1] of the cathedral, its most objective or dramatic development. See again the note at the bottom of page 380.

[1] Fig. 41, page 81, Fig. 150, page 227, and Fig. 220, page 392, "Paint., Sculpt., and Arch. as Rep. Arts"; Fig. 2, page 17, Fig. 68, page 207, Fig. 78, page 235, "The Genesis of Art-Form."

CHAPTER XXII.

SIGNIFICANCE AS ATTRIBUTABLE TO THE ELEMENTS OF ART-FORM IN TIME AND SPACE COMBINED: IMPORT, LIFE, AND ORGANISM AS SUGGESTED IN POETRY.

Résumé of the Line of Thought in this Volume—Have still to Compare Significance as Represented by the Underlying Elements of Form in Art with the Same in Nature—Import, Life, and Organism as Represented in Nature through Combined Effects of Movement or Operation in Time and of Matter or Arrangement in Space—Objects in Time Suggesting Space Manifest Progress—Objects in Space Suggesting Time Manifest Unity—Poetry and Music Manifest Progress Suggesting Unity—Of the Two, Poetry Suggests More Unity ; Words Having More Meaning than Single Notes—Poetry Suggests Unity also through Verse, Metre, Rhyme, Alliteration, Assonance, Refrains, Choruses—Through Repetition of Epithets and Phrases in Blank Verse—Through Parallelism, Causing Expression to be Prolonged and Reiterated—Two Extremes to be Avoided : One the Disproportionate Emphasis of Conditions Tending to Progress : Doggerel—Corrected by Breadth of View, Introducing Suggestions of Space—Other Extreme to be Avoided is Disproportionate Emphasis of Conditions Tending to Unity—How Avoided in a Shakespearian Soliloquy—By the Poetic Hiatus or Ellipsis.

AS we turn in this chapter from comparatively generic to more specific results of art-significance as manifested in the form, the reader will perceive that the course of thought in this volume, having boxed the compass, as it were, of all the possibilities of expression, is returning to its starting-point. Our endeavor to detect the methods of representing significance through the forms of art began with a study of the ways in which it seems to be represented through the forms of nature. In these latter, it was shown that the elementary suggestions of space and of time are gradually developed into suggestions of organism, life, and import; and, through the latter, into conceptions of the infinite, the eternal, and the absolute, or, as one may say, of truth in the abstract. Having reached this point, as preliminary to retracing our steps, in order to show how that which had been discovered to be suggested through the forms of nature could be made by man to be suggested through the forms of art, it was found necessary to consider three different departments in which, for different purposes, the truth or the significance embodied in form is differently derived, characterized, and expressed—namely, religion, science, and art. After this, having separated the conceptions of art from those of the other two, it was shown that even in this there can be detected three distinct tendencies, the first *religious*, leading through the *good*, the *sublime*, and the *grand*, to *epic* art; the second, *scientific*, leading through the *true*, the *picturesque*, and the *simple*, to *realistic* art; and the third, *artistic*, leading through the *beautiful*, the *brilliant*, and the *striking*, to *dramatic* art; and the preceding three chapters have indicated the influence of each of these tendencies upon products in the higher arts of poetry, music, painting, sculpture, and architecture.

The reader will recognize that the work of showing how significance may be represented in the same way in the forms of art as in those of nature, cannot be completed till, in our applications of the subject, we have retraced all our steps back to the very first one with which we started; back, that is, to the elementary forms of nature in which significance begins to be suggested. In order to do this logically we should consider—reversing the order of arrangement in each triad of suggestions mentioned on page 6—how the forms of art as well as of nature can represent conceptions of

Import	Method of Operation	Force	Existence
Life	Operation	Movement	Time
Organism	Arrangement	Matter	Space

To dwell upon all these terms, and thus to repeat what was said in Chapter I., is not necessary in this place. It will be sufficient to remind the reader that the suggestions respectively indicated in each triad of terms are cumulative, and depend upon those in each of the triads preceding them; also that all the suggestions mentioned first in each of the triads—and the same is true respectively of those mentioned second and third—are connected. In other words, the suggestion of *import* is conveyed through that of *life*, which itself is conveyed through that of *organism*. Besides this, *import* is mainly represented through a *method of operation* produced by *force* upon *existence; life*, by an *operation* produced by *movement* in *time;* and *organism*, by an *arrangement* produced by *matter* in *space*. For our present purposes, much of this, especially that which is in the second and third columns, need not be considered. We may confine attention mainly to that which is in the first and fourth columns, *i. e.*, to the suggestions in art, corresponding to those in nature, of *import, life*, and *organism* as conveyed through appearances having *existence* in *time* and in *space*. In Chapters XXII. to XXIV. we shall consider the representations of *import, life*, and *organism* in each art-form, owing to its suggestions of effects in *time* and in *space* combined;

and in the remainder of the book we shall consider the suggestions predominantly made either in *time* alone or in *space* alone, which need to be considered thus, inasmuch as the effects of poetry and music are mainly manifested in the one, and those of painting, sculpture, and architecture are mainly manifested in the other.

To take up the first of the topics thus indicated, Chapter I. has shown us that impressions of *organism* and through them of *life* and *import* are conveyed by objects in nature, and therefore presumably by those in art, in the degree in which they appear to be subjected when separated from others in space, to successive movements or operations—to what we may term changes in *time;* or in the degree in which successive changes, perceptible in *time*, seem to have affected objects as separate portions of *matter*, which is what we mean by separate objects in *space*. Notice now that the former of these conditions, when, notwithstanding successive changes in an object, it is still perceived to be one object, or to be an *organic* whole, is that which is mainly instrumental in producing an effect of *unity;* and that the latter condition, when, notwithstanding the object is one, or an *organic* whole, it is perceived to be subject to change, is that which mainly produces an effect of *progress*. Whether unity or progress be the more apparent depends less upon the intrinsic nature of an object than upon our individual way of viewing it. If we regard a tree at any single moment of time, all that render it apprehensible are outlines separating it from other things in *space*. These cause it to seem a *unity*. The moment, however, that we come to inquire what has caused these outlines to appear as they do, we attribute their appearances to former *processes* of growth; in other words, although the *unity* of the tree is what is chiefly noticed, the very appearance of this unity suggests *progress*. Again, if we observe the changes that time has wrought upon the tree, we at once have our minds directed to the fact that the *progress* noticed is effected in some one thing which, because it is one, possesses *unity*. Thus we may accept it as a general principle, that, when objects in nature that manifest *import* through *life* and *organism* appear to be a *unity*, they suggest *progress ;* and that when they appear to have *progress*, they suggest *unity*. And our inference with reference to the forms of art is that they must manifest primarily either *unity* suggesting *progress* or *progress* suggesting *unity*. In this and the two chapters following, this principle is to be applied to the methods of expressing significance through the forms of the different arts. The reader who may be interested in noticing how the same may be applied to the methods of constructing each form as a form, will find this indicated on pages 131, 270, 299, and 300 of the volume of this series entitled "The Genesis of Art-Form."

Before we pass on, it is important to notice particularly the words *suggest* and *suggested*, as used in the sentences above. Doing this will save one from the error of supposing that the arts of sound should attempt to give form to subjects that can be adequately delineated in only space, or that the arts of sight should attempt to give form to subjects that can be adequately reported in only time. Concerning this error, more will be said in Chapters XXV. to XXVII. At present, let us confine ourselves to the question in hand. Let us notice how each of the art-forms may be made suggestive of *import* through being suggestive also of *life* and *organism*. In doing this, we shall begin with the arts of sound,—poetry and music. The forms of these are apprehended through successive effects that appear, moving one after another, in time, and thus manifest primarily *progress* suggesting *unity*.

Of the two arts, poetry can, in a certain sense, be said to be more naturally suggestive of *unity* than music. No separate musical note can be so complete in itself, or so representative of a form in space, as a separate word. When we say *tree* or *man*, for instance, the word recalls an object in space. Even when we use words that do not recall such an object, the flow of ideas during the time in which each word is being uttered stands still, as it were, for a moment ; and this fact of standing removes it somewhat from the sphere of progress in the sense of movement. Notice too, that, in part, it is this fact also that gives a word as contrasted with a note more *import*. Music moves forward like a wheel when its spokes are revolving, the united influence of the tones being far more marked than the significance of separate tones. Poetry moves forward like one walking, step by step, the united influence of sentences being scarcely more perceptible than that of separate words.

Accordingly when we come to inquire how unity, which is primarily a condition of space, may be suggested in connection with progress which is mainly represented in poetry, the answer is easier than when we apply an analogous question with reference to music. In trying to find the answer, let us start by recalling exactly what it is that constitutes *form* in poetry. " Notwithstanding all that has been advanced by some French critics," says Whately in his " Rhetoric, " " to prove that a work not in metre may be a poem, universal opinion has always given a contrary decision, and when that which is poetical is put into the form of verse we have poetry." According to this critic, then, poetry is a form of verse. But what is verse? A little reflection will reveal that every known phase of it is a method of causing the flow of the words as they present themselves in *time*, to be interrupted sufficiently and with sufficient regularity to convey an impression like that produced when objects appear side by side in space. Lines, feet, alliteration, assonance, rhyme,—all have the effect of retarding or preventing an absolute change; and thus of causing the composition to manifest not movement only, but unity of movement. Consider, for instance, the lyric. Its thought usually moves on very impetuously. The artistic requirement in its mode of expression, therefore, is that it manifest, in some way, that there is unity in the movement. But, how can this be done better than by arranging the sounds in certain like groups, indicating unity of method? And how can we find like groups more clearly indicated than in the regular recurrence of accents, as in feet, or of tones as in alliteration or assonance, and especially as in rhymes at the ends of lines. These latter, in particular, cause the thought, at like intervals, to pause, as it were, and to connect the sound heard with a like sound that has preceded it. A similar impression is also conveyed when successive stanzas end with a like refrain or chorus. Notice the poems on page 341. The refrain and the chorus, therefore, are not superfluous. Without them, the thought of the lyric might often seem to roll forward as lifelessly and with as little evidence of organism as a log. These make it step and fly,—give it a regularly recurring motion like that of a living creature. As contrasted with the thought of the lyric, that of the epic is less impetuous. In assuming form, therefore, the latter can afford to a greater degree to disregard the suggestion of space. It can advance, as in blank verse, with very much less aid than is afforded by the regular recurrence of the accents and tones just mentioned.

At the same time, the only metrical effect that is really absent from the ordinary epic is that of rhyme. All the other effects, even something that is similar to the refrain or chorus of the lyric, blank verse includes. In the "Iliad," for instance, time and again we meet with the same phraseology. Sometimes whole lines are repeated. Juno, "large eyed and august," Agamemnon, "king of men," "swift-footed" Achilles, the "white-armed" Helen, "winged words," and other epithets like these, are reiterated with a frequency that in our age might be considered monotonous and redundant. Tennyson, however, has done the same thing with fine effect in his "Idyls." In "Morte D'Arthur," the king is made to say:

> Watch what thou seest, and lightly bring me word.

Sir Bedivere replies:

> Yet I thy hest will all perform at full,
> Watch what I see, and lightly bring thee word.

And still again, farther on, the king says:

> I bade thee watch, and lightly bring me word.

An artist like Tennyson would not have repeated these Homeric methods, unless he had perceived a subtle reason for doing so. What is it? What but to convey to the ear and also to the mind an impression of unity as well as of progress,—an impression, as we shall find presently, similar to that conveyed through the repetition of similar strains in a composition of music?

Another more intimate analogy between musical and poetic forms of expression is also worth noticing. It will serve to reveal as well the very close connection that exists between versification and poetic thought. In the following parallelism we have one of the oldest poetic expressions on record :

> I have slain a man to my wounding
> And a young man to my hurt,
>
> *Gen. iv., 23.*

Examination will show that these two lines sustain to the single idea of murder, a relation exactly the same as that which will be pointed out presently between different notes of melody and the single chord of harmony from which these notes are developed. The two lines prolong and reiterate, and thus reveal in succession, according to the order of sequence in experience, what might be stated in a single phrase. This prolongation or presentation in succession is necessary because the medium of poetry must manifest movement or *progress*. It is, moreover, a prolongation, and a manifest *prolongation*, of what might be stated in a *single* phrase, because poetry must indicate also certain effects of *unity*. Here then, in this simple parallelism of early poetry are very clearly manifested these two suggestions which it has been said that this form of art must convey.

The very fact, however, that it may convey either of them involves the possibility of its conveying one of them to an overbalancing extent ; and shows the necessity of maintaining in this art the mean between the two extremes, at the one of which the conditions tending to progress are exclusively emphasized, and at the other the conditions tending to unity. As has just been indicated, it is the ability to evolve an idea, rather than to state it, which, more than anything else, perhaps, renders poetic art-production possible. Notice, too, that a large number of words and phrases can do no more than state an idea, while few words, however rapidly uttered, can keep pace with the processes of ideas. From this fact it follows that there is much less liability in poetry than in music, that the movement be too rapid. There is, however, some danger of it. What is doggerel? At times, nothing more nor less than verse so intently driven toward the expression of one idea that the writer of it ignores all other ideas. He looks straight at his goal and at nothing on either side of him. The result is a narrow line of thought, devoid of any of those suggestions of associated things in space, *i. e.*, in heaven or earth or under the earth, with which poetry that really stimulates the imagination is always crowded. Verse may represent movement to perfection and still be doggerel, *e. g.*:

> And still I him pursued with speed,
> Till at the last we mett;
> Whereby an appointed day of fight
> Was there agreed and sett:
>
> Where we did fight, of mortal life
> Eche other to deprive,
> Till of a hundred thousand men
> Scarce one was left alive.
>   *The Legend of King Arthur: Percy's Reliques.*

> Before we parted, one kind friend,
> And then another talked so free;
> They went from table-end to end,
> And spoke to each, and spoke to me.
>
> Books, pretty books, with pictures in,
> Were given to those who learn to read,
> Which showed them how to flee from sin,
> And to be happy boys indeed.
>   *The Climbing Boy's Soliloquies: Montgomery.*

> On and on through many cities,
> Through Bologna to Ancona,
> Stopping off to see the places
> Mentioned in the classic history,
> Down the eastern coast of Italy
> By a route not much frequented,
> Therefore far more interesting,—
> Finally they reached Brindisi.
>
> *Sketches in Palestine: Hammond.*

The primary condition needed in order to make lines like these poetic, is that the mind should, once in a while, glance off from the course which it is pursuing, and show how its thoughts are connected with thoughts in other associated courses. That is to say, the words should suggest space through which the thought is moving, and thus give to the whole the effect of outlook or breadth, in which, as in all true art, imagination has compared one thing with another. Is it not a fact that in the following the vitality, freshness, warmth, glow, charm, and all those qualities that are associated with *life* and *organism*, as well as those that are connected with depth and breadth of *import*, are owing to the presence of the characteristics that have just been said to be lacking in the verses above? Notice how the poet, by referring to the "scream of the curlew," "yawning," "subterranean host," "loose crags," "infant touch," "adder," "wolf," "maiden," etc., draws suggestions from every side of the channel which the main thought is following, and makes them all do service in augmenting the amount of force which is dashing on like a flood in one general direction:

> "Have thou thy wish!" He whistled shrill,
> And he was answered from the hill;
> Wild as the scream of the curlew
> From crag to crag the signal flew.

> . . . .
> That whistle garrisoned the glen
> At once with full five hundred men,
> As if the yawning hill to heaven
> A subterranean host had given.
> Watching their leader's beck and will,
> All silent there they stood and still.
> Like the loose crags whose threatening mass
> Lay towering o'er the hollow pass,
> As if an infant's touch could urge
> Their headlong passage down the verge,
> With step and weapon forward flung,
> Upon the mountain-side they hung.
> . . . .
> Like adder darting from his coil,
> Like wolf that dashes through the toil,
> Like mountain-cat who guards her young,
> Full at Fitz-James's throat he sprung,
> Received, but reck'd not of a wound,
> And lock'd his arms his foeman round.—
> Now, gallant Saxon, hold thine own!
> No maiden's hand is round thee thrown!
> *Lady of the Lake*, v.: Scott.

But as poetry is an art, the words of which follow one another in time, the poet should be careful to have these effects in space merely suggested and not in any sense detailed. There is a special liability to violate this requirement, whenever the main thought to be presented is not naturally associated with movement, as when one is describing something actually perceived in space, as in quotations on pages 343 and 438, or is expressing a sentiment or belief discoursive or didactic in nature, rather than narrative. But even though the main thought be not associated with movement, the subordinate thought may be. And if the poet will bear this in mind, he may direct attention to that which exists in space, and yet by referring constantly, while doing so, to actions which can take place in only time, he may have his language full of the representation of movement.

Notice how this fact is exemplified in the use of the words that are italicized in the following:

> For instantly a light upon the turf
> *Fell* like a *flash*, and lo! as I looked up,
> The Moon *hung naked* in a firmament
> Of azure without cloud, and at my feet
> *Rested* a *silent* sea of hoary mist.
> A hundred hills their dusky *backs upheaved*
> All over this still ocean; and beyond,
> Far, far, beyond the solid vapors *stretched*,
> In headlands, tongues, and promontory shapes,
> Into the main Atlantic, that appeared
> To *dwindle* and *give up* his majesty,
> *Usurped upon* far as the sight could *reach*.
> *The Prelude; Conclusion: Wordsworth.*

Notice, too, how Shakespeare in the following gives effects of life and organism as well as of import to the discoursive character of his main thought—which otherwise would have merely given him "pause" in space. Notice the allusions which he makes to things that move in time; and which have no interest nor even existence except as actions:

> To be or not to be, that is the question:—
> Whether 't is nobler in the mind to suffer
> The slings and arrows of outrageous fortune;
> Or to take arms against a sea of troubles
> And by opposing end them? To die,—to sleep,
> No more;—and by a sleep to say we end
> The heart-ache and the thousand natural shocks
> That flesh is heir to,—'t is a consummation
> Devoutly to be wished. To die,—to sleep;—
> To sleep! perchance to dream;—ay, there's the **rub;**
> For in that sleep of death what dreams may come,
> When we have shuffled off this mortal coil,

> Must give us pause. There's the respect
> That makes calamity of so long life;
> For who would bear the whips and scorns of time,
> The oppressor's wrong,. . . .
> But that the dread of something after death,—
> The undiscovered country from whose bourn
> No traveller returns,—puzzles the will;
> And makes us rather bear those ills we have
> Than fly to others that we know not of?
> Thus conscience doth make cowards of us all.
>
> Hamlet, iii., 1: Shakespeare.

There is a significant connection between these effects and the use of the rhetorical hiatus and ellipsis which are so general in poetry, and so generally regarded as legitimate. These figures of speech are suggestions to the reader that the thoughts of the writer are moving forward in time, and that he must not try to elaborate them. He must hurry on to something else. In the majority of cases, too, hiatus follows a reference to something that is aside from the main line of thought, something that the writer conceives of as existing side by side with that with which he is dealing. In other words, these figures of speech suggest space as well as time. This fact explains why it is that they alone so often add effects of import and life to what would otherwise seem very insignificant and lifeless. One secret of Robert Browning's power lies in this use of the ellipsis. But he sometimes carries the figure too far. Compare his handling of it in the following with that of Shakespeare in the passage last quoted. See also page 214.

> Alcamo's song enmeshes the lulled isle,
> Woven into the echoes left erewhile
> By Nina, one soft web of song: no more
> Turning his name, then, flower-like, o'er and o'er!

> An elder poet in the younger's place —
> Nina's the strength — but Alcamo's the grace;
> Each neutralizes each then ! Search your fill ;
> You get no whole and perfect Poet — still
> New Ninas, Alcamos, till time's midnight
> Shrouds all — or better, say, the shutting light
> Of a forgotten yesterday. Dissect
> Every ideal workman — (to reject
> In favor of your fearful ignorance
> The thousand phantasms eager to advance,
> And point you but to those within your reach) —
> Were you the first who brought (in modern speech)
> The Multitude to be materialized?
> That loose, eternal unrest — who devised
> An apparition i' the midst ? The rout
> Was checked, a breathless ring was formed about
> That sudden flower : get round at any risk
> The gold-rough, pointel, silver-blazing disk
> O' the lily ! Swords across it ! Reign thy reign
> And serve thy frolic service, Charlemagne !
>
> *Sordello, bk. 5 : Browning.*

CHAPTER XXIII.

SIGNIFICANCE AS ATTRIBUTABLE TO THE ELEMENTS OF ART-FORM IN TIME AND SPACE COMBINED: IMPORT, LIFE, AND ORGANISM AS SUGGESTED IN MUSIC AND ORATORY.

Unity, or the Effect of Arrangement in Space can be Suggested in Connection with Progress in Music—By Melody when its Progress is not too Rapid or Slow ; and is Subject to a constantly Recurring Rhythm—By Harmony, when its Simultaneous Tones are Compounded of the Successive Notes Developed in the Melodies—Same Principles Apply to Developments of Themes in Long Compositions—Extreme of Disproportionate Emphasizing of Effects of Progress to be Avoided : Illustration—Extreme of Disproportionate Emphasizing of Effects of Unity to be Avoided : Illustration—Tendency of Wagner to Emphasize Unity by Subordinating Melody to Harmony—Application of these Principles to Oratory which must Manifest Progress not too Rapid or Slow, and Unity by Regularity in Pauses and Rhythm, and in Modulation—Gesture as Delivery in Space, and its Influence upon Effects of Life, Organism, and Import—Must not Go to the Extreme of too much Movement or too little.

IN order that musical tones as they follow one another may seem to constitute a tune, and thus may seem to be musical in the highest sense, it is evident that they must possess certain characteristics in addition to the mere fact of being consecutive. In the first place, the tones must move neither too rapidly nor too slowly. In the former case, the mind cannot separate the notes ; in the latter, it cannot connect them ; and hence in neither case will they manifest those characteristics that make music intelligible, vital, and organic. All who have applied themselves to the task know how difficult it is to learn passages that represent either of these two extremes of movement. They prevent the mind from readily perceiving—and, for this reason alone, from remembering—the relationships of the notes. Moreover, those whose attention has been directed to the subject must have noticed that, as a rule, notwithstanding superior facility in the execution of difficult runs, great performers upon musical instruments usually execute the same passage in slower time than inferior performers do; and also that the slower rendering of the passage usually enhances greatly such effects as it may manifest of import, life, and organism. The slower rendering enhances these, because, if the movement be too rapid, it fails to suggest anything that can check it. While this is true, however, it is also true that, if the movement be too slow it suggests something that checks it too much. Anything of substance sufficient to check movement suggests an effect produced by something that does not move. As the mean between the two extremes is the one in which musical art becomes most expressive, as we say, it evidently becomes this in the degree in which it conveys suggestions both of movement which is represented in time, and of non-movement, which, as a rule, is represented in space. Notice again, however, that it is not only the fact of moving with just the right degree of deliberation that conveys these impressions, but still more, perhaps, the fact of moving rhythmically with different changes and interruptions of movement recurring at regular intervals. Look at the following:

Très Jolie Waltz: Emile Waldteufel.

It is hardly necessary to call attention to the fact that these recurrences in rhythm and in movements of pitch produce unity of effect in music, in the same way as in poetry do alliteration, assonance, feet, lines, and rhymes. See page 394.

But there is another more literal sense in which the effects of music may be suggestive of something else than movement. In the chord several notes are sounded at one time. By consequence they are not apprehended in succession. When, therefore, we come to ask how music, though appearing in time, may suggest effects not requiring different intervals of time, we may get one clue to an answer from the chord. We apprehend this to be what it is, because its notes are sounded simultaneously; and we apprehend the resemblance between a chord and a melody in the degree in which the different notes which, when sounded together, constitute the chord, are in the melody sounded at near intervals. The melody, in this case, seems, more than anything else, like the chord pulled apart; and its notes, though separated, are comprehended as if united. In other words, the separate notes, though apprehended in time, are comprehended, as it were, in space. It is important to notice also that unless the different notes of the melody or the notes of its different phrases can be thus comprehended, they convey no impression of their relationships. If the movement be too slow or too involved for the notes constituting the one chord, or constituting other chords naturally associated with this chord, to linger in the memory, or if the movement be so regardless of these notes as not to sound them at all, then the tune will have little import; it will not be intelligible, because it will not appear to be a tune, or to have organic life. Accordingly, it is not alone on account of its deliberate movement, but on account also of its relation to the chord, *i. e.*, to sounds not apprehended in succession, that the ordinary hymn or ballad can be easily retained in memory. Here is the first phrase of a hymn all the notes of which are in a single chord, which is printed at the right:

Ovio: L. Mason.

And all the notes of the following are in two chords, also printed at the right:

Old Melody.

But the vast majority of simple melodies are composed of the notes of three chords and of no more, the last two chords at the right of this next example being merely modifications of one and the same chord:

I Know that my Redeemer Liveth: Handel.

The chief reason why it is less difficult to remember melodies like these than the melodic movements of ordinary symphonies, is because the latter contain notes from a greater number and variety of chords, and are, therefore, more irregular and complex.

The same principle is applicable to longer compositions. In operas like Beethoven's "Fidelio" or Wagner's "Lohengrin," on account mainly of consistency in the methods of development, a somewhat similar though greatly varied general effect is felt to pervade all the melodies; and, as these follow one another, they are felt to be suggestive of something connected and cumulative. In other words, the music seems to have body and an end in view. The body conveys the impression of *organic vitality*, and the end in view that of *import*. In mere operettas, like those of Offenbach or Lecocq, we hear only separate snatches of melody with effects which, if varied, seem disconnected, and, if not, monotonous. In other words, the compositions appear to have little unity or progress, —little, that is, to suggest either one kind of movement or one aim for all movements.

These two kinds of music will serve to illustrate the necessity in this art, as well as in others, of avoiding the two extremes, in the one of which the conditions tending to progress are too exclusively emphasized, and in the other the conditions tending to unity. Several years ago —it may not be true now—when music of the kind last mentioned was played by the bands in Paris, one would hear the lighter passages performed by a chosen few, while, when it came to the heavier passages, all the musicians, with a great flourish of trumpets and beating of drums, would play together. For such compositions, this method of rendition was apparently appropriate. It certainly represented very strikingly their lack of continuity and of climax. But the general method of such performances, at that time, had had such an influence in France, that it had come to be applied to the execution of music of a higher order, and, as in the case of other executions, was usually successful in taking all the life out of it. This was so, as will be noticed, because everything was subordinated to the requirements of the melody as distinguished from the harmony, or, as this use of terms has been explained, to the requirements of the effects of movement, as distinguished from those of non-movement.

On the contrary, when at that time the Austrian bands would render even light music, as if influenced by a reminiscence of the requirements of more serious music, the quality and quantity of their tones, though greatly lessened in force, were seldom sacrificed, and were not always even subordinated to the requirements of the different melodies. The result was a sustained unity of effect wholly different from what was possible according to the French method. Of course the Germans sometimes carry this other effect too far. When an opera like Gounod's "Faust" is produced in one of their opera-houses, the passages in recitative are usually rendered far more dramatically and powerfully than by the French or the Italians, but not so with passages like the flower-song or the soldiers' chorus. In these, the German tendency to subordinate the melody to that which is not the melody, seems at times to make them overlook certain requirements of rhythm and tune essential to the effects intended by the composer. While, therefore, it is true that, in some respects, an opera may be improved by being rendered according to the method of Wagner, it is also true that in some respects it may be impaired. No one can deny that Wagner was a great composer of melodies. He throws away more of these in the orchestration of the second act of the "Meistersinger" alone than would suffice to immortalize almost any other composer. In fact, one peculiarity of his harmonic movements is the degree in which they are developed exactly as were the very earliest harmonies, *i. e.*, from a simultaneous production, in many different parts, of many different melodies. But he does not always seem to bear in mind that harmony was developed from melody which was also, at first, sung. He too frequently seems to confine the singer's part to mere intonation, or *recitative*. The followers of Wagner would say that, in such cases, he is subordinating the melody to emotive expression, because the singer's part is always accompanied by orchestration representing, by way of analogy, association, or imitation, the feelings natural to the sentiment. But notice that, as a rule, an accompaniment is an arrangement not of melody but of harmony. It is in reality to this latter, therefore, that Wagner is subordinating what other composers would put into the form of melody. In doing this he and his followers evidently represent the other tendency in music, which it has been said must be avoided, namely, that of emphasizing too exclusively the requirement of unity, which is what harmony in music mainly represents. The result is just what, according to the theories of this volume, we should expect. However little may be confessed in these days when Wagner is the fashion, a good many people get very tired of listening to certain parts of his operas. These parts they find lifeless and meaningless, dull and uninspiring. A little examination, too, will convince most of us that they are all parts in which the tendency just mentioned has been carried to excess. On the contrary, the parts most universally popular, like the choral of "Tannhauser," the wedding march of "Lohengrin," the sword song of "Siegfried" and the prize song of the "Meistersinger," all show the influence of the counterbalancing tendency. Absolutely successful music, as in the case of all other absolutely successful art, is that which occupies a middle ground between the two extremes.

To show how analogous are the methods applicable whenever there is any necessity for artistic effects, it will be interesting, before passing from the arts that address us through the ear, to notice how the principles under consideration apply to the partially æsthetic art of *oratory*. So far as this art is dependent upon vocal effects, the sounds of successive words, like those in music and poetry, must be uttered rhythmically—flowing onward without too much either of rapidity or of hesitation, of abruptness or of monotony. If the thought flow too rapidly, it fails to reveal sufficiently the separate import of the words; if too slowly, it fails to reveal their consecutive or cumulative import. All successful orators, upon analysis of their styles, will be found to manifest a mean between these two extremes. Sometimes an exact measurement of time is evident between the utterance of successive emphatic and unemphatic words, producing, in this way, a rhythmic effect. Of course, as the subject changes from grave to gay, the general time becomes more rapid, but the relative time, as indicated by the proportion of it given to emphatic as contrasted with unemphatic words, often remains the same. This feature was especially noticeable in the elocution of Edward Everett. It was so very apparent, in fact, that during the first five minutes of his speaking the effect seemed artificial. But before long, as sentence after sentence rolled upon the ear, each laden successively with those accumulating suggestions with which he knew so well how to build up a climax, the effect was something more than animating. It was electrifying and transporting. His words, owing largely to their rhythmic regularity, were literally winged. And yet he spoke always with deliberation. But the evenness of the flow of the whole conveyed the impression that the fountain was living, never exhausted nor to be exhausted, and, like the current of a mighty river, it bore irresistibly upon its tide, the thoughts and feelings of his hearers. Probably no orator of the present, in this regard, resembles Mr. Everett; but frequently one listens to stump-speakers or to clergymen who, with unmusical voices, ungainly gestures, and crudely conceived themes, hold the attention of their audiences simply through manifesting this single virtue of a rhythmic flow of syllables. And where an orator does not accomplish this result habitually, it will be noticed, nevertheless, that in most of his climaxes that are particularly effective his elocution assumes the trait. Sometimes it is particularly emphasized by an unusually regular introduction of phrases, similar pauses being always observed between these. This was very apparent in the oratory of Wendell Phillips and of George W. Curtis; and largely accounts for the æsthetic and finished effects of their delivery. Other orators, again, as was the case with Henry W. Beecher and John B. Gough, appear to have very little regard for exact measurements of time. But notwithstanding the broken, disconnected impression that many isolated portions of their delivery convey, examination will discover even with them a similar method of making pauses and a similar method of intonation in connecting these, which in the end convey the same general effect of unity.

The word intonation introduces us to another feature of successful elocutionary delivery, modulation. With its various forms of pitch and slide, this may be said to produce effects which, as contrasted with those just considered, are a result of a vertical movement up and down rather than of one that is horizontal or forward. These elocutionary effects, therefore, of modulation or of inflection, as often called, seem to bear the same relation to the forward movement as the chord to the melody—in other words, to be the suggestion in elocution of an influence other than that produced by an effect in time. When all the words of an oration appear to move upon the same key, or when, in spite of many variations of this key, successive words, phrases, or sentences all seem to be emphasized or to end on the same key, the result is a lifeless monotony. Opposite conditions lead to an opposite result. In the mean between the two, we find that excellence which develops neither into a ministerial tone nor into bombastic ranting, nor, as sometimes is the case, into both. Did any of the orators that have been mentioned lack ability to modulate their voices properly, with all their excellence as regards time they would not have deserved the name applied to them. A very artistic illustration of modulation in delivery was afforded, a few years ago in this country, by the elocution, when he was in his prime, of Dr. E. H. Chapin of New York. His voice swelled and sank literally like waves, billow after billow breaking into a spray of rhetoric about the listener with all the effect of an intellectual and emotional surf-bath. But the orator who, with the least appearance of effort, could produce the most satisfactory effects both of time and of modulation was Wendell Phillips. He could measure off his rhythm without any suggestion of monotony in recurrence; and could pass over all the notes of two octaves so subtly that half of his audience would be willing to take oath that he had not varied his intonations by more than two or three intervals. If a natural effect be the perfection of art, then he was the most artistic elocutionist of his day.

Similar facts may be affirmed of gesture. Gestures actually appear in space. And, as we should expect, a due regard for them may at times counterbalance defects in vocalization. There is delivery in which neither voice nor action in itself would seem satisfactory, yet both when combined do seem so. This is the case because the mind, regarding the result, perceives the effects of time in the language, and of space in the gestures, and, as we have found, the two, when manifested together, are able, as would not be possible for either by itself, to convey impressions of organic life as well as of import. It is doubtful whether the Italian Father Gavazzi, who, some years ago, attracted such crowds in this country, would have been able, with his imperfect knowledge of English, to hold the attention of his American audiences in any unusual degree, had it not been for the marvellously expressive nature of his gestures. In the histrionic art, with the violent extremes of passion that are expressed in the language of many plays, few characters could ever be made to seem consistent throughout, were it not for the acting. It is this that adds, to what otherwise might seem an endless variety of language, the effect of unity. Hence, as distinguished from the orator, whose thoughts are usually so closely connected, whose subjects are so much of a unity, that he needs little action, the histrionic artist is properly called an actor. When we have the excellences of the orator and the actor combined, we have a product that is rare, but—as proved in the cases of Gough and

Beecher — one to which all men concede extremely high intellectual rank.

As for gesture considered by itself, after so much has been said to the same effect, it is almost superfluous to add that it too must manifest a mean between influences suggestive of progress and of unity, *i. e.*, between too much movement and too little. If there be too much, the orator lacks unity, in the sense of a manifestation in all parts of his discourse of individual force of character; if there be too little, he lacks progress, in the sense of *abandon* directed toward an impersonal end.

CHAPTER XXIV.

SIGNIFICANCE AS ATTRIBUTABLE TO THE ELEMENTS OF ART-FORM IN TIME AND SPACE COMBINED: IMPORT, LIFE, AND ORGANISM AS SUGGESTED IN LANDSCAPE-GARDENING, PAINTING, SCULPTURE, AND ARCHITECTURE.

Landscape Gardening—How it may Suggest both Progress and Unity—One Extreme to be Avoided—Also the Other—Painting: The Scene and its Precedences and Consequences—Painting must Represent a Single View — How Progress, as in the Allegoric Painting, may be Appropriately Treated—Immobility in Space must not be too Exclusively Represented—The most Suggestive Moment must be Represented: Illustrated from Titian's Methods—Same Principles Applied to Landscapes—Sculpture: Suggestions of Progress in this more Difficult than in Painting, yet not Impossible—Two Extremes to be Avoided—The Foremost Statues, even of Single Figures, are Full of Organic Life and Import—A Building may Suggest Progress or Growth—The Idea or Plan of it Is the Seed—The Suggestion of Effects in Time or Growth must not be too Prominent—Nor must the Suggestion of Effects of Fixedness or Space—Neglect of these Principles in Irregularity of Outline and Color on American Streets—Of Buildings amid Scenery which are Apparently out of Place—Effects of Appearances of Nature on the Growth of Styles of Architecture.

PASSING on now to the arts that appear in space, and recalling that in these we must have, instead of progress suggesting unity, unity suggesting progress, it will be of interest, especially in view of the bearings of the subject upon landscape-painting, to consider, for a little, the conditions that confront us in the allied, but not wholly fine, art of landscape-gardening. That this art manifests effects in space, and thus tends to unity, is self-evident. It will seem almost equally evident to those who have followed our line of thought, that it may also suggest effects in time, or progress.

In external nature, effects in time are evinced in what we term growth, as manifested in the conformations of the surface of the land, or in the distributions or developments of shrubs or trees that spring from it. Applying these ideas to landscape-gardening, it is simply a fact recognized by all, that any given plot may be so graded and laid out that hills and valleys, lawns and lakes, avenues and flower-beds, shall appear to be the results of nature as much as of artifice. In the degree in which such is the case, landscape-gardens may be said to suggest effects in time. And yet if, in connection with these, there be no evidences that the results perceived were contrived and constructed through an exercise of ingenuity and skill ; if, in other words, there be no evidences of a human mind which, accepting certain natural features of landscape as developed in time, has given unity to the whole in space, and this as a result of thinking,—then manifestly the landscape will not appear artistic.

Accordingly here again, in these two facts, we have indicated the necessity of avoiding the same two tendencies — the one in the direction of effects in time, and the other in space—that were considered in poetry, music, and oratory. The artist, while suggesting effects in time, must not make them too prominent. Where human intellect is supposed to have graded the hillocks and cultivated the lawns, neither of these can appropriately present too great an appearance of ruggedness or unculture. Lakes that are acknowledged to be the results of contrivance should not seem swamps, nor should streams that are made to flow into them seem sluggish. Trees that have been transplanted should not appear illy selected as to sizes, nor illy arranged as to groups or rows. Walks that every one knows to have been planned, however adroitly they may be adjusted to the conformations of the land, should never violate the mathematical laws controlling the formation of curves; nor should flowers that have been placed in beds be disposed otherwise as to sizes and colors than in a manner suited to produce effects that are æsthetic.

On the other hand, the artist, while striving to avoid the tendency just mentioned, can scarcely be too cautious in his endeavor to guard against infidelity to such effects as may be supposed to have developed naturally. It is possible to grade the land so that the outlines and positions of mounds, lawns, and lakes shall seem too much the products of design. The trees may be too nearly of a size, and arranged with too much regularity. If in addition, as in some French gardens, they be clipped in order to seem uniform, or be made to imitate tents, spires, or what-not that a man may fancy, or if they be ranged like fence-poles about walks suggesting nothing but a square and compasses, or stuck into the edges of flower-beds, wherein all the colors are as carefully matched as in the mats of a French parlor, then, while artifice has had its perfect work, nature may seem to have been so painfully distorted and misrepresented that the result has been the death of her.

Let us look now at painting. Here again we have an art that appears in space. As such, the medium for the embodiment of its theme is a fixture. It cannot move. Therefore, of course, painting cannot delineate succession. But all ideas or events depend for their interest very largely upon that which has preceded them or which may follow them. Accordingly, the question to solve in this art is, How can preceding or following conditions be indicated with a due regard to representation legitimate to space alone? Evidently only so far as they can be suggested. And so far as thus indicated, the tendencies to be avoided must be the same as in the other arts already considered, namely, that of making the suggestion of succession, or of progress, too prominent; and that of making too prominent the representation of fixedness, or of unity.

Let us glance at these tendencies in their order. A work of art, which represents a scene in nature, must appear, of course, like such a scene, and therefore it must not include anything which could not be perceived, or legitimately supposed to be perceived, in a single view. As already suggested on page 354, it is a question whether we do not find a violation of this principle in the so-called allegoric painting. An allegory, it is said, is a continuous metaphor; and, as anything continuous must takes place in time, an allegory must represent different intervals of time. But need it do this? Why need time be any more than suggested? And why can it not be suggested in ways that do not interfere with that effect of unity which is dependent upon fixedness in space? When we try to answer these questions, we find ourselves forced to decide that, whether or not a painting be artistic, depends not upon the fact of its being allegoric or the contrary, but upon the mode in which the allegory is presented. In Cole's well-known series of paintings called "The Voyage of Life," the allegory is embodied in four distinct pictures, each of which presents but a single scene, the only connection between the one and the others being supplied by the imagination. Delaroche's allegorical painting in the Hall for the Distribution of Prizes in the School of the Fine Arts in Paris reveals the figure of Fame distributing wreaths of laurel to artists grouped about her as a centre. This arrangement causes an effect of unity. But the artists are those of all time. This fact suggests, though it does not delineate, progress; while the combination of the effects of unity and progress is such as to produce—what has been said here to be a legitimate result in such cases—an effect that is interpretive of *import* because manifesting *life* and *organism*. To an extent, a similar effect may be said to characterize Kaulbach's "Reformation" and Raphael's "School of Athens,"[1] mentioned on page 354. Of course all these paintings represent forms that never met the eye of a living man at any one moment. But their appearance in a single picture may be defended upon the ground that, when the mind recalls "The Reformation" or "Athens," it thinks of the different characters not as existing in different places and periods, but in that one conception of its own imagination. Why, therefore, should not the representation of the imagination reveal them all as present together? Nevertheless one would be untrue to all the facts of the case, did he not acknowledge a liability to confusion in such paintings. For instance, Kaulbach's composition in the Berlin Museum, termed "The Destruction of Jerusalem by Titus," introduces both men and angels, both the material and the heavenly Jerusalem. This confusion may be so great, too, as to prevent the picture from suggesting *unity*, or *organic life*, or from being, in any full sense, interpretive of its own *import*. On this subject, the reader may consult Chapters XIV.

---

[1] Fig. 156, page 249, "Paint. Sculpt., and Arch. as Rep. Arts."

and XV. of "Painting, Sculpture, and Architecture as Representative Arts," and may notice, also, what is said further of this same painting, as well as of others, on pages 476 to 478 of the present volume.

But again we have to note in painting the tendency to make fixedness, or effects in space, too prominent, and, doing so, to disregard the suggestions of movement or of effects in time. This tendency is the cause of the dead or lifeless impression left by many family portraits and groups, and by most pictures representing prominent men assembled in council, a president with his family or cabinet, a senator in the chamber of state, or reformers in convention. In these, there are presented likenesses and perhaps accurate ones, but the arrangements of the figures often contain no suggestions of the influence of preceding intentions or of following incidents. In single figures, it is frequently difficult to secure these suggestions without a sacrifice of naturalness. But it can be done. Fig. 169 on page 299 of "Painting, Sculpture, and Architecture as Representative Arts" contains the "Leaving for Work" by J. F. Millet. In this picture one of the legs of a peasant who is walking is made longer than the other for the purpose of suggesting two different positions which the eye is obliged to take in at one glance. In other words, the picture represents the effect of movement. On pages 298 to 302 of the same book other representations of the same effect are described. Where figures are grouped, the possibilities of indicating an interchange between them of thought, emotion, or action are, of course, much greater. Yet they are too often entirely neglected. The result is that, however accurately the figures may reproduce the outlines of their models, all stare out from the canvas, looking as inanimate as do Punch and Judy

religious, scientific, and artistic, then artistic alone, and then only phases of the artistic,—and showing how each is represented through methods common to all the arts. We have now reached a point where we can analyze no further without taking up such phases as can be represented in only a single art. In the chapters remaining, attention will be confined to these phases, our object being to detect, if possible, how to distinguish each of them from all others. That this object is important, needs no arguing. Only in the degree in which it is correctly solved by the artist, will he be able to correlate his subject-matter to his form, and his form to his subject-matter, in such ways as to render both in the highest degree effective. "The aim of a work of art," says Taine in his "Ideal in Art," "is to make known some leading and important character more effectively and clearly than objects themselves do." "Distinctiveness and richness of idea," says Prof. H. N. Day, in his "Science of Æsthetics," "are indispensable in all art. . . . The first work of the artist is to shape this ideal into more complete and definite outline." Evidently the earliest step toward imparting effects of clearness and definiteness of idea must be taken by distinguishing the phase of significance appropriate for one art from that appropriate for another.

As we start out to do this, we are reminded of what was indicated in Chapter XXII., namely, that poetry and music are composed of words or notes that follow one another, and are thus fitted to reproduce movement in time, but only to suggest arrangement in space; and that painting, sculpture, and architecture are composed of colors or outlines that appear side by side, and are thus fitted to reproduce arrangement in space, but only to suggest movement in time. But, apart from this very clear line of demarcation between the arts that are apprehended in time and in space, all the arts on either side of this line have characteristics separating them from one another. Poetry is composed of articulated words, each of which conveys to the intellect a definite meaning. Music is composed of inarticulated notes not one of which, of itself, conveys a definite meaning, and several of which, joined together, convey a meaning which, while approximately definite to emotion, is not necessarily so to the understanding. Painting is composed of colors and outlines made to resemble definitely those of nature; sculpture, of outlines and bulk made to do the same; but architecture, of colors, outline, and bulk, which, while fulfilling the general principles of construction in nature, do so in only an indefinite way, in a way analogous, therefore, to that in which music fulfils the laws of intonation in speech. Hence the appropriateness of the term applied to architecture by Madame de Staël,—"frozen music."

Now let us take up each of the arts in order, and try to determine those characteristics which separate its form from the forms of the other arts, and which, by so doing, limit the phase of significance that the form can appropriately represent. That this phase should be limited thus, is no new conception. It is as old, certainly, as the time of Plutarch. In modern times, Lessing has expanded it in his "Laocoön," emphasizing particularly the difference due to the fact that certain arts appear in time, and others in space. "The rule is this," he says (Sec. 18, Frothingham's translation), "that succession in time is the province of the poet," and of course, he would have added, had he been referring to music, of the musician also; "coexistence in space, that of the artist,"—by which he meant, one who produces works distinctively of painting or sculpture. "Objects which succeed one another, or whose parts succeed one another in time," he says in Sec. 16, "are actions. Consequently actions are the peculiar subjects of poetry. . . . Objects which exist side by side, or whose parts so exist, are called bodies. Consequently, bodies with their visible properties are the peculiar subjects of painting." . . . And again (Sec. 18), "To try to present a complete picture to the reader by enumerating in succession several parts or things, which in nature the eye necessarily takes in at a glance, is an encroachment of the poet on the domain of the painter. . . . To bring together into one and the same picture two points of time necessarily remote, as Mazzuoli does in the 'Rape of the Sabine Women,' and the reconciliation effected by them between their husbands and relations; or, as Titian does, representing in one piece the whole story of the prodigal son . . . is an encroachment of the painter on the domain of the poet." It will be perceived that the force of this criticism is derived from the supposition that the arts are representative. Lessing argues that as effects are presented in nature, whether in time or in space, so must they be presented in art. There must be no attempt, therefore, to represent through music and poetry effects that can be presented adequately only in space, or in bodies; nor to represent through painting and sculpture, those that can be presented adequately only in time, or in movement.

There is an objection to the theory of Lessing thus stated, which is met and obviated by the further development of the general principle underlying it, which is unfolded in Chapters XVI. to XIX. of "Art in Theory." The objection is, that a literal application of the theory seems to necessitate the artist's invariably representing in a story something that is heard in time—in other words, something that is received by him in the form of a story; as also his invariably representing in a picture something that is seen in space, or that is received by him in the form of a picture. As a fact, however, it often happens that the forms through which effects have been exerted upon the mind have lingered so long in it, and experienced so many modifications there, that, though critical analysis may detect, as in architecture and music, that the effects have been suggested by forms in nature, the artist himself is unconscious of what these forms were. Often, too, even though not unconscious of this, the effect upon his imagination has been such that what was experienced as the result, say of hearing a story, can be represented truthfully only through a picture, and *vice versa*. Indeed, as shown in Chapters XVI. to XIX. of "Art in Theory," exactly the same experience, at different stages of the development of its influence upon the mind, can be represented appropriately only as represented through the medium of a different art. Therefore, though there is a general truth in Lessing's principle, when one comes to apply it practically, the question to be asked is not whether the conception was derived from a form appearing in time or in space, but whether, as it has affected the mind, it can be represented to others in time or in space. But notice that, when we ask this question, it necessitates our asking another. This has reference to the mental condition legitimately expressed in a form in time or in space. Let us apply the question, first, to a form of poetry as contrasted with one of painting. When a man uses words, as he does in the phase of consciousness represented in poetry, he thinks of certain scenes in the external world because they are suggested not by anything that he is actually, at the time, perceiving there, but by his memory that is recalling them. To one likening his actions to those of Nelson at Trafalgar, or of Dewey at Manila, these men are not really present, only ideally so. As objects of thought, they are not outside of the thinker's mind, they are in it. In the phase of consciousness represented in painting, however, a man thinks of external scenes because they are actually before him. He is much more clearly aware than in the former case, of two different sources of thought—one within and the other without. The objective world is really present. If he wish to represent this fact, he must do it in some other way than through words alone; because words contain only what is in the mind, or is ideally present there. He must use an external medium, as in painting, sculpture, or architecture.

Notice now that, as applied to poetry, the facts just mentioned seem to rule out of its domain any descriptive details other than those of such prominence that a man observing them might reasonably be supposed to be able to retain them in memory,—other than details—to state it differently—which have been stored in the mind, and are brought to consciousness because, apparently, the most important factors entering into the general mental effect. There is, of course, a certain interest, though sometimes not above that which is merely topographic or botanic, awakened by minute descriptions of fields and flowers, such as a painter on the spot would be able to give while carefully scrutinizing these in order to depict them. But descriptions of this kind do not accurately represent the processes of thought of which, when using words, the mind is conscious. Such descriptions do not represent, as words should, the mental results of the action of the poetic imagination, and, therefore, they do not appeal, as poetic words should, to the imaginations of others. Here, for instance, is a passage written with the motive of the painter. The readers of it instinctively think of a plot of ground, *i. e.*, of a mindless thing standing between their thoughts and the thought of the writer. They are not brought into immediate communication with the living mind from which the words come, and therefore their minds are not addressed directly by this mind, as, through the use of words, they should be addressed:

> From the gate
> Of this home-featured inn, which nestling cleaves
> To its own shelf among the downs, begirt
> With trees which lift no branches to defy
> The fury of the storm . . .
> the heart-soothed guest
> Views a furze-dotted common, on each side
> Wreathed into waving eminences, clothed
> Above the furze with scanty green, in front
> Indented sharply to admit the sea
> Spread thence in softest hue—to which a gorge
> Sinking within the valley's deepening green
> Invites by grassy path.
>
> *Alum Bay: Thomas Noon Talfourd.*

Now let us notice a passage in which the description of the external world is subordinated to the thought in the same way in which a scene of nature is, when it is recalled by memory. As contrasted with the last quotation, the reader will recognize in the following a far more immediate communication of thought and feeling between mind and mind, while, at the same time, nothing is described which in a picture could be any more than suggestively represented:

commonly but a single epithet. A ship is to him at one time the 'black ship,' at another the 'hollow ship,' and again the 'swift ship.' . . . Further painting of the ship he does not attempt. But of the ship's sailing, its departure and arrival, he makes so detailed a picture that the artist would have to paint five or six, to put the whole on canvas. . . . He wants, for instance, to paint us the bow of Pandarus. It is of horn, of a certain length, well polished, and tipped at both ends with gold. What does he do? Does he enumerate these details thus drily, one after another? By no means. . . . The poet shows us in the process of creation what the painter can only show us as already existing." ("Laocoön," Sec. 16, trans. by E. Frothingham.)

> He uncovered straight
> His polished bow made of the elastic horns
> Of a wild goat, which from his lurking place,
> As once it left its cavern lair, he smote,
> And pierced its breast, and stretched it on the rock.
> Full sixteen palms in length the horns had grown
> From the goat's forehead. Then an artisan
> Had smoothed, and aptly fitting each to each,
> Polished the whole and tipped the work with gold.
>
> *Iliad, iv. : Bryant's Trans.*

But to leave Lessing and Homer, let us pass on to the drama. In the works of Æschylus, Euripides, and Sophocles, as well as in those of Racine and Corneille in the age of Louis XIV., everything is usually made to conform to what is termed the law of the three unities, *i. e.*, the unity of time, of place, and of action. According to this law, the events must not extend over a period much longer than would be occupied by similar actual occurrences. They must take place in the same locality, and must not mix the comic and the tragic. We all know how the French are

nine cases out of ten he must violate the law of the unities. This is a fact illustrated clearly by the methods chosen by those who gave form to the English drama of the age of Elizabeth. As we know, there is little in their writings to suggest conformity to this law. What is the reason? Can we not attribute it partly to the fact that England had, at that time, no great painters or sculptors; and that her age of architecture, after having expended itself almost exclusively upon churches and palaces, and, very fortunately, having exerted no influence at all upon places of amusement, had passed? There was therefore no extensive contemporary interest with reference to methods employed in arts other than the drama, and, of course, it never entered into the mind of any dramatist, any more than into that of Homer, to imitate the modes of presentation practised in paintings, statues, or buildings. The play-writer thought only of representing words and deeds in such a way that they could be recognized to be natural and would appeal dramatically to those who patronized the theatres. No wonder, therefore, that the methods of the English drama have, in every country, virtually supplanted those of the classic. The latter, like Goethe's "Iphigenia in Tauris," may contain excellent dramatic passages, and, for the sake of these, many may be willing to sit through the intervening explanations. But people in general have less patience. In a drama the only unity that, as a rule, they really desire is dramatic.

Another illustration from the realm of poetry. In speaking of the plan of his "Excursion," Wordsworth, in several places, tells us that his conception of it was that of a cathedral to which his minor poems should stand related like chapels opening from the aisles. In other words, he acknowledges that a method of thought or expression not natural to poetry, but to another art, an art, too, necessitating a body filling space, was present to his mind when considering the general form of his poem. So far as this method had influence, his motive, therefore, was that not of the poet but of the architect. A poem modelled after a cathedral! One might as well talk of a picture modelled after a symphony, or a statue after a running stream. To be sure, if the stream were frozen stiff, and so far lifeless, the statue might image it. Only so far as thought were in a similar condition could a poem that was really like a cathedral, embody it.

Analogous criticisms might be made with reference to many other of our English poems. Crabbe's "Borough," Cowper's "Task," and Thomson's "Seasons," are modelled apparently upon the methods of a man who is preparing a set of village photographs or a country guide-book. As a result, notwithstanding many admirable passages, who does not feel that, considered as wholes, the poems are inartistic? Or, as contrasted with them, who does not feel that works like Scott's "Marmion," Byron's "Corsair," and Bulwer's "Lucile," however deficient in passages, nevertheless, considered as wholes, are artistic? But what is the essential difference between the poetry represented by these two classes of products? Not merely that the former are explanatory and naturalistic, and the latter narrative. Scott abounds in information and description, and Crabbe in anecdotes. The difference lies in the fact that while, as a rule, poets like Scott portray actions in such ways that the successive events described keep pace with the movement of thought, even if they do not lead it onward, poets like Crabbe portray actions, if at all, as if stopping often, with pencil in hand, to sketch in detail, or explain and elaborate the scenes observed. While doing so, the descriptions, of course, fail to keep pace with the movement of thought. Hazlitt's criticism on Wordsworth's "Excursion" might be applied to all of them. "It is more than anything in the world like Robinson Crusoe's boat, which would have been an excellent good boat, and would have carried him to the other side of the globe, but that it could not get out of the sand where it stuck fast."

To observe this effect of lack of movement, notice the passage from the "Excursion" in which a cathedral is described. The reader can judge for himself how far the story, the movement, the animation of the poem, is in danger of standing still, in order to give place or rather space for such descriptions; as well as how far they are more appropriate for a guide-book, or a report to be handed to an architect, painter, or antiquary, than for any other purpose.

> As chanced, the portals of the sacred Pile
> Stood open; and we entered. On my frame,
> At such transition from the fervid air,
> A grateful coolness fell, that seemed to strike
> The heart in concert with that temperate awe
> And natural reverence which the place inspired.
> Not raised in nice proportions was the Pile,
> But large and massy, for duration built;
> With pillars crowded and the roof upheld
> By naked rafters intricately crossed
> Like leafless underboughs in some thick wood
> All withered by the depth of shade above.
> Admonitory texts inscribed the walls,
> Each in its ornamental scroll inclosed;
> Each also crowned with wingèd heads,—a pair
> Of rudely painted cherubim. The floor
> Of nave and aisle, in unpretending guise,
> Was occupied by oaken benches ranged
> In seemly rows; the chancel only showed

POETRY INFLUENCED BY THE PAINTER'S MOTIVE

> Some vain distinctions, marks of earthly state
> . . . . A capacious pew
> Of sculptured oak stood here, with drapery lined;
> And marble monuments were here displayed
> Thronging the walls; and on the floor beneath,
> Sepulchral stones appeared, with emblems graven,
> And foot-worn epitaphs, and some with small
> And shining epitaphs of brass inlaid.
> *Excursion, v. : Wordsworth.*

Some of Wordsworth's descriptions of natural scenery have the same characteristics. For instance, in the following, how essentially the poet is conceiving of nature as so much space which he must divide into distinct portions; how evidently he is thinking of the way in which a painter would divide off his canvas in order to reproduce the scene!

> —A point that showed the valley, stretched
> In length before us; and not distant far,
> Upon a rising ground, a grey church tower,
> Whose battlements were screened by tufted trees.
> And towards a crystal mere that lay beyond
> Among steep hills and woods embosomed, flowed
> A copious stream with boldly winding course;
> Here traceable, there hidden,—there again
> To sight restored and glittering in the sun.
> On the stream's bank and everywhere, appeared
> Fair dwellings, single, or in social knots;
> Some scattered o'er the level, others perched
> On the hillsides, a cheerful, quiet scene
> Now in its morning purity arrayed.
> *Excursion, v. : Wordsworth.*

Here are other descriptions of the same character:

> That lonely dwelling stood among the hills
> By a grey mountain-stream; just elevate
> Above the winter torrents did it stand,
> Upon a craggy bank. An orchard slope
> Arose behind. . . . The narrow vale which wound

> Among the hills, was grey with rocks that peered
> Above its shallow soil ; the mountain-side
> Was loose with stones bestrewn, which oftentimes
> Clattered adown the steep, beneath the foot
> Of struggling goat dislodged ; or towered with crags.
> *Madoc in Wales, xiv. : Southey.*

>   'T was a spot
> Herself had chosen, from the palace walls
> Farthest removed, and by no sound disturbed,
> And by no eye o'erlooked ; for in the midst
> Of loftiest trees umbrageous, was it hid.
> Yet to the sunshine open, and the airs
> That from the deep shades all around it breathed
> Cool and sweet-scented. . . .
>   To a graceful arch
> The pliant branches, intertwined, were bent ;
> . . . . With fragrant moss the floor
> Was planted, to the foot a carpet rich,
> Or for the languid limbs a downy couch,
> Inviting slumber.
> *Fall of Nineveh : Atherstone.*

With these lines, let us now contrast two descriptions from Tennyson. Notice how little there is in them which a painter could reproduce with accuracy ; and this because the motive to expression, although influenced by certain scenes to which allusion is made, is not that of the painter but that of the poet. In each the movement of thought is the main object of representation. We hear of a court and a sunset ; but we scarcely do so before other things are so crowded upon attention as to obviate at once any suggestion of a desire to delineate outlines as they appear in space.

>   There rose
> A hubbub in the court of half the maids
> Gathered together ; from the illumined hall,
> Long lanes of splendor slanted o'er the press
> Of snowy shoulders, thick as herded ewes,

POETRY NOT INFLUENCED BY PAINTER'S MOTIVE 451

> And rainbow robes and gems and gem-like eyes,
> And gold and golden heads; they to and fro
> Fluctuated, as flowers in storm, some red, some pale,
> All open-mouthed, all gazing to the light,
> Some crying there was an army in the land,
> And some, that men were in the very walls,
> And some, they cared not, till a clamor grew
> As of a new-world Babel, woman-built,
> And worse-confounded; high above them stood
> The placid marble Muses looking peace.
>
> *The Princess: Tennyson.*

> The charmèd sunset lingered low adown
> In the red West; through mountain clefts the dale
> Was seen far inland, and the yellow down
> Bordered with palm, and many a winding vale
> And meadow set with slender galingale;
> A land where all things always seemed the same!
> And round about the keel with faces pale,
> Dark faces pale against that rosy flame,
> The mild-eyed, melancholy Lotus-eaters came.
>
> *The Lotus-Eaters: Tennyson.*

Two more quotations will illustrate the possibility of describing a scene without enough movement even when in itself it involves movement. For the same reason they will show still more clearly than any quotations that have preceded them, the poet's liability, even when circumstances do not seem to favor it, to follow the methods of the painter. In the first quotation, notice the accuracy and minuteness of the descriptions—descriptions that cannot, by any stretch of imagination, be supposed to represent what a person interested in all the series of events transpiring, would be able to observe. The minuteness is conceivable on only the supposition that the observer intends afterwards to make something, or to paint something, precisely like some object seen, which therefore he has examined with special attention. In other words, the description is not a natural representation of the movement of thought in the mind of a poet. Notice, too, that during all the time that the writer is explaining the details, his story stands still:

> And lo! the gorgeous pageant like the sun
> Flares on their startled eyes. Four snow-white steeds
> In golden trappings, barbèd all in gold,
> Spring through the gate; the lofty chariot then,
> Of ebony, with gold and gems thick strewn,
> Even like the starry night. The spokes were gold,
> With fetters of strong brass;

The idea of his being able at a glance to detect the difference between gold and brass!

> the naves were brass
> With burnished gold o'erlaid, and diamond rimmed;
> Steel were the axles in bright silver case;
> The pole was cased in silver; high aloft,
> Like a rich throne, the gorgeous seat was framed,
> Of ivory part, part silver and part gold;
> On either side, a golden statue stood;
> Upon the right, and on a throne of gold,
> Great Belus, of the Assyrian empire first,
> And worshipped as a god; but, on the left,
> In a resplendent car by lions drawn,
> A goddess—
>
> *The Fall of Nineveh: Atherstone.*

The other passage is a description of something very similar, by Shelley. But following the delicate poetic instincts of his nature, the writer reveals hardly a suggestion of a painter's view-point.

> Hark! whence that rushing sound?
> 'T is like the wondrous strain
> That round a lonely ruin swells
> Which, wandering on the echoing shore,

The enthusiast hears at evening;
'T is softer than the west wind's sigh;
'T is wilder than the unmeasured notes
Of that strange lyre whose strings
The genii of the breezes sweep;
Those lines of rainbow light
Are like the moonbeams when they fall
Through some cathedral window, but the **tints**
Are such as may not find
Comparison on earth.
. . . . .
Behold the chariot of the Fairy Queen!
Celestial coursers paw the unyielding air;
Their filmy pennons at her word they furl,
And stop obedient to the reins of light.
These the Queen of Spells drew in,
She spread a charm around the spot,
And leaning graceful from the etherial car,
Long did she gaze and silently
Upon the slumbering maid.
Queen Mab: Shelley.

Of course, in the movement of a poem there may be many different degrees of rapidity. In the lyric the thought may rush through its course like a mountain cataract, and in the epic may advance slowly and grandly as a river near the ocean; but, in either case, the evolution of the ideas should be the principal thing, and the descriptive details subordinate, while all together should represent movement.

CHAPTER XXVI.

SIGNIFICANCE MAINLY ATTRIBUTABLE TO THE ELEMENTS OF ART-FORM IN TIME ALONE, AS DIFFERENTLY REPRESENTED IN POETRY, MUSIC, AND ORATORY.

Definite Thought as Expressed in Poetic Words, and Indefinite Emotion in Musical Tones—Words Cause Imagination to See as well as to Hear what is Referred to—Poetry of the Highest Order Presents a Vision of an Ideal Realm—Even when Describing Objects Vague in Themselves—Lack of these Effects in that Poetry which Subordinates the Verbal to the Musical—Such Poetry Common in our Own Day—And does not Exert the Legitimate Influence of Poetry—Contrast between Tennyson and Byron—Reasons why Foreigners Prefer the Latter—Comment on Byron's Methods—Explanations—Expression Appropriate for Musical Tones—Printed Explanations of Scenery Accompanying Musical Compositions no Proof that Limitations of this Form of Expression should not be Recognized—Pleasure from Musical Effects is Independent of these Explanations—And of the Words and Acting in Ballads and Operas—As Shown by Various Facts with Reference to Lovers of Music—Expression in Oratory as Limited on its Poetic or Musical Side—And on its Picturesque Side.

AS indicated in the preceding chapter, Lessing, in his "Laocoön," did a permanent service for sound criticism by distinguishing the method of representation in poetry from that in painting and in sculpture. In this chapter it will be shown that, owing largely to new developments in both arts, it is now of equal importance to distinguish the methods of poetry from those of music. On page 434 it was pointed out that the differences between sounds and sights, while greater in degree, are no more actual than between kinds of sounds. The effects of poetry are produced by articulated words, those of music, so far as it is " pure music," by unarticulated tones. Words represent conceptions of which the mind is made conscious through definition, and which are therefore sufficiently intelligible to be clearly distinguished. Tones represent conceptional tendencies of which the mind is made conscious without definition, and which, therefore, are not always sufficiently intelligible to be clearly distinguished. See Chapters XVI. to XVIII. of " Art in Theory."

The consequent difference between the effects of the two arts, whether considered as produced in the mind or expressed in the form, is this: Both influence the imagination, and, while doing so, conjure pictures which pass in review before it; but while poetry indicates definitely what these pictures shall be, music leaves the mind of the listener free to determine this, the same chords inclining one man, perhaps, to think of his business, and another of his recreation, one of a storm at sea, and another of a battle-field. Now notice a further reason for this difference: Words make thought definite because they appeal to the imagination as is done through the sense not only of hearing but also of sight; and this, not only because they can be printed as well as spoken, but because, as a rule, they refer to objects, as in the cases of *hut, farm, road*, and *horse;* or to actions, as in the cases of *come, go, stop*, and *hurry;* or to other conditions, as in the cases of *near, far, with*, and *by*, that can be seen, and that are seen by imagination whenever the words are used. Musical tones, on the contrary, appeal to imagination almost exclusively as is done through the sense of hearing irrespective of sight. This is a difference which will be shown, as we go on, to be radical, and extremely important. The effect of words in causing the imagination to perceive that which is mentioned, may be observed by noticing those that are italicized in the following:

> Lost in the *labyrinth* of thy fury.
> *Troilus and Cressida, ii., 3 : Shakespeare.*

> *Riveted,*
> *Screwed,* to my memory.
> *Cymbeline, ii., 2 : Idem.*

> Thou art all *ice*, thy kindness *freezes.*
> *Richard III., iv., 2 : Idem.*

> I'll *queen* it no inch further
> But milk my ewes and weep.
> *Winter's Tale, iv., 3 : Idem.*

One test of poetry of the highest order is that, as we read it, it calls attention to these visible objects. Through doing this, the lines transport us into a realm of imagination, and this not of our own making, as in music, but of the poet's making. So far as he fails to lift us into this realm, and to keep us in it, his poetry fails of one of its highest possibilities. Notice in the following how clean-cut and concrete every figure is, how it stands out in relief, rising visually before the mind, the moment that the words are heard:

> Like one that stands upon a promontory,
> And spies a far-off shore where he would tread,
> Wishing his foot were equal with his eye ;
> And chides the sea that sunders him from thence.
> *3 Henry VI., iii., 2 : Idem.*

> New honors come upon him
> Like our strange garments ; cleave not to their mould,
> But with the aid of use.
> *Macbeth, i., 3 : Idem.*

> Ay, marry now, my soul hath elbow-room.
> *King John, v., 7 : Idem.*

He has strangled
His language in his tears.
Henry VIII., v., 1 : Idem.

Like a glow-worm golden,
  In a dell of dew,
Scattering unbeholden
  Its aërial hue
Among the flowers and grass which screen it from the view.
To the Skylark : Shelley.

She was a Phantom of delight
When first she gleamed upon my sight ;
A lovely Apparition sent
To be a moment's ornament ;
Her eyes as stars of Twilight fair ;
Like twilight's too her dusky hair ;
But all things else about her drawn
From Maytime and the cheerful Dawn ;
A dancing Shape, an Image gay,
To haunt, to startle and waylay.
She was a Phantom of Delight : Wordsworth.

Her feet beneath her petticoat
Like little mice, stole in and out,
  As if they feared the light ;
But O, she dances such a way,
No sun upon an Easter-day
  Is half so fine a sight.
A Ballad upon a Wedding : Sir John Suckling.

But let my due feet never fail
To walk the studious cloisters pale,
And love the high embowered roof,
With antique pillars massy proof,
And storied windows richly dight,
Casting a dim religious light :
There let the pealing organ blow,
To the full voiced choir below,
In service high and anthems clear,
As may with sweetness through mine ear
Dissolve me into ecstasies.
Il Penseroso : Milton.

And the night shall be filled with music,
   And the cares that infest the day
Shall fold their tents like the Arabs,
   And as silently steal away.
The Day is Done : Longfellow.

Art is long and time is fleeting,
   And our hearts, though stout and brave,
Still like muffled drums are beating
   Funeral marches to the grave.
The Psalm of Life : Idem.

These last two stanzas are characteristic of Longfellow. Does the visual effect of the style give us one reason for his wide popularity? Observe now that this clean-cut, concrete visualization can be conjured in the imagination even by a description of something which, in itself, is not clean-cut or concrete:

                    The other shape,
If shape it might be called that shape had none
Distinguishable in member, joint, or limb,
Or substance might be called that shadow seemed,
For each seemed either ; black it stood as night,
Fierce as ten furies, terrible as hell,
And shook a dreadful dart ; what seemed his head
The likeness of a kingly crown had on.
Paradise Lost, ii. : Milton.

Then saw they how there hove a dusky barge,
Dark as a funeral scarf from stem to stern,
Beneath them ; and descending, they were ware
That all the decks were dense with stately forms,
Black-stoled, black-hooded, like a dream,—by these
Three Queens with crowns of gold,—and from them rose
A cry that shivered to the tingling stars,
And, as it were one voice, an agony
Of lamentation, like a wind that shrills
All night in a waste land, where no one comes,
Or hath come since the making of the world.
Morte d'Arthur : Tennyson.

MUSICAL POETRY APPEALING ONLY TO THE EAR. 459

With these quotations in mind, let us examine the following. As we read them, are we not far more conscious of certain audible sensations of great delicacy and sweetness than of any definite and distinct pictures rising, one after the other, into consciousness; and, just in the degree in which this is true, is it not a fact that we fail to be lifted out of our actual visible surroundings into that realm of the imagination, no less visible, into which it seems the peculiar function of poetry of the highest order to transport one?

>Round thee blow, self-pleachèd deep,
>Bramble roses, faint and pale,
>And long purples of the dale.
>>Let them rave.
>These in every shower creep
>Through the green that folds thy grave.
>>Let them rave.
>>>*A Dirge : Tennyson.*

>A slow-developed strength awaits
>>Completion in a painful school ;
>>Phantoms of other forms of rule,
>New Majesties of mighty States—
>
>The warders of the growing hour,
>>But vague in vapor, hard to mark ;
>>And round them sea and air are dark
>With great contrivances of Power.
>
>Of many changes, aptly joined,
>>Is bodied forth the second whole.
>>Regard gradation, lest the soul
>Of Discord race the rising wind.
>>>*Love thou thy Land : Idem.*

>Praise him, O winds that move the molten air,
>>O light of days that were,
>And light of days that shall be ; land and sea,
>>And heaven and Italy ;

> Praise him, O storm and summer, shore and wave,
>   O skies and every grave;
> O weeping hopes, O memories beyond tears,
>   O many and murmuring years,
> O sounds far off in time and visions far,
>   O sorrow with thy star;
> And joy with all thy beacons; ye that mourn,
>   And ye whose light is born;
> O fallen faces, and O souls arisen,
>   Praise him from tomb and prison.
>   *A Song of Italy: Swinburne.*

The following is not, as might be supposed, a part wrested from a stanza in order to be used as an illustration. It is a complete stanza:

> So much we lend, indeed,
>   Perforce, by force of need,
> So much we must; even these things and no more,
> The far sea sundering and the sundered shore
>   A world apart from ours,
>   So much the imperious hours,
> Exact and spare not; but no more than these
> All earth and all her seas
> From thought and faith of trust and truth can borrow,
> Not memory from desire, nor hope from sorrow.
>   *A Parting Song: Idem.*

Notice the following too,—a remarkably successful description, so far as concerns the method of representation possible to sound alone:

> And gentler the wind from the dreary
>   Sea-banks by the waves overlapped,
> Being weary, speaks peace to the weary
>   From slopes that the tide-stream hath sapped;
> And sweeter than all that we call so
>   The seal of their slumber shall be,
> Till the graves that embosom them also
>   Be sapped of the sea.
>   *By the North Sea: Idem.*

In our own day, the general effects of this kind of verse are exceedingly familiar and popular. It is not too much to say that its cadences so ring in the ear that, in the opinion of some, new verse that fails to echo them almost fails to manifest any poetry at all. Indeed, in their minds, the distinctively poetical is confounded with this style, almost as completely as in the days of Pope it was confounded with the balance of rhythm in lines like the following:

> Where small and great, where weak and mighty, made
> To serve not suffer, strengthen not invade;
> More powerful each as needful to the rest,
> And, in proportion as it blesses, blest;
> Draw to one point, and to one centre bring
> Beast, man, or angel, servant, lord, or king.
> *Essay on Man, iii.: Pope.*

This balance of rhythm, however, is now recognized to have been artificial and inartistic. Is it possible that our own frequent subordination of all other poetic effects to the musical may be the same? Of course it is not recognized to be so by our popular critics. The style of Pope was not recognized to be what it was by their representatives of his day. Popular critics, like other popular people, give voice to popular opinion. They are on the crest of its wave for the very reason that they have the full support of the opinion that is about and below them. For this reason, paradoxical as it may seem, those esteemed the best critics of an age are often its worst critics. Nor, as applied to poetry, has this fact in our own times been otherwise than detrimental. "When I get my girls together and try to read to them," said a friend of the author, referring to his three daughters, all Eastern college students, "the only expression in which all universally join is, 'Don't read poetry.' Now you and I," he went on, "when we were young, would have preferred poetry. Why don't the young of to-day prefer it?" Such a question usually suggests a homily about its being a scientific age. The homily may have relevance, but it does not deal with the sole reason for the result, nor with the one most important. Science and art are different, and they satisfy different mental cravings, one demanding stimulus for knowledge and the other for imagination. Nor was there ever a time when the normal mind did not demand both. To suppose that it can be satisfied with one of them is like supposing that thirst can be assuaged by giving food. If anything have taken the place of the poem, it is more likely to be the novel, which, like it, appeals to the imagination. But why should the novel take the place of the poem? What imaginative effect attends it that was formerly produced by poetry, and which, apparently, modern poetry does not produce? This can be best answered, perhaps, by mentioning another "modern instance."

At an evening gathering, a professor of literature had been reading and explaining some of Tennyson's poems. Later in the evening, a retired banker, a college graduate and an omnivorous reader, said to him, "That kind of poetry is all very fine, but it is too fine for me. When I want poetry, I read Byron," to which remark he added in an undertone a phrase or two about the lurid light in front of which, according to him, Byron was accustomed to arrange his characters in relief. This comment conforms in spirit to that which an unprejudiced mind must acknowledge to represent the best critical judgment of continental Europe. As a rule, its writers and scholars fail to assign as high rank to the poetry of Tennyson and his school as do the English and our own people. Probably many of us who are enthusiastic admirers of Tennyson can recall foreign friends, given to literary criticism, with whom we have had long controversies on this subject. It would not be accurate to say that the poet contrasted with Tennyson is always Byron. It can only be affirmed that, as a rule, the English poetry for which they express preference, is of a kind affording certain contrasts to that of the great laureate; and that, if Byron be mentioned at all, he is mentioned in superlatives. Now is there any need of arguing about what is the reason for this? Is it not because Tennyson and writers of his school depend so largely upon musical effects? These effects are either, as in those on page 459, entirely substituted for visual effects, or are allowed to overbalance the visual to such an extent as to obscure them, especially to the mind of a foreigner too unaccustomed to either the sounds or the associations of English words for them to reveal to him their subtlest suggestions. In other words, the outlines of this style of poetry are not large enough or broad enough for him; not like those of Shakespeare, or of Byron, for instance, as illustrated in the following:

> 'T is midnight. On the mountains brown
> The cold round moon shines deeply down;
> Blue roll the waters, blue the sky
> Spreads like an ocean hung on high,
> Bespangled with those isles of light,
> So wildly, spiritually bright;
> Who ever gazed upon them shining,
> And turned to earth without repining?
> *The Siege of Corinth: Byron.*

> Up rose the Dervise with that burst of light,
> Nor less his change of form appalled the sight:
> Up rose that Dervise—not in saintly garb,
> But like a warrior bounding on his barb,

Dashed his high cap, and tore his robe away—
Shone his mailed breast and flashed his sabre's ray !
His close but glittering casque, and sable plume,
More glittering eye, and black brow's sabler gloom,
Glared on the Moslem's eyes some Afrit sprite,
Whose demon death-blow left no hope for fight.
The wild confusion, and the swarthy glow
Of flames on high, and torches from below ;
The shriek of terror, and the mingling yell—
For swords began to clash and shouts to swell—
Flung o'er that spot of earth the air of hell !
Distracted, to and fro, the flying slaves
Behold but bloody shore and fiery waves ;
Nought heeded they the Pasha's angry cry
They seize that Dervise !—seize on Zatanai !
He saw their terror—checked the first despair
That urged him but to stand and perish there,
Since far too early and too well obeyed,
The flame was kindled ere the signal made ;
He saw their terror—from his baldric drew
His bugle—brief the blast—but shrilly blew ;
'T is answered—" Well ye speed, my gallant crew !
Why did I doubt their quickness of career ?
And deem design had left me single here ? "
Sweeps his long arm—that sabre's whirling sway
Sheds fast atonement for its first delay ;
Completes his fury what their fear begun,
And makes the many basely quail to one.
The cloven turbans o'er the chamber spread,
And scarce an arm dare rise to guard its head :
Even Seyd, convulsed, o'erwhelmed with rage, surprise,
Retreats before him, though he still defies.
No craven he—and yet he dreads the blow,
So much Confusion magnifies his foe !
His blazing galleys still distract his sight,
He tore his beard, and, foaming, fled the fight;
For now the pirates pass'd the Harem gate,
And burst within—and it were death to wait ;
Where wild Amazement shrieking—kneeling—throws
The sword aside—in vain—the blood o'erflows!
The Corsairs, pouring, haste to where within

> Invited Conrad's bugle, and the din
> Of groaning victims, and wild cries for life,
> Proclaimed how well he did the work of strife.
> They shout to find him grim and lonely there,
> A glutted tiger mangling in his lair !
> But short their greeting—shorter his reply—
> " 'T is well—but Seyd escapes—and he must die—
> Much hath been done—but more remains to do—
> Their galleys blaze—why not their city too ? "
>
> *The Corsair : Byron.*

Byron's poetry, with its abrupt, if not ungrammatical, transitions of tense, its inharmonious successions of syllables, and its inaccuracies of diction,[1] the German critics prefer to the poetry of Tennyson. If we ourselves do not prefer it, would it not, at least, be wise for us to try to perceive why others should do so, and to ask ourselves whether this style does not meet a legitimate imaginative demand which the poetry of our own time is neglecting? In this age there is no great danger that any large number will give to the English poetry of the early part of this century, of which, perhaps, Byron is the foremost representative, the supreme literary homage once accorded it. But let us not go to the opposite extreme. Let us acknowledge that the artistic possibilities of many of our younger poets might be greatly broadened by giving to this poetry a certain amount of very cordial literary recognition.

In this book we are considering the representative effects of poetry and of music for no other purpose than to distinguish them from one another. Those who wish to study the manner in which effects in each of these arts

---

[1] Notice " behold . . . nought heeded," " completes his fury what their fears begun," " spread . . . dare rise," " distract his sight, He tore," and " career," in the above.

may be represented in each detail of form, will find the subject amply discussed in the volume of this series entitled " Poetry as a Representative Art," and in the essay upon " Music as a Representative Art," which latter is printed in the volume entitled " Rhythm and Harmony in Poetry and Music."

It follows from what has been said that, as distinguished from poetry, music should be representative of only such indefinite and emotive mental effects as can be expressed in unarticulated sounds. This inference suggests, at once, a reason for certain well-known facts with reference to the effects of this art. It shows us, for instance, why the music invariably conceded to rank highest is instrumental; is—to quote the words of Mr. Dwight, late editor of " The Journal of Music "—" pure music, which lives and moves in purely musical ideas"; and again, it shows us why it is that all men, well-nigh with unanimity, recognize a superlative sweetness in the midnight serenade. In both cases there is experienced a distinctive effect of sound, and of this only. In connection with the former, there is no distraction from words; in connection with the latter, none from sights.

Of course, some other facts apparently controverting this principle may be instanced. There is a certain style of instrumental music, especially among the Germans, which, to draw our inferences from explanations printed on programs, seems to be the embodiment of phases of thought which can be appropriately expressed in poetry also, and even in painting. It seems to be distinctly stated in connection with certain of these compositions, as of some, for instance, of Liszt, that they represent poems, and of others, as of the Pastoral Symphonies of Beethoven and Haydn, that they represent scenes in nature. It is a question, however, whether we are not doing an injustice to the composers of such music when we infer that their so-called explanations are intended to imply that the phase of significance represented might be as well expressed in poetry or in painting. Would the authors of these compositions admit that their works are imitative merely, or imitative at all in any slavish sense? Do the explanations imply any more than this,—that the compositions to which they refer are musical developments representative of natural conditions analogous to such as, in certain circumstances, which are not those actually realized, might be expressed, but differently expressed, in poetry or in painting? If this be the true meaning of the composers, then they desire merely to explain their work, as all admit that they can do legitimately, according to the methods, as we might term them, of comparative æsthetics; and if this be so, their compositions involve no violation of the principle here unfolded. No attempt is made in them at representation in a manner appropriate only in poetry or in painting. Their composers have merely indicated the existence of relationships, which, in other conditions, or with a different development, might be differently represented.

Again, judging this style of music from its effects, as we ourselves experience them, let those of us who can analyze the sources of our enjoyment of it inquire whether we are pleased with this or that composition because it is an imitation—*i. e.*, because it sounds so much like the roaring of a storm, the rustling of a forest, or the bleating of sheep; or, because, aside from any resemblances to other things, from any connections with subjects that might be depicted or described in other ways, the composition is enjoyable in itself, on account solely of the way in which, starting with a theme suggested by some sound in nature, the melodies and harmonies have been developed, one after another, according to those strictly musical methods which cause the whole to be music and not something else. Or suppose that in any given product we really take delight, and our main delight too, in the imitation, let us ask ourselves again whether we take delight in the imitation for its evidences of ingenuity, or for the musical sweetness and beauty which this imitation has succeeded in bringing to our notice. A few such questions will probably convince us that the æsthetic effect, which is alone the legitimate effect of art, is always produced in the degree in which a musical composition is an expression of something distinctively musical.

Again, the ballad or the opera may be instanced as controverting the principle that we are considering. But can it be said that these prove that the highest style of music is dependent for success upon the words or actions of a performer of it? With some persons, of course, it is. But let us recall that songs and operas are often enjoyed immensely by persons to whom music as music is a sealed art. Their pleasure in the song is similar to that which attends the utterance of very rhythmical poetry; and in the opera, the gaudy playhouse, the gayly dressed people, the glittering stage, and the movements of the actors are all entertaining on their own accounts. A real musician, however, frequently regards everything of this sort as a distraction; and he enjoys the music connected with it just as much — sometimes more — when the words used on the stage are in a foreign language which he does not understand, or when the harmony is played, apart from either words or scenery, by an orchestra in a concert room. It is true, of course, as brought out in Chapter

without slipping off, to follow a line of cracks along the side of a steep roof covered with ice.

A word, too, might be added with reference to the fault of making elocution too picturesque; of confounding representation in action with painting. As we all know, in connection with expression in language, only a moderate degree of action is natural. To overstep the boundary of moderation in this regard is to transgress those limits where the dignity of appropriate characterization passes into the ludicrousness of incongruous caricature,—a result that we may laugh with in comedy, but can only laugh at in a serious performance.

in so many copies and photographs that are made of the group of the "Young Pilgrims" taken from "The Destruction of Jerusalem."

From what has been said, however, it need not be inferred that painters can never draw their subjects from poetry, or poets from painting. It need merely be inferred that there should be a difference in the ways in which the two arts treat the same subject. An illustration of this difference has been mentioned already in connection with what was said on page 418 of the series of paintings by Cole entitled "The Voyage of Life." Hogarth's series of paintings, entitled "The Rake's Progress" and "The Harlot's Progress," exemplify the same principle. In these, each of the separate pictures represents only a single situation. Yet all placed side by side accomplish a result similar to that which would be reached if the successive details were unfolded in a representation in time.

An illustration of the same difference in method has been noticed by certain of the German critics, in connection with what is said of the shield of Achilles in the eighteenth book of the "Iliad." We know how the shield would be perceived in space; but the poet, instead of saying merely that this and that were to be seen on it, assumes a time when they were not; represents Thetis, the mother of Achilles, journeying to Vulcan to request him to forge it; and then mentions the actions of the god of the anvil while he fulfils the request.

>So speaking he withdrew, and went where lay
>The bellows, turned them toward the fire, and bade
>The work begin. . . . .
>And first he forged the huge and massive shield,
>Divinely wrought in every part,—its edge
>Clasped with a triple border, white and bright,

>A silver belt hung from it and its folds
>Were five ; a crowd of figures on its disk
>Were fashioned by the artist's passing skill,
>For here he placed the earth and heaven, and here,
>The great deep and the never setting sun
>And the full moon, and here he set the stars.
>
> *Iliad, xviii : Bryant's Trans.*

That which is appropriate for representation in painting needs to be distinguished from that appropriate not only in poetry but also in landscape-gardening, sculpture, and architecture. When we recall what an inartistic impression is frequently conveyed by the reproducing in a picture of a highly cultivated park, or of a gentleman's homestead,—the house architecturally correct, and the avenues leading to it as clearly drawn as the lines of a geometric figure,—then we may understand with some definiteness what is meant by confounding the conceptions to be expressed in landscape-gardening and in painting. Both ought to represent, as all art should, the effects of nature at first hand; but, in the case of pictures such as those just mentioned, there is danger that the main impression conveyed will be of the effects upon nature of some man, of some landscape-artist. And reflection will convince us that this is the reason—certainly a sufficient one—why such pictures often appear inartistic. They manifest, to too great an extent, the influence of a method of representation appropriate to another art.

The difference between that which is appropriately represented in painting and in sculpture is very truthfully suggested, though not entirely indicated, by the difference, which all recognize, between the meaning of the terms *picturesque* and *statuesque*. The *picturesque*, as defined on page 280, involves a conception of much and minute variety. And this is just what painting involves. The color that is used in it, and not in sculpture, is never well applied unless it imitates the influences of light and shade in nature to such a degree as to cause slight differences at almost every perceptible point. Besides this, color enables the artist to separate, one from another, and thus to represent clearly, a very large number of small details most of which would be indistinguishable if an attempt were made to indicate them in sculpture. On the other hand, the *statuesque* involves the conception of something that stands out by itself,—something that, because it has bulk or body, can be looked at from every side. Even when the term applies to the sculpture of mere relief, the solidity of the medium that is used in it, and not in painting, tends to separate every contour from every other by emphatically defined outlines. These outlines, too, must be comparatively few in number and the objects which they delineate comparatively large in size. Thus the limitations of the material used in each of the arts determine the limitations of the subjects which it and it alone can appropriately embody. On account of the minute representative possibilities of color, one can make a painting of a landscape, and can crowd into a small compass a large number of figures and faces, appearing almost immediately beside or behind one other. In sculpture, landscape is well-nigh impossible, and so is any extensive grouping of figures. Even such figures as can be brought together, must, owing to the uniformity of color, be very distinctly separated, and, as artistic effects produced through variety of hues are impossible, compensating artistic effects through the use of outlines become imperative. Hence parallelism, continuity, balance, symmetry, and kindred methods of æsthetically accenting the requirements of contour become more prominent. For instance, in the group of "Niobe and her Children,"[1] none of the figures touch one another, and all are separated by apparently equal spaces; besides which, on each side of the centre, they lean in exactly the same directions. In the relief called "The Soldier's Return,"[2] on the National Monument near Bingen, Germany, the figures, though apparently touching, are all separated by approximately like distances, and, on each side of the centre, their trunks and limbs produce effects of exact parallelism. In painting, such uniformity of arrangement, through the use of outlines alone, suggests artificiality, unless intended to imitate effects of sculpture. Why? Because an art is always fulfilling its best possibilities when it is doing that which it and it alone can do. What painting can do and sculpture cannot, is to produce effects through the use of pigments. What sculpture can do and painting cannot, is to produce effects through the use of bulk, including outlines representing length, breadth, and thickness. When the painter is trying to produce effects of bulk such as can be better produced in sculpture, or of outlines such as can be just as well produced where there is no color, he is, consciously or unconsciously, under the influence of methods necessitated where those of color are wanting. These statuesque effects in painting are most common upon walls. In almost any decorated interior, we come upon figures, either alone or in groups, some of them, if not highly colored, hardly distinguishable, at a distance, from statues. Often, even when grouped, they stand apparently alone, looking not at one another but at ourselves, showing that the chief object of their artist was

---

[1] Fig. 45, page 146, "The Genesis of Art-Form."
[2] Fig. 52, page 176, "The Genesis of Art-Form"; Fig. 23, page 51, "Paint., Sculpt., and Arch. as Rep. Arts."

to call attention to the beauty of the contour or pose of each individual figure, rather than to the blendings of the outlines and colors of all the figures of the composition considered as a whole. In other words, such paintings produce a statuesque rather than a picturesque effect. Undoubtedly, in certain cases, they are the only forms of painting adapted to the circumstances. But in other cases they are out of place, and appear stiff and unnatural. Especially do they seem out of place in certain products which carry to an extreme the conception that a painting should never even suggest a story. As will be shown on page 484, there is some reason for holding this view as applied to grouping in statuary. But, as applied to painting, it is questionable whether the conception in its extreme form is not very largely a result of confounding the picturesque with the statuesque.

There are other paintings, usually developments, too, of decoration, which may be said to manifest not so much a statuesque as an architectural effect. Some of the altarpieces and religious compositions of the old masters show an absolutely symmetrical disposition of the figures.[1] These appear balanced against one another in such ways that it is almost impossible to compare them to anything except the wings of a building; while the symmetrical framework of pillars, pediments, and steps actually surrounding the figures in many instances, not only suggests but literally proclaims the architectural motive. These architectural effects, if there be a reason in the subject excusing them, as is the case, for instance, in Raphael's "School of Athens,"[2] may add interest to the composi-

[1] See Fig. 15, page 71, also Fig. 58, page 185, of "The Genesis of Art-Form."

[2] Fig. 10, page 41, "The Genesis of Art-Form"; Fig. 156, page 249, "Paint., Sculpt., and Arch. as Rep. Arts."

tion; but otherwise they not infrequently do the opposite.

The methods of sculpture differ, of course, just as do those of painting, from the methods of poetry. A good illustration of the difference may be noticed by contrasting the statue of the Dying Gladiator or Galatian,[1] probably well known to all of us, with Byron's description of the statue. Here are his words:

> I see before me the Gladiator lie;
> He leans upon his hand — his manly brow
> Consents to death but conquers agony,
> And his drooped head sinks gradually low—
> And through his side, the last drops, ebbing slow
> From the red gash, fall heavy, one by one,
> Like the first of a thunder-shower; and now
> The arena swims around him,— he is gone,
> Ere ceased the inhuman shout which hailed the wretch who won.
>
> He heard it; but he heeded not — his eyes
> Were with his heart, and that was far away.
> He recked not of the life he lost, nor prize,
> But where his rude hut by the Danube lay,
> There were his young barbarians all at play,
> There was their Dacian mother— he, their sire,
> Butchered to make a Roman holiday.
>
> *Childe Harold: Byron.*

Nothing needs to be added with reference to confounding sculpture with landscape-gardening beyond that which was said on page 475. But, at the risk of some unavoidable repetition, the line of thought already suggested when separating painting from sculpture may, so far as it refers to the limitations of the latter, be somewhat extended. The word *statue* seems to indicate still more distinctively than the word *picture* that there must be a representation of that which is stationary. With this suggestion in mind,

[1] Fig. 166, page 283, "Paint., Sculp., and Arch. as Rep. Arts."

we shall find that, as a fact, the principle applied to painting on page 477 is yet more applicable to sculpture. The continuous stages in which the hero is constantly reappearing, which is delineated in the spiral band surrounding the column of Trajan, is probably even less interesting in itself than is the pictorial story of the life of Joshua mentioned on page 476.[1] Nor is there much doubt that the different separate pictures in the series by Hogarth, entitled "The Rake's Progress" or "The Harlot's Progress," are more interesting than the different single scenes, all together representing the "Life of Columbus," which constitute the sections of one of the pairs of bronze doors of the Capitol at Washington. Another reason for this fact will be suggested on page 486. At present, let us notice that what sculpture can do, and painting cannot, is to produce effects through the use of bulk, *i. e.*, of outlines, including those of length, breadth, and thickness,—outlines that one can sometimes walk around and regard from every side. It follows that sculpture is at its best in the statue, or, so far as in the relief, in that in which the figures project to the greatest degree possible. This condition is represented in significance by giving to each figure even of a group an individual rather than a collective, associative, or communicative interest. To explain what is meant, the figures depicted in the frieze surrounding the Parthenon,[2] whether in the procession or not, indicate an individual interest in the sense of not representing any great interchange, between one figure and another, of thought, feeling, or action. In this regard, they

---

[1] See also "An Epitome of the Lives of Isaac, Jacob, and Esau," as it is represented in one of the reliefs in the door of the Baptistery at Florence, Fig. 155, page 247, of "Paint., Sculpt., and Arch. as Rep. Arts."

[2] Fig. 148, page 223, "Paint., Sculpt., and Arch. as Rep. Arts,"

present an entirely different appearance from figures in such paintings as Rubens's "Descent from the Cross,"[1] or Raphael's "Death of Ananias."[2] So, in the group of "Niobe and her Children,"[3] described on page 481, there is no interchange of feeling or action; yet, at the same time, because each figure, in its own way, gives expression to the same general emotion of grief, its position is interpretive of the meaning of all the figures. Or take a more marked example. The German scholar, Ludwig Preller, says that the "Apollo Belvedere,"[4] or the statue after which this is modelled, probably stood originally on the apex of the pediment of a temple at Delphi, with the statue termed "Diana of the Louvre"[5] on one side of it, and the statue termed "Athena of the Capital"[6] on the other side. This would be in accordance with the answer said to have been given, when the Gauls approached Delphi, to the question of the people whether the treasures of the temple should be removed. The answer was, "I myself [meaning Apollo] and the White Maidens [meaning Athena and Diana] will take care of that." Now if we can recall the appearance of these three statues as thus situated, we shall be able to comprehend how their postures, full of movement as each is, should mutually add to one another's interest, and at the same time not interfere at all with the statuesque character of the effect of each. When, however, we come to such products

---

[1] Fig. 163, page 277, "Paint., Sculpt., and Arch. as Rep. Arts"; Fig. 16, page 73, "The Genesis of Art-Form."
[2] Fig. 39, page 79, "Paint., Sculpt., and Arch. as Rep. Arts"; Fig. 94, page 288, "The Genesis of Art-Form."
[3] Fig. 45, page 146, "The Genesis of Art-Form."
[4] Fig. 28, page 62, "Paint., Sculpt., and Arch. as Rep. Arts."
[5] Fig. 19, page 75, "The Genesis of Art-Form."
[6] Fig. 37, page 76, "Paint., Sculpt., and Arch. as Rep. Arts."

as the well-known bronze doors of the Baptistery[1] at Florence, or those of the Capitol at Washington, mentioned on page 484, we seem to be upon more doubtful ground. Different sections of these are made to represent different parts of a continuous narrative. Perhaps a trustworthy method through which to estimate the æsthetic value of the result is to ask ourselves whether we admire such products on account of the story which they reveal, or, as is true of the statues mentioned a moment ago, on account of the grace or significance of the individual figures represented in connection with the story. Upon reflection, we probably shall find the latter reason to be the true one. Even in statues, merely symbolic, as on the silver monument to Marshal Saxe by Pigalle at Prague, and on that to Maria Christina, Duchess of Saxe-Teschen,[2] by Canova at Vienna, the former of which represents the mailed form of Maurice of Saxony surrounded by all sorts of living creatures,—an eagle, a lion, a Cupid, etc.,—and the latter the sepulchral pyramid of the deceased, in which heaven and earth are represented by an angel leaning on a lion, and the mourning people by the four ages of life, depositing the ashes of the princess,— even in such works we probably shall find our interest centring mainly in the individual figures. Notice, too, how much more true this is apt to be in the case of sculpture than of painting. We seldom see in a picture a figure that stands out from all surrounding figures, asserting such claims to preëminent and exclusive attention as is common in groups of statuary. Continuing this line of thought, we shall soon recall how superlatively we have enjoyed certain statues, for the very reason, apparently,

[1] Fig. 155, page 247, "Paint., Sculpt., and Arch. as Rep. Arts."
[2] Fig. 22, page 50, *idem*.

that they were placed so that we could view them apart from anything else,—statues that stand in rows, as in the Vatican, or in alcoves by themselves, as is the case at Rome with the "Apollo Belvedere,"[1] and the "Venus of the Capital," and at Frankfort-on-the-Rhine with the "Ariadne." These facts may aid us in forming a conception of what is meant by the phase of significance represented in the statue, and by the statue's significance being less dependent than is that of a painting upon the suggestion of cause and effect as operating in time.

But there is yet a more important limitation to the subject-matter in sculpture. As said on page 434, sculpture differs from painting in not representing color, and in representing bulk or body. By consequence, painting that depicts leaves, flowers, fruit, and children, or grown people as doing very trifling things, may rank high, because manifesting a high degree of skill in drawing and coloring. The more minute the factors with which both of these deal, the more difficult, often, is it to attain success. Besides this, almost any scene which painting depicts includes a very large number of different objects; and these to an extent may compensate in quantity for what the general subject lacks in quality. But in sculpture the conditions are different. There is almost no comparison between carving the wreath of a column's capital and the contour of a human body; and, if the latter have to be carved at all, the difficulty of the work, the permanence of the material, and the fact that the body, when completed, is to be the sole object of attention, all combine to make it seem especially inappropriate to have it represent a trivial subject. It ought to be a dignified subject, or, in lieu of that, at least a subject treated in a dignified

---

[1] Fig. 28, page 62, "Paint., Sculpt., and Arch. as Rep. Arts."

way. As for the dignity of the subject, notice that, in a sense not true of painting, it is appropriate that the figure delineated should be represented in a form greatly exaggerated. Very large pictures, like those of West in the Philadelphia Academy of Fine Arts, sometimes offend us by their very size; and it is almost impossible to conceive of an attractive picture with figures of heroic proportions. But the "Moses" of Angelo or the "Liberty Enlightening the World" in New York do not offend us. On the contrary, very small pictures, as in miniatures, are often extremely pleasing and valuable. But most of us cannot avoid feeling, when we see the bronze doors of the Capitol at Washington, that the small size of the figures makes the work expended upon them hardly worth while, because such subjects could have been represented so much more satisfactorily in pictures.

As for dignity of treatment in lieu of dignity of subject, the influence of this was indicated in what was said, on page 480, of the very extensive use made in sculpture of effects produced by regularity of lines, as in parallelism, continuity, balance, and symmetry. The prominence of these effects is noticeable even in a group like that of "The Laocoön,"[1] where they are partly concealed by the complexity of the arrangements. But in other products they are not concealed. Often in sculptured reliefs the repetition of similar directions in the outlines is so apparent as to produce a rhythmic effect,[2] corresponding to that produced by men marching; and this effect imparts as much greater dignity to each individual figure as it

[1] Fig. 21, page 49, "Paint., Sculpt., and Arch. as Rep. Arts"; Fig. 75, page 226, "The Genesis of Art-Form."

[2] See "Romans Besieging a Fortress," Fig. 6, page 27, "The Genesis of Art-Form"; also "The Soldier's Return," Fig. 52, page 176, *idem.*; also Fig. 23, page 51, "Paint., Sculpt., and Arch. as Rep. Arts."

does to an ordinary man when he is put into line with others in a military company. Such effects, too, for reasons given on page 481, are frequently entirely out of place in paintings.

Turning now to architecture, perhaps it might be affirmed that in no other art is it more necessary to apply principles like those under consideration. Not, of course, that there is any danger of confounding its method of representation with that of poetry or music; but there is danger of confounding it with that of painting or sculpture. When our race, with no models to direct them, first began to build houses and temples, the external forms of each were determined by the design for which it was constructed,— a design suggested, as reflection will show that it must have been, by the modes of attaining in nature ends like those of support, protection, and shelter. This being the case, the desire to attain these ends was evident to every one who saw the building; in other words, the building's effects were artistic in the sense of being genuinely representative of the design of the builder.

In process of time, however, after many such structures had been erected, and some of them had come to be especially admired for their appearance, a class of artists arose more intent to imitate this appearance than the methods in accordance with which the older architects had designed the buildings and caused them to appear as they did. As a consequence, there came to be no apparent connection between the outward form of a building and that for which it was designed;— in other words, architecture ceased to be representative, in the sense in which the word has been used in this essay. But besides this, after the arts of painting and sculpture had been developed, architects began to manifest a tendency to imitate the methods, if not the appearances, employed in these arts. In accounting for the inferiority of the architecture of the Renaissance, Fergusson, in the introduction to his "History of Modern Architecture," says: "Most of those who first practised it, at the time the revolution took place, were either amateurs, sculptors, or painters. Alberti may be named as among the earliest and the most distinguished of the first class. Among the latter, it is hardly necessary to name Michael Angelo, Raphael, Giulio Romano, Peruzzi, Leonardo da Vinci, etc. . . . All painters can make architectural designs for the backgrounds of their pictures. . . . But if any one supposes that such a design will make a permanently satisfactory building, he knows little of the demands of true art, and how little its requirements are to be met by such child's play. . . . Perfection was reached in architecture in the Middle Ages; and the attempt to supersede this, and to introduce the plan of designing by the sketches of an individual, is really the root of the difference between the two systems."

In this passage, Fergusson ascribes inferiority to modern architecture as contrasted with mediæval,—though he does not employ these words,—because of the prevailing tendency in this art to derive its methods from painting and sculpture rather than from the natural promptings and requirements of architecture itself. This tendency often causes the builder to be entirely satisfied with an "elevation" that merely makes a satisfactory picture when drawn on paper. But, as will be shown in the volume of this series entitled "Proportion and Harmony of Line and Color," the requirements of perspective often prevent the parts of a building, which, when so drawn, seem to fulfil the principles of proportion, from fulfilling them when put into the building itself. Besides this, the tendency leads to other forms of confusion between the kinds of conceptions appropriate for producing effects in this art and of conceptions that find legitimate expression in the other arts only. One element of successful architecture undoubtedly is the mere external appearance of a building. And yet, if this alone be regarded, is it not evident that the building, according as it is constructed with exclusive reference to its position or proportions, will be the embodiment of a motive less legitimate distinctively to architecture than to landscape-gardening, painting, or sculpture? And is it not because of this confusion of motives that we find in our modern buildings—in their cornices, roofs, windows, and walls—so much that is false, in other words, so much that is merely on the outside, put there to look well, not to fulfil or to give embodiment to any such significance as it is the peculiar function of architecture to represent? This is not to say that, in this art, the external form should violate the laws of proportion or harmony; but it is to say that these latter should be made subordinate to the general design, that they should cause the outlines to be so disposed as to indicate this design, and not, as is true in too many cases, to conceal it.

Enough has been said, however, with reference to this and to the other arts, to indicate the truth of that which has been maintained in this chapter, namely, the necessity, when a work of art is to be produced, of first distinctly separating the conception to be expressed in it from all that cannot be embodied appropriately in the form of art that has been chosen for the medium of representation.

This discussion has now reached a point where it can go no farther in the direction which has been pursued without confining attention for a time to each art by itself, in order to show thus the different phases of thought and emotion which its various elements of form are fitted, singly and conjointly, to represent. The results of an endeavor to do this will be found in the volumes of this series, entitled " Poetry as a Representative Art," " Painting, Sculpture, and Architecture as Representative Arts," and in the essay entitled " Music as a Representative Art," which latter, for convenience, is printed in the volume entitled " Rhythm and Harmony in Poetry and Music." Later on in the development of the general line of thought, after this subject of significance in form has been fully considered, the subject of form as form is taken up and discussed in three volumes, namely, " The Genesis of Art-Form," " Rhythm and Harmony in Poetry and Music," and " Proportion and Harmony of Line and Color in Painting, Sculpture, and Architecture."

INDEX.

Absolute, the, as suggested in nature, 13-21 ; is conformity to an absolute method, 32, 38, 56 ; not inconsistent with suggestions of change, 51-56 ; or of the eternal and infinite, 19-21 ; revealed through single specimens, 56-59 ; truth, 32, 38, 54, 56-59.
Achilles, shield of, described by Homer, 478.
Adoration of Magi, Luini, 477.
Æneid, 263, 265, 327, 331.
Æschylus, 443.
Æsthetics, comparative, iii. ; Science of, Day, 276, 280, 433.
Africa, religion of, 89, 100, 102.
Age, influence of the, on artistic inspiration, 129 ; on religious inspiration, 31, 112-115 ; on works of genius, 247.
Akenside, 333.
Alcamenes, 204.
Alexander, panel-paintings of, 363.
Alexander's Feast, Dryden, 345.
Alhambra, 386.
Allegoric and Allegory : music, 325, 350 ; painting, 325, 354, 418-420, 476-478 ; poetry, 325, 330 ; sculpture, 325, 367, 368.
Alum Bay, Talfourd, 438.
Analogical Representation, 64 ; cause of continuing influence of art-products, 206, 207 ; distinguished from logical formulation, 193-196 ; from spiritually influential suggestion, 175, 189-191 ; necessitates form as does all art, 194.
Analogy, 194-207 ; involves likeness in methods of formation, 196.

Analysis of thought in this volume. 388, 389.
Ananias, Death of, Raphael, 364.
Anarchy, Vedder, 354.
Ancient Mariner, Coleridge, 236.
Anderson, Charles, trance speaker, 101.
Angelo, Michael, 48, 231, 266, 277, 321, 355-357, 368, 379, 488.
Animals, their methods of communication, 97-99 ; their thinking processes, 97 ; the subconscious in, 95-99 ; why sinless, 95, 96 ; why worshipped, 95, note.
Antoinette, Marie, 78.
Apollo Belvedere, 485, 487 ; significance, how represented in, 425.
Appearances, meaning of word as used in art, 3.
Arabesque Architecture, 325, 386.
Arbuthnot, Epistle to Dr., Pope, 236.
Arch, pointed, architecture of, 325, 377, 381, 383, 384, 386, 387 ; round, architecture of, 325, 377-379, 385.
Architectural Styles, Rosengarten, 386.
Architecture, as affected by surrounding scenery, 430, 431 ; commemorative, 325, 382 ; constructed according to analogies of nature, 204, 205 ; distinguished from other arts, 434 ; distinguished from painting and sculpture, 434, 489-491 ; distinguished from poetry, 446-448 ; dramatic, 325, 371-376, 383-387 ; effects confounded with those of drawing, 489-491 ; effects of outline in,

Architecture — *Continued.*
370–376; epic, 325, 371–376, 378–380, 385–387; of horizontal support or entablature, 325, 377, 380–382, 385–387; of perpendicular support or pointed arch, 325, 377, 380, 383–387; of vaulted support or round-arch, 325, 377–380, 385–387; realistic, 325, 371–376, 380–382, 385–387; significance in, 426–431; time-effects in, 425–427; unity and progress in, 425–431; unity of effect in street and campus, 428, 429.

Architecture, History of Modern, Fergusson, 490.

Ariadne, statue, 487.

Aristotle on epic art, 324; on dramatic, 317.

Arnold, Matthew, 95.

Arrangement, and method of, as suggested in nature, 6–11.

Art, aided by religion, 136, 230–232; aided by science, 154, 211, 212, 229–232; an aid to religion, 135, 136; an aid to science, 151–154, 171–173; characterized by blending of conscious and subconscious mental action, 87, 94, 129, 133–135, 155, 156, 159–161, 210, 211, 271; considers objects as wholes, 147; continued influence of, 206, 207; derives emotions, thoughts, and forms from nature, 5, 133; distinguished from religion, 62–64, 87, 94, 130–134, 155–165, 189–191; distinguished from science, 62–64, 87, 94, 137–154, 164–180, 193, 194, 253, 254; effects peculiar to those of suggestion through representation, 189–191, 241; effects on culture, 252–254; effects on materialism and traditionalism, 135, 136; does most for religion and morals when attending to its own business, 131–134, 162, 163, 190, 191; includes the painful, 267–269; in hypnotism, 68, 69, 132; its aim as pleasure, 267–269; its effects natural when analogical, 198–205; its effects related to hypnotism, 68, 69, 132; its limitations a source of strength, 206, 207; its forms appeal to the mind, 2, 3, 196; its use of ethics and learning, 256–265; not injured by culture and learning, 227–232, 265; no substitute for religion, 136; observation and information help it, 133, 135, 265; personal effects of, 234–240; subject-matter of, 141; tends to ideality rather than faith, 159–163.

Art in Theory, Raymond, 4, 5, 69, 94, 203, 210, 272, 273, 320, 376, 435, 436, 455, 469.

Art, its Laws and the Reasons for Them, Long, 326, 353, 355, 359, 374.

Art of Poetry, Horace, 332.

Artist, the, as born, 217–220; as made, 131–133, 220–232, 265–267; characteristics of, 129, 131–134, 238–240, 246–250; characterized by sentiment, 255, 256; characterized by subconscious mentality, 71, 72, 129, 131–134, 149–154, 210–229; emotive susceptibility of, 217, 244, 246; ethical and religious aims of, 263–266; harmony in, between conscious and subconscious mental action, 133–135, 155, 156, 159–161, 210, 211, 271; information of, 133; interested in technique, 244; memory of, 228, 229; mental ability of, 133, 134; need of education and training in, 220–229, 265, 266; *versus* scientist, 129, 133, 139, 140, 144, 148–150, 172, 211–220, 234, 235, 253, 254; *versus* teacher of religion, 131–136. See Art, Artistic, Genius, and Subconscious.

Artistic-Artistic tendency in art, 271–274, 311, 384.

Artistic Conceptions, owing to comparatively harmonious blending of conscious and subconscious mental influences, 62–64, 87, 94, 129, 133–135, 155, 156, 159–161, 210, 211, 271; *versus* religious, 62–64, 87, 88, 94, 133–135, 155, 156,

Artistic Conceptions — *Continued.*
159–161, 174, 175, 210, 271; *versus* scientific, 62–64, 87, 88, 94, 137, 139, 146, 151–155, 164, 165, 171–180, 193, 194, 211–213, 271, 272.
Artistic Inspiration, 65, 107, 227; *versus* religious, iv., 72, 131–136.
Artistic Mind *versus* scientific, their methods, 148–150, 153, 154, 172, 218–220.
Artistic Observation *versus* scientific, iv., v., 164–178.
Artistic Significance, 62–64, 208–268. See Artistic Conceptions.
Artistic Temperament, 210, 216–220; all children have, 218; differs from scientific in degree of emotive susceptibility, 219; individual, yet reflective of nature, 234, 235; or of other men, 248; not injured by cultivation, 227–232; not manifested physically alone, 216, 217.
Artistic Truth, source of, 94; *versus* religious and scientific as affected by temperament and training, 224–232, 234, 235.
Arts, the, as distinguished from one another in motive, 434–491; in time and space, 434, 435.
As You Like It, Shakespeare, 264, 321.
Assyria, religion of, 89, 100.
Athena of Capitol, statue, 485.
Atherstone, 450, 452.
Atonement, necessity for, exemplified in hypnotism, 183.
Attila, Defeat of, Raphael, 364.
Aurora, Guido, 354.
Aurora Leigh, Mrs. Browning, 323, 346.
Australia, religion of, 89, 100.
Automatic writing of spiritualists, 80, 104.

Bain, 296, 303.
Baptistery at Florence, 368.
Baptists, Seventh-Day, 132.
Barateau, 342.
Bardeen, 299, 303.

Barry, 374.
Bascom, 280, 378.
Baudelaire, 328.
Bavaria, statue, 367.
Beattie, 336.
Beautiful, the, 274, 276, 284, 299, 311; includes the sublime, 284–286.
Beauty, 205, 206; in art not inconsistent with representing analogy, 205; relative use in art of it, and of ugliness, 206.
Beauty, Science of, Bascom, 280, 378.
Beecher, H. W., 84, 236; his oratory, 411, 413, 414; his training, 226.
Beethoven, 201, 231, 247, 309, 351, 466; his training, 223, 224.
Beggar Boys, Murillo, 361.
Bias of mind interferes with obtaining spiritual truth, 108, 109.
Bible, cannot be interpreted as scientific statements, 177–181; Coleridge's test of its truth, 46; criticism of its poetry by Huxley, 138; development of truth in, 112–114; discrepancies appear because of literalism of interpretation, 180, 181; explained by suggestive interpretation, 176–181, 184, 185, 187, 188; expression of truth in, 41–49, 54, 55, 114, 115; higher criticism of, 42, 119; how inspired, 109–128; how to be interpreted as shown by its arguments, 43–45; its history, 41, 42; its injunctions, 45–48; its prophecies, 42, 43; its use of the word *truth*, 48, 49; legends and myths in, 119–121; no objection to associating it with occult mental action, 115–118; statements in, as affected by environment, 109, 110, 113, 114; tests of its truth, 122–128.
Bigotry, 123, 188.
Bingen on Rhine, monument, 481.
Biographia Literaria, Coleridge, 67.
Bishops, On the Irish, Swift, 306.
Blair, 312, 326.
Blanc, C., 374.

Bodily influence upon artistic significance, 208–268.
Borough, Crabbe, 447.
Brain, two lobes in, 65; size of, as determining ability, 221, 222.
Bridge, The, Longfellow, 197.
Bridge of Sighs, Hood, 289.
Brilliancy, characteristic of genius, 250, 307.
Brilliant, the, 274, 281–290, 293, 294, 299, 301, 302, 307, 311, 389; its relation to the sublime and the picturesque, 274, 282.
British Quarterly, 299, 303.
Brown, J. G., 361.
Browne, C. F., 301.
Browning, E. B., 323, 346.
Browning, R., 242, 243, 323, 346, 347; his obscurity artistic, 214; use of ellipsis, 214, 401, 402.
Brunelleschi, 266.
Bryant, 143, 335.
Buddhist religion, 64, 89.
Bull, the rhetorical, 292.
Bulwer, 324, 447.
Burke, 277–279, 284.
Burlesque, the, 292, 295, 296, 305.
Burning of Borgo, Raphael, 364.
Burns, 321, 336, 337; realistic, 337; not wholly uneducated, 266.
Bust, the, 203.
Butler, 306.
Byron, 237, 324, 336, 337, 447, 483; defects in his poetry, 465; preference of foreigners for, 462, 463; *versus* Tennyson, 462–465.

Campbell, 333, 336.
Canon, 350.
Canova, 486.
Canterbury Tales, 337.
Capitol at Washington, 368, 484, 486.
Capriccio, 350.
Caravaggio, 363.
Card Players, Caravaggio, 363.
Caricature, 305, 306, 309.
Carlyle, 195, 214.
Catholics, 108, 128.
Ceremonial, not religious but artistic, 176, 177.

Chadbourne, 229.
Chaignet, 278, 285, 286, 339.
Chaldee account of Creation, 119–121; seer, 120, 121.
Chamouni, Hymn in the Vale of, Coleridge, 278.
Change not inconsistent with absoluteness or eternity of truth, 51–56.
Chapin, E. H., oratory of, 412.
Character, as manifested in deeds, 23, 24; divine, as manifested in nature, 23–25.
Character-painting, 325, 361, 362; -sculpture, 325, 369.
Charge of Light Brigade, Tennyson, 345.
Charity, Intellectual, 123.
Chaucer, 337.
Chesterfield, Letter to, Johnson, 307.
Chevy-chace, ballad, 344.
Childe Harold, Byron, 336, 483.
Children, naturally artistic, 212, 218.
Childhood, second, owing to physical weakness, 222.
Chinese religion, 89.
Chord, musical, as basis of melody, 405, 406.
Choron, musical writer, 350.
Chorus, producing effect of unity, 394, 395.
Christ, the, his arguments, 44, 45; parables, 42, 44; use of word *truth*, 48, 49; was the truth because full of love, and was the life, 49, 56, 57.
Christian, faith, 157, 158, 160; Scriptures, 89, 103, 104, 110, 111. See Bible.
Christians, 64, 111.
Christmas carols at Rome, 202.
Churchill, J. W., 74.
Churchman, zealous, justified, 123.
Clairvoyants, 129.
Claude, 356, 422.
Claude-Lorraine-glass, 422.
Clemens, S. L., 299.
Cliffs, On the, Swinburne, 335.
Climbing Boy's Soliloquies, Montgomery, 397.
Cloud, The, Shelley, 344.

INDEX.

Clouds, To the, Wordsworth, 139.
Cole's Voyage of Life, 418, 419, 478.
Coleridge, 46, 67, 236, 278.
Cologne Cathedral, 381.
Color, harmony of, as resulting from harmony in vibrations, 68, 69.
Columbus, Life of, on bronze doors, 484.
Comedy, pure, 297.
Comic, 308, 309.
Commemorative Architecture, 325, 382 ; Sculpture, 325, 368.
Communications of animals, 97–99.
Comparison, superficial and organic, 197, 199, 200.
Compilation of the Bible, 121.
Conceptions, 63. See Artistic, Religious, and Scientific.
Confucius, 111.
Congenial, the, as manifested in genius, 249, 250.
Conscience, as related to the subconscious, 109, 110, 156–161 ; meaning of, 156–159 ; the wise and good least conscious of, 109, 110.
Conscious mental action, as related to subconscious, 64–66, 86–88, 93–98 ; comparatively harmonious blending of it with subconscious action in imaginative art, 62–64, 87, 94, 129–136, 155, 156, 159–161, 210, 211, 222–229, 271 ; corrects that which comes from subconscious action, as in hypnotism, 106, 108–111, 113 ; developed at same time as subconscious, 222–230 ; exerts a strong influence in the educated or the good, 92, 109, 110 ; its influence subordinate to that of the subconscious in religion, 87, 93, 94, 131, 156–162, 175, 271 ; supreme over that of the subconscious in science, 87, 88, 94, 137, 139, 144–146, 148–151, 153, 155, 271, 272.
Consciousness as related to conscience, 156–161 ; coming to, 157.
Constructive elements of outline underlying effects in all arts of sight, 370–385.
32

Contrast, artistic effects of, 202, 203.
Conversion, through hypnotism, 182, 183.
Coriolanus, Shakespeare, 290.
Corneille, 443, 476.
Cornhill Magazine, 302.
Correggio, 245, 356, 379.
Corsair, The, 324, 447, 465.
Cotter's Saturday Night, Burns, 336.
Coupland, W. C., 70.
Cours d' Esthétique, Jouffroy, 278.
Course of Time, Pollok, 163, 257, 327.
Cowper, 304, 332, 447.
Crabbe, 237, 439, 447.
Crawford, 369.
Creation of world from nothing, explained according to hypnotism, 184 ; order of, according to psychometry, 120.
Creeds, cannot contain all the truth, 40, 41, 50, 51, 113–115 ; may tend to spiritual death, 187–189 ; necessity for freedom from formulæ, 50–60, 187–189 ; not religious but scientific, 176, 177 ; significance of, is beneath the form of statement, 30, 31, 40, 46, 47, 50–60, 114, 115. See Freedom.
Criticism, higher, 42, 119–122.
Critics, popular, 461 ; often the worst, 461.
Critique of Judgment, Kant, 277, 278, 284, 286.
Crucifixion, Rubens, 364.
Cultivation as related to artist, 227–232.
Culture, as resulting from art-study, 253 ; meaning of, 252, 253 ; not produced by study of science alone, 253.
Cupid Bending Bow, statue, 369.
Curtis, G. W., oratory of, 411.
Customs, religious, as showing primitive beliefs, 100.
Cymbeline, Shakespeare, 456.

Dallas, E. S., 228, 267.
Dante, 154, 163, 190, 200, 213, 231, 263, 321.
Darwin, 29, 138.

Davies, C., 302.
Day, H. N., 276, 280, 433.
Death of Ananias, Raphael, 485.
Decline of Carthage, Turner, 356.
Decorative, painting, 325, 331, 357, 358; sculpture, 368.
Delaroche, 354, 419.
Demon Possession and Allied Themes, Nevius, 81.
Demosthenes, 225.
Denner, 359.
Denton, W., 120.
Dervishes, Mohammedan, 102.
Descent from the Cross, Rubens, 162, 364, 485.
Descriptive, poetry, 325, 331-336; music, 351.
Deserted Village, Goldsmith, 201, 336.
Design, Lectures on, Opie, 475.
Destiny-Maker, Raymond, 329.
Destruction of Jerusalem, Kaulbach, 419, 420, 478.
Diana of the Louvre, Statue, 485.
Dickens, 231, 237, 296.
Didactic poetry, 325, 331-333.
Dirge, A, Tennyson, 459.
Discernment, spiritual, 41, 43, 114.
Discobolus, 369.
Discrepancies of the Bible, 113-115, 180, 181.
Distance, subconscious apprehension of, 74-77, 98, 99.
Divine Comedy, The, 163, 200, 265, 331.
Divine Life, Intelligence, and Character as Represented in Natural Forms, 15, 21-25.
Dog, Methods of thought of the, 97, 98.
Doggerel, what it is, 397, 398.
Dogmas, 40, 187, 188. See Creeds and Formulæ.
Dogmatism, 52.
Dome, its architectural meaning, 426.
Domestic Asides, Hood, 307.
Dora, Tennyson, 330.
Doubt as means of grace, 51.
Drama, Greek *versus* English, and law of unities, 443-446.
Dramatic, 273, 311-313, 320-**332,** 389; character of, in art, 315-317; in architecture, 325, 371-387; in music, 325, 351, 352; in painting, 325, 353, 360-366; in poetry, 325, 338-348, 443-446; in sculpture, 325, 369-375.
Droll, the, 295, 297, 298 309.
Drunkard's Progress, engraving, 476.
Dryden, 345.
Dunciad, Pope, 330.
Duncombe, 294.
Dwight, 466.
Dyer, J., 343.
Dying Galatian, or Gladiator, 369, 483.

Ear, musical poetry appealing to it and not to eye, 454-465.
Earthly Paradise, Morris, 337.
Eccentricity attributed to artists, 239, 240.
Education, poem by West, 143.
Education, what it means, 220-226.
Egypt, religion of, 89.
Egyptian, religion, 100; temples, 102.
Elements, of Art-Criticism, Samson, 147; of Criticism, Kames, 254.
Eleusinian Mysteries, 101.
Elizabeth, Drama of Age of, 446.
Elliot, portrait of, Reynolds, 359.
Elocution, its gestures, 413, 414; modulation, 412, 413; movement, 411, 412; unity and progress in, 410-414; *versus* poetry, 471-473; with musical motive, 472; with pictorial motive, 473.
Elyseum conceived by ancients, 89.
Emerson and Transcendentalists, iv.
Emotion, artistic, not merely physical, 216, 217; always strong in the artist, 217, 244, 246; an element of sentiment, 254, 255; as addressed in art, 2-5; as associated with nature, 5; as stimulating imagination, 211-220; not in distinction from thought, the source of art, 212-214; often means the same as soul, 211.

INDEX.   499

Emotive, the, *versus* the instinctive and reflective, 210, 211, 273.
Encyclopædia Britannica, 301.
English Composition and Rhetoric, Bain, 296, 303.
Entablature, architecture of, with horizontality, 325, 377, 380–382.
Epic, 311–322, 389; an early form of art, 315, 316; character of, 313, 314; in architecture, 325, 370, 371, 373–380, 385; in music, 325, 349–351; in painting, 325, 352–357, 360; in poetry, 325, 323–331, 338; in sculpture, 325, 367, 368; lack of rhyme in its poetry, 395; relative rank of, 317–321; *the*, painting of the world, 355.
Episcopalians, 128.
Equipment of Cupid, Titian, 421.
Essay on Man, Pope, 332, 461.
Eternal, the, as represented in nature, 13–21.
Ethan Allen, ballad, Raymond, 338.
Ethical, the, as used in art, 257–265.
Euripides, 443.
Evening, Claude, 356.
Everett, E., oratory of, 410, 411.
Excursion, Wordsworth, 257, 335, 448, 449; general plan of, 446, 447.
Existence as suggested by nature, 6.
Expression, arts of, 209; its meaning, 209, 272.
Eye, poetry should appeal to it, as words do, 454–465.

Faerie Queen, Spenser, 330, 350.
Faith, 40, 64, 155–163; Christian, 157, 158, 160; free, 124, 181, 182, 184; influenced by suggestion, 176–190; living and progressive, 51–53, 187–189; relation to fidelity and faithfulness, 158; to hypnotism, 176, 181–183; to practice, 158, 181–189; to salvation, 185, 186; *versus* ideality, 155–163; *versus* knowledge, 55, 56, 155, 187, 188.

Faithless Sally Brown, Hood, 295.
Fakirs, Indian, 102.
Fall of Nineveh, Atherstone, 450, 452.
Fantasia, 325, 350.
Farce, the, 293, 294, 305.
Farewell, The, Tennyson, 343.
Fawn, statue, 369.
Fergusson, 490.
Fernando and Elvira, Gilbert, 300.
Fine Arts, Wyatt, 380.
First Break with the British, Raymond, 338.
First Principles, Spencer, 165.
Florence, Baptistery at, 486; tomb of Giuliano de' Medici, 368.
Flower in the Crannied Wall, Tennyson, 145.
Force as suggested by nature, 6–11.
Form, as connected with ideality, 161, 165, 167; essential to an artistic conception, 133, 160, 161, 190, 194; essential to an ideal, 165, 167; meaning of the word as used in art, 1–3, 5, 12.
Forms, of art as suggesting significance, 1–4, 69, 190, 191, 195–207; of nature as representing the divine life, intelligence, and character, 15, 21–25; of nature as representing the infinite, eternal, and absolute, 15–21; of nature as representing truth, 26–32, 51–55, 114, 115; of nature as suggesting significance, 5–11, 15–32, 54–58, 198; of nature do not infallibly embody divine purposes, 114, 115.
Formulæ, cannot contain all the truth, 40, 41, 50, 51, 113–115; may tend to spiritual death, 187–189; necessity for freedom from, 50–60, 187–189; not religious but scientific, 176, 177; significance of, is beneath them, 30, 31, 40, 46, 47, 50–60, 114, 115.
Formulation, logical, 64, 139, 146, 150, 174, 175, 177–179, 192, 193, 206, 207; not possible to the phases of truth needed in art and religion, 152, 153, 175–181.
Fox, C. J., 228.

Freedom of mind when controlled by art, 241 ; by faith, 124, 181, 182, 184.
Freeman, E. A., 377, 378, 380, 382–384.
Friends, the, or Quakers, 108, 132.
Friendship, as connected with knowledge of God and truth, 57, 58.
Fugue, 325, 350.
Fuseli, 313, 353, 355, 358, 360, 364.
Future, foretold, 77–79 ; life determined by present life, 185, 186.

Galatea and Pygmalion, 217.
Garden of Cymodoce, Swinburne, 335.
Gardener's Daughter, Tennyson, 242, 282.
Gavazzi, Father, oratory of, 413.
Gay, J., 141.
Gay Science, Dallas, 228, 267.
Genesis, description of knowledge of good and evil, 96 ; poetry in, 396.
Genesis of Art-Form, The, Raymond, 340, 392, 492.
Genial, geniality, significance of, and connection with genius, 249, 250.
Genius, allied to insanity, 107 ; creative and divine, 186 ; eccentricity of, 239, 240 ; methods of work of, 218, 219 ; needs training and practice, 131, 223–227 ; related to subconscious and unconscious mental action, 131, 225–229 ; what it is, 147, 247–250. See Artist.
Genre painting, 362.
Gérôme, 361.
Gertrude of Wyoming, Campbell, 336.
Gesture in oratory, 413, 414.
Ghiberti, 368.
Ghost in Macbeth, 75.
Gifts, spiritual, 129.
Gilbert, 297, 300.
Gilpin, John, Cowper, 304.
Giuliano de' Medici, tomb of, 368.
Glasse of Time, Peyton, 327.
Gnosticism, 102, 103.
Goethe, 154, 213, 220, 230, 231, 247, 254, 265, 321, 445, 446.
Goldsmith, 201, 298, 336.

Good, the, 274, 275, 284, 297, 311, 389.
Good-Natured Man, Goldsmith, 298.
Gothic Architecture as dramatic, 383–387.
Gough, J. B., oratory of, 411, 413, 414.
Government, Vedder, 353.
Grammar of Painting and Engraving, Blanc, 374.
Grand, the, 274, 275, 284, 286–288, 290, 293, 295, 297, 311, 312, 389.
Gray's Elegy, parody on, 294.
Greece, 89, 104.
Greek, architecture, 325, 380, 382, 385, 386 ; law of unities, 443–446.
Greeks, the, 100.
Gregorian chant, 162.
Grongar Hill, Dyer, 343.
Grotesque, the, 295, 296, 305, 308, 309.
Guido, 354.
Gurney, 77, 308.
Guy Mannering, Scott, 141, 236.

Hades, Greek and Roman, 89.
Hallucinations, 99.
Hamilton, Sir W., 154, 170, 172, 279, 280, 284, 285.
Hamlet, Shakespeare, 287, 288, 298, 305.
Hamlet's Soliloquy, parody on, 294.
Hammond, 398.
Handel, 201, 351.
Harlot's Progress, Hogarth, 478, 484.
Harmony, 69.
Hart, 326.
Hartmann, Von, 70.
Haydn, composer, 309, 351, 466 ; poem, 441.
Hazlitt's Criticism of Wordsworth, 448.
Hebraic, Compilers of Bible, 121 ; laws against sorcery and witchcraft, 82–85 ; prophets and Scriptures, 89, 104, 110–114, 119–121.
Hebrews, 104 ; their character as influenced by written Scriptures, 111.
Hegel, 29.

Henry VIII., Shakespeare, 263, 457; 1 Henry IV., 201, 258, 283; 1 Henry VI., 307; 2 Henry VI., 263; 3 Henry VI., 289, 456.
Herder, 43.
Heroic, poetry, 325, 330, 331; painting, 325, 355, 356; sculpture, 325, 367, 368. See Epic.
Hidden Region of Mind, 64, 65. See Subconscious.
Higher Criticism, 42, 119-122.
Hindoos, their religion, 64.
Historic, art, 312, 325; painting, 325, 353, 359-361, 363; sculpture, 325, 368.
History in the Bible, its inspirational purpose, 41, 42.
History of Ancient Art, Winckelmann, 286.
Hogarth, 309, 478, 484.
Holy Night, Correggio, 356, 379.
Homer, 143, 247, 321, 326, 331; his descriptions, 442, 443, 446.
Hood, 289, 295, 300, 307.
Hope, Guido, 354.
Horace, 332.
Horatii, The, Corneille, 476.
Horatius at the Bridge, Macaulay, 471.
Horizontal Support, architecture of, 325, 380-382.
Horrible, the, 275, 287, 289, 290, 311.
Hudibras, Butler, 306.
Hudson, T. J., 83, 176, 181.
Human Form, as expressing significance in movements and postures, 373-375; physical as influencing art-conceptions, 208-269.
Humanities, the, 3, 242.
Humanity, influenced in art, 209.
Humor, 294, 295, 298-304, 306-309.
Huxley, 138, 139, 144, 150, 164.
Hypnotism, 67, 68, 176, 181; as affording possible explanations of certain religious doctrines, 120, 181-187; as related to faith, 176, 181-186; its control over mind exercised through suggestion, 68-70, 105-110, 176, 177, 181-186; method of communication of animals, 97-99; of spiritualism, 79, 83, 107-109; partakes of nature of art, 68, 69, 132; physical in character, 68, 182; the truth of its reports from the subconscious depends on the truth of the premise suggested to the one hypnotized, 105-109, 150, 151; subconscious processes of memory and logic revealed by it, aside from premise, seem flawless, 105, 106, 150, 221; while controlling the mind, leaves it free and individual, 181, 182, 184.
Hypnotizer, his methods, 68, 69.

Ideal in Art, The, Taine, 317, 433.
Idealism, 273, 274, 312, 324.
Ideality, 64, 190, 191, 195, 196, 234; as related to religion, 159-163, 166-169; as related to science, 170-173; *versus* faith, 155, 159-163; *versus* knowledge, 165-173.
Idealized Realism, 273, 274, 324.
Ideals, 234; defined, 161, 165, 167; in this world determine life in next, 186.
Ideals Made Real, Raymond, 441.
Idyls, of the King, Tennyson, 330, 331; of Theocritus, 330.
Iliad, 143, 263, 265, 327, 331, 395, 442, 443, 476, 478, 479.
Il Penseroso, Milton, 248, 457.
Image in the mind in imagination, 2, 3.
Imagination, 2, 3, 63, 87; an aid to science, 151-154, 170-173; creative when, in form and significance, continuing work of creation, 198; connected with emotion, 211-220; developed from subconscious in connection with conscious mental action, 129, 130, 149-155, 210, 211, 213-215, 223-227, 229; divine because creative, 186; improved by training, 226-229; individuality of effect of artist's, 234-250; not injured by scientific study or learning, 230, 231; not untrue nor irrational, 149, 150, 212; perceives definite pictures in

Imagination—*Continued.*
  poetry, 455–465 ; one source of belief in immortality, 90, 152–154 ; *versus* religious inspiration, 127–136, 155, 159, 271, 272 ; *versus* investigation, 137–155, 165, 170–172, 193, 194, 210, 211, 271, 272 ; why a substitute for investigation, 149, 167, 170 ; why for experience, 212, 213. See Art, and Artistic Conceptions.
Imaginative minds as unpractical, intuitive, prescient, inventive, spiritual, 151–154.
Immaculate Conception, Murillo, 356, 379.
Immortality, 89. See Life after Death.
Immortality, Intimations of, Wordsworth, 96, 145.
Import, as suggested in art, 388–431 ; in nature, 13–25 ; spiritual, 64.
Incongruity, the basis of the playful in art, 292, 293, 299, 300, 308, 309.
Indians, religion of, 99, 110.
Individual interest awakened by the statue, 484–487.
Individuality of effect in art, 234–240 ; not in conflict with representing natural appearances, 238–240; nor with general effects, 245–250.
Inferno, Dante, 265. See Divine Comedy.
Infinite, as represented in nature, 13–21.
Information, previous, as a test of truth, but to be used with charity, 122–125 ; indispensable to artist, 133, 228, 229.
Innocence, Raphael, 354
Innocents Abroad, Clemens, 299.
Innuendo, 307.
Insight, spiritual, as a test of truth, 31, 125, 126.
Inspiration, 63, 87, 133–136 ; allied to results of hypnotism, 107 ; artistic, iv., 65, 71, 72, 107, 131–134, 226, 227 ; attributed to insanity, idiocy, and genius, 107; attributed to subconscious action, 107, 131–133, 226, 227 ; Biblical, 109–128;

divine and not divine, 75 ; improved by practice, 227 ; in compilation of the Bible, 121 ; influence of environment on divine, 112–114 ; its spiritual influence is by way of suggestion, 175–184 ; religious *versus* artistic, 65–72 ; religious, is rational, 109–113 ; tests of truth of Biblical, 122–128; truth of, interpreted by conscious action of some mind, 103, note, 107–118, 122–128 ; truth of, modified by character and thought of the inspired person, 112–114 ; truth of religious, does not always depend on intelligence or ability of inspired person, 133 ; *versus* imagination, 87, 88, 128–136, 155, 159–161, 272 ; *versus* investigation, 155, 271, 272. See Bible, Religion, and Religious Conceptions.
Inspirational Preachers and their training, 227.
Instinct and Reason, Marshall, 92.
Instinct in animals and man, 93.
Instructive tendency, 93–95, 229 , allied to religious, 94–100 ; *versus* the emotive and the reflective, 93–95, 210, 211, 272.
Introduction à l' Étude de la Musique, Choron, 350.
Intuitive insight as a test of truth, 125, 126.
Investigation, 63, 87, 138, 164 ; aided by art, 151–154, 171–173, 218, 219 ; an aid to art, 133, 134, 229, 231; *versus* imagination, 137–155, 165, 170–172, 193, 194, 211, 271, 272. See Science, and Scientific.
Iphigenia in Tauris, Goethe, 445, 446.
Irony, 306.
Italy A Song of, Swinburne, 460

Jago, 294.
Japanese Religion, 89.
Jessen, 70.
Jesus. See Christ.
Jewess, story of a, 76.

INDEX

Jewish Cemetery, The Ruysdael, 356.
Joan of Arc, 105.
Jocular, the, 295, 297.
Johnson, 307.
Josephine, Empress, 78.
Joshua, a relief, 476, 484.
Jouffroy, 278, 285.
Journal of Music, 466.
Julius Cæsar, Shakespeare, 178.
Justice, Raphael, 354.

Kames, 254.
Kanawha, 78.
Kant, 104, 277, 278, 284, 286.
Kargé, 75, 76.
Kaulbach, 354, 419.
Keats, 337.
Kepler, 71.
King John, Shakespeare, 456.
Kingsley, 341.
Klopstock, 163.
Knight, 144.
Knowledge, characteristic of Science, 64, 155, 156, 164, 165; of God, what it is, 56–58; of good and evil, 96; *versus* faith, 155, 156, 187, 188; *versus* ideality, 164-172.
Kugler, 362, 421.

Lady of the Lake, Scott, 346, 399.
Landscape-Gardening, in England, 333, 334; significance of, distinguished from that of painting or sculpture, 474, 475; time suggested in, 416, 417; unity and progress in, 415-417.
Landscapes, dramatic, 364–366; epic, 356, 357; realistic, 358.
Laocoön, criticism, vii., 236, 285, 421, 434–436, 442, 443, 454; statue, 204, 285, 369, 375, 424, 488.
Last Judgment, Angelo, 48, 277.
Law of Psychic Phenomena, The, Hudson, 83, 176, 181.
Lawrence, A., Size of Brain, 221, 222.
Lay Sermons, Addresses, and Reviews, Huxley, 138.

Learning, as expressed in art-products, especially poetry, 256–266; as influencing the artist, 226–232.
Leaving for Work, Millet, 420.
Legend of King Arthur, 397.
Legends of the Bible, 119–121.
Lemon, Mark, 304.
Leonardo, 213.
Les Principes de la Science du Beau, Chaignet, 278, 285, 339.
Lessing, vii., 51, 236, 285, 421, 443, 454; theory of, 434–436, 442.
Liberty, Christian, 177, 181, 182, 187, 188.
Liberty Enlightening the World, statue, 367, 488.
Life, as suggested in art-forms, 390–431; by nature, 9–11; character of, after death, determined by belief and character in this world, 185, 186; on earth as connected with that above, 56–60; sources of belief in future, 89–92; spiritual, dependent on freedom from formulæ, 50–60; spiritual, influenced by suggestion, 187–190; truth involves it, 48–60.
Lightning Calculators, 72, 93, 105.
Lincoln, 181, 184; his dream, 79.
Lion Hunt, Rubens, 364.
Liszt, 351, 466.
Literalism in interpreting the Bible, and its evils, 176–184, 187.
Literary Interpretation of the Bible, 177–179, 181.
Lochinvar, Scott, 471.
Locksley Hall, Tennyson, 343.
Logical Inference, or reasoning, a test of truth, 126, 127. See Formulation.
Lohengrin, Wagner, 410.
Long, 326, 338, 353, 355, 359, 374.
Longfellow, 197, 199, 202, 203, 342, 458.
Lost Love, The, Wordsworth, 288.
Lotus Eaters, The, Tennyson, 142, 451.
Love, connection between it and the truth, 56–58.
Lover's Journey, Crabbe, 439.
Love thou thy Land, Tennyson, 459.
Lowell, 284.

Lucile, 324, 447.
Ludicrous, the, 292, 293, 295-305.
Ludlow, 75.
Luini, Bernardino, 477.
Lyric, cry, 339; poetry, 325, 339-345, 364, 365.
Lytton, 324.

Mab, Queen, Shelley, 453.
Macaulay, 471.
Macbeth, Shakespeare, 289, 348, 456; ghost in, 75.
Madoc in Wales, Southey, 450.
Making of a Book, Alexander, 363.
Malebranche, 51.
Manfred, Byron, 237.
Marjorie, Little, Sargent, 362.
Marmion, Scott, 447.
Marquand, 362.
Marryat, F., 66.
Marshall, H. R., 92.
Martin Chuzzlewit, Dickens, 237.
Mason, Dr. R. O., 182.
Materialism, and belief in the Bible, 116; evils of, and effects of art upon, 135, 136.
Mathematics, subconscious, 72, 73. See Lightning Calculators.
Matter, 6.
Maud, Tennyson, 242.
Mazzuoli, 435.
Measure for Measure, Shakespeare, 200.
Medicine Man of Indians, 100.
Medium, spiritual, 79-85, 100-103, 108-111; untrustworthiness of communications of, 82-85.
Meissonier, 359.
Meistersinger, The, Wagner, 308, 409, 410.
Melody deriving suggestions of organism and import from its connection with the chord, 405, 406.
Memory, as influenced in hypnotism, 66-71; its influence in art, especially poetry, 227-229.
Mendelssohn, 231.
Merchant of Venice, Shakespeare, 308.
Merrill, 328.
Messiah, The, Klopstock, 163.

Metaphysics, Lectures on, Hamilton, 154, 170, 279, 280.
Method of operation, as determined by appearances in time and space together, 7-9; as determining impressions of life, organism, and import in nature, 9-11; as determining meanings of words, 35-37; as determining significance in art, 390-393; as determining truth in the Bible, 41-49; as indicating the divine in nature, 22-25; as suggesting the infinite, eternal, and absolute, 16-21; connection between a single and the universal, 13, 29, 30, 32, 38, 42, 45; connection between it and truth, 25-27, 29-62.
Meyers, 77.
Midsummer Night's Dream, Shakespeare, 167.
Millet, J. F., 361, 365, 420.
Milton, 24, 130, 134, 154, 163, 185, 200, 226, 230, 247, 248, 260, 261, 276, 277, 321, 336, 457, 458, 471.
Miltonic character of poetry, 23, 24.
Mind, as addressed in art, 2, 3, 196; conscious, hidden, occult, subconscious, 64, 65; of man and in nature as representing the divine, 22-25; receiving truth subconsciously, modifies it, 106, 108-113. See Conscious and Subconscious.
Mind Readers or Reading, 79, 97-100, 102, 129.
Minerva, Pheidias, 204.
Minstrel, The, Beattie, 336.
Miracles and Modern Spiritualism, Wallace, 108.
Miserere sung at Rome, 202.
Mock Heroic, the, 293, 294.
Modulation in oratory, 412.
Mohammed, 105.
Mohammedan Architecture, 325, 386.
Mohammedans, 64, 104, 105, 128.
Montgomery, 397.
Moorish Architecture, 325, 386.
Mormons, 64, 128.
Morris, 337.

Morte d'Arthur, Tennyson, 258, 331, 395, 458.
Moses, Angelo, 277, 368, 379, 488.
Moses, W. S., 80.
Movement, accompanying suggestions of non-movement, or space-effects in elocution, 411–414; in music, 403–406; in poetry, 260, 399–401, 435–444, 448–453; natural, 6–11; offsetting space-effects in painting, 435–437, 475–479; sculpture, 424, 425.
Mozart, his subconscious facility, 73, 223, 224, 247.
Müller, Max, 90.
Murillo, 356, 361, 379.
Music, 162, 201, 202, 223–225; dramatic, 325, 351, 352; distinguished from poetry, 455–472; German *versus* French, 407–409; movement and non-movement as represented in, 403–406; must not move too slowly or too rapidly, 403–406; possible developments in future presentation of, 470; realistic, 351; source of enjoyment in imitative and naturalistic, 467, 468; unity and progress in, 403–410.
Music as a Representative Art, Raymond, 349, 352, 466, 492.
Musical effects not all that poetry needs, 459–485.
Myths of the Bible, 119–121.

Napoleonic characteristics, 23, 24.
Narrative poetry, 331, 333.
National Library, Washington, 363, 367.
Natural, the, in art, is analogical, 198–205; not all the, is legitimate in art, 206; scenery, as it should be presented in poetry, 333–337; theology, and the verification of its claims, 21–25.
Naturalistic, 325; music, 325, 351; painting, 325, 357–359; poetry, 325, 331–336; sculpture, 325, 368.
Nature, as regarded by the artist and scientist, 139, 140; including the non-human and human, 5;
is a source of the significance of art, 5, 130, 160, 161. See Art, Artistic.
Nevius, J. L., 81.
New Monthly Magazine, 214.
Newsboys, Brown, 361.
Newton, 219.
Night and Day, Angelo, 368, 379.
Night Thoughts, Young, 333.
Nile of the Vatican, statue, 368.
Niobe and her Children, statue, 369, 424, 481, 485.
North American Review, 182.
Notre Dame, Paris, 379.
Novel, reformatory influence of, 191.

Obscurity, in imaginative works the appropriate expression of subconscious intellection, 213–215; of Browning and Carlyle, 214.
Occult region of the mind and nature, 64, 65; theories with reference to its results, 83–85. See Subconscious.
Odyssey, 331.
O Mary, Go and Call the Cattle Home, Kingsley, 341.
Opera, 325, 351, 352, 408–410, 468–470.
Operation as indicated in nature, 7–11, 13. See Method of Operation.
Opie, 352, 353, 475.
Oracles of ancients, 104.
Oratorio, 325, 351.
Oratory, gestures in, 413, 414; modulation in, 412; time, movement, and rhythm in, 410–414; unity and progress in, 410–414; *versus* musical, poetic, or pictorial effects, 471–473.
Organism, as suggested by art-forms, 390–431; by natural forms, 9–11.
Origin and Growth of Romanesque Architecture, Freeman, 377.
Origin of Species, Darwin, 138.
Othello, Shakespeare, 264, 278, 283.
Outlines as determining significance in arts of sight, 370–385.
Oxon, M. A., 80.

Painful, the, in art, justification for, 267-269.
Painters, individuality of great, 238, 246.
Painting, 146-148, 162, 191, 203, 204, 238, 246, 266, 267, 277; distinguished from other arts, 434; can derive subjects from poetry sometimes, but must treat them differently, 436, 476-478; cannot treat all poetic subjects, 475, 476; its treatment must be distinguished from that of architecture, 482; of landscape-gardening, 479; of poetry, 434-444, 475-479; of sculpture, 479-482, 484-489; space-effects delineated in, 418, 420-425; time-effects delineated in, 435-437, 475-479; time-effects suggested in, 418-420; unity and progress in, 417-425.
Painting, Sculpture, and Architecture as Representative Arts, Raymond, 94, 352, 376, 420, 422, 426.
Paintings must not be too large, 488.
Pantomimic art, 325; painting, 325, 362, 363; sculpture, 325, 369.
Pallas of Pheidias, 423.
Parables of Jesus, what they imply that truth is, 42, 44.
Paradise, Lost, Milton, 134, 163, 185, 200, 226, 259, 261, 265, 277, 327, 331, 458; Regained, 260.
Parallelism, in painting, 480; in poetry, 395, 396; in sculpture, 488.
Parallels or Parables, 44.
Parody, 293, 294.
Parting Song, Swinburne, 460.
Pastoral Symphonies of Beethoven and Handel, 351.
Pathetic, the, 275, 288, 289, 302, 303.
Patience, Sullivan, 297.
Peace and Prosperity, Vedder, 353.
Percy's Reliques, 344, 397.
Permanence in truth, 52-55.
Perpendicular Support, architecture of, 325, 380, 383-387.
Personal effects of art, 234-240.

Perugino, 354.
Peter Bell, Wordsworth, 169.
Peyton, T., 327.
Phantasms of the Living, Meyers and Gurney, 77.
Pheidias, 204, 247, 266, 423.
Phillips, W., oratory of, 411, 412.
Philosophy, Kaulbach, 354.
Phraseology of art and religion not literally true, 177-181. See Bible Inspiration and Literalism.
Physical human action, conscious and subconscious, 65, 66; effects of hypnotism on, 68, 69.
Physiological effects of art, 2.
Pickwick Papers, Dickens, 296.
Picturesque, the, 274, 280-283, 286-290, 293, 294, 299, 301, 302, 311, 389; *versus* statuesque, 479-482, 484-489.
Pierce, 98.
Pigalle, 486.
Pilgrim's Progress, engraving, 476.
Piloty, 361.
Pisano, 368.
Plato, 154.
Platonic, 101.
Platonism, 102.
Playful, the, in art, 275, 291-309.
Pleasurable interspersed with non-pleasurable effects in art, 275, 287-289, 293, 305-308.
Pleasure as the aim of art, 267-269.
Pleasures, of Hope, Campbell, 333; of Imagination, Akenside, 333.
Pliny, 103.
Plutarch, 434.
Poème Sympathique, Liszt, 351.
Poetic, effects not the same as musical, 454-465; language that of perception, 143, 144; language not that of prose, 236-238; repetition of words, phrases, and thoughts in the, 394-396.
Poetry, 134, 138-148, 154, 162, 163, 167-169, 177-179, 181, 190, 191, 197-201, 236-238, 256-266, 276-278, 281-290; appeals to imagination visually, 455-465; descriptive, 437-453; distinguished from other arts, 434; doggerel, 397, 398; importance of movement in,

INDEX. 507

Poetry — *Continued.*
437-443, 446-453 ; not popular to-day, 462 ; novel has taken its former place, 462 ; of Bible, 138, 395, 396 ; space-effects important in, 435-444 ; subjects different from painting and sculpture, or, if not, treated differently, 436, 476-479, 483 ; *versus* elocution, 471 ; *versus* music, 454-465 ; *versus* oratory, 471-473 ; *versus* painting, 435-444, 475-478 ; *versus* prose, 236-238 ; *versus* Sculpture, 483.
Poetry, Kaulbach, 354.
Poetry as a Representative Art, Raymond, 94, 340, 466, 492.
Poets, and memory, 228 ; born, not made, 216, 217, 247-249 ; great, have been men of education, 154, 230, 265, 266 ; of individuality, 235, 236, 240 ; sympathetic, 240-246 ; *versus* scientists, 139-141, 167-171, 256-261.
Pointed Arch, architecture of, 325, 377, 383-387.
Pollice Verso, Gérôme, 361.
Pollok, 163, 257, 327.
Polytheism, its rise, 102, 103.
Pope, Alexander, 236, 293, 330, 332 ; his balance of rhythm, 461.
Pope, the, 128.
Popper, D., 308.
Popular critics, 461 ; often the worst, 461.
Popularity in art, 245.
Portraits, character of Titian's, 362, 421, 422.
Poussin, 364, 374.
Practical, the, reformer, 166.
Practice, effects of, on mind as well as body, 222-227 ; leading to do things unconsciously, 70-72 ; necessary to artist, 131, 220-229.
Prague, monument at, 486.
Praxiteles, 266, 369.
Preller, 485.
Prelude, Wordsworth, 168, 169, 265, 335, 400, 440.
Presbyterians, 132.
Presentation at the Temple, Luini, 477.

Princess, The, Tennyson, 281, 324, 451.
Principles of Psychology, Spencer, 94.
Progress, art-effect of, 391-430 ; reproduced in elocution, music, and poetry, 391-414 ; suggested in architecture, landscape-gardening, painting, and sculpture, 415-431.
Progress, necessary to spiritual life, 51-55 ; of truth not inconsistent with permanence, 51-55.
Prophecy, artistic, 151 ; its purpose and interpretation in the Bible, 42, 43 ; spiritualistic, 77, 79, note.
Prophets in sense of inspired teachers, 110, 112 ; most trustworthy when writers, 110. See Inspiration.
Proportion, 68.
Proportion and Harmony of Line and Color, Raymond, 69, 490, 492.
Prosaic *versus* poetical, 142, 143, 256-261.
Protactic poetry, 325, 345, 346.
Protestant, 111, 128.
Prudence, Raphael, 354.
Psalm, My, Whittier, 200.
Psalm of Life, A, Longfellow, 458.
Psychical Research, English Society of, 77.
Psychic Experience, 99.
Psychic Phenomena, The Law of, Hudson, 83, 176, 181.
Psychography, Oxon, 80.
Psychology, Jessen's, 70 ; Principles of, Spencer, 94.
Psychometrist, 77, 129.
Psychometry, 120.
Publican, why better than the Pharisee, 50.
Pun, the, 293, 294, 305.
Pygmalion, 217.
Pythagoras, 8.

Quackenbos, 299, 324.
Queen Mab, Shelley, 453.

Racine, 263, 443.
Rake's Progress, Hogarth, 478, 484.

Rape of the Lock, Pope, 293.
Rape of the Sabines, Poussin, 364.
Raphael, 204, 213, 231, 245-247, 266, 354, 361, 364, 419, 482, 485.
Rational action of mind, 94; in inspiration, 109-113.
Raymond, 329, 338, 441.
Realism, 273, 274; idealized, 273, 274, 324.
Realistic art, 311-315, 319-322, 389; in architecture, 370-378, 380-382; in painting, 357-360, 364, 365; in poetry, 331-338, 342-345, 364, 365; in sculpture, 368; ranks high in arts of sight, 357, 381.
Reason *versus* instinct, 92-100.
Reasoning as a test of truth, 126, 127.
Reflective *versus* instinctive and emotive, 93, 94, 210, 211, 272, 273.
Reformation, The, Kaulbach, 354, 419.
Refrain, the effect of, in poetry, 394, 395.
Religion, allied to the instinctive, 94-100; an aid to art, 136, 231, 232; art no substitute for it, yet an aid to it, 135, 136; distinguished from art, 62-64, 87, 94, 130, 134, 155-165, 189, 190; distinguished from science, 62-64, 87, 94, 137-165, 174-180, 193, 194; must be rational and intelligent, 109-115, 166, 167; not expressed representatively, 176, 177, 189, 190; source of, 62-129; source of its thought and emotion, 62-64, 87-136; tending to faith not ideality, 159-163; tending to suggestion not knowledge, 175-189. See Inspiration, Religious, and Subconscious.
Religion, Kaulbach, 354; Raphael, 354.
Religious-Artistic tendency, 271-274, 311.
Religious Conceptions, as expressed in art, 256, 257; characterized by subordination of conscious mental action to subconscious, 87, 93, 94, 131, 156-162, 175, 271; creeds

and ceremonials are not necessarily expressive of, 176, 177; dependent upon suggestions of material surroundings, 88, 89, 166, 167; *versus* artistic, 62-64, 84, 88, 94, 133-135, 155, 156, 159-161, 174, 175, 210, 271; *versus* scientific, 62-64, 87, 94, 137-154, 174-180, 193, 194.
Rembrandt, 361.
Renaissance Architecture, 325, 386.
Repetition, of rhythm and phrase in music, 404-407; of sounds, feet, lines, words, phrases, and thoughts in poetry, 392-396.
Representation, analogical, 64, 175, 189-191; artistic, must be distinct, 322, 433; cause of continuing influence of art-products, 206, 207; peculiar to art, not religion, 189-191; reformatory influence of, in art, 190, 191; suggestive influence of, 190, 191, 241.
Resentment, Crabbe, 237.
Revelation, believed to be closed and not closed, 128, 132.
Revived Grecian Architecture, 325, 386.
Reynolds, Sir J., 146, 203, 359.
Rhetoric, Blair, 312, 326; Hart, 326; Whately, 393; Complete, Bardeen, 299, 303; Welsh, 299, 302, 303; Composition and, Bain, 296, 303; Quackenbos, 299, 324.
Rhymes, poetic effect of, 394, 395.
Rhythm and Harmony in Poetry and Music, Raymond, 69, 349, 352, 466, 492.
Rhythm, allied to hypnotism, 68; musical effects of, 404, 405; poetic, 394, 395.
Richard II., Shakespeare, 263; Richard III., 178, 456.
Richter, 231.
Ridiculous, the, 292, 293, 295, 305-307.
Ring and the Book, Browning, 242, 323, 346.
Rogers, 369.
Romanesque Architecture, 325, 385.
Romans, ancient, religion of, 100.

Rome, art of modern, 230 ; religion of ancient, 89, 104.
Romeo and Juliet, Shakespeare, 283, 305.
Rosengarten, 386.
Rottmann, 204, 366.
Royal Academicians, Lectures before, Barry, 374.
Rubens, 162, 266, 361, 364, 485.
Rural Sports, Gay, 141.
Ruysdael, 356.

Sacred Writings, 89, 104, 110, 111 ; influence on religious and intellectual progress, 111. See Automatic Writing, Bible, and Inspiration.
Salient points alone brought out in art, 147.
Samson, 147.
Sarcasm, 306-309.
Sargent's portraits, 362.
Satan, Milton's, 276, 277.
Satire, 306-309.
Saxe, Marshal, monument, 486.
Scenery as affecting architecture, 430, 431. See Architecture and Descriptive Poetry.
Schiller, 230, 231, 254, 255, 263, 265.
School of Athens, Raphael, 354, 419, 482.
Science, an aid to art, 154, 211, 212, 229-232 ; contrasted with art, 62-64, 87, 94, 137-155, 164-180, 193, 194, 206, 213, 253, 254, 271, 272 ; contrasted with religion, 62-64, 87, 94, 137-155, 164, 165, 174-180, 193, 194 ; helped by imagination, 151-154, 170-173 ; its characteristic, knowledge, 64, 94, 155, 164 ; its method, investigation, 63, 87, 137, 155 ; not necessarily causing culture, 253, 254 ; subject-matter *versus* that of art, 141, 146.
Science, of Æsthetics, Day, 276, 280, 433 ; of Beauty, Bascom, 280, 378 ; of Religion, Müller, 90.
Science, painting by Kaulbach, 354.
Scientific-Artistic tendency in art, 271-274, 311, 389.

Scientific, art in architecture ranks high, 381, 382 ; conceptions conditioned by dominance of conscious over subconscious intellection, 87, 88, 94, 137, 139, 144-146, 148-151, 153, 155, 271, 272 ; significance, how derived, 62-64 ; source of truth, 94 ; *versus* artistic conceptions, 62-64, 87, 88, 94, 137, 139, 146, 151-155, 164, 165, 171-180, 193, 194, 211-213; *versus* religious conceptions, 62-64, 87, 94, 137-165, 174-180, 193, 194.
Scientist *versus* the artist, 129, 133, 140, 144, 148-150, 172, 211-220, 234, 235, 253, 254.
Scott, Sir W., 141, 236, 346, 399, 445, 447, 471 ; his poetic description, 447.
Scriptures, 89, 104. See Bible.
Sculpture, 162, 191, 203, 204, 266 ; distinguished from painting, 479-489 ; distinguished from poetry, 483 ; dramatic, 325, 369 ; epic, 325, 368 ; realistic, 325, 368 ; significance as indicated in, 424, 425 ; space-effects must not exclude suggestion of time-effects, 424, 425 ; statues may be large, 488 ; subjects must be dignified, 487, 488 ; symbolic, 325, 367 ; unity and progress in, 424, 425.
Séances, spiritualistic, 81, 100-103.
Seasons, Thompson, 201, 447.
Second childhood as related to control of subconscious powers, 222.
Self-Consciousness fatal to artistic success, 219.
Self-Dependence, M. Arnold, 95.
Senses, appeal of art to the, 1, 2.
Sensual in art, 2.
Sensuous in art, 2.
Sentence, a, represents in words a mode of operation, 35-37.
Sentiment, as expressed in art, 254-269 ; characterizing the artist, 255, 256 ; what it means, 254, 255.
Shakespeare, 143, 167, 168, 178, 200, 201, 220, 230, 231, 246, 258, 263, 266, 278, 283, 287-290, 298, 305,

512   REPRESENTATIVE SIGNIFICANCE OF FORM.

Technique, importance of, vi. ; why artists seem supremely interested in, 244.
Temperament, Artistic, 210, 216–220 ; all children have, 218 ; differs from scientific mainly in degree of emotive susceptibility, 219 ; individual, yet reflective of natural and human surroundings, 234, 235, 248 ; not destroyed by cultivation, 227–232 ; not manifested in the physical alone, 216, 217.
Tempest, Shakespeare, 201.
Teniers, 245, 309, 321, 361.
Tennyson, 142, 145, 242, 258, 281, 282, 330, 334, 343, 345 ; his descriptions, 450, 451, 458 ; his Homeric repetitions, 395 ; his musical effects, 459, 462 ; his poetry *versus* that of Byron, 462–465 ; why not appreciated by foreigners, 462, 463, 465.
Thanatopsis, Bryant, 335.
The Day is Done, Longfellow, 197, 458.
Theology, natural, claims and arguments of, 21–25.
Theosophists, 82.
The Three Ages, Titian, 421.
Thompson, 201, 334, 335, 447.
Thought and emotion necessarily go together, 3, 212, 213 ; as derived from nature, 5 ; as influenced by art, 2–5 ; in essence is comparison, 212. See Significance.
Time, arts appearing in, *versus* space, 434, 435 ; as reproduced through movement in elocution, 410–414 ; in music, 403–410 ; in poetry, 393–402 ; is suggested through forms of architecture, 426–431 ; of landscape-gardening, 415–417 ; of painting, 417–423 ; of sculpture, 423–425 ; suggests, in connection with space, methods of operation, organism, life, and import, 7–11 ; the divine intelligence and character, 22–25, 59, 60 ; the infinite, eternal, and absolute, 15–21, 58–60 ; truth, 28, 29, 58–60.

Tintern Abbey, Lines Composed a few Miles above, Wordsworth, 95, 153, 172.
Titian, 203, 245, 266, 435 ; his character-portraits, 362, 421, 422.
Tom, Blind, 73.
Tradition and insight, 122–125.
Traditionalism, 135.
Trajan, Column of, 484.
Trance, conditions, 100–103, 107–109 ; speakers, 100–103 ; truth as obtained through, 107–109.
Transcendentalists of New England, iv.
Travesty, 295, 298.
Troilus and Cressida, Shakespeare, 201, 348, 456.
True, meaning of the adjective, 27, 32–38 ; the, 274, 275, 284, 294, 295, 297, 299, 300, 311, 389.
Truth, as derived from nature, 27–30 ; as derived from trance-conditions dependent on lack of bias in the mind receiving it, 108, 109 : as its meaning is determined by arguments of the Bible, 43–45 ; by its history, 41, 42 ; by its injunctions, 45–48 ; by its parables, 44, 45 ; by its prophecies, 42, 43 ; by its uses of the word *truth*, 48, 49 ; by the words of the Christ, 44, 45 ; change in its form not inconsistent with its absoluteness and eternity, 51–56 ; conformity to an absolute method, 32, 38 ; connection between it and a method of operation, 25, 27–38, 62 ; danger of confounding it with a formula, 52–54 ; degree of it derived from subconscious intellection, 105–127 ; from inspiration of the Bible, 109–115 ; general discussion of its nature, 26–60 ; its progress and permanence, 52–55 ; of life, its conformity to right methods, 55 ; of the Bible, is literary and suggestive, not literal and formulative, 176–181, 183–188 ; personal bias of artistic, 234, 235 ; results of, as expressed in language and life, 39–60 ; signs and wonders no test of, 102, 117,

INDEX. 513

Truth — *Continued*.
118 ; source to which men attribute it, 27–32 ; tests of, 122–127 ; terms applied to, 32–38 ; the absolute, eternal, or infinite, 32, 38, 46, 47 ; the word *truth* as used in the Bible, 48, 49 ; to the spirit, what it is, 50, 51.
Truths and the truth, 46.
Tucker, Dr., 74.
Turner, 356.
Twain, Mark, 299.
Twelfth Night, Shakespeare, 143, 264.
Twenty Years, Barateau, 342.
Typical nature of Biblical characters, 43, 44.

Unconscious, Philosophy of the, Von Hartmann, 70.
Unconsciousness, associated with inspiration, 132, 133 ; as distinguished from self-consciousness, a characteristic of the true artist, 71, 72, 225, 239, 246. See Subconscious.
Unities, the law of, in the drama, 443–446.
Unity, and progress in art-form, 390–392 ; illustrated in the different arts, 390–430 ; portrayed in architecture, landscape-gardening, painting, and sculpture, 415–431 ; suggested in poetry and music, 390–414 ; wanting in many streets and public buildings, 428, 429.
Unknowable, philosophy of the, Spencer, 14, 24.
Up the Rhine, Hood, 300.

Van Beers, 363.
Vaulted Support or round arch, architecture of, 325, 377–380.
Vedder, 354.
Velasquez, 203.
Venus of the Capitol, statue, 487.
Venuses, their significance, 425.
Verse effects of unity and space produced in connection with movement, 394–398.
33

Vibratory nature of nervous excitation, 68.
Vienna, monument to Maria Christina at, 486.
Violent, the, 275, 289, 290, 302, 304, 311.
Virgil, 204.
Vision, of Constantine, Raphael, 364 ; of Sir Launfal, Lowell, 284.
Visions of animals and men, 97–100 ; communication by means of, 97–100.
Voice, influence of a musical, 202.
Voisin, M. A., 182, 183.
Voyage of Life, Cole, 418, 419, 478.

Wagner, 201, 308, 351, 352, 407–410, 469 ; a great composer of melody, 409 ; composed harmony from melodies, 409 ; subordinated melody to harmony, 409.
Wallace, A. F., 108.
Wallenstein, Death of, Piloty, 361.
Ward, Artemus, 301.
Washington, 84 ; prophecy about, 78, 105.
Washington, doors of Capitol at, 368, 484, 486 ; National Library at, 367.
Way, truth as the, 48, 49.
Webster, 221, 222.
Wedding, Ballad on a, Suckling, 457.
Welsh, 299, 302, 303.
West, Benjamin, 488 ; Gilbert, 143.
Westminster Bridge, Wordsworth, 336.
Whately, 393.
When Sparrows Build, song, 201.
Whipple, 301–303.
Whittier, 200.
Willems, 359.
Winkelmann, 286.
Winter's Tale, Shakespeare, 456.
Wit, 295, 298–309.
Wit and Humor, Lectures on, Smith, 299, 301 ; Whipple, 301–303.
Witchcraft and Sorcery, Hebrew laws against, 82, 84, 85, 110, 111.

OTHER WORKS BY PROF. GEO. L. RAYMOND

The Essentials of Æsthetics. 8vo. Illustrated . . Net, $2.50

This work, which is mainly a compendium of the author's system of Comparative Æsthetics, previously published in seven volumes, was prepared, by request, for a text-book, and for readers whose time is too limited to study the minutiæ of the subject.

"We consider Professor Raymond to possess something like an ideal equipment. . . . His own poetry is genuine and delicately constructed, his appreciations are true to high ideals, and his power of scientific analysis is unquestionable." . . . He "was known, when a student at Williams, as a musician and a poet—the latter because of taking, in his freshman year, a prize in verse over the whole college. After graduating in this country, he went through a course of æsthetics with Professor Vischer of the University of Tübingen, and also with Professor Curtius at the time when that historian of Greece was spending several hours a week with his pupils among the marbles of the Berlin Museum. Subsequently, believing that all the arts are, primarily, developments of different forms of expression through the tones and movements of the body, Professor Raymond made a thorough study, chiefly in Paris, of methods of cultivating and using the voice in both singing and speaking, and of representing thought and emotion through postures and gestures. It is a result of these studies that he afterwards developed, first, into his methods of teaching elocution and literature" (as embodied in his 'Orator's Manual' and 'The Writer') "and later into his æsthetic system. . . . A Princeton man has said of him that he has as keen a sense for a false poetic element as a bank expert for a counterfeit note; and a New York model who posed for him, when preparing illustrations for one of his books, said that he was the only man that he had ever met who could invariably, without experiment, tell him at once what posture to assume in order to represent any required sentiment."—*New York Times.*

"So lucid in expression and rich in illustration that every page contains matter of deep interest even to the general reader."—*Boston Herald.*

"Its superior in an effective all-round discussion of its subject is not in sight."
The Outlook (N. Y.)

"Dr. Raymond's book will be invaluable. He shows a knowledge both extensive and exact of the various fine arts and accompanies his ingenious and suggestive theories by copious illustrations."—*The Scotsman* (Edinburgh).

Published by G. P. PUTNAM'S SONS, 27 West 23d St., New York.

The Psychology of Inspiration. 8vo . . . . Net, $1.40

An attempt to distinguish Religious from Scientific Truth and to Harmonize Christianity with Modern Thought.

Dr. J. Mark Baldwin, Professor of Psychology in John Hopkins University, says that its psychological position is "new and valuable"; Dr. W. T. Harris, late United States Commissioner of Education, says that it is sure "to prove helpful to many who find themselves on the border line between the Christian and the non-Christian beliefs"; and Dr. Edward Everett Hale says "no one has approached the subject from this point of view."

"A book that everybody should read. . . . medicinal for profest Christians, and full of guidance and encouragement for those finding themselves somewhere between the desert and the town. The sane, fair, kindly attitude taken gives of itself a profitable lesson. The author proves conclusively that his mind—and if his, why not another?—can be at one and the same time sound, sanitary, scientific, and essentially religious."—*The Examiner*, Chicago.

"It is, we think, difficult to overestimate the value of this volume at the present critical pass in the history of Christianity."—*The Arena*, Boston.

"The author has taken up a task calling for heroic effort; and has given us a volume worthy of careful study. . . . The conclusion is certainly very reasonable."
Christian Intelligencer, New York.

"The author writes with logic and a 'sweet reasonableness' that will doubtless convince many halting minds. It is an inspiring book."—*Philadelphia Inquirer.*

"Interesting, suggestive, helpful."—*Boston Congregationalist.*

"Thoughtful, reverent, suggestive."—*Lutheran Observer*, Philadelphia.

Published by FUNK & WAGNALLS COMPANY, 44 East 23d St., New York.

The Orators' Manual, a Text-Book of Vocal Culture and Gesture . . . in constant demand for years. . . Net, $1.12
The Speaker, a Collaborated Text-Book of Oratory. . . Net, $1.00
The Writer, a Collaborated Text-Book of Rhetoric. . . Net, 90 cts.

Published by SILVER, BURDETT & COMPANY, 231 West 39th St., New York.

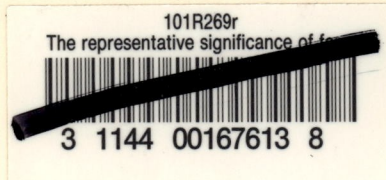